Heidegger and Dao

Daoism and the Human Experience

Series Editor: David Chai
Associate Professor of Philosophy, Chinese University of Hong Kong

Editorial Advisory Board
Lisa Raphals, University of California, Riverside (USA)
Robin Wang, Loyola Marymount University (USA)
Franklin Perkins, University of Hawaii (USA)
Eric S. Nelson, Hong Kong University of Science and Technology (Hong Kong)
Thomas Michael, Beijing Normal University (China)
James Sellmann, University of Guam (USA)
Chris Fraser, University of Toronto (Canada)
Bret Davis, Loyola University Maryland (USA)
Zongqi Cai, University of Illinois Urbana-Champaign (USA)
Zhihua Yao, Chinese University of Hong Kong (Hong Kong)

Daoism and the Human Experience creates a platform to explore, question, and learn about the ways Daoist thought elucidates the human experience in its philosophical, literary, aesthetic, and spiritual manifestations. We welcome contributions focusing on Daoist thought itself, as well as those that explore it within the broader context of China, East Asia, continental Europe, India, Africa, the Americas, and the Islamic world.

Titles in the series include:
Daoist Resonances in Heidegger, edited by David Chai

Heidegger and Dao

Things, Nothingness, Freedom

Eric S. Nelson

BLOOMSBURY ACADEMIC
LONDON • NEW YORK • OXFORD • NEW DELHI • SYDNEY

BLOOMSBURY ACADEMIC
Bloomsbury Publishing Plc, 50 Bedford Square, London, WC1B 3DP, UK
Bloomsbury Publishing Inc, 1385 Broadway, New York, NY 10018, USA
Bloomsbury Publishing Ireland, 29 Earlsfort Terrace, Dublin 2, D02 AY28, Ireland

BLOOMSBURY, BLOOMSBURY ACADEMIC and the Diana logo
are trademarks of Bloomsbury Publishing Plc

First published in Great Britain 2024
This paperback edition published 2025

Copyright © Eric S. Nelson, 2024

Eric S. Nelson has asserted his right under the Copyright, Designs and Patents Act, 1988, to be identified as Author of this work.

For legal purposes the Acknowledgments on p. viii constitute an extension of this copyright page.

Cover image: Lui Shou-kwan 呂壽琨, 1919–1975, "Zhuangzi" 1974.
Hong Kong Museum of Art Collection.

All rights reserved. No part of this publication may be: i) reproduced or transmitted in any form, electronic or mechanical, including photocopying, recording or by means of any information storage or retrieval system without prior permission in writing from the publishers; or ii) used or reproduced in any way for the training, development or operation of artificial intelligence (AI) technologies, including generative AI technologies. The rights holders expressly reserve this publication from the text and data mining exception as per Article 4(3) of the Digital Single Market Directive (EU) 2019/790.

Bloomsbury Publishing Inc does not have any control over, or responsibility for, any third-party websites referred to or in this book. All internet addresses given in this book were correct at the time of going to press. The author and publisher regret any inconvenience caused if addresses have changed or sites have ceased to exist, but can accept no responsibility for any such changes.

A catalogue record for this book is available from the British Library.

ISBN: HB: 978-1-3504-1190-6
PB: 978-1-3504-1194-4
ePDF: 978-1-3504-1191-3
eBook: 978-1-3504-1192-0

Series: Daoism and the Human Experience

Typeset by Integra Software Services Pvt. Ltd.

For product safety related questions contact productsafety@bloomsbury.com.

To find out more about our authors and books visit www.bloomsbury.com
and sign up for our newsletters.

To Shengqing

Contents

Acknowledgments	viii
Introduction	1
Part One *Dao*, Thing, and World	11
1 Way, Thing, and World in Laozi, Zhuangzi, and Heidegger	13
2 The Autopoietic Self-Transformation of Things in Ziranist Daoism and Heidegger	37
3 Heidegger and Laozi's *Daodejing*: The Gathering Emptiness of Thing and Place	59
4 Heidegger and the *Zhuangzi*: The Uselessness and Unnecessariness of Things	85
5 Heidegger's Dao amidst Thing and World	107
Part Two Nothingness, Emptiness, and the Clearing	131
6 Daoist Nothingness, Buddhist Emptiness, and the Myth of "Oriental Nothingness"	133
7 Nothingness, Emptiness, and the Clearing: An Intercultural Interpretation	147
8 The Nothing, Nihilism, and Heidegger's East Asian Entanglements	167
9 Reimagining the Ethics and Politics of Emptiness	187
Notes	199
Bibliography	228
Index	245

Acknowledgments

A book does not belong solely to its author. Hermeneutical transmissions, the research of others, and myriad conversations and encounters have helped inform my thinking and make this present work possible. I am grateful to all the teachers, scholars, and friends who have shaped my way. I would particularly like to express my gratitude to Emilia Angelova, Charles Bambach, Mark Cabural, David Chai, Charles Chan, Chung-ying Cheng, Kim-chong Chong, Bret Davis, Joshua Derman, William Edelglass, Timo Ennen, Saulius Geniusas, Siby George, Fabian Heubel, Jean-Yves Heurtebise, Jenny Hung, Patricia Huntington, Curtis Hutt, Leah Kalmanson, Sophia Katz, Halla Kim, Hye Young Kim, Theodore Kisiel, Sai Hang Kwok, Kwok-ying Lau, David Michael Kleinberg-Levin, Chenyang Li, Manhua Li, Dan Lusthaus, Rudolf Makkreel, John McCumber, Thomas Michael, Ronny Miron, Anish Mishra, Kyung-ah Nam, Richard Nelson, On-cho Ng, Franklin Perkins, Dennis Prooi, François Raffoul, James Risser, Frithjof Rodi, Jana Rošker, Frank Schalow, Dennis Schmidt, Martin Schönfeld, Brian Schroeder, Yumi Suzuki, Kellee Tsai, Qingjie James Wang, Robin Wang, Youru Wang, Mario Wenning, Ann Pang-White, Jason Wirth, Simon Wong, Tung Tin Wong, and especially Shengqing Wu.

I am also thankful for the following research opportunities and funding sources: the Herzog August Bibliothek (Wolfenbüttel) and the University of Hawai'i at Mānoa where I wrote the initial draft of this book; HKUST IEG20HS01, Hong Kong Research Grants Council (RGC) GRF 16631916, and Hong Kong Research Grants Council (RGC) HSSPFS 36000021 for funding archival, library, and other research activities.

Readers should keep in mind that this book is a sequel to Nelson 2017 that can, of course, be read independently as a related "intercultural genealogy." Note that there is some slight repetition in the text to remind readers in later chapters of earlier significant points. Some of the short discussions of Daoism, Buddhism, other German thinkers and writers, social-political philosophy, and Heidegger's broader life and thought might strike some as excursions, but they serve to contextualize, illustrate, and support the overall argument and interpretation offered in this book. As I interpret Heidegger in an intercultural, anarchic-egalitarian, and participatory democratic context, this requires confronting Heidegger's worst moments and tendencies while intensifying the thinking of freedom as releasement.

Also note, lengthier quotations from Chinese and German language sources have been placed in the endnotes. With both early ziranist or generative Daoism and Heidegger, it is difficult to think with and through their sources without encountering and engaging their words and linguistic strategies in their own sense and context.

Finally, note that parts of Chapters 1, 4, and 8 appear in substantially different forms in Nelson 2022c: 141–62; Nelson 2022: 787–806; and Nelson 2023b.

Introduction

1. Heidegger and the Way

Martin Heidegger (1889–1976) is a philosopher of being under and on the way. "Way" is arguably a more elemental guiding word than being, beings, or meaning to express the twists and turns of his thinking.[1] Heidegger insisted throughout his writings that the way toward a more decisive questioning of being, the unthought matter to be thought, is more fundamental than any given determinate answer or expected result. Each anticipatory indicative response remains provisional as the way itself overturns expectations and compels reposing the question of being anew. Heidegger's early methodology of formal indication and its continuation as wayfaring explains the variety, originality, and intensity of his reflections that cannot be reduced to a method or a doctrine.[2] This interpretive situation compels his readers to repose and enact for themselves the questionability and perplexity of that which is to be thought and enter a condition of being underway without a predetermined destination and purpose.

Thinking anticipates through expectations that can be upturned and reoriented by what is encountered. There is no uninterrupted "royal road" of conceptualization from thought and the subject to the truth of being. Heidegger himself confessed that he was confronted with—playing on the senses of "*Holzwege*," wooden or forest paths—unexpected twists, turns, and dead ends. The dead end is the place where one is forced to double back, repeat one's steps, and take new ones. He also spoke of his own errors and stupidities, as his pathways traversed freedom and fixation, good and evil, and truth and errancy. Numerous publications have reconstructed these pathways through narratives of unconcealment and concealment, social-political errancy and offense, and private reticence and hiddenness. The thinker is not only persistently concealed from others but remains concealed and unknown to himself. The philosopher of the unthought in the history of metaphysics does not necessarily sufficiently confront his own unthought. Nevertheless, thinking that would be appropriate to what is to be thought in its event cannot sidestep arduous walks, narrow passages, and steep ascending and descending paths. In Heidegger's twisting byways and sideways, in the play of shadow and light conveyed in his favorite passage from the *Daodejing* 道德經, a path emerges in which thing and world would be released through their emptiness into the free mystery of their own ways of manifesting and being. This is why philosophy, inveterately wrapped up in its own self-referential conceptuality without adequately recognizing that which addresses and motivates it, should ruthlessly criticize without abandoning Heidegger's thinking. More than this, it should be approached as an imperfect yet insightful exemplary model that continues to speak to the present condition.

Why then write or read about Heidegger and the *dao*? What is this *"dao"*? An initial clue is found in the *Zhuangzi* 莊子 that states a way is made by walking it. The Chinese *dao* 道 character is composed of the radicals related to walking (辶) and head (首). Some explanations accentuate the head as directing the feet. But the accent here is on walking and moving, as the head follows the passage of the feet stepping along the path and encountering the myriad things in their varying circumstances. Relational freedom and unanxious ease (*xiaoyao you* 逍遥游) occur in a wandering that recognizes and forgets things, values them in their uselessness and lets them go in their departure, and transitions with the transformations of self and world. This way as walked cannot be disconnected from that which is encountered on the way: changing things, localities, seasons, and birth and death. According to the *Zhuangzi*, these occur in an elemental generative nothingness (*wu* 無) from which attunement occurs by emptying and forgetting the heart-mind (*xin* 心). Emptiness can signify a gloomy absence of meaning in ordinary language. But, as linked with humility, simplicity, and sincerity in early Chinese thought, it is constitutive of a free and responsive way of life.

It is not accidental that Heidegger, who already began to think about the Daoist way in 1919 and 1930, and early Daoists accentuated questions of the thing as that which is to be encountered and nothingness as a way of living freely that undoes the fixities of the self and identity. This inquiry will recount and radicalize their tactics of questioning identity and undoing fixation. It is an attempt to critically reactivate and reimagine Heidegger's way in view of the early Daoist *dao* and, to a lesser but still significant extent, the Buddhist dharma by (1) historically tracing and situating Daoist and Buddhist influences operative in Heidegger's German contemporaries and his own thinking, (2) reinterpreting his thought from these sources (including those unfamiliar to him), and (3) articulating the senses of the thing, generative nothingness, and the open empty clearing for the sake of a renewed *ethos* of openness to things and world, as a way of freely and responsively wandering and abiding amidst them and the places they shape. This *ethos*, more elemental in its demand than recent object-oriented philosophy and thing-theory, would recognize how things have their own environing places and changing pathways, even if they are thought to have no well-being or sentience of their own.

This threefold task demands a specific intercultural practice of hermeneutics (the art of interpretation) in response to the tensions between historical circumstances and philosophical questions. Interculturality challenges the orthodox identity-based presuppositions that continue to dominate philosophy and its history. The heterodox interpretive strategy deployed here is a mixture of historiographic and philosophical inquiry, and Asian and European discourses, as we consider a variety of historically positioned exemplary cases and traverse shifting perspectives with and beyond Heidegger. First, archival and historical inquiry frees us to study the purportedly "small," semi-forgotten, and problematic questionable figures of an epoch that can lead to a more appropriate hermeneutical contextualization and historical sensibility in contrast to pure forms of theorizing and moralizing. The hermeneutics of words and concepts entails examining multiple generations rather than only a single renowned author. Engaging forgotten and semi-forgotten texts and authors can help facilitate generational contextualization as well as their further rediscovery. Secondly, Daoist and Buddhist texts should not only deliver raw data for European conceptual reasoning. They offer a variety of argumentative and interpretive strategies with their own situated specificity and philosophical stakes. Working through unthought hiddenness and the anxieties of influence, this analysis reveals how Heidegger is unique among European philosophers in learning from ways enacted in these sources.

What follows can be read as a reflection on Heidegger's statement: "Releasement toward things and openness for the mystery belong together. They grant us the possibility of residing in the world in a wholly other way" (GA 16: 528). This constellation of releasement, openness, mystery, things, and other ways of relational dwelling appears throughout his discussions of Daoist sources and was developed in conversation with them. Heidegger's pathways to the releasement and freedom of things (*Gelassenheit der Dinge*)—through the uncanniness of nothingness and the open emptiness of the clearing—are informed by his explicit engagements and unthought resonances with East Asian philosophies, particularly the *Daodejing*, attributed to the mysterious figure of Laozi 老子 and the *Zhuangzi*. The early forms of these two anthologies, composed from disparate sources, have been dated from the chaotic Warring States period (475–221 BCE). The redacted transmitted editions, used by the German translators read by Heidegger and his contemporaries, stem from the post-Han Wei-Jin period (220–420 CE). It is still insufficiently appreciated how the images and words employed in late-nineteenth- and early-twentieth-century German editions reverberate throughout Heidegger's writings, giving them an aura of both familiarity and strangeness in comparison with contemporary translations and readings.

How did this remarkable conjuncture and its concealment come to pass? Answering this question, the first task of this study, requires a situating and singularizing historical description. Heidegger's interest in Daoism was part of a generational movement—shared by Martin Buber and others—and unique in how it was adopted into his thinking. Heidegger was aware of Daoism since at least 1919. He repeatedly directly cited and indirectly evoked multiple translations of its two classics from 1930 (GA 80.1: 370; Petzet 1993: 18) to the final years of his life (GA 91: 667–8). It is noteworthy, given the remarkable shift in his thinking in 1942–1944, how he explicitly referenced and tacitly echoed—occasionally from 1919 to 1942 and with regularity beginning in 1943—their thought-images and interpretive strategies. His pivotal crisis and transformation of the mid-1940s, coinciding with the defeat of National Socialism, might be described as a quasi- or semi-Daoist turn. It incorporates and systematically reconfigures several distinctive Daoist elements based on German translations, his translation activities and conversations with a visiting Chinese scholar, and his own philosophical categories.

The significance of this adaptation of early Daoist sources into European philosophy remains contentious. First, a formerly prevalent view sees this intersection as a fortuitous personal idiosyncrasy that does not play a serious systematic role in his thinking. Second, another—increasingly widespread—analysis holds that these are crucial concealed sources from which his modes of speaking and thinking draw insight, orientation, and—in the crises of the closing years of the Second World War and early postwar period—healing and renewal. Earlier research on Heidegger and the "East" prepared the way for this change in perceptions but are often Orientalizing, mythologizing, and inadequately hermeneutically situated.[3] They frequently fail to appropriately recognize how these transmissions can dialogically speak back and help us question and reimagine key themes and categories not only in Heidegger but in European philosophy.

2. Shifting Perspectives: Heidegger's Daoism and Daoism's Heidegger

The present interpretation of Heidegger and the *dao* has three interwoven objectives. Its first aim is to convey a more multifaceted historical and intercultural sense of Heidegger's way, the Daoist *dao*, and the Buddhist dharma. It contests both Orientalist fantasies about Heidegger and "Eastern wisdom" and the opinion that Heidegger had myriad yet ultimately incidental Daoist affinities by tracing his Daoist encounters and intersections and how they helped guide key aspects of his philosophical journey in an elemental and systematic way. Its first mission is to map out Heidegger's explicit and implicit engagements with East Asian discourses concerning the thing, nothingness, and world with the intent of articulating the conditions of an elemental encounter with them. Second, this strategy makes it necessary to examine Daoist and Buddhist constellations beyond Heidegger's historically circumscribed acquaintance with them and allow them the freedom to speak back to European transmissions and shift European perspectives. A third interrelated undertaking, existentially the most vital as it is compelled by our contemporary situation, is to indicate prospects of responsively attuned and ecomimetic relations with things and within the world and, on that basis, the critical unfettering potential of ways of being environmentally and publicly attuned in response to existing ecological and social crisis-tendencies. These crises consist of the devastation of earth and thing, the obscuring of sky and world, environmental degradation and destruction, and the global climate predicament. Early Daoist philosophy and moments in Heidegger's thinking point toward different modes of attunement and dwelling that can "leap ahead" (*vorspringen*) in "being-with" (to expand Heidegger's early categories beyond human existence) and nurture life in responsive attunement by sympoietically (to adopt Donna Haraway's expression) co-appropriating and collaborating with others and things, self-patterning environing localities and ecosystems.

To accomplish this threefold task, this book's opening part focuses on elucidating the thing in its specificity and priority and Part Two on nothingness and how they mutually form the locus of sense and world. More specifically, Part One presents a historically informed intercultural description of Heidegger's philosophical journey in the context of an expansive analysis (beyond the German editions mentioned by Heidegger) of Daoist practices of undoing fixations. Daoist discourses accentuate generativity and fluidity, natality and mortality, responsive attunement (*wuwei* 無為) to spontaneous self-naturing (*ziran* 自然), thingly transience and transformation (*hua* 化), and the generative nothingness that nourishes the myriad things (*wanwu* 萬物). These expressions and thought-images, which defy the bifurcation of concept and picture, emerged in ancient Chinese sources mostly unfamiliar to Heidegger and other early European readers. These documents encompass recently excavated pre-Qin era silk and bamboo manuscripts, such as the Guodian and Mawangdui *Laozi* manuscripts that have dramatically altered contemporary studies of early Chinese thought. Heidegger also did not systematically investigate the transmitted Wei-Jin era mysterious learning editions and commentaries of Wang Bi 王弼 (226–249 CE) and Guo Xiang 郭象 (252–312 CE). The Sinologist and translator Richard Wilhelm (1873–1930) did study them, construing Daoism as a philosophy of the "sense of life," and these two editions served as the basis of every German translation available in Heidegger's milieu.

Part Two shifts and expands the horizons of this inquiry from the Daoist thing to nothingness, emptiness, and the clearing, drawing on Daoist, Buddhist, and modern East Asian discourses. Heidegger's earlier dismissiveness of Buddhism was adjusted in the postwar period, especially regarding Zen Buddhism. This changed appreciation is witnessed in his postwar conversations with visiting Japanese intellectuals and his interview with the Thai Buddhist monk Bhikku Maha Mani. His modified understanding is most evident in the 1953–1954 essay "From a Dialogue on Language." It marks the culmination of Heidegger's turn from the fear and trembling of existential nothingness to the clarity and freedom of emptiness, the open, and the clearing. Accordingly, in Part Two, we delve into the roles of Daoist nothingness, Buddhist emptiness, and East Asian discourses and interlocutors that helped mold postwar Heidegger's understanding of emptiness and clearing.

The project unfolded here offers a unique and innovative contribution in four ways: (1) a systematic reexamination of the German language translations and interpretations that shaped Heidegger's linguistic context and individual engagement with Daoism and the thing (in Part One) and Daoism, Buddhism, and nothingness (in Part Two); (2) an analysis of the linguistic and conceptual shifts in Heidegger's thinking that correlate with his interactions with Daoist, Buddhist, and East Asian texts and interlocutors; (3) a critical interpretation—with and beyond Heidegger and his generation—of early Daoist and classic Buddhist sources as indicating models of the self-nature of the thing and comporting oneself toward thing and world through practices of emptiness; and (4) a Zhuangzian Daoist and "Flower Garland" (*Huayan* 華嚴) Buddhist inspired critique and reimagining of the thing, nothingness, releasement, and their contemporary import.

3. A Preliminary Overview of the Chapters

Part One's five chapters examine varying answers to a question that recurs throughout Chinese and German discourses: What is a thing? First, the thing in the restricted sense signifies what is available, ready at hand, and useful. These "mere things" are of bare significance in the availability of daily use and consumption. These are the conventional anthropocentric categories of usefulness parodied and undermined in the *Zhuangzi* and by the mature Heidegger. Second, the thing in its expansive sense denotes "all beings" and encompasses all that is and might potentially be atoms, stones, plants, animals, humans, spirits, gods, and heaven and earth. Chapter 1 unfolds Daoist philosophy for the sake of resituating Heidegger's thought, tracing the expansive image and conception of things in texts associated with Laozi and Zhuangzi and their early Chinese context. The expression *wanwu* (myriad things) points toward all existents in their own concrete, plural, relational, and transformational generativity. Informed by this "ziranist" or "generative" clarification of the thing, Chapters 2 to 5 track Heidegger's journey from a (predominantly yet not exclusively) pragmatically instrumental and objectively represented thing (as useful instrumental tool and representational object) to the fullness of the thing *as* thing that gathers place and world.

This proposed reading of Heidegger's thing touches on a contested issue that can be preliminarily addressed here: the appropriateness and inappropriateness of the analysis of the thing and nature in *Being and Time*. I concur with Heidegger's later self-critique that this seminal, brilliant, and incomplete work is overly transcendental and pragmatic, requiring a more radical step toward being and the thing that only fully emerged after the Second World War.[4] Heidegger mentioned but barely articulated a "third" more primordial "power of nature" in *Being and Time* (GA 2: 70, 211) and "nature in an originary sense" in the 1929 "The Essence of Ground" (GA 9: 155). Heidegger noted that criticisms of the absence of nature in *Being and Time* were in part correct in later self-reflections and retorted that this work did not aim at a complete philosophical system (GA 82: 8, 293). Further, the thing cannot be simply identified with nature, and nature with power, as Heidegger increasingly problematized in his 1930s genealogies of *phúsis* and more fully recognized in the 1940s. The mature Heidegger insisted on a turn from a still too Dasein-centric approach in the late 1920s, in which things are primarily perceived in their availability and serviceability, toward the priority of the thing as "carrying and opening the there" (GA 82: 493–4). This transition—whether understood as a gradual adjustment or fundamental break—suggestively intersects with his readings of the *Daodejing* and the *Zhuangzi*. The *Zhuangzi*, for instance, discloses through parables and perspectival shifts how the pragmatically and conceptually available thing (labeled and fixed as an isolated object) is not the dynamic thing encountered and followed in its transformations. The "useless" free thing and the sustaining nourishing earth cannot be pragmatically or theoretically dictated, and the very paradigm of the anthropocentric constitutive subject is inadequate to them.

This is not the only example. Heidegger returned to Daoist-inflected interpretive strategies and thought-images of letting beings and things be themselves, preserving the darkness that nourishes, entering the silence in which genuine hearing happens, emptying the heart-mind for the sake of the encounter and event, and the mystery beyond mystery. Heidegger's mature thinking of the ontological "event" (*Ereignis*) is connected to his most mentioned line from the *Daodejing*. The event refers to what is hidden coming into view, or the matter to be thought entering thinking, while it inevitably retains dimensions of hiddenness and being unthought that escape the subject. Heidegger's resonances with the *Daodejing* and the *Zhuangzi*, based on a partial degree of direct influence, allow for a reevaluation of Daoist *ziran* and Heidegger's "ziranist" leanings that culminate in the releasement of things.

The *Daodejing* states that all things, even the *dao*, follow their own *ziran*. What is *ziran*? This expression emerged in a specific historical constellation that is profoundly unlike yet still can speak to our situation. Two prevalent translations are spontaneity and nature. "Nature" is inadequate to express what is meant by "*ziran*" and can only be used in a highly qualified sense. Unlike the "nature" that is frequently opposed to the human world in modern thought, and thus has an ideological and mythological aura, *ziran* is enacted in all things human and nonhuman. "Ziranism" (in contrast to reductive naturalisms) refers to the centrality of the multiplicity, spontaneity, and transformation of self-generation and self-patterning. Daoist *ziran* signifies generatively being self (*zi* 自) so (*ran* 然), autopoietic self-emerging and self-patterning, or nature in the qualified sense of self-naturing. This sense of *ziran* is fundamental albeit incompletely thought in Heidegger's Daoist encounters. These engagements occurred in the context of his understanding of *Abendland* (Occident, the evening land, Greek *hésperos* and *dúsis*, which referred to Europe and not the "West" in the current sense) and *Morgenland* (Orient, the morning land, Greek *anatolḗ*, the land of the rising sun). Naturalism seeks to dictate the nature of the thing through a determining theory or picture of what it considers true nature. It inadequately recognizes human participation within nature. "Ziranism" expresses in contrast the need to attend to the self-unfolding or self-dynamic of the thing that is possible through practices of emptying and realizing the humility of the heart-mind (*xuxin* 虛心) and attuned non-coercive action (*wuwei*).

Daoist generativity does not entail naive oppositions between the organic and the artificial, the primitive and the civilized, or the passive and the active, as inaction is enacted in action, clarity in mystery, and simplicity in complexity. It likewise cannot be reduced to a first principle or to causality, at least in their standard explanations, owing to the elemental spontaneity and transformability in things themselves. Instead of an unbroken determinate sequence, or resignation before an indifferent necessity, there is an adaptive sense of generational change in natality and mortality that gives each singular life its due while letting it go in death. This *ziran*-directed guiding strategy entails the reconstruction of several core, and arguably the most transformative, elements in Heidegger's philosophy. Indeed, as this book demonstrates, Heidegger's anarchic and Daoist tendencies are closely interconnected in accentuating the generative self-patterning of things. *Ziran* can be understood in the *Zhuangzi* through images of dark watery chaos.[5] This free self-patterning chaos has anarchic (without *arché* or *dao*-archic) and—if reimagined under modern conditions—participatory democratic implications in stressing adaptive spontaneity and collaborative or sympoietic self-ordering by human and non-human individuals and communities; this strategy necessitates critiquing Heidegger's most problematic philosophical and social-political commitments while recovering and extending moments of truth.

Chapter 6, analogous to the contextualization of Chapter 1, resituates Heidegger's thinking by shifting perspectives to Daoist generative nothingness (*wu*) and Buddhist emptying emptiness (Sanskrit: *śūnyatā*; Chinese *kong* 空). These have their own specificity and are not merely instances of a monolithic "Oriental nothingness" or nihilism. Daoist nothingness and Buddhist emptiness have a variety of senses within

Daoist and Buddhist teachings that differ from the monotheistic *creatio ex nihilo*, the "nonbeing" of classical Greek philosophy, and the mystical nothingness of Occidental metaphysics and onto-theology. The systematic clarification of varieties of nothingness and emptiness in Chapter 6 situates Chapter 7's reenvisioning of Heidegger's earlier existentially oriented philosophy of nothingness and its subsequent transitions to the emptiness and the clearing of his postwar thinking.

Chapter 8 concerns the intercultural position of Heidegger's nothingness in its early reception in the 1930s and 1940s by East Asian philosophers and intellectuals. This chapter contains an exploration of the controversial and inconvenient existential Buddhist and transnational fascistic intellectual Kitayama Junyū 北山淳友 (1902–1962) whose philosophy of nothingness provides a counterargument to my interpretation. Kitayama studied philosophy in Freiburg and Heidelberg during the 1920s and remained active in Germany until 1944, providing significant clues to Heidegger's intercultural contexts. There are several reasons for this unusual retrieval. First, he was directly involved in Heidegger's German milieu, as one of the first authors to extensively engage with the discourses of Heidegger and phenomenology, South and East Asian Buddhism, and Japanese philosophy for two decades in Weimar and National Socialist Germany. Secondly, Heidegger was familiar with him, and several passages in Heidegger's later interpretations echo Kitayama's earlier uses of Heideggerian categories. Thirdly, Kitayama's problematic identification of the nothingness of Daoism, Buddhism, and the Kyōto School with the destruction of the liberal individual for the sake of collectivist nationalist, militaristic, and authoritarian politics is valuable to illustrate the perils of incomplete elucidations of nothingness and practices of emptiness.[6] Emptiness does not loosen the borders between the self and society for the sake of a determinate collective identity in classical Daoism and Buddhism. It radically unfixes forms of substantive identity in, for instance, the different strategies of equalizing things in nothingness (Zhuangzi) or reciprocal interpenetration in emptiness (Huayan Buddhism) that releases both the specific singular and the relational whole.

The concluding chapter draws out implications for a new philosophy of nothingness, thing, and world. It reassesses the historical and political tensions of modern discourses of nothingness by adopting the relational singular of Zhuangzi and Huayan (which are distinctive yet complementary) to contest essentialized individual and social realities. As collective identities are just as constructed and illusory as individual identities, if not more so, it is a mistake with perilous consequences to destructure and decenter the individual subject while fetishizing the collective subject as a monological identity removed from communicative gathering and the existential dynamics of personal and interpersonal life. The challenge is to encounter and express connection and relatedness, and dismantle binary oppositions, without disregarding environing locality and particularity or—to be clear—reducing them to either particular or universal identities that systemically exclude and subjugate what is non-identical. Since it would be negligent to avoid critical discussion of ideology and politics in the current climate, even as ideology and culture-industry impact the most critical consciousness and practices, the complex philosophical and social-political contexts traced in the closing chapters entail learning from Heidegger's insights and failures to resituate the ethical and political roles of nothingness and emptiness, reconsidering them with and beyond their previous incarnations.

4. *Dao* and *Ethos*: Critical Intercultural Implications

Heidegger has left a troublesome and thought-provoking legacy. The agrarian utopianism that informed his interest in Daoism demands a differentiated ideology-critical interpretation. His hermeneutical situation requires thinking through ambiguity and complexity, as good and bad only appear in the finitude and imperfection of life. Heidegger is one of the few modern European philosophers to seriously engage with and adaptively learn from East Asian philosophy, breaking with philosophy's Eurocentrism in practice even if he could not do so within his conception of Occidental philosophy (*abendländische Philosophie*). Heidegger, despite himself and his problematic anti-democratic nationalist political commitments in the 1930s that ziranist Daoism and Heidegger's more thoughtful critics place in question, helps to confront the continuing Eurocentrism of philosophy, its systematic distortion of the history and practice of philosophy, and disclose other freer possibilities for thinking and dwelling.

Daoist generative nothingness, Buddhist emptiness of form, and Heidegger's open clearing of being convey exemplary orientational models of being relationally free and responsive in the world with things and environments. They disclose in their radical moments three distinctive ways of transformatively undoing experiential and linguistic hypostatization and of releasing self and things. As unfolded in this ziranist philosophical reconstruction, each expresses ways of contesting sedimented formations of reified life and thought. Daoist nurturing care (*ci* 慈) for things, Buddhist loving-kindness and compassion for sentient beings, and Heidegger's care (*Sorge*) suggest distinctive indicative ways of leaping-ahead for and critical exemplary models of caring for things and nourishing life.

There are two initial problems that confront this approach to Heidegger. First, his formally indicative categories of care, being-with, and leaping-ahead were restricted to human existence in *Being and Time*. Secondly, Heidegger described the analytic of Dasein as ethically neutral and suspends the language of ethics, morality, and value. This is a problem if interpreters are bound solely to *Being and Time*. The Berlin philosopher Katharina Kanthack has argued that this neutrality does not entail ethical indifference, which would signify a forgetting of care, but leads to an *ethos* of relational being-with and ethical knowledge of self and other (Kanthack 1958 and 1964). This formally emptied neutrality opens the concrete nexus of ethical questionability, deliberation, and decision. It allowed for questioning the ethical modalities of leaping-in (*einspringen*) to coercively dominate the other and leaping-ahead to care for and nurture the other's self-individuation. The later Heidegger provides instructive ways to reorient and expand his earlier discourse. He speaks not of ethics, with its fixed rules and virtues, but of *ethos* or "originary ethics" (GA 9: 356). He articulates an *ethos* more fundamental than ethics and a worldly mortal abiding in openness to mystery that is more originary than *ethos* (GA 98: 345). Most significantly, this *ethos* encompasses things and their spaces. At the same time, factical existence is another key piece of the puzzle, as intersubjective and interthingly comportments are complexly mediated by material and social forms of life in which they serve apologetic ideological as well as critical transformational roles.

The guiding aspiration of these chapters is to reinterpret and reimagine Heidegger's thinking of being and his originary ethics given their ziranist elements and our hermeneutical situation. Its primary thesis is that, entangled with Daoist and other intercultural sources, Heidegger's path proceeds from the paradigmatic Occidental philosophy of available givenness and mere presence—which conceals the open spacing of things and seeks to logically exclude and dialectically subordinate negativity and the nothing—to nothingness, emptiness, and the clearing in their coming to presence and withdrawal in absence or, to accentuate its mutable verbal sense, presencing-absencing. The nurturing darkness and mystery of nothingness and the concealing-unconcealing openness that characterize Heidegger's thinking of being are, when interpreted as bearing and *ethos*, elemental to responsively encountering and dwelling with things in the world-clearing. Zhuangzi's vision of free and easy wandering indicates ways of practicing philosophy as contesting and unraveling fixations. These practices allow rethinking Heidegger's pathways and reimagining for ourselves things, nothingness, and world in the specificity of our existential condition.

Part One

Dao, Thing, and World

1

Way, Thing, and World in Laozi, Zhuangzi, and Heidegger

I. Introduction

1. Phenomenology, Daoism, and the Thing

What is a thing? To provide a preliminary description, the thing appears to be that which presents or manifests itself. Ordinary language and philosophical discourses of the thing oscillate between the narrow sense of the "mere thing" as available tool and present object, the epistemic sense of a presently existing object, and the plenitude of the thing in its way of being. The first sense contrasts things with human beings and living creatures. The thing is characterized by its accessibility and usefulness. The second sense signifies anything and everything that exists. In modern German philosophy, to introduce one example, Hermann Lotze began his metaphysics with the question of the thing and defined ontology as the study of the real that consists of things that "are," and their nexus of events and relations, in contrast to those that "are not" (Lotze 1879: 1). There is an additional third sense of things in which they are not merely available for use or present for thought. There is an inkling in moments of beauty, sublimity, and terror that things and the world have their own sense that demands attentiveness. The thing places a claim on human language and thought in these and other moments, calling for patience, reticence, and silence in encountering it in its plain and unadorned other-power or self-so-ing.

In Hugo von Hofmannsthal's poetic words, the encounter is with the "reluctant beauty of small things" (Hofmannsthal 1979: 65). German language poets, such as Hofmannsthal and Rilke, allowed the thing to shape the words and mood of the poem. The epistemic and metaphysical thing of theorizing seems barren and deficient compared with the encountered thing of the poets. Heidegger paired Daoists and poets to stress their contact with things, being amidst the world, and thoughtfulness that he adopted as models for thinking. The first five chapters trace the transitions and implications of Heidegger's philosophical journey from the instrumental thing of use and the representational thing as object to the gathering thing keeping in view Daoist sources of the self-generative *creatio continua* of the thing.[1]

His early philosophy of the thing emerged in the context of debates between idealist and realist philosophies of the thing and his training in phenomenology as a methodology that describes consciousness and its objects. His teacher Edmund Husserl described phenomenology as a movement "toward the things [or matters] themselves" (*zu den Sachen selbst*), defining the thing (*das Ding*) in the *Philosophy of Arithmetic* (1891) as that which bears characteristics with unity through temporal and spatial variation and—as what is experienced points back to who experiences—in *Ideas* (1913) as the correlational object of intentional consciousness.[2]

Husserl's phenomenological strategies produced several dilemmas for Heidegger. First, the thing would seemingly designate what is most concrete while—in the thing as object—abstracting away from the specific features and qualities that make particular things uniquely what they are. Second, given the material, social-historical, pragmatic, and conceptual mediations of the thing, given the mediated referential and interpretive nexus through which it is experienced, the thing cannot be simply intuited and described, yet we (or, at least, some) wish to encounter it as something of its own that exceeds an anthropocentrically constituted and constructed object.

Phenomenology simultaneously promoted and prevented answering the question of thing *qua* thing for Heidegger. He repeatedly reposed the question "what is a thing?" He inquired in response to these tensions between concrete thing and intentional object in the context of (1) phenomenologically encountering and describing the thing, (2) confronting "Occidental" (*abendländische*) philosophical conceptions of the thing (particularly in Aristotle and Kant), and—most extraordinarily—(3) engaging the Daoist emptiness of the thing in the *Daodejing*, attributed to Laozi, and its uselessness in the *Zhuangzi*.[3]

Before proceeding further, we might want to ask: what is Daoism and why is it significant for Heidegger and his generation? The expression has a variety of historical meanings. First, Daoism (*daojia* 道家) was applied to Laozi in a retrospective construction and categorization of schools in the *Historical Records* (*Shiji* 史記) of the Han dynasty historians Sima Tan 司馬談 (c. 165–110 BCE) and his son Sima Qian 司馬遷 (c. 140–86 BCE) for whom it signified Huanglao 黃老 biopolitical-cosmological discursive formations. Second, types of "religious Daoism" (*daojiao* 道教) emerged during the late and post-Han eras that were associated with biospiritual arts of internal alchemy (*neidan shu* 內丹術), the way of immortals (*daoxian* 道仙), and the way of spirits/gods (*shendao* 神道). Third, and most pertinently here, it referred to the teachings of Laozi and Zhuangzi, whose historical connections are unclear and controversial, for generations of Chinese literati and modern European intellectuals. This sense can be designated early, Lao-Zhuang, or ziranist.[4]

"Ziran" is a key interpretive term throughout this inquiry. What I designate "ziranism" should not be construed as "naturalism" insofar as naturalism misses what it would signify by limiting nature to a fixed positioned image in an enframing (i.e., positioning into a determining frame) world-picture that deworlds things and human existence. *Ziran* is explored as an *ethos* and interpretive orientation that prioritizes recognizing the spacing of the thing and the interthingly nexus in their own ways of manifesting and being. *Ziran* is "nature" only in the most anti-reductive and expansive sense of calling for an attuned and responsive comportment and recognition of the autopoiesis in sympoiesis of the myriad things. Autopoiesis is not applied to but rather reimagined through Daoist sources, as are other key expressions such as *ethos*. It signifies here a dynamic, generative, plural self-formation irreducible to a closed determinate system (which would exclude questions of *ethos* and ethics constitutive of the first- and second-person perspective) or a fixed, essential individual or collective identity. It indicates the myriad things in their relational self-so-ness, or self-generative naturing, and interthingly nexus without reduction to restrictive epistemic and metaphysical constructions of nature and the thing. This book proposes in this light a ziranist interpretation and critique of Heidegger's long-standing engagement with early Daoist sources.

2. The Art of Tea, the Safeguarding Darkness, and the Joy of Fish

When did this encounter begin to emerge? Two anecdotes help answer this question. An old Japanese anecdote of a gift in 1919 recounts how the young Heidegger initially encountered Daoist conceptions of the thing and being-in-the-world in the German edition of *The Book of Tea* by Okakura Kakuzō 岡倉覚三 (1862–1913). He received this popular book as a gift in 1919 from Itō Kichinosuke 伊藤吉之助 (1885–1961).[5] Okakura fuses motifs from Laozi-Zhuangzi, the Chan/Zen Buddhist dharma, and Shintō together to draw a picture of the East Asian spirit of tea as it is enacted in concrete ritual practices that carefully attend to the smallest details of tea, water, utensils, and environment. One meets the world in a sip of tea.

According to Okakura, the way and art of tea-making and drinking realizes the Daoist "art of being-in-the-world" (*Kunst des In-der-Welt-Seins*). This appears to be the first hyphenated use of this expression in German. It expresses the Daoist awareness of how self and world are relationally bound together, and it is only in practices that freedom occurs. Freedom is not a quality of the self but is thoroughly relational. This Daoist worldly art consists of an *ethos* of continual adaptation and readjustment to the environment where one maintains relationships and makes room for things and others without abandoning one's position (Okakura 1919: 29). In Okakura's chapter on Daoism, he accentuates the role of emptiness (*die Leere*) in the *Daodejing*'s imagery of the spatial vacuum. The reality of the room is found in its emptiness, the usefulness of the water jug dwells in its emptiness rather than its material form, and emptiness is all-encompassing as the space and possibility of movement (Okakura 1919: 30). Conspicuously, and not fortuitously given the historical and linguistic evidence, these descriptions reverberate throughout Heidegger's thinking.

A second anecdote tells of Heidegger's Daoist affinities a decade later in the closing years of the ill-fated Weimar Republic. Heidegger's friend, the art critic Heinrich Wiegand Petzet (1909–1997), recounted how Heidegger visited Bremen in October 1930 to hold the lecture that eventually became "On the Essence of Truth" (*Von Wesen der Wahrheit*) that elucidated truth as unconcealment (Petzet 1993: 18). Heidegger enthusiastically discussed the *Daodejing* during the lecture and the *Zhuangzi* at the subsequent dinner.

Heidegger incorporated the *Daodejing* into early versions of this pivotal lecture: "those who know lightness wrap themselves in darkness" ("Der seine Helle kennt, sich in sein Dunkel hüllt") (GA 80.1: 370). This is Victor von Strauss's translation of an expression (*zhi qi bai, shou qi hei* 知其白, 守其黑) in chapter 28. It depicts the sage as a streambed and template image for the world who preserves the feminine in the masculine, childlikeness in virtue, darkness in light, and *dao*-like qualities amidst the mundane world (Strauss 1870: 140; Lou 1980: 74). Heidegger elucidated here the play of unconcealment-and-concealment, referring to the *dao*'s movements between lightness and darkness. In the next sentence, he introduced another expression he recurrently linked with the *Daodejing*: "the genuine search is not for that which is only unveiled, but exactly on the contrary for the mystery (*Geheimnis*)" (GA 80.1: 370). The freedom of the mystery is the unconcealing-concealing "letting be of beings" (*Seinlassen des Seienden*).

Heidegger referred to Strauss's translation of chapter 28 in the third Freiburg and Marburg version of the lecture (GA 80.1: 397), in letters and notes, and decades later in *Identity and Difference* (GA 11: 138). Indeed, Heidegger persistently returns to Daoist-inflected thought-images of letting beings and things be themselves, preserving the darkness that nourishes and regenerates, entering the silence in which genuine hearing transpires, emptying the heart-mind for the sake of the encounter and event of being (instead of *dao*), and the twofold mystery beyond mystery.

Petzet depicts how Heidegger was still pondering Daoist thought-images after his 1930 lecture on truth. Heidegger surprised the attendees of a dinner party by requesting a copy of a book called the *Speeches and Parables of Zhuangzi* (*Reden und Gleichnisse des Tschuang-tse*). Buber had translated this selection around two decades earlier based on English translations by Frederic Henry Balfour (1881), Herbert A. Giles (1889), and James Legge (1891) and it was a familiar book among Weimar era intelligentsia.[6] Otto Pöggeler adds that Heidegger appears to be deeply familiar with Buber's translation of the *Zhuangzi* and perhaps even of his *Tales of the Hasidim* as well.[7] Pöggeler does not provide sufficient detail here. A second indication of this relationship is that Buber's "Afterword" to the *Zhuangzi* discussed the same sentence concerning darkness and light from Strauss's *Daodejing*. Buber writes of hiddenness (*Verborgenheit*) and unhiddenness, the generative hiddenness that nurtures life, speaks to the sages, and is encountered in abyssal solitude (Buber 2013: 110). According to Buber, enacting hiddenness in both word and action constitutes the history of Laozi's teaching.[8]

Heidegger proceeded to read and interpret the narrative of the joy of fish (*yule* 魚樂) from Buber's translation of the "Autumn Floods" (*qiushui* 秋水) *Zhuangzi* chapter. Zhuangzi (Zhuang Zhou 莊周) and his friend the skeptic Huizi 惠子 (Hui Shi 惠施) debated possibilities for genuinely recognizing the joy of fish while watching their playful movements from the bridge above. Richard Wilhelm, whose translation Heidegger also cites, construed Zhuangzi as offering a Kantian-like critical resolution of Huizi's dogmatic "Humean" skepticism (Wilhelm 1912: 9). This scene might be understood as presenting a skeptical problem of knowledge in which Zhuangzi, a proto-Wittgenstein, skeptically outdoes Huizi's skeptical doubts about knowing, throwing the doubter into doubt. The dogmatic skeptic assumes a priori that one cannot know, presupposing the game of knowing and not knowing that Wittgenstein exposed in *On Certainty* (Wittgenstein 1969), while Zhuangzi freely followed the fish in their changing movements without anxiously being confined by the game of knowledge and ignorance. Whereas the dogmatist presumes to inherently grasp the givenness and essence of things, and the skeptic imagines all is text and interpretative projection, Zhuangzi recognizes that there can be no fixed borders between interpretation and world or fish and non-fish. That is, we are not able to establish this distinction in a fashion that could ground either absolutism or skepticism. Huizi and the dogmatic skeptic fixate on what is known and not known based on the hypostatization of self and non-self as isolated substantive identities. But Zhuangzi contests the boundaries of self and non-self, being or not being a fish, or knowing and not knowing. The Zhuangzian exemplary genuine person (*zhenren* 真人) freely adopts to and responsively moves along with the transformations of perspectives, things, and their own self.

Heidegger appears to have realized that this dialogue concerns intersubjective and interthingly relations. Petzet describes how, on this evening in Bremen, Heidegger delved into the implications of this encounter with the otherness of the fish for being-with (*Mitsein*).[9] Heidegger analyzed being-with as ethically neutral in *Being and Time*. Yet this analysis is not ethically indifferent as it discloses forms of ethical and relational knowledge of self, others, and the world (Kanthack 1958). Did Heidegger construe the story as an allegory for interhuman encounters? Probably yes, as being-with designates in *Being and Time* the sociality of Dasein, in the prospect of an authentic "we" and in the fallenness of the "they." It did not encompass relations with—as he described them in 1929–30—worldless things and world-poor animals. Even so, the inkling of an alternative way of interacting with—albeit not yet leaping-ahead for the sake of—animals and things is glimpsed here in 1930, even if it primarily served as an image for intersubjective interaction. Possibilities of encountering and interacting with living and nonliving things (i.e., thing in the expansive sense that encompasses any entity) reoccur in passages in the 1930s (such as in GA 45: 3, 29). They would be radically transformed in Heidegger's 1940s engagements with the *Daodejing* and the *Zhuangzi* and postwar philosophy in which he questions the anthropocentric priority of the human and emphasizes the centrality of the thing vis-à-vis the subject as a moment and place of gathering world.[10]

3. The Thing and the Worlding of the World

We do not know how Heidegger specifically responded to Okakura's *The Book of Tea*. The thirty-year-old Heidegger was already thinking in 1919 of the verbal character of the world, as he sought to depersonalize and verbalize reified substantives in formally indicative (as he would soon call them) expressions such as "it worlds" (*es weltet*) and "it values" (*es wertet*) introduced in the 1919 lecture-course *The Determination of Philosophy*. He proposed there that "living in an environing world, it signifies for me everywhere and always, it is all worldly, 'it worlds.'"[11] But this worlding character of the world is suppressed in ordinary experience, and environmental meaningfulness (*das Bedeutungshafte*) loses its meaning (*ent-deutet*). The living-experiencing of the environing worlding of the world (*Umwelt erleben*) is de-vitalized or "de-lived" (*ent-lebt*). The "it worlds" undergoes processes of substantialization as it is distilled into and concealed in the objectness of things (*res*) that René Descartes had divided into the extended thing (*res extensa*) and the thinking thing (*res cogitans*).

Heidegger examined in the next 1919/20 lecture-course *Basic Problems of the Phenomenology* how world is engulfed in the reifications of lived-experiences (*Verdinglichungen der Erlebnisse*) and the devitalization of life (*Entlebung*) (GA 58: 183). Reification signifies becoming "thinglike" in Karl Marx's paradigmatic assertion that persons become things and things become persons through commodification. Typically, reification is characterized as a loss of the subject's sense of being an active subject and cannot apply to nonhuman beings (e.g., Lukács). But reification is a fixation in the flow of experience, language, and environment. It is not merely a lapse by the subject but a systematic loss of relational openness and possibilities. In Heidegger's analysis, by contrast, there is also a reification of things (*res*) and world. Already in this early lecture-course, the thing is separated from its environing relational worlding character and posited as an object for the subject. The thing is "only there as such," as a correlate of the ego, and reduced to the real as purely existing, in the distancing theoretical attitude that he attributed to Husserl. Still, "it worlds" is intimated in specific ways of encountering things in questions such as when one asks (perhaps in surprise) "What sort of thing is that?" (GA 56/57: 89). The "real" constructed in idealism, which strives to overcome the fixated "dead thing" with the life of subjectivity, and in realism, which fixates it as ontic, is impoverished in losing contact with the superabundance and multiplicity of the life of the thing. The life of the thing functions as an implicit norm that shaped Heidegger's early philosophy of the thing. But the self-emerging thing is increasingly conceived as either a pragmatically useful or worldless theoretical object.

Things are understood in the lecture-courses of the 1920s as objects of a constrained notion of immediate external experience and natural scientific and theoretical inquiry (GA 58: 51). Such objectivizing knowledge of things is an inappropriate modality for grasping the self-world (GA 58: 223). The reification of relations is extended to the reflexive nexus of the self-world (which is neither subject nor object) when it is seen as consisting of an ontic nexus of things in which the self-world loses both its "self" and "world" character (GA 58: 232). The self exists in reification when it is subsumed like a mere thing in this instrumental nexus as a mere object among other objects. The objectivized neutralized thing as object in his winter semester 1929–30 lecture-course is said to lack world: "The stone is worldless, without world, has no world" (GA 29/30: 289). The stone, the stream, and the mountain are not world-disclosive, not world-events. They are not the worlding of the world of "it worlds" and—unlike in Heidegger's later thought—cannot address me or their perceiver.

The object has two primary dimensions, and a third inadequately thought one of non-anthropocentric nature that haunts Heidegger's early project and compels his subsequent turn (GA 2: 70, 211; GA 9: 155). The object is predominantly (1) instrumentally ready-to-hand (*zuhanden*) in pragmatic routine in an ontic nexus of tools and equipment or (2) objectively present-at-hand (*vorhanden*) for theoretical inquiry (GA 23: 24). Things as ready-to-hand serve in *Being and Time* the function of an instrumental "in order to" (*um-zu*) in its manipulable handiness (*Handlichkeit*), conduciveness (*Beiträglichkeit*), serviceability (*Dienlichkeit*), and usability (*Verwendbarkeit*) that constitute an equipmental whole (*Zeugganzheit*) through which things are encountered as equipment available for routine use (GA 2: 68).

Things are experienced and perceived primarily as objects of use, exchange, and—as present-at-hand—objective inquiry. Yet things are still beyond this objectification in a subterranean third dimension that stretches from the life of the thing in 1919 to the few insufficient remarks about the natural thing (*Naturding*) in the late 1920s to the thing that gathers, says (*Sagen*), and addresses me (*spricht mich an*) in the 1950s. At this juncture, however, the practical referential nexus of significance (*Verweisungszusammenhang der Bedeutsamkeit*) determines the world of Dasein, and the equipmental nexus determines things in their instrumental obtainability to be used, only interrupted by their uselessness in breakdowns and malfunctions. This approach is undoubtedly groundbreaking, yet it is not entirely satisfying.

Simply stated, Heidegger's early version of relational holism centered around the being-there of human existence and his later version centered around the thing. This early analysis was inadequate according to his own later remarks that gave greater priority to the thing as generating the sense of place and world. Emmanuel Levinas noted how Heidegger's incomplete account in *Being and Time* presupposes without appropriately articulating the elemental as an inappropriable atmosphere and milieu of air, earth, rain, sunlight, and wind that "suffice for themselves" (Levinas 1969: 132). In freely wandering, one enjoys the fresh breeze and the sunlight not for a purposive goal but for themselves, as the stone and the blade of grass appear in the elemental interplay of light and shadow. Heidegger ignores how the elemental nourishes me and things as they are encountered in non-purposive enjoyment (*jouissance*) (Levinas 1969: 134). Despite the pragmatic instrumental tendencies criticized by Levinas and his later self, Heidegger's late 1920s explication of the thing is not merely pragmatic. Even as things are interpreted as dominated by a referential nexus of usage and usefulness, Heidegger also analyzes the facticity of interruptive breakdown, disorienting questionability and uncanniness, and possibilities of other forms of relational attunement in encountering things. There are moments that point toward a fuller philosophy of the thing.

In the 1935–37 "The Origin of the Work of Art," the apparently natural thing, the thing as instrumental equipmental objectness (*Zeug, Gebrauchsding*), and the work (*Werk*) are differentiated as the artwork discloses the thing that bears and opens the "there" and liberates it from the nexus of instrumentality. The work discloses the constitutive role of things in the thereness of human existence (GA 82: 484–7). Even prior to the ostensive turn (a notion Heidegger introduced in his auto-critiques of the middle and late 1930s) to the poetic thinking and saying of being, there are indications of intimate relations with things and their life in his account of the atmosphere of attunement and mood—such as the thing as encountered in situations of extreme utter boredom (GA 29/30: 132), existential anxiety, resigned indifference, or astonished wonder—that increasingly draws Heidegger toward poetic and Daoist ways of addressing and being responsively attuned with the thing in releasing it through emptiness into its way of being.

4. Releasement and Being on the Way: *Ethos* without Mysticism

The primary objection against Daoism's import for Heidegger appeals to German poets and mystics. Does Heidegger's embrace of the sensibility of the thing signify a form of religious mystical experience or poetic "thing-mysticism" (*Dingmystik*)? The latter category, popularized by Walther Rehm (1930: 297–358), has been applied to poets of humility before reality (as in Hofmannsthal or Rilke) and the later Heidegger who appears to share this sentiment. Heidegger's thing primarily motivates, without doubt, the poetics and climate of Heidegger's discourses; it also, nonetheless, signals an immanent elemental co-relational *ethos*. But what of the modern Occidental category of religious mysticism?

Buber and Heidegger avoid and suggest alternatives to the Orientalist mystical and occultist appropriations of their era. Buber shifted from mysticism to ethics, a shift in which Daoist impulses played an underexplored role. We see in Heidegger's reflections a justified suspicion of the category of mysticism as he transitions in his later thinking to *ethos* or that which is more primordial than *ethos*. This transformation involves an intercultural reinterpretation of German mystical and Daoist sources. Earlier discourses of releasement concerned the soul or the self rather than things. This is palpable in multiple nineteenth-century and twentieth-century comparative readings of Laozi and Meister Eckhart. Despite their distinctive contexts, these sources link Daoist "acting without acting," or acting from a responsive attunement of minimal assertion and calculation (*wei wuwei* 為無為), and Eckhart's "releasement" (*Gelassenheit*) under the banner of mysticism.

Examining such sources reveals how the cross-cultural matching and classification of meanings within the same linguistic community can arrive at strikingly divergent results.[12] This problematic led Schleiermacher to conclude that hermeneutics requires both a contextualizing linguistic interpretation as well as an individualizing psychological interpretation to form a holistic perspective on an author or text (Schleiermacher 2012). It might be objected that this hermeneutical strategy is overly reductive. However, although Schleiermacher's specific interpretive model and its psychological presuppositions are no longer adequate, interpretation still demands both contextualizing and particularizing historical and linguistic strategies to elucidate the said and unsaid of texts and discourses. Secondly, historically and linguistically situating Heidegger's thinking, as pursued here, need not lead to mere historiography and reductive misinterpretation, since it can illuminate the being-historical event and truth of this thinking while not ignoring its historical complicities and mediations.[13]

Let us reflect on a few contextualizing examples and digressions that can help situate this analysis. In his 1870 translation of the *Daodejing*, Victor von Strauss translated the "highest vacuity" (*xuji* 虛極) at the beginning of chapter 16 as the pinnacle of renunciation (*Entäußerung*) and, in a note, added that this was what Eckhart called secluded detachment (*Abgeschiedenheit*) (Strauss 1870: 85). The German American public philosopher and pioneering intercultural thinker Paul Carus identified the simplicity, quietude, and unity of Laozi and Eckhart in the introduction to his 1898 English edition of the *Daodejing* (Carus 1898: 24). It was in the comparative religious works of the theologians Hermann Mandel and Friedrich Heiler that Laozi's *wuwei* and Eckhart's *Gelassenheit* were interpreted as ways of emptying the soul (Mandel 1912: 256; Heiler 1918: 252).

The transcultural linking of *Gelassenheit* with the *Daodejing* is not new with Heidegger. The expressions *Gelassenheit* and, more frequently, *gelassen* are already found in German editions familiar to Heidegger to refer to a calm undisturbed quietude, such as the *Daodejing* translations of Strauss and Wilhelm and the *Zhuangzi* editions of Buber and Wilhelm.¹⁴ This expression is also seen in the commentary of other renditions published during the Weimar Republic. Hertha Federmann's 1920 *Tao teh king* compares it with the inaction of the divine releasement of the Neo-Platonic one and with Martin Luther's justification through faith in contrast to justification through works (Federmann 1920: 95). Although the *Daodejing* is about how sage-kings and sages relate to things through nonaction and affairs (*shi* 事) through nonentanglement, these comparisons shaped by modern Occidental constructs of mysticism and spiritualism are not primarily concerned with things and the interthingly nature of reality.

The thing orientation of Heidegger's conception of releasement is notably different than typical mystical discussions that accentuate soul and self, including German mystical discourses and the early German translations of Daoist classics accessible to Heidegger. Heidegger's releasement is without doubt informed by its senses in Eckhart, Jakob Böhme, and German mystical traditions. *Gelassenheit* is understood there as the calmness and serenity of the self that takes precedence over *Gelassenheit* as the freedom—not of self and God but—of worldly things. The latter sense denotes freedom as a generative, relational, and interthingly participation between existents without any need for assertion or affirmation. Heidegger insisted on Eckhart's centrality, whose works he read since 1910, when Paul Shih-yi Hsiao (Xiao Shiyi 蕭師毅, 1911–1986) and Karl Jaspers asserted the Daoist and Asian resonances of his later thinking of the clearing of being.¹⁵ Nonetheless, as a bearing (*Haltung*) related to the self-becoming and self-essencing of things, instead of the self mystically uniting with God, Heidegger does more than evoke Daoist *wuwei* that was already long associated with the French word *laisser* as early as the physiocrats and the German word *lassen* since the nineteenth century. *Wuwei* is a letting that is frequently conjoined with things and affairs in the world such that it does not only signify a minimal activity of the self, much less a sinking of the self into itself and God. *Wuwei* is minimalism in an art or way of being-in-the-world that releases and responds to affairs and things in their self-happening (*ziwei* 自為).¹⁶

There are several indications yet to be elucidated that the *Laozi* and *Zhuangzi* provide not only historical raw data or content but orientational guiding models of what Heidegger designates poetic thinking that is closer to the happening and unconcealing of truth than philosophy as metaphysics, onto-theology, and positivistic technique. Laozi and Zhuangzi consequently appear to have an exemplary status alongside the more frequently discussed Anaximander, Heraclitus, Parmenides, and Hölderlin. Poetic ways of thinking and saying indicate possibilities of—as Heidegger articulates in a 1955 talk—a responsively attuned disposition and way in "the releasement of things" and "openness for the mystery" in contrast to the bureaucratic and technological reduction of persons and things to instrumentalized usefulness.¹⁷ As an opening association with things and mystery, it evokes if not directly utters the noncoercive or receptive doing of *Daodejing* 64 as well as the "mystery upon mystery" (*xuanzhi youxuan* 玄之又玄) of *Daodejing* 1 (Lou 1980: 2, 165–6). He directly contemplates Laozi's utmost mystery enfolded in mystery (*Geheimnis aller Geheimnisse*) in the 1957–58 Freiburg lectures "The Essence of Language."¹⁸

Heidegger's articulation of releasement has a distinctive tone and *ethos* in emphasizing the relationship with things in addition to one's dispositional comportment, a connection that is found in the *Daodejing*. Chapter 64 distinguishes two modalities that correlate with Heidegger's early conception of intrahuman being-with and his later conception of dwelling with things. This chapter describes neither acting nor intervening in affairs (in human relations, not leaping-in) while simultaneously assisting the myriad varieties of things in their self-nature (in human relations, leaping-ahead).[19] In the situation of Heidegger's early thought, the solicitude (*Fürsorge*) of not leaping-in (*einspringen*) to take away but leaping-ahead (*vorspringen*) to assist individuation analyzed in *Being and Time* matches such passages in the *Daodejing* except that it is restricted to intrahuman being-with. Heidegger's later thought extends this relationality beyond the human sphere. It is expansive in contrast with the still too anthropocentric model *of Being and Time* in rethinking being-with and language regarding things. Not only do human others have their unique ways of being and paths of individuation. Things have their own concealed mystery, revealed in stillness, in their showing forth that calls for reticence, releasement, and responsiveness.

Heidegger's transformation is shaped by his persistent engagements with early Daoist sources. Drawing on his co-translation of the *Daodejing* with Paul Shih-yi Hsiao, who attended his Heraclitus and Parmenides lecture-courses in 1943–44, Heidegger describes in other writings both *Gelassenheit* and *dao* in the same language of "way" as a bringing underway (*auf den Weg bringen*) and moving on the way (*Be-wegung*).[20] Letting (*Lassen*) is a genuine bringing about (*zuwege bringen*) and releasement (*Gelassenheit*) into the essencing of the thing (GA 99: 31, 41). They concern the worlding of the thing and not merely a subjective human comportment (GA 99: 40). As examined throughout Part One, Heidegger's most groundbreaking turning is not the way from being to beings in the mid-1930s, but his twists and turns through his confrontation with the philosophy of the will that emerges in the late 1930s toward the releasement of thing and world in emptiness in the 1940s. In his mature conception of releasement after 1943 his thought shifts away from the self's dispositional state toward the priority of the thing. It is during this same period that he detected a connection between his own problematic of technology and releasement, of instrumentally enframed things and self-so things, and the texts ascribed to Laozi and Zhuangzi that is unfolded from 1943 (GA 75: 43) through his final reflections (GA 91: 667).[21]

II. The Thing and Self- and World-Naturing

5. *Wu* 物 as Sacrificial, Ritual, and Patterned Event

Two Chinese books caught Heidegger's attention during the Weimar Republic—to which he returned with renewed dedication in the closing years of the Second World War—through Okakura Kakuzō's reflections on Daoism and tea (in which the thing is natural as well as artistically sensed and cultivated) and the translations of Wilhelm (Laozi and Zhuangzi), Strauss (Laozi), Buber (Zhuangzi), and perhaps others such as Federmann (Laozi).[22]

Before returning to Heidegger's thing below, two preparatory questions should be posed: what were the early Chinese and Daoist senses of the thing such that they could eventually interest Heidegger and his generation?[23] And what are these senses on their own terms that can help us to reevaluate Heidegger's discourse of the thing?

The early formation of the Sinitic language during the Shang dynastic period (c. 1600–1046 BCE) is interlinked with practices of divination, ritual, and sacrifice.[24] Etymology, their shifts in meanings and contexts, and linguistic and experiential positionality help clarify words and the senses they have gained and lost. The earliest identified uses of *wu* 物 in Shang divination inscriptions signified a speckled cow killed in sacrifice.[25] The character "物" combines the radicals for cow (*niu* 牛) and to cut/blood on the knife (*wu* 勿) associated with sacrificial ritual practice, and etymologically its early meaning was any type of moveable entity used in ritual sacrifices.[26] Sacrifice meant the death and destruction of the specific thing and the continued reproduction of things and the cosmic ritual order as a whole.

This sacrificial and ritual context is significant for the development of early Chinese conceptions of the thing and its forms of world-disclosure. A sacrificial entity has its allotted time culminating in the ritual cosmic event of its sacrifice. The expression *wu* became interlinked with the arising, persisting, and disappearing of the thing in its own allotted time and with what is changing and perishable. *Wu* indicates accordingly a temporalizing duration as the thing is depicted in subsequent sources as formed in flow (*liu* 流) and transformation (*hua*).

The excavated manuscript *All Things Flow in Form* (*Fan Wu Liu Xing* 凡物流形) from the Warring States period provides an example of the flowing and temporalizing character of the thing.[27] The text begins by posing two questions: how do things flow into taking form and shape? How does the thing inexorably dissipate after having taken on form? Given the mutability and conflict of contrary vital powers, the author of the text inquires, how do constant forces operate generating form and the thing and then disperse? That is, how is the thing individuated and fixed for a time? *Wu* expresses a temporalizing formation of a changing finite form between birth and death. The momentarily persisting thing expresses a cosmological order that transpires through the flow of elemental primordial forces (*qi* 氣) and is regulated through "natural" or "heavenly" criteria (*tiandu* 天度): "The hundred things do not perish as they depart and return, dissipate and remerge."[28]

Along with generation and transformation, carving and cutting, and leaving uncarved and uncut, are images that reappear in early Chinese philosophy. The thing was carved away from the whole of things as a particularized form in an early form of abstraction and fixation. Yet the microcosmic thing was aligned with a macrocosmic harmony and ritual order as is evident in the early classics and "Confucian" erudite (*rujia* 儒家) sources. The semantic range of *wu* unfolded to include concrete forms such as color, person, natural phenomena, living creatures (specified as *shengwu* 生物), and the nonliving thing. *Wu* indicated by the late spring and autumn (*chunqiu* 春秋) period "a thing" no longer specifically bound to sacrificial practices while often retaining an interconnection with a ritually reproduced cosmic order (Pines 2002: 697–8).

There are, undoubtedly, diverse ways of contesting stratified dualities. A specific interpretation of Nietzschean genealogy envisions the origin as fatefully determining and implicitly governing all permeations: a religion born of cruelty remains cruel even in its highest moments of love and tolerance. But his point does not only concern "lowly origins." As Nietzsche's critique exposes, the highest ideas of love and tolerance function not only as masks but as justifications for hatred and destruction against those considered other and deemed unworthy of this totalizing love; as when Christian universal love results in frenzied pogroms against stubbornly resistant particularity that is posited as the negation of love. However, early Chinese genealogical thinking of origins is concerned with different issues. It embraces all things in their differences and transformations. It recognizes that things arise in transitional incipience (*ji* 幾): they are born small and low, rise and face their zenith, and descend back into their origins. Genealogy can trace transformations that suspend and reverse the initial meaning: the sacrificial entity becomes its opposite by being linked with self-becoming in an *ethos*, irreducible to fixed rules and virtues, of nourishing living and nonliving things. How did this transformation occur?

The history of the thing in early Chinese philosophy offers several clues. First, *wu* designated a naturally arising thing, and reality consisted of "all things" (*baiwu* 百物, literally "hundred things") in early Confucian sources and the "myriad things" (*wanwu* 萬物, literally "ten thousand things") in the literature that informed the *Daodejing*'s development. Early Confucian and Daoist texts can be distinguished to an extent by the uses of *baiwu* and *wanwu* to express the entirety of things. The former is more characteristic of extant early Confucian materials, although not later ones such as the *Xunzi* 荀子 that presupposes and critiques Lao-Zhuang discursive formations, and the latter of extant Laoist materials in which the phrase *baiwu* does not appear.

The early Confucian "all things" expressed both the temporal and the ritual character of the thing. In the *Analects*' *Yang Huo* 陽貨 chapter, section 19, Confucius (Kongzi 孔子) famously asks, "[H]ow does heaven speak at all as the four seasons follow their courses and all things arise?"[29] Seasons and things take their generational turns, as seasonality serves as the principal image of time in the *Book of Changes* (*Yijing* 易經) and other early Chinese sources.[30] The ritual and cosmic character of the thing is expressed in early sources such as the *Book of Rites* (*Liji* 禮記). In its nineteenth chapter, the *Record of Music* (*Yueji* 樂記) sections 12 and 14 (2.3 and 2.5), "all things" are portrayed as constituting a fluctuating harmonizing whole maintained through a ritual and sacrificial order that is enacted through music and rites (Cook 1995: 45, 47). In music as in natural harmony, things transform, discord, and are reconciled. In ritual as in natural order, each thing finds its appropriate place and role. Music and ritual are consequently exemplary models of governance that reproduce cosmic harmony and maintain its order.[31] For Xunzi, 'thing' is the most general and inclusive name.

Early Confucianism accordingly demanded looking at and reflecting on worldly things. In the "Expansive Learning" (*daxue* 大學) chapter of the *Book of Rites*, the "extension of knowing" (*zhizhi* 致知) in the "investigation of things" (*gewu* 格物) implies discovering their ritual role and order in self-cultivation (*shenxiu* 身修). Song-Ming Neo-Confucianism offers its own distinctive discourses of the thing. Zhu Xi 朱熹 (1130–1200) construed the inquiry into things as an experiential inquiry aiming at the clarification of the fundamental cosmological pattern and principle (*li* 理) that organizes vital material and bodily forces (*qi*) and constitutes the order of things. The Song era Neo-Confucian philosophy of "investigating things and extending knowledge" (*gewu zhizhi* 格物致知) advocated by Zhu Xi to comprehend the patterning principle that configures vital forces to explain the thing is a movement away from the ziranist thing as it is of itself.

The history of ancient and medieval Chinese philosophical discourses reveals shared overlapping yet distinctively deployed vocabularies and interpretive strategies formed in interpretive conflicts concerning the thing and its onto-cosmological significance. They do not have one idea of what it is to be a thing. In non-ziranist discourses, the thing is an object of technique and mastery to be reshaped, used, and consumed; in others, it is secondary to the investigation and self-knowing of the heart-mind. There are sacrificial, ritual, and patterning principle cosmological explanations of things. We now turn to the principal focus of this work, the ziranist elucidations of the thing, as having its own self-generating sense as a transitioning relational nexus, articulated in the *Laozi*, the *Zhuangzi*, and related excavated and transmitted sources.

6. Straw-Dogs and Ziranist Models of the Myriad Things

How then is the self as being-in-the-world disposed and attuned to things in Lao-Zhuang discourses? Different models of nourishing the self and nurturing things occur in the texts attributed to the enigmatic figures of Laozi and Zhuangzi, each revealing distinct constellations between self and the thing, temporality, and the cosmos.

The received rendition of the *Daodejing* retains connections between the thing and sacrifice, temporal duration, and cosmic ritual order. One passage evokes both the sacrificial role of things and their own generational life. In *Daodejing* 5, heaven and earth are described as "lacking benevolence and regarding the myriad things like straw-dogs" (天地不仁, 以萬物為芻狗). This passage has been interpreted as conveying the sage's neutral indifference or even a cruel sacrificial inhumaneness toward things and people. It has also been read as having an ethical meaning. It was explicated in the *Xiang'er* 想爾 commentary (c. 190–220 CE) in moralistic language as asserting "the good with humaneness and the bad without humaneness" (仁於諸善, 不仁於諸惡). This commentary made sense of the passage by correlating the nurturing aspects of *dao* with being in accordance with it and its indifferent aspects with lack of accordance. The sacrificial straw-dog served accordingly as a warning established by the Yellow Emperor (Huangdi 黃帝) of people's futile and useless expenditure of vital forces and life as they increase and destroy themselves and heaven does not hear them as they fail to integrate their natural vital substance in accord with the heavenly.[32]

The image of the straw-dog appears to evoke cruelty and indifference in contemporary readers yet indicates the appropriate and inappropriate timing of the life of the thing. It is exemplary of the temporal event of the thing in its gathering and dispersing. The thing in its self-unfolding gathering cannot be fittingly encountered if it is conceived as a static objectified identity and presence or according to a predetermined instrumental use and purpose. A drastically different sense of the thing's import is expressed in the *Zhuangzi*. As expressly noted in one of the narratives regarding Confucius in the *Zhuangzi*'s "Heavenly Revolutions" (*Tianyun* 天運) outer chapter, "straw-dog" (*chugou* 芻狗) is a sacrificial object that is elegantly clothed and taken care of during the duration of the ritual and afterward left aside and trampled back into the earth or used for kindling (Ziporyn 2020: 121). The figure of the straw-dog in the *Laozi* and the *Zhuangzi* serves as an image of the generational life and death of the thing.[33] The *Tianyun* chapter clarifies this sense as it then equates Confucian teachings to a flawed endeavor to preserve the scattered remnants of the straw-dog after their allotted time has passed. The pursuit to hold on to the dead and the past can only result in the living being haunted by nightmares.

Notwithstanding the sense of temporality conveyed in the "all things" passage considered previously above, Confucius in the *Tianyun* could not adequately recognize the generational revolving nature of things as events or moments in time that form and dissipate in transformation. Rituality, righteousness, law, and measure alter over time (禮義法度者, 應時而變者). The straw-dog functioning as the image of the thing discloses a world and its criteria in incessant generation, formation, and dissolution.

The excavation and study of pre-Qin to early Han silk and bamboo texts have revolutionized the study of early Chinese thought. They have proven the antiquity of the *Laozi* materials that contain small yet notable differences. The close connection between thing, generation, and transformation is expressed in the excavated Guodian 郭店 (c. 300 BCE) and Mawangdui 馬王堆 (c. 200 BCE) renditions of the *Laozi*. These materials indicate more complex configurations of the thing operative in the early "Laoist" context, as the thing is related to the reflexive "self" or "so of itself" (*zi* 自) in expressions that can be translated as the self-so-ing, self-transforming, self-steadying, and "self-guesting" of the myriad things.[34]

7. The Self-Naturing of the Thing

What is the early significance of the character for "self" and "of itself" used in such expressions? It is thought to initially signify the nose and is used in Shang oracle inscriptions to signify "to start from." Concerning the thing, it refers to the face and point of departure of the thing. The impersonal self-relational *zi* is not the personal self of human agency, identity, or subjectivity (*wo* 我). It encompasses cosmic, human, animal, and material entities. It signifies not only the "my ownness" (*Jemeinigkeit*) of the self-world phenomenologically described by Heidegger but the "its ownness" of each thing-world. Unlike ordinary English and German language usage, the thing (*wu*) encompasses sentient and insentient beings, and each thing has its own way of being itself (*zi*). The thing's own self-relational self-world (expressed in *zi*- expressions in the Chinese context) is not considered in Heidegger's early thought, where the thing is experienced as either instrumentally ready-to-hand (*zuhanden*) or objectively present-at-hand (*vorhanden*), nor is it fully articulated in his later thinking, evocative of early Daoist sources, of the responsive remembering (*das andenkende Denken*) of the thing in writings such as the 1950 essay "The Thing" examined in later chapters.

Early Chinese philosophy, as seen in the early strata of the *Book of Changes*, was inspired by the constantly changing natural, spiritual, and sacrificial world. The language of the thing and the self-occurring both originate in the context of ritual sacrifice. The natural and sacrificial orders were initially the same. The "*ran*" of *ziran* appears to initially refer to the spirit of the thing in its ritual burning, or what remains in its sacrificial transformation, and later identifies only the naturally changing thing. *Ziran* signifies the temporal transformative self-so in early Daoism and is subsequently fixed and objectified into nature as object. In its earlier senses, it does not so much name an object or set of objects ("nature") as much as the way in which something verbally ("naturing") and adverbially ("naturally") occurs in its movements (compare Liu 2015: 75). The discourse of the myriad things and self-naturing appears to have been systematically articulated initially in the *Laozi* materials, functioning as its key concepts and becoming fundamental to ensuing Chinese philosophy, bioethical life, and aesthetic culture.

Lao-Zhuang discourses, despite their differences, can well be described as ziranist given their recognition of the priority of *ziran* and the inadequacy of translating it as naturalism. The conclusion to *Daodejing* 25 (in Guodian A 11) asserts that *ziran* is the key to understanding the way: *dao* follows or patterns itself according to its own self-naturing (*daofa ziran* 道法自然). The late Han era *Heshanggong* (河上公, Riverside Elder) commentary describes how this means that *dao* follows its own naturing (*daoxing ziran* 道性自然). The myriad things are self-sufficient in their self-becoming and self-accomplishing (*wanwu zicheng* 萬物自成).³⁵

The rediscovered *Heng Xian* 恆先 text (300 BCE) regards letting the thing happen (*wuwei*)—in "neither avoiding nor partaking in it" (無舍也，無與也)—as an accordance with the thing's self-happening (*ziwei* 自為).³⁶ Does the early history of the thing's "selfing" or "self-so-ing" (*zi*) imply that the sage-kings and sages do or do not step back and assist the thing in allowing it to determinate itself? Both possibilities of responsive nurturing and neutral indifference are implied in different renditions and interpretations of the *Laozi*, an assembled source formed from a textual and interpretive multiplicity. There are noticeable differences between the Guodian and received *Laozi* texts that some translations accentuate more than others. In Guodian A 6, according to Henricks's translation, the ancient sages are "able" (the first use of *neng* 能) yet are "unable to act" (its second use in *funeng wei* 弗能為), allowing the myriad things to be themselves in their own self-so-ing or self-naturing.³⁷ In *Daodejing* 64, and in Cook's translation of A 6 (Cook 2012: 245), the sages do not dare to (coercively or calculatedly) act (*fu gan wei* 弗敢為) while they expressly complement or assist (*fu* 輔) the myriad things to be themselves.³⁸ That is, the exemplary sages act and do not act by assisting and nourishing the life of things without forced purposive intervention that is constrained and undone by the restrictions of its aims.

Guodian A 6 could be read as implicitly stating the same message as *Daodejing* 64 if its first use of "able" implies able to complement and its second use unable to coercively act (Cook 2012: 245). It could also be read to suggest the neutrality of following *dao* with respect to the self-generative naturing of things, a model found in Huanglao 黃老 and so-called "legalist" (*fajia* 法家) discourses.³⁹ The received version of *Daodejing* 64 indicates a correlational co-responsive attunement without compelled or artificial action (*wei*) in following *dao* in its caring, maternal, and nurturing functions by complementing and assisting things to occur as themselves.⁴⁰ The nurturing function that supports self-nurturing applies to persons as well as things. Guodian A 16 and *Daodejing* 57 describe how the sage-kings practice noninvolvement in affairs, non-doing, quieting, and desiring without desiring as the people self-enrich, self-transform, self-rectify, and self-simplify of their own accord.⁴¹ How does the sage-king let the inevitably myriad and plural people order themselves? According to chapter 49, the sages empty and have no invariable heart-mind of their own to impose on others; they responsively take the people's heart-mind as their own. They do not preferentially prejudge, treating the good and bad, the sincere and insincere alike.⁴²

Heidegger's distinction between the two extremes of solicitude (*Fürsorge*) in *Being and Time* reminds us of Okakura's description of Daoism as making place for others. Heidegger differentiates care as (1) leaping-ahead and liberating (*vorspringend-befreiend*) for the sake of promoting the other's self-care and self-individuation, that is, potentiality-for-being (*Seinskönnen*) of an individuated self and (2) leaping-in and dominating (*einspringend-beherrschenden*) so as to strip away the other's self-care and thus possibilities of self-individuation.⁴³ Unlike Okakura's description of Daoism, this making place for others applies exclusively to human being-with in *Being and Time*. We will inquire later whether Heidegger eventually arrives at a making place of living and nonliving things that intersects with the self-happening of the thing revealed in the *Laozi*. What then of the thing's temporality?

The opening lines of Guodian A 7 and *Daodejing* 37 express the temporalizing constancy of *dao*'s operating without purposive activity as things transform themselves (*zihua* 自化) and determine and settle themselves (*ziding* 自定). Lords and kings emulate *dao* in knowing the limits of what is sufficient and in quietude. The constancy of *dao* is described respectively as *daoheng* 道恆 and *daochang* 道常. *Heng* was tabooed, as part of the given name (Liu Heng 劉恆) of the fifth Han dynasty emperor, and altered to the semantically overlapping *chang*. Neither word designates an eternity outside of time but rather extended and potentially infinite duration.

The earlier usage of *heng* signifies the temporalizing of the waxing moon and a fecund generative and potentially infinite perpetuity; *chang* the temporality of continuing and extending regularity.⁴⁴ The moon goes through its phases, the earth its seasons, and the repeating pattern is extended. The temporalizing of constancy is not an indeterminate neutral arena. It is one wherein vital forces and things wax and wane according to their own natures. *Heng* signifies persevering, long continuance, and prosperity in the explication of the thirty-second hexagram of the *Book of Changes*. If *heng* is interpreted as a generative temporalizing according to its early sense, then the affective dispositional state (*daqing* 大情) of continuing and prospering things (*hengwu* 恆物)—often translated as the enduring reality of the eternal thing from Legge to Ziporyn—should be noted in the "Great Teacher" (*Da Zongshi* 大宗師) chapter of the *Zhuangzi*: "to hide the world in the world, so that there is no place to escape, is the great affection that prospers things."⁴⁵

The *Daodejing* teaches the generative and nourishing function of *dao* that sages and kings emulate. This is not unrelated to the sacrificial sense in a text such as Mawangdui *Laozi* A 13. It states, "the way generates" (*daosheng zhi* 道生之) and "virtuosity nourishes" (*dexu zhi* 德畜之) "governed things" (*wuxing zhi* 物刑之) and "useful devices" (*qicheng zhi* 器成之). The corresponding line in *Daodejing* 51 reads that they generate and nourish "formed things" (*wuxing zhi* 物形之) and "potentiality" (*shicheng zhi* 勢成之). While characters such as *xing* 刑 (to punish, govern, or form), *xing* 型 (model, formed pattern), and *xing* 形 (form, shape) were linguistically interchangeable characters in antiquity, the different characters in A 13 intimate two different forms of order expressed in the succeeding lines. Generative *dao* operates in Mawangdui A 13 through "ceaseless self-offering" (*heng ziji* 恆自祭) instead of the more typical (in other renditions) "constant self-naturing" (*chang ziran* 常自然).

The language of Mawangdui A 13 hearkens to the older sacrificial signification of thing with its discourse of governing/punishing things, useful instrumental products, and self-offering/sacrifice. It also points toward the *ziran* of the thing. In the expression *ziran*, "*ran*" indicates temporalizing self-generativity, the entity's being self-so in its own temporal moment of life. This is not an underlying essence or constant substance but an arising and dissipating nexus of relations calling for our humility and gratitude to recognize it. Pertinently, *ran* is etymologically related to burn, or ignite, referring to sacrificial burnt meat. Again, early Daoist sources show a movement from the earlier sacrificial meaning to the integral meaning of the moment of life. In both cases, the temporality of the thing and its relation to the cosmic whole of *dao* is elemental. The way generates and nourishes the life of things, allowing them their determinations and transformations, and their own significance in life and death. The kings and sages emulate and participate in the generative temporalizing of *dao* by complementing and nurturing things in their life and letting them depart in their death. This intergenerational ziranist *ethos* entails that each generation has meaning in its own finitude and in allowing the old to be buried and the new to be born. Such moments in early Chinese thought intersect with the thinking of natality, generation, and mortality in Wilhelm Dilthey (an earlier thinker of finitude and generation), Heidegger, and Hannah Arendt.

The *Heng Xian* further contextualizes the senses of constancy operative in the Guodian *Laozi*. The opening line asserts that in the originary state of constancy (*heng*), there is no being (*hengxian wuyou* 恆先無有).[46] This contested line could be understood as the nothingness of or—as it has no spatial or temporal differentiation—prior to primordial constancy. Spatiality arises from emptiness and temporality arises from beginning such that the vital generative forces are self-generating and self-arising (氣是自生自作) and things self-reproducing and self-reverting (*zifu* 自復).[47] Given subsequent interpretations of the generativity of nothingness, it could indicate the generative spatializing and temporalizing of being emerging from emptiness and beginning from nothingness as the indistinct and muddled is differentiated and individuated into the temporalizing being of primal forces, things, and names that each has its own time. This resonates with the much later "Heaven's Portents" (*Tianrui* 天瑞) chapter of the *Liezi* 列子 (c. 300 CE, although incorporating earlier materials), in which the initial state of things is described as muddled without separation (萬物相渾淪而未相離) and the temporality of things as one of generative metamorphosis (*wanwu huasheng* 萬物化生).

Guodian A 10 and *Daodejing* 32 state that "[s]hould lords and kings be able to uphold [the way], the myriad things will bring themselves in line."[48] The myriad things are self-ordering. More literally, *zi* 自 refers to self and *bin* 賓 visitor or guest. The lords and kings allow the thing to be the guest of itself, allowing the thing to occur in its own course. Its own course has been interpreted as its way of being or role in the moral-political order of things. The *Heshanggong* commentary takes being a guest as spontaneous moral obedience and submission (*fucong yude* 服從於德).⁴⁹ Wang Bi elucidates in his commentaries on *Daodejing* 10 and 32 the functioning of the self-relation of things as a condition of the self-sufficiency, self-tranquility, and self-contentment of things. The sovereign ruler nurtures them to this condition guided by the example of *dao*.⁵⁰

The early *Laozi* materials do not radically differentiate between interacting with things and persons, as persons appear as a special case of rather than an exception to things. The Laozian *ethos* of the sage's letting and the thing's naturing or selfing is articulated in Guodian 16 (*Daodejing* 57): "I engage in no affairs and the people are self-enriching. I do not (coercively) act and the people are self-transforming. I practice quietude and the people are self-rectifying. I desire without desiring and the people self-simplify."⁵¹ Letting, quieting, and simplifying, concomitant with the self-becoming of things on their own, are in the context of the *Laozi* practices of the self and political rule that have multifaceted relations with Daoist biospiritual meditative practices as well as Huanglao, so-called power-oriented "legalist" (in the work attributed to Hanfei 韓非 with its "Sovereign's Way" chapter and two chapters on the *Laozi*), and anarchic (in Zhuangzi, Liezi, and Bao Jingyan 鮑敬言) biopolitical models that contest and dispel supremacist identarian configurations of the political.⁵²

III. Freedom, Allotment, and Self-Naturing after the *Zhuangzi*

8. Freedom and Fate in Self- and World-Naturing

Ziranist Daoism is a philosophy of radical relational freedom and responsive participation in the world. But, as reversal is part of the very movement of things and any constellation can assume an ideological form, freedom is perpetually betrayed. It can fall into obsessive fixation or indifferent fatalism, and anarchy into totalitarian order (i.e., strong holism suppressing alterity and singularity), as the highest values devalue themselves. In this section, and in Chapter 4, we consider the larger context and consequences of Zhuangzian freedom that would eventually inspire Heidegger, for whom "freedom is admittance into the disclosure of beings as such" (GA 9: 192), and that allows us to critically and interculturally resituate this discourse of worldly freedom amidst things.

What is the context and status of the *Zhuangzi* with its radical teaching of anarchic, immanent, this-worldly freedom amidst the facticity of existence? The Han dynasty historian Sima Qian in the *Shiji* 史記 affiliates Zhuangzi with Laozi, stating that he illustrates the same teaching through metaphor and parody. Although the relationship between the *Laozi* and *Zhuangzi* remains historically unclear, and they should not be conflated given their differences, these two collections are related in expressing variations on the prominence of the self-naturing (*ziran*) of things disclosed through noncoercive responsive attunement (*wuwei*).⁵³ *Ziran* only occurs ten times in the *Zhuangzi*, and the *ethos* of the self-letting/other-selfing correlation is often conveyed in other *zi*- expressions and in the enactment of responsive resonance (*ying* 應) with the thing. While *ying* is only used twice in the ordinary sense of reply or response in the

Daodejing, it has a more vital role in the *Zhuangzi* and in the *Heshanggong* and Wang Bi *Laozi* commentaries. The sages respond when affected (*gan erhou ying* 感而後應) in *Zhuangzi* chapter 15 "Engraved Meanings" (*Keyi* 刻意). This chapter concerns undoing engraved meanings as constructed fixations.

The freedom and ease of worldly responsiveness of the exemplary genuine person arise through bracketing intentional calculative action (*wuwei*) and attuned or resonant being affected (*ying*). This is glimpsed in the thought-images of Butcher Ding (Paoding 庖丁) nourishing life and responding to the intrinsic nature of the ox with the cutting of his blade or (in an example Heidegger referred to in a 1960 lecture on art) the woodcutter's responsive working with the wood.[54] Such responsiveness has been understood in early Chinese interpretations as (1) an undetermined free wandering and sojourning; (2) an uncoerced music-like attunement with the thing and its situation; (3) a (more or less deterministic) process of adaptation and accommodation to things; or (4) an automatic reflex fatalistically determined by the stimulus.

First, given their blending of indifference and responsiveness, how are sages and persons affected to respond by stimuli? The Wei-Jin period saw a controversy over the emotions of sages concerning whether they completely overcame them in affective indifference (He Yan 何晏, c. 190–249 CE) or harmoniously balanced them from nothingness (Wang Bi). As considered below, responsive resonance as attuned releasement in Chinese philosophical and artistic traditions resituates the subject and subjectivity. It suggests other modalities of being affected and attuned by things to Heidegger's conception of *Befindlichkeit* (attunement, disposedness) manifested through *Stimmung* (mood) through which things and world are disclosed in his examples of encounters with disorienting disrelational limit-situations of radical anxiety, profound boredom, as well as other oriented situations of joy, love, wonder, and—in a complex mediated way—the poetic word and saying of his later thought.[55]

Secondly, given the stimulus-response model, how should freedom and determination be understood? Zhuangzian freedom has appealed to intellectuals searching for an alternative relational freedom distinct from German ideas of freedom as embracing duty, necessity, and the state. It has been construed as an effortless playful freedom that is independent of while responsive to things, as an adjusting and adaptation to the self-nature of the thing and its interbodily and interthingly situation or as the tranquil acceptance of the vicissitudes of one's particular fated allotment and whatever alteration of life and death might transpire. Adaptation raises questions, articulated in Count Hermann von Keyserling's 1919 *A Travel Diary of a Philosopher*, concerning whether Daoist adaptation to changing circumstances is external or whole (encompassing one's internal and external comportment), whether it is genuine freedom or subordination to an objective depersonalizing world order.[56] The Sinologist F. E. A. Krause more carefully differentiates strains of Daoism in his 1923 work on East Asian philosophies and religions, identifying moments of the *Zhuangzi* and the *Liezi* with "practical fatalism."[57]

In addition to the remarkable appearance of J. G. Weiss's 1927 *Daodejing* edition in the second 1942 leaflet of the White Rose student resistance movement, which emphasized good governance through the noncoercive self-ordering of affairs, others linked the *Zhuangzi* with anti-totalitarian freedom.[58] As stated in a 1942 *Sinica* article by the Sinologist Werner Eichhorn, to give an example of the hermeneutics of freedom and fatedness in the *Zhuangzi* in Heidegger's linguistic situation, *dao* signifies the freedom (*ziran*) of things in principle (Eichhorn 1942: 141). This profoundly relational freedom is opposed to linguistic and conceptual essences and fixations such that Daoism is fundamentally incommensurable with "Occidental" philosophy. The dao-ness of the thing can only be measured according to and by following its changing behaviors in the comportment of *wuwei* (Eichhorn 1942: 142). This freedom of the *dao*, as fallen in the ordinary world, is concealed in the entanglements and affairs of that world in which things appear lifeless and fixed and destiny as inescapably fated without free and easy responsiveness. The perspective of freedom is blurred in the perspective of differentiation and determination. The exemplary Daoist way of life in freedom and releasement has its own critical and transformative potential vis-à-vis the reification and alienation reproduced by the existing social-political order. These critical categories unfolded in Marxist and existential transmissions, including—on some readings—Heidegger's *Being and Time*, take on new senses in relation to Daoism.

Axel Honneth and Rahel Jaeggi defined reification and alienation respectively as a forgetting of recognition (Honneth 2005) and a relation of relationallessness (Jaeggi 2005).[59] These two diagnostic concepts are frequently conceived according to essentialized concepts of identity and the subject, disputed by Honneth and Jaeggi, and as anthropocentric, which they fail to adequately overcome. The recognition of the generative and transformative plurality of things offers a more suggestive non-anthropocentric model as any autopoietic nexus, such as an ecosystem, can undergo reification with destructive consequences and, to return to the *Dialectic of Enlightenment* of Theodor Adorno and Max Horkheimer, be experienced as the alienation of the domination of nature. No underlying collective or individual identity or subject is required, as these reproduce the very reification under question. Ziranist ways of dwelling, or being-in-the-world to recall Okakura's expression, do not conceptually negate but rather consist in shifting through these limiting conditions and standpoints in which the freedom of *dao* is discovered in situations and things themselves. *Ziran* does not exclusively apply to one's own self and its freedom, except in hedonistic and egotistical interpretations of the Warring States era philosopher Yang Zhu 楊朱. It is disclosed in the *Daodejing* and the *Zhuangzi* in genuinely encountering things in their own freedom. In the Daoist setting, there is a thingly autonomy that requires appropriate attunement and recognition, contesting reification and alienation. The dereification of thing and place is a condition of the dereification of human existence.

The self-determination of the thing appears in the *Zhuangzi* in their self-transforming (*zihua*) and self-acting (*ziwei*). The adaptive and receptive disposition of *wuwei* is correlated with the thing's self-transformation by itself in chapter 11 (*Zaiyou* 在宥) and chapter 17 (*Qiushui* 秋水). The recognition of the self-acting of the thing occurs when one does not self-act in the thirteenth "Heaven's Way" (*Tiandao* 天道) *Zhuangzi* chapter. Things occur and act of their own by "not self-acting" such that "heaven does not bring the myriad things forth and they transform, earth does not grow the myriad things and they are nurtured, the lords and kings do nothing and all under heaven is achieved."[60]

The *Zhuangzi* contested subordinating the thing's way of being itself in its environment, such as chaos freely existing without openings or the turtle enjoying the muddy riverside, to an external role, e.g., having holes drilled or being displayed at court, by emphasizing its own self-becoming that would be construed as an allotted and singularly determined self-nature (*zixing* 自性). However, in addition to issues of external adaptation and conformity, there are questions concerning internal conformity and whether Zhuangzian freedom transcends only the former (for the sake of internal authenticity or genuineness) or both external and internal determination.

9. Freedom with Things: Zhuangzian and Buddhist Reflections

The Wei-Jin era mysterious learning discourses of Wang Bi and Guo Xiang center around nothingness and the thing. They are pivotal in modifying and transmitting the ziranist *Daodejing* and *Zhuangzi*. Wang Bi's *ziran*-oriented interpretation of nothingness is examined later in Part Two. Guo Xiang stressed the singularity of the thing. In his commentary on the *Zhuangzi*, he linked "lone" (*du* 獨) with "transformation" (*hua*). In "lone-transformation" (*duhua* 獨化), the sole singular (*du*) and self (*zi*) retain identity while transforming: the self retains itself and its own self-nature in becoming other than itself in transformation.[61] In Guo Xiang, the relation of the thing to itself (as a guest of itself), individuated and potentially isolated as uniquely lone and sole (*shenqi duhua* 神器獨化), is possible in interthingly mutual dependence (*xiangyin* 相因). Such a vision of interdependence and independence, of harmony and monadic self-determination to describe this relation in the categories of Leibniz, risks for his critics bifurcating the thing between other-determined and self-determining, identity and difference, and host and guest. The sole spontaneously self-generating thing (*zisheng* 自生) is in jeopardy of monadic separation from the dynamic relational responsive resonance of the myriad things in which its own self-determination as world determination occurs.[62]

Zhi Dun 支遁 (Zhi Dao Lin 支道林, 314–366 CE), Dao'an 道安 (312–385 CE), and fourth-century Chinese Buddhist sources informed by Lao-Zhuang and mysterious learning teachings offer salient reference points for reconstructing philosophical controversies involving Lao-Zhuang argumentative and hermeneutical strategies. The Buddhist philosopher and monastic Zhi Dun fused the discourses of mysterious learning and Buddhist "perfection of wisdom" (*Prajñāpāramitā*) literature prior to the systematic formation of Chinese Madhyamaka from Kumārajīva 鳩摩羅什 and Sengzhao 僧肇 to the Tang era three treatises school (*sanlun* 三論) associated with Jizang 吉藏. To jump ahead for a moment, Chinese Madhyamaka reappears in Part Two in the context of distinguishing Daoist nothingness, Buddhist emptiness, Heidegger's nothing, and nothingness in Nishida Kitarō 西田幾多郎 (1870–1945) and examining Heidegger's lifelong interactions with Japanese intellectuals that led to a 1919 gift, a 1924 declined invitation conveyed by Miki Kiyoshi 三木清 (1897–1945) to teach in Japan, and myriad conversations.

Zhi Dun's thought might be described as a "Daoistic Buddhism," a category invented by modern scholars, in which early Lao-Zhuang Daoism is fulfilled in Buddhism and Buddhism is deployed to resolve Daoist and mysterious learning philosophical questions. Zhi Dun criticized Guo Xiang's interpretation of Zhuangzi in his lost "Discourse of Free and Easy Wandering" (*xiaoyao lun* 逍遙論) for the complacency, determinism, and fatalism of its notion of complying (*yue* 約) with one's endowed particular allotment (*fen* 分) in the myriad transformations (*wanhua* 萬化). Fated self-nature stands in tension with the freedom expressed in the joy of the fish playing without a fixed determinate purpose, a narrative that—as noted earlier—fascinated Heidegger and that he interpreted in relation to being-with in 1930.[63] If taken as the fixity of a predetermined character, it subverts the independence of free and easy meandering that, it might be added, continues to resonate with the freedom of forms of shamanistic and poetic "far-roaming" (*yuanyou* 遠遊) that meld spontaneity and responsiveness and interior and exterior landscapes.[64]

Is freedom the freedom of enacting one's fated self-nature and inborn character, whatever it might be, or a freedom of transforming—in Buddhist discursive terms—the seeds of self-nature that is ultimately empty of itself? Zhi Dun identified Zhuangzian freedom with Buddhist *prajñā*. The latter perceives things as things without being fettered by things in recognizing the self-emptiness of both somethingness and nothingness.[65] Zhi Dun's conceptual blending contrasts with subsequent Buddhist scholars, such as Guifeng Zongmi 圭峰宗密 (780–841 CE) in his *Inquiry into the Origin of Humanity* (*Yuanren lun* 原人論) from the late 820s or early 830s. He criticized the teachings of Laozi and Zhuangzi as fatalistic and unable to motivate disciplined spiritual transformation and liberation (Zongmi 708b4; Gregory 1995: 44). If Zhi Dun's criticisms of Guo Xiang's determinism are valid, then *ziran*, which promised in the *Zhuangzi* to equalize and liberate things in their anarchic self-determination from serving as mere sacrificial and instrumental objects, has become the self-determination of the thing's predetermined self-nature (*zixing*) in its allotted fated share. The next chapter will examine a parallel problem of the absorption of worldly freedom into destiny (*Geschick*) in Heidegger's thinking of the 1930s.

To remain with the Chinese situation at this time, the problematic of determinism and freedom that emerged between Guo and Zhi presents numerous interpretive difficulties. First, the *Zhuangzi* itself articulates in the Inner Chapter "Great Teacher" the significance of the self-occurring of *dao* rather than fixed nature in discussions of the thing. *Dao* is without forced activity and fixed form (*wuwei wuxing* 無為無形) and self-originating and self-rooting (*ziben zigen* 自本自根). The life of things transforms without its direction being known and the exemplary sages participate and wander amidst transforming things without escape or separation (聖人將遊於物之所不得遯而皆存) and without calculation and anxiety regarding their purpose and outcome. Second, the *Zhuangzi* does not only indicate the sole singular monadic self-determining transformation of the thing but also mutual co-determination (sympoiesis) in the synchronization and integration of the myriad things that Guo Xiang treats, as it were, like a preestablished harmony that leaves each thing to solely determine itself.[66] That is, *ziran* refers to the self-happening of the thing as well as to its natureless and selfless (in any fixed or substantialized sense) world-happening as a singular moment that dynamically mirrors and reflects the whole.

10. Self-Relationality

The equalizing (*qi* 齊) of the *Zhuangzi* is described in the "Autumn Floods" chapter as the "coherence and equality of the myriad things" (*wanwu yiqi* 萬物一齊). This equalizing is more a transforming flowing musical harmonizing than subordination to a fixed determinate uniformity.[67] Equalization transpires in temporal and transformative relationality and its recognition, in which "heaven, earth, and I live side by side together, and the myriad things and I are one" (天地與我並生, 而萬物與我為一), in relational world-naturing as well as in singular and sole self-naturing.

Kierkegaard's Anti-Climacus claimed that the self is a relation between a relation and a relation. The relationality of reality is even more radically expressed in Laozi and Zhuangzi. Daoist expressions with "*zi-*" convey a profoundly different model of reflexive self-relation than the self-reflection of a thinking subject that is only one of its forms. This early variety of zi-expressions in early sources such as the Guodian *Laozi* and the *Heng Xian* is flattened out into a notion of *ziran* that increasingly becomes fixated as an objective order and object, in which the thing appears determined by a fixed nature. This development weakens the dynamic verbal and transformative character of early *ziran* discourses conveyed in the *Laozi* and the *Zhuangzi*: the thing as irreducibly self-so of itself or self-naturing in its own transformations and flow.

In conclusion, to briefly reiterate, *ziran* signifies the self- and, if not monadically isolated, the world-naturing of the thing. It is the relational thing in its temporal and transformative self-naturing that distinguishes the thing in the *Daodejing* and the *Zhuangzi* and indicates an aesthetics and culture of care for things in their own self-so thereness. This need not presuppose either their sentience or internal sense of well-being. Chapter 1 has traced the senses and philosophical implications of early Chinese conceptions of the thing. The following four chapters examine the transformative relational thing in Daoism, Heidegger, and his generational context.

2

The Autopoietic Self-Transformation of Things in Ziranist Daoism and Heidegger

I. *Phúsis* and the Thing

1. Nature, *Phúsis*, and *Ziran*

The letting releasement and responsive attunement of the thing in *wuwei* in early materials related to the formation of the *Daodejing* and the *Zhuangzi* presuppose a cosmological natural-political order of the self-generativity of things and a seasonal temporality in which they operate. What can they signify apropos Heidegger's ontology or to a contemporary audience who can read both? In Heidegger's corpus, the modern construction and technological enframing of world, as an arena of universally fungible and exchangeable things, are intimately interwoven with the history of Occidental metaphysics and its early Greek origins, seemingly excluding premodern Asia.[1]

"Nature" and the "natural thing" are primarily interpreted from "world" in *Being and Time* and are derivative concepts abstracted from Dasein's world-relations and way of being-in-the-world (GA 2: 60, 63). The "homogenous space of nature" is a "deworlded" space (GA 2: 112). A pure natural thing (*Naturding*) without Dasein's world is incomprehensible (GA 82: 52). *Being and Time* already introduces a "prior release" (*vorgängige Freigabe*) of letting the thing rest (*Bewendenlassen*) and a third more elemental "power of nature" (GA 2: 84–5 and 70, 211), even while accentuating the instrumental referential context instead of his later thingly oriented relational context. These undeveloped alternative hints prepare the way for his more radical thinking of nature as power in relation to *phúsis* in the mid-1930s, the releasement of nature from the confines of power in the 1940s, and then his critique of an enframed world that obstructs life by obscuring the sense of things. First, the "there" belongs to Dasein. Later, the "there" is the gathering of the thing.

The experiential and discursive functions of *ziran* entail a distinctive yet intersecting form of world-event and disclosure from Heidegger's retrieval of the early Greek experience and conception of *phúsis* (φύσις) as more elemental than any experience or concept of "nature." *Natura* is a derivative and problematic concept that he used with reluctance. Heidegger repeatedly reimagines nature as *phúsis* in works such as the 1935 lecture-course *Introduction to Metaphysics*, revised and published as a book in 1953, as determinate of the history of Occidental metaphysics:

what does the word *phúsis* say? It says what emerges from itself (for example, the emergence, the blossoming, of a rose), the unfolding that opens itself up, the coming-into-appearance in such unfolding, and holding itself and persisting in appearance—in short, the emerging-abiding sway.

(GA 40: 16)

The early Greek *phúō* (φύω) is related to archaic Indo-European words for birth, earth, dwelling, and being. It designates that which is brought forth, generated, and produced. The meaning of *phúsis* is that which arises and disperses (akin to *ziran* to this extent). *Phúsis* was only later distinguished from what is artfully produced (*tékhnē*, τέχνη) and from the normatively lawful (*nómos*, νόμος) as *phúsis* came to refer only to that which materially exists. This expression encompasses in its early Greek context not only the natural, the material, and the physical (in the subsequently reduced senses of these words) but heaven, earth, stones, plants, humans, gods, and their works (GA 40: 17).

Phúsis further signifies in Heidegger's provocative reading that which is as an emerging upsurge from being's hiddenness and concealment, an abiding holding sway (*Walten*, which typically means reign, preside, prevail), and essence (*Wesen*) as essencing (*Wesung*) rather than as the determinate underlying idea or principle of the thing.[2] While the metaphysical concept of "essence" intones that there is something else determining the thing, self-essencing indicates that it is in fact its own way of existing. Such qualities of self-becoming are expressed in Daoist sources where things emerge and transform according to their own nature, place, and time. Even the *dao* of things cannot be fixed into or imposed as a determinate principle. Once more, we find correlations between Heidegger and the *Daodejing*. *Dao* is called concealed and nameless (*daoyin wuming* 道隱無名) in *Daodejing* 41. It holds sway without coercion or violence (*buzai* 不宰) in *Daodejing* 10 and 51. Reinhold von Plaenckner, Wilhelm, Georg Misch, and other German interpreters deployed the expressions "reign," "prevailing," or "holding sway" (*Walten*) to speak of *dao*.[3] It is a crucial feature of Greek *phúsis* in Heidegger that becomes intertwined with questions of power and violent creation in the mid-1930s. This differs from the pluralistic self-ordering of *ziran* where power and violence are signs of loss and failure. Yet, as Heidegger clarified in a later note, in which these two terms share greater affinity, *phúsis* is in the first place "the self-unfolding emergence in and through which a being first is what it is" (GA 73. 1: 85).

2. *Phúsis* and Its Unconcealment and Saying

The word *phúsis* operates as a name for being itself, as that by which beings appear (GA 40: 17), referring to being's emerging event, emerging beings and things, and their unconcealed truth. The emerged and the submerged, the unconcealed and the concealed are interconnected, and truth (*alḗtheia*, ἀλήθεια) is thought negatively in Heidegger's etymological reconstruction as "not hidden" (*a-lḗtheia*). *Lḗthē* means concealment, forgetfulness, and oblivion. It is the name of a goddess and a river in Hades. It refers for Heidegger to a primary nonderivative refusal, obstruction, and unsaid, while truth (or *alḗtheia*, which is more originary than and only inadequately called truth) refers to that which emerges into the openness from hiddenness and into saying from the unsaid.

According to Heraclitus's fragment 123, "nature tends toward hiddenness" (φύσις κρύπτεσθαι φιλεῖ). Heidegger translated this as "emerging gives favor to self-concealing" (GA 55: 110, 121). It might be thought that *phúsis* names the self-emergence (*von ihm selbst her*) of beings from being, such that ontic beings can be questioned from the ontological perspective of being and intersects with *ziran* as the self-emergence of things from *dao*, as it shifts through things without being limited by them. The *dao* nourishes and has its freedom in things, following its own self-nature and generating exemplary models to be emulated by sages and non-sages without being confined to one fixed rule, in *Daodejing* 25 (Lou 1980: 65).

Several questions should be addressed now. Heidegger mentions *lógos* (λόγος) and not *phúsis*, in conjunction with *dao*. A basic guiding word (*Leitwort*) such as *dao* operates as an originary world orienting word, as Heidegger noted (GA 11: 45; GA 12: 187). It is striking that Heidegger reflectively and adaptively engages with Daoist language and does not follow the widespread practice of drawing comparisons between facets of Daoist and Occidental philosophy, beyond the statements that *dao*, *lógos*, and *Ereignis* (the non-ontic appropriative event of being) operate in their own ways as elemental untranslatable guiding words (GA 11: 45; GA 12: 187).

Heidegger's "From a Dialogue on Language," a key text explored in part two, expresses hesitancy and warns of all-too-easy identifications that give an appearance of mutual understanding without a genuine encounter occurring between two interlocutors. As basic guiding words, each discloses a distinctive world. The relation between Heidegger's being and *dao* is much more complicated, as *phúsis* signifies being as emergence and self-naturing the way *dao* arises of itself and generates all things from nothingness. It is from the self-generative watery yet fecund depth of nothingness that things emerge in early *Laozi*-related sources excavated in the archaeological sites Guodian and Mawangdui. If *dao* functions akin to *lógos* (language as saying), then in early Daoistic contexts it is nothingness (the guiding word of part two) that evokes and structurally parallels the generative functions of *phúsis*.

3. The Hermeneutics and Politics of *Phúsis* and the Thing

Intercultural philosophy, which contests the fixated identities of orthodox philosophy, needs to recognize both proximity and distance, resisting both totalizing fusion and isolated particularity. It should not only co-illumine diverse perspectives and discursive configurations. It can also self-reflectively and critically engage, confront, and dialogically differentiate in communication (*Auseinandersetzung*). Heidegger began to address this hermeneutical problem in his 1937 "Ways to [Dialogical] Discussion."[4] In this short essay, he considers the barriers to a genuine understanding between peoples and reformulates, at the collective level of the French and German peoples, the earlier themes of making room for and leaping-ahead for the other in mutual individuation, actions that require both a lasting will to listen to each other and a reserved courage for one's own self-determination (GA 13: 21). Self-determination plays a multivalent role since it is ideologically entangled with both freedom and oppression. Autonomous self-determination has had an emancipatory import in relation to oppression. Such concepts can also contest pathological, oppressive forms when the other is not heard and eclipsed in ideologically driven formations of the individual and popular will, as Arendt exposes in her 1951 *The Origins of Totalitarianism*.[5]

In Heidegger's 1937 essay, he appears caught between the self-determining willing of the German people (*das deutsche Volk*), which dominated his thinking during the 1930s, and *Gelassenheit* toward others, as self-determination is problematically connected with decisions about creatively determining the destiny and mission of the Occident (no doubt in distinction from the Soviet East) (GA 13: 16). The prospect of genuinely making room for and hearing toward the other in mutual co-illumination and co-individuation is thereby distorted and undermined. It is only adjusted in Heidegger's shift in 1943 from the paradigm of the self-assertion and self-determination of the will, which lacks an appropriate sense of measure and limit, to the freedom of letting releasement that recognizes its limits vis-à-vis others.

Can Lao-Zhuang ziranist political models of sympoietically self-ordering communities and environments be deployed to not only co-illuminate but also transcend Heidegger's political thinking and philosophy of nature and art? The anarchic self-measuring social-political tendencies of specific threads of Daoist discourses are best approximated in democratic self-organization of social-political life through the interactions of a plurality of individuals (better articulated by Arendt than Heidegger). These points suggest (to think with and beyond Heidegger and his agrarianism and linguistically defined "people") an alternative *ziran*-oriented philosophy of nature and society to his conception, during the National Socialist era, of violent creative founders and the collective identity of the people.[6] Noncoercive action (*wuwei*) and nonintervention in affairs (*wushi*) were formulated in the Warring States environment of debates over coercive politics, in which (to summarize) "legalists" advocated law, punishment, the force of the state, and the ultimate power of the sage-king; Confucians endorsed the exemplary role of virtue in the moral ordering of society; and the *ziran*-oriented Daoists conceived of the self-generative autopoiesis of social-political life in which people ordered themselves with or—in more radical anarchic moments in the *Zhuangzi*, the *Liezi*, and the admonishment of Bao Jingyan by Ge Hong 葛洪 (283–343 or 363 CE)—without sage-kings. Heidegger is at this juncture closer in proximity to the legalist assertion of power than anarchic (or *dao*-archic) self-generation and nearer to the coercion of things in a new formation of life than their releasement into their own self-openness.

Early Greek *phúsis* is depicted in Heidegger's reconstruction as the "first beginning" (GA 69: 142), from which Occidental metaphysics emerges. There is also the "other beginning" that confronts this first beginning. In the postwar period, various readers discovered the "other beginning" in early Chinese and other forms of thought. In the period of its initial articulation, the other beginning concerns the early Greeks and contemporary Germans (Bambach 2003). It is described in the 1935 *Contributions to Philosophy* as the referral and offering/sacrifice of beings to being that—in Heidegger's language—essences and holds sway as an event in the clearing of self-hiddenness.[7]

Modern European thought has been shaped in its interactions with its others that it typically endeavors to exclude from its own sense of history and otherless self-identity. The Indian and Islamic sources of science and mathematics (such as infinity and zero as discussed later) should be too obvious to deny. There are also intriguing intersections between the politics of nature and Chinese philosophy in earlier forms of European thought. First, for instance, French physiocrats such as the Sinophile François Quesnay, the "Confucius of Europe" to his admirers, had called for "physiocracy" as government by *phúsis* that blended minimizing the mercantilist state, the promotion of agriculture and agrarian communities, and economic" laisser passer, laisser faire" and free trade, inspired in part by (a French Enlightenment appropriation of) Confucianism and *wuwei*. Second, the agrarian-agricultural facets of the *Daodejing* and the *Zhuangzi* were construed as supporting an anarchistic communal socialism in fin-de-siècle intellectuals such as Julius Hart and Buber. If the previously discussed accounts of Heidegger's 1919 encounter with Daoism are accurate, it is conceivable that Heidegger linked Daoist motifs with leaping-ahead and making room and space for the other and, as he describes in 1937, for the thing in its openness (GA 45: 3, 29). As in Quesnay, Buber, or Ernst Bloch, who wrote an essay (published in 1962, but which he dates to 1926) on Johann Peter Hebel, Jeremias Gotthelf, and the agrarian utopianism of rustic *dao* ("bäurisches Tao"), Heidegger would no doubt have noticed the agrarian-environmental elements of Chinese philosophical and poetic discourses, if not their anarchistic and libertarian Marxist self-generative spontaneity respectively accentuated by Buber and Bloch.[8]

Agrarian utopian images of fields, forests, and rivers dominate many of Heidegger's writings. But, conspicuously, such considerations are not the focus of Heidegger's vision of German Dasein's decision in 1933 or of great leaders poetically creating and forming a people in their own self-determination from the *phúsis* of being in the mid-1930s. Heidegger advocated his own distinctive version of the politics of *phúsis*, a "physiocracy" interpreted in his own ontological sense, during his initial engagement on behalf of the new totalitarian regime in which alienating dispersion, separation, and division become the originary negativity confronting the people's Dasein (GA 91: 184–5). *Phúsis* and the emergence of the National Socialist state as its expression are enmeshed in his early Nazi-era notes on metapolitics and advancing effort (GA 91: 172–87) and in the 1934–35 lecture-course *Hölderlin's Hymns "Germania" and "The Rhine"* (GA 39).

Jacques Derrida, among others, explicated in *The Beast and the Sovereign* the imposition of violence, power, and "sovereign potency" in Heidegger's conception of *phúsis* as holding sway (*Walten*) in a way that can underwrite political commitments through the philosophy of nature.[9] In the mid-1930s the establishment of beings is conceived through "work and deed and sacrifice" ("Werk und Tat und Opfer") (GA 65: 298). It is interconnected with the creativity and violence of nature that is activated in order to attain the authentic self-determination and we-being of the collective Dasein of the German people. The sources, dynamics, and consequences of this problematic "metapolitical" and onto-political deformation of the ancient Greek notion of the independent *pólis* and the modern republican notion of the popular self-determination of a unitary general will, with its faith in a collective national will directly choosing itself, unconcerned with individual rights and participatory public spheres, calls for its own specific ideology-critical analysis.

Heidegger is at this moment near and far away from the *wuwei-ziran* insights of the 1920s or the semi-Daoist turn of the mid-1940s. During this politically and philosophically problematic period, Heidegger asserts the self-ordering of the people and its imagined communal identity in contrast to individual Dasein, pluralistic society, or mortals and things in their gathering and resonance. His thought appears motivated by active and coercive acting (*wei* 為) and aggressively intervening in entangled affairs (*shi* 事), as he claims that authentic transformation requires (in place of the "anticipatory liberating solicitude" of *Being and Time*) a "liberating violence," leadership, and enduring formation.[10] His thinking is at its farthest removed from the openness and responsive releasement of things in their own self-becoming. The latter turn is provoked (at least in part) by his subsequent engagement with the *Daodejing* and its *dao* that encompasses and nourishes things without violating them in their plural self-generative and mutual autopoiesis.[11]

An important clarification is necessary here: autopoiesis will be interpreted here through Daoism rather than imposed on it. Daoist autopoiesis only occurs through singulars (things) in their interaction (*dao*) through emptiness. It is inherently communicative, mutual, or sympoietic. Collective organicism (as in romantic and vitalist natural philosophy) and closed systems (as in the systems theory of Niklas Luhmann) signify a reification, since the autopoiesis of a collective nature or society, without alterity and singularity, is governed by a fatalistic totalizing *arché* rather than an anarchically open and interactive self-ordering. Ziranist autopoiesis signifies sympoiesis as it releases rather than imprisons the myriad things.

The thing shifts from its heretofore passive and static pragmatic characterization, as an object for human eyes and hands, into a novel role in creative making (*poēsis*, ποίησις) and the work during the early and mid-1930s. It is no longer only available as a useful product or theoretically represented object as it now discloses world through the work of art—albeit not yet potentially of and by itself in addressing and saying as it does in 1949–50. The thing in Heidegger's 1935 works is not exclusively determined by usefulness and questionable in its breakdown. However, it is not yet autopoietic as it is still defined by the work of being through sagely poets, philosophers, and lawgivers. This resonates with Hanfei's "legalist" way of legitimating the sovereign more than the antipolitical and "anarchistic" politics of the *Zhuangzi* and *Liezi* which refuses the sovereign and disentangles fixating perspectives.

Heidegger in his better moments (that prioritize existent beings) recognizes the being of the thing as its existential autopoiesis such that the ontic operates in relation to the ontological without being reduced to it. In other moments, the thing is impoverished in relation to human existence, as in *Being and Time*, or subsumed in being, as in the 1930s. The thing emerges in the latter context from being, and is potentially sacrificed to it, or a given historical configuration of the event of being, in what, in the politically highly problematic context of National Socialist totalitarianism, Heidegger portrays as the creativity of originary "poets, thinkers and state creators, who actually ground and establish the historical existence of a nation."[12]

What then is the relation between *phúsis* (as upsurging and emerging holding sway) and the particular thing? Already in the 1930s, Heidegger calls for liberating the thing from being a particular carrier of properties and from the paradigm of representational thinking and truth as correctness and correspondence. The thing is at work in emergence, art, and sacrifice and no longer merely sunk in impoverished worldlessness, as in 1929. Yet is the thing ever genuinely liberated from its pragmatically mediated and anthropocentrically determined nexus of significance? Does Heidegger ever arrive at an appropriate interpretation of the thing as it is happening of itself (in its *ziran*) and in its own world openness? Can we appropriately conceive the self-naturing and worlding of the thing through Heidegger's reflections?

4. The Thing, the Work, and the Poetic

There are already indications pointing toward the prioritization of the thing in his later thought. *Phúsis* is called the first beginning and *da-sein*, as the "openness of the there," the other beginning, in his notes for the 1935 Frankfurt lectures version of "The Origin of the Work of Art" that was eventually reworked for publication in 1949 (GA 82: 494). In this work, earth is the emerging, the upsurge, and the showing forth of that which is hidden. The clearing is an "open middle" or center that is not enclosed or encircled by beings, as it "circles around all beings like the nothingness that we hardly know" (GA 5: 40).

The thing can only be encountered amidst the clearing (*Lichtung*). This does not primarily signify light but rather thinning out, as in an open area in a forest in which light can then shine forth. Heidegger gives two apparently different (at least in emphasis) yet perhaps complementary interpretations of the relationship between clearing and the thing. One strategy prioritizes the clearing as an event of being over things that arise and disappear within it: "In the midst of beings as a whole an open place occurs. There is a clearing. Thought of in reference to beings, this clearing is more in being than are beings" (GA 5: 39–40; Heidegger 2002: 30). The thing is in danger of being concealed and lost in being, as the ontological difference moves toward overweighing being against existent beings, whether taken sacrificially (e.g., for the sake of transforming earth and things into a people's homeland) or generationally—through natality and mortality—as a "taking turns" with earth, things, and others.[13] A being in its own generation and death should be honored and celebrated rather than transmuted into a sacrifice for the sake of legitimating idols of gods and peoples.

Another hermeneutical strategy diverges more powerfully from the degradation of the thing for the sake of the idea and the soul in Occidental metaphysics. This strategy prioritizes the thing as it shapes moment and place. It centers opening and clearing in the unique relational worlding and gathering of the thing: "the thing things world." We think the thing in its own terms when we let the thing be in its thinging out of the worlding of world (GA 7: 173). In the latter text, Heidegger evokes an almost Daoist sensibility of *ziran*, as it is no longer the thing in the artwork (e.g., the shaped and positioned stone in the *poiesis* of the sculpture) but the thing as thing (e.g., the uncut unpositioned stone itself in its autopoiesis) that forms meaningful worlds. Each stone can disclose from its own moment and place an interrelated environmental nexus.

How did Heidegger's modified thinking of the thing take place? Revealingly, in the "Origin of the Work of Art," the thing in its thingliness, as carrying and opening "the there" (GA 82: 494), plays an increasingly noteworthy role from the lecture's initial

1935 version until its eventual 1949 publication. Heidegger contends, with Kant and Dilthey in the background, against aesthetics and the precedence of subjectivity, genius, and the artist. He emphasizes instead the role of elemental thingliness, earth, and world in the priority of the work that discloses them. The thing is situated between thingliness, equipmentality, and work articulated in relation to emergence and holding sway (*phúsis*), craft, technique, and eventually technology (*tékhnē*), and creation and creative action (*poēsis*) in 1935.

What about the thing in the work? Thinking confronts the greatest resistance to determining the thingness of the thing as the inconspicuous thing intractably withdraws from it (GA 5: 16–17). The artwork has a thingly basis and functions as a pragmatically and symbolically mediated thing.[14] The thing is not intuited or given in itself. It is mediated in the work through equipmentality. In articulating the "thingly character" of the work of art, Heidegger interrogated three prevailing expositions concerning the thing: (1) as bearer of characteristics or properties (a subject with predicates), (2) as the unity of a manifold of sense perceptions (as *aesthesis*), and (3) as formed matter. The first two definitions express modern theoretical models of objectified objectness (*Gegenständlichkeit*). The third, Aristotelian, conception of the thing as formed matter was formulated according to the model of creation and making through equipment, such that the thing is experienced as objectively present-at-hand (1 and 2) and as pragmatically ready-to-hand (3). The equipmental tool-being of the thing is determined by its qualities of availability, reliability, and usability.

The materiality and equipmentality of the thing are appropriated in the artwork such that the thingly work can bring, set forth and become world-disclosing and world-building. Van Gogh's boots, which Heidegger likely misinterpreted, "disclose the world of the peasant as related to the earth"; the ancient Greek "temple arises from the earth toward the sky disclosing a world." The painting and the temple as truth-in-the-work are specific manifestations of being's emergence and unconcealing's disclosure.

Things are derivative to work and truth, which are interlinked in a sacrificial economy of the truth of being and its enactment in creative and violent works:

> One essential way in which truth establishes itself in the beings it has opened up is its setting-itself-into-the-work. Another way in which truth comes to presence is through the act which founds a state. Again, another way in which truth comes to shine is the proximity of that which is not simply a being but rather the being which is most in being. Yet another way in which truth grounds itself is the essential sacrifice. A still further way in which truth comes to be is in the thinker's questioning, which, as the thinking of being, names being in its question-worthiness.
>
> (GA 5: 49; Heidegger 2002: 37)

In this context, *tékhnē* is not merely technology or technique; it is a practical way of knowing things. *Poēsis* is a making, forming, and creating things that can violently enact—and gains its power from—the emergence, upsurge, and sovereign holding sway of *phúsis*.

Heidegger's thinking in this essay continues to be inadequate to the ziranist truth of the thing. This thing in the work is not the self-generative thing that offers a measure, and this poetic creation is not the intimate word responsively bound to the happening of the thing. The thing of the "Origin of the Work of Art" is closer to the dominion of the instrumental and representational object of *Being and Time* than it is to the formation of the free region of released things in the *Bremen Lectures* and related notebooks (GA 99). In between these two points are his critical self-reflections on this earlier account of earth, thing, and the work (GA 82: 494) and the 1943 engagement with Daoism (GA 75: 43–4).

II. Heidegger's Later Thinking of the Thing in Relation to Daoism

5. The Historical and Philosophical Emergence of the Fourfold

In the 1949 *Bremen Lectures*, in many ways his most Daoist-inspired work, Heidegger describes the gathering of the fourfold (*das Geviert*) taking place between earth and sky, mortals and immortals. The established definition of "*Geviert*" is quadripartite or four-quartered, evoking the boundless four-cornered *dao* without corners (*dafang wuyu* 大方無隅) of *Daodejing* 41 (Lou 1980: 112). Wang Bi's commentaries on *Daodejing* 41 and 58 state that this fourfold encompasses and enfolds all things without cutting and wounding any of them (不以方割物).

This usage was not unfamiliar to Heidegger's linguistic community. Two Weimar-era German translations already name this as the fourfold. Wilhelm's translation reads: "the great fourfold has no corners" ("Das große Geviert hat keine Ecken") (Wilhelm 1911: 46, 103). Federmann's translation has "a great fourfold without limiting angles" ("ein groß Geviert, ohn Winkel endend") (Federmann 1920: 47). A Daoist-informed fourfold was articulated in Heidegger's contemporary linguistic community in works that were in part familiar to him. It is not used by Hölderlin and rarely by other poets.

Heidegger's conception of the fourfold evokes Chinese discourses of the four-cornered world and the world as consisting of heaven and earth (*tiandi* 天地), humans and spirits (*renshen* 人神).[15] The more typical classical Chinese expression is "heaven, earth, and humans." There are other sources from which Heidegger could have drawn. *Daodejing* 25 adds, as Wilhelm discusses in his commentary, *dao* as a fourth (Wilhelm 1911: 99). The chapter speaks of the greatness of *dao*, heaven, earth, and the sage-king in a fourfold relationship in which humans model themselves on earth, earth on heaven, heaven on *dao*, and *dao* models itself on its own self-naturing. Wilhelm's comments on the preceding chapter identify "creatures" (Wilhelm's translation of the Chinese word for things) with gods and humans ("die 'Geschöpfe' = Götter und Menschen") and the "with-world" (*Mitwelt*) (Wilhelm 1911: 99).

What is an exemplary model in *Daodejing* 25 (Lou 1980: 65)? *Fa* 法 can signify law, rule, method, exemplary model, and later the Buddhist dharma. In "legalism," it means method or tactical sensibility in ruling and invisibly deploying power. "Legalism" is thus a misnomer. In the *Daodejing*, it is emulating and patterning oneself on the way and the sages. In the German linguistic context that informed Heidegger's understanding, Victor von Strauss translated *fa* as correct measure (*Richtmass*). Wilhelm's 1911 translation uses *Vorbild* which can be understood as an exemplary model but also as a primordial archetypal image for all things, including humans and gods.[16] Whereas Strauss's translation uses square (*Quadrat*) instead of fourfold and typically spirits (*Geister*) in preference to gods, Wilhelm's language is closer to Heidegger's way of speaking of the fourfold.

Other variations on varieties of earthly and spiritual entities appear in German accounts of Chinese sources. A post-Han-era religious Daoist expression is "humans, spirits, and immortals/transcendents" (*ren shen xian* 人神仙). Such immortals are not Heidegger's gods. They are biospiritually realized humans rather than natural spirits. In the German context, the influential nineteenth-century Austrian Sinologist and Japanologist August Pfizmaier describes in his 1870 book *The Tao-Teaching of Genuine Persons and Immortals* how religious Daoist teachings encompass heaven and earth ("Himmel und Erde"), genuine humans and immortals ("wahren Menschen und den Unsterblichen"), and humans and gods ("Menschen und Götter") (Pfizmaier 1870: 229). A different variation of the cosmic whole is seen in Ernst Faber's 1877 work on the Daoism of the *Liezi*, construed as pantheistic naturalism. He notes how humans complete or perfect themselves situated between heaven, earth, and things (Faber 1877: 6).

The exemplary image—interpreted along the lines of a Daoist *Vorbild* rather than a Jungian *Urbild*—of the fourfold is shaped in part by Heidegger's intensive engagement with the *Laozi*, *Zhuangzi*, and conceivably other Chinese and Japanese sources and interlocutors in the 1940s. Pöggeler attributes this influence to "Chinese literature" in *Martin Heidegger's Path of Thinking* and elsewhere to the *Daodejing*, maintaining that it plays an understated yet undeniable and striking role in Heidegger's thinking.[17] In the confluence of the fourfold, it is not being or human existence, but the thing that gathers and discloses world.[18] Things now partake in an elemental being of their own, a dimension missing in the predominantly instrumental analysis of the thing in *Being and Time*, or the creative poetic violence of *Introduction to Metaphysics* and the various 1935 lecture versions of "The Origin of the Work of Art." Although threatened and circumscribed by its ordering in metaphysical and technological enframing (*Gestell*), the thing can come to word (*zu Wort kommen*) in the attuned saying that conveys the thing in its own sense.

6. The World-Gathering Thing

How can the once worldless thing come to gather words around itself in saying? As noted earlier, Heidegger introduced the phrase "it worlds" in his 1919 lecture-course to indicate the verbal character of world as worlding. He proposed "the nothing nothings" in his 1929 lecture "What is Metaphysics?"; only later did he arrive at the theme of the first 1949 Bremen lecture, revised as the 1950 essay "The Thing." In these latter works, he notes how "the thing things" in statements such as "the thinging gathers" ("das Dingen versammelt") and—contrary to the 1929 static worldlessness of the thing—"the thing things world" ("das Ding dingt Welt") (GA 7: 175, 182;

GA 79: 13, 24). The thing is not a correlate of intentional consciousness, the projection of temporalizing human existence, or the emerging sway of being. It is the thing's lingering time spent and earthly dwelling place (i.e., both senses of *ver-weilen*) that gathers and brings near earth and sky, mortals and immortals into the fourfold (GA 7: 170; GA 79: 17).

The word "thing" in its modern usage can signify an indeterminate object, somethingness, or in its plural form reality. The archaic meanings of the Germanic word ding/thing (*þenga-) include a moment or duration in time and gathering as, for instance, in the assembling of the populace or a court to authorize a judgment and decision. It is this sense of the thing's temporalizing and gathering that Heidegger accentuates in "The Thing." Heidegger's reformed elucidation of the thing consequently breaks with his earlier temporal idealism that identified ekstatic Dasein as the locus of temporalizing.

In Heidegger's shift against the lingering transcendental idealism of his analytic of Dasein, and toward the thing in its own ways of being as more than an intentional correlate, time and space are then not given as merely objectively present as a neutral arena for that which phenomenally appears as bearing qualities, as in the paradigm of representational thinking. In distinction from the temporalizing of human being-in-the-world in the 1924 lecture *The Concept of Time*, in which the "in each case for a while at a particular time" (*Jeweiligkeit*) constitutes the "I am" (GA 64: 113), Heidegger articulates in 1949 the prominence of things in the duration of "a while" (*Weile*) and the nearness and proximity of place wherein humans reside. The lingering of things gathers time as an encountered duration and their dwelling gathers space as an encountered locality (*Gegend*) with its own singular configuration and life. Temporality and spatiality are not merely external frames in which things are placed; they consist of the co-presencing and mutual interconnecting and mirroring of things as world. The verbal sense of the thinging of the thing is the nearing in which "world as world" is held near (GA 7: 179; GA 79: 24). The thing discloses world and, further than this, it gathers, carries, and opens the worlding of the world in the specificity of a durational "for a while" and the locality of a place.[19] This localizing place is simultaneously self-generatively world-forming and world-opening. It might be the place on the way where the wanderer tarries under the canopy of the useless tree, encountering anew the earth below and the sky above.

What then is the relation of thing, earth, and world first thought of in terms of strife and contest in the mid-1930s and now as nourishing generosity of the "there is / it gives" (*es gibt*)? According to their archaic roots, as guiding hints for thinking, earth means ground; the earth as the dwelling place of mortal things was named the middle enclosure (Midgard) as distinct from the enclosure of the Æsir gods (Asgard). World is the generational existence of the "age of man" (*Welt* as from old Germanic *weralt*) or "world-age" (*Weltalter*). This etymology reveals a particular sense of place and time. A world-age and its world-picture consist not only in a human generation; it is a configuration of things. The thing, great because it does not live merely for itself, generously opens and discloses world and world conceals the event of the thing as it becomes an object (whether with or without value) in what Heidegger earlier described as a practically determined referential nexus of significance.

7. Enframing and Releasing Things

Heidegger diagnosed in his December 1949 Bremen Lecture "Das Gestell" and in the 1954 essay "The Question Concerning Technology" how the collecting formation (*Gestalt*) of modernity is an enframing positionality (*Gestell*) in which things and humans are available as a standing-reserve (*Bestand*) of useful resources. *Ge-stell* is a condition of world-denial and the neglect of things (GA 100: 23). It signifies a totalizing collecting (*ge-*, which signifies gathering, in expressions such as *Ge-viert*, the fourfold) and placing and positioning (*stellen*). It obscures and excludes other ways in which things disclose themselves. It conceals—in an objectively fixated presence (*Präsenz* as distinguished from self-presencing as *an-wesen*) and the apparent givenness of availability—the occurrence of truth in the dynamic of mystery and disclosure, concealment and unconcealment. *Ge-stell* functions through positioning things as purely useful or useless. It operates as the enframing or enpicturing structure, the totalizing framework, and technical apparatus in which things lose their thingly character in being purely given, obtainable, and disposable in—to step beyond Heidegger into critical social analysis—processes of production, exchange, and consumption.[20] Heidegger's anti-totalizing analysis of enframing can serve as a formal indicative and critical template for diagnosing and confronting the degradation of things and their environing worlds.[21]

Heidegger's analysis of enframing entails a significant shift in his thinking of the thing. Heidegger was concerned foremost with the reification of human existence in the 1920s, submerging the thing in instrumentality. He is concerned in 1949 with the hardening fixation of thingly existence in which natural and human lives have become objectified and instrumentalized, their presencing substantialized into available givenness. These expressions involve two problems. First, according to Heidegger, they hint at yet do not reach the hidden essencing of technology. This means that the analysis of instrumentality and availability must lead to the question of presencing as such. Heidegger's elucidation of being in its coming to presence and withdrawal in absence challenges being experienced as mere given presence. Secondly, given that reification means to be reduced to a thing-like role, it could be asked whether the thing can be reified. The thing can be reified if the thingness it is fixed and limited to is different than its own manner of thingness. Heidegger marks the difference between the thing as instrumentally and objectively present (as enframed in a fixed position and use) and the thingliness of "it things" as world-gathering. The thing gathers world and grants nearness in stillness; yet the thing as object-entity obscures and disfigures the thing that it would represent (GA 98: 114–15, 119). Heidegger speaks in the 1949 *Bremen Lectures* of the danger of the enframing picturing of world in which things are frozen in their positionality.[22]

The intimate bonds between thing, place, and world remain a key task for Heidegger, as his notion of the thing shifts in relationship to instrumentality and usefulness. The worldlessness of the thing is diagnosed as an absence and lack of the thing as thing in Heidegger's later thinking. The world-picture as enframing the thing positions, fixates, and obfuscates the thing *qua* thing, leaving it and us in our encounter with it without world. The ordering of enframing places itself above the thing that it encompasses and positions. Enframing positionality obscures the proximity of the world that approaches in the thing (GA 11: 122). Things become mere facets of a reality consisting of a standing-reserve of disposable inventory, thereby leaving the thing unnourished, unprotected, and without its own event and truth.

The thing is necessary for nearing and encountering world and the world that hides and violates things is a world-picture. This analysis of the enframing of things could be called a formal indicative or critical model that indicates the missing nearness and reality of the thing. Heidegger's early conception of formal indication (*formale Anzeige*) is of an emptying formalizing that opens the concrete facticity and variety of ways of being.[23] Formal indication is not only Heidegger's early conception of way. It could also be conceived of as a way of forming critical models, to apply Adorno's expression, to the extent that, as Heidegger articulates it in the 1920s, it necessitates destructuring fixation (*Destruktion*) and differentiating encounter (*Auseinandersetzung*). It thereby points toward that which is missing, discloses closed-off and hidden possibilities. It intimates alternative ways of caring-for and individuating existence. Heidegger's early method of emptying through formal indication is expanded and reoriented from human existence toward thing, place, and world in his ensuing thinking of way that radicalizes this unfixing-opening structure.

The picturing, enframing, and positioning of the thing contrasts with its freedom in the letting-releasement and saying that protects the thing and its truth (GA 76: 338). Arendt notes how: "To thinking there belongs '*Gelassenheit*'—security, composure, releasement, a state of relaxation, in brief, a disposition of 'lets be'" (Arendt 2018b: 430). In German mystical traditions, there are moments for God's things to speak to us. In that context, the letting be of things primarily means abandoning entanglements and affairs that one learns to tolerate and accept, to open the soul to God. That is not the Lao-Zhuang spontaneous embracing of the myriad things and the world in their own self-becoming. Heidegger strikes a more Daoist than mystical tone in his postwar thought in embracing one's quotidian world-relations and pointing toward things in a nonacting or nonintervention that allows the thing to be seen and heard. In addition to the mystical state of mind of letting be, there is the *Gelassenheit* in and of things in their own worldly occurring rather than in my own mental releasement. Releasement, not unlike Daoist *wuwei* with which it is in dialogue, expresses not only a comportment but further possibilities of things themselves granting mortals a guiding measure (GA 13: 215).

8. The Measure of Things

Is there a measure on earth? In a range of early Chinese sources, which can help situate early Daoism, thingly and environmental patterns provide models and measures for humans. The legendary sovereign Fu Xi 伏羲 is said to have drawn the *Book of Changes*'s eight trigrams based on observing the patterns of heaven and earth. Cang Jie 倉頡 is said to have formed written characters based on the tracks of animals and birds. The genuine measure (*yidu* 一度), according to the *Yuandao*, is following the tracks (*xungui* 循軌) of things themselves (Lau and Ames 1998: 110–11).

The consummate measure, as expressed in the Daoistic *Zhuangzi* and the eclectic *Guanzi* 管子 collections, is found in water (an image of the most indeterminate, flexible, and encompassing of things) in its stillness, evenness, and clarity. Swirling water undoes what is fixed, gathering and dispersing things through its movements. Yet it is its stillness and emptiness that set the measure. In the *Zhuangzi* "Heavenly Way" (*tiandao* 天道) chapter, water is taken as an exemplary measure for sages just as the still level water (*shui jing you ming* 水靜猶明) provides the measure for carpenters (*dajiang qufa yan* 大匠取法焉). The *Guanzi* "Water and Earth" chapter states that "the water level is first among the five measures," and as an elemental image of equalizing and evenness, "water is the level for all things, the quality of tranquility in all life, and the quality of impartiality between right and wrong, profit and loss."[24]

For Heidegger, so-called modern Occidental thinking underscores in a variety of ways the preeminence of the human, the mind, and the subject as the measure of things.[25] The deworlding of things is consummated in enframing. It signifies the removal of the orientation of place, measure, and meaningfulness that is granted by things and the localities and regions that gather around them. The modern crisis of meaning is not due to the death of God or the subject. It transpires through the loss of the sense of meaning-generating gathering things and the words that express their encounter. Consequently, world, enacted and embodied in specific moments and places, is viewed as a bare identity in the repetition of indifferent unfulfilled time and the homogeneity of vacant space.

As Heidegger conveyed in his October 1955 lecture "*Gelassenheit*," commemorating the hometown musician Conradin Kreutzer, human releasement with respect to things signifies making room for the releasement occurring in things themselves and in their words prior to and after the questions and answers that restrain—evoking the *Daodejing*—things and their mystery (GA 16: 527). This dimension of Heidegger's conception of releasement evokes the relational thing orientation of early Daoist sources. In the language of the *Heng Xian* and the *Zhuangzi*, as shown in Chapter 1, the "inaction" and letting of *wuwei* express a comportment that acknowledges the self-acting (*ziwei*) of the thing.

Heidegger describes the prospect of the reflectively mindful and thoughtful encounter with the thing: "we think of the thing as thing when we release the thing in its thinging from the worlding of the world. In this way we thoughtfully let ourselves be approached by the encompassing essencing of the thing" (GA 7: 182; GA 7: 20). Heidegger's expression "thoughtfully let" (*andenkend lassen*) means to allow the thing (as it is of itself) to approach in responsive reminiscence of it in its lingering duration and dwelling place. Genuine thoughtful thinking is an enactment of letting. To let means the releasing-free of things and place; it is described as giving occasion to, bringing about as bringing underway (*zuwege-bringen*), and releasing the enregioning of the free region (GA 99: 61; GA 100: 23). *Being and Time* was centered on the ekstatic-existential temporality of human existence. Now the temporalizing and spatializing gathering of things, such as the stone and other "small things" that silently make up a country path, is its moment and place. The stone expresses a world, and the dewdrop reflects the universe. The saying of thinking is the echo of silence, the occurrence of which remains a mystery (GA 97: 247).

9. The Moment and Place of the Thing

Heidegger's later expansive notion of the thing appears to intersect with Chinese images and models of the thing and the gathering of the elemental in the thing. Nonliving and living things are understood as a gathering of material and biospiritual forces (*qi*) in the Chinese context. They do so such that there is no ultimate distinction between internal and external, self and other, and kinds of being, insofar as they consist of a temporary configuration of changing forces that form and dissipate. Each thing has its own moment and place as it gathers and harmonizes in emptiness and oscillates between the darkness (*yin*) from which they emerge and the brightness (*yang*) that they hold.[26] Strauss and Wilhelm translated *qi* (elemental force) as soul of nature and life-breath, and *yin-yang* respectively as dormancy and activity and darkness and light. Perhaps Heidegger's attempts to translate the *Daodejing* with Paul Shih-yi Hsiao contained this passage and reimagined it with a less metaphysical and more poetic significance.

Darkness, hiddenness, mystery, and concealment are intertwined throughout Wilhelm's works. In his translation of *Daodejing* 65, pure life signifies concealed life (*verborgenes Leben*, as he translates mysterious virtuosity [*xuande* 玄德]), which means deep, far-reaching, and effective life (Wilhelm 1911: 70). Wilhelm describes elsewhere how wonder swells up from the dark mystery of *dao* (Wilhelm 1925: 45). This mystery is also described as concealment (*Verborgenheit*) from which the forces of life arise (Wilhelm 1925: 61). *Dao* is the swelling primeval empty ground (*chongxu* 沖虛) in the title of his 1921 translation of the *Liezi*. The thing emerges from the generative fecund darkness of *dao* into the light in Wilhelm's translation of *Daodejing* 42, which mentions neither emptiness (*chong* 沖, rinsed or washed away), in affinity with Heidegger's earth and world of the 1935 "Origin of the Work of Art," nor the earth and sky of the 1949 *Bremen Lectures*. Heidegger expressed little interest in discourses of life-forces in European vitalism, which remained biological and ontic, or in East Asian *qi*-philosophy that was frequently connected with vitalism and pantheism in his linguistic community. Nonetheless, this interculturally entangled imagery in works familiar to Heidegger suggestively intermingles with his own discourse of earth, world, and the moment and place of the gathering thing, even as the *Daodejing* is only specifically mentioned, particularly between 1943 and 1950, in relation to the thing and its emptiness.

Lao-Zhuang Daoism is often misinterpreted as a philosophy (or family of philosophies) of the eternal *dao*. It is not about static atemporality but the continuing *dao* (*hengdao*) operating through temporalizing things. In contrast with bifurcating and fixating *dao* and thing, the constancy of the self is to be in accord—without anxiety and disturbance—with the temporalizing meandering flow of things and affairs. Inflexibility, rigidity, and fixation mean death for the embodied heart-mind that is nourished and freed through an unrestricted communication and exchange. Heidegger's later notebooks explicitly recognize the theme of undoing fixation and frozenness in the *Daodejing*. *Winke I und II* (his notebooks from 1957 to 1959) begins by quoting *Daodejing* 43 on how the softest overcomes the hardest, the healing hidden in stillness counters the fixated frozenness of things in restlessness (GA 101: 3).

Daodejing 43 describes how the softest breaks and overwhelms the hardest, how what is without being (*wuyou* 無有) can enter even that which has no entrance (such as the hardened and fixated), and how the benefits of acting without action and teaching without words contrast with forced coercive active and speaking.

Did Heidegger's extensive engagement with the *Daodejing* in the mid-1940s help therapeutically undo hypostatization in his own thinking? There are questions concerning bifurcation in Heidegger's earlier thinking: issues of the potential bifurcation and fixation of being and beings, the ontological and the ontic, which threaten—as asserted by Heidegger's critics—to coercively subsume and commit violence to the particularity of persons and things. This is a genuine problematic in Heidegger's works of the 1930s. Heidegger's late wartime and postwar reflections on the thing point toward a different pathway: they demand—in a language that strongly alludes to and periodically overtly refers to the *Daodejing* and the *Zhuangzi*—the releasement of things and openness to their mystery (GA 16: 528).

What then is the mystery of the thing? It is bound to the thing's own way of temporalizing, spatializing, and speaking world. Neither time nor being can be construed as things. They differ from the thing insofar as it is ontic and the ontological cannot be conflated with the ontic. Nonetheless, Heidegger approaches the thing in its own temporalizing as an ontic-ontological event irreducible to Dasein: "Each thing has its own time" (GA 14: 6). Likewise, according to the 1969 lecture "Art and Space," "we ought to be able to recognize that the things themselves are places and do not merely belong to place" (GA 13: 208). Each thing has its own "existential" moment and place in which it is gathered and gathers world. This was an impossibility in *Being and Time* and in his early period in which the primordial meanings of language (*Urbedeutungen der Sprache*) relate to Dasein and not the thing (GA 17: 318). The thing now can speak to and address me ("Das Ding spricht mich an") even if not in a human language (GA 89: 249). Human saying is entangled with the communication and meaningfulness of things that open and configure places and localities for human building and dwelling. One way of being-in-the-world is to inhabit, reside amidst, and cultivate things and the environing world; the other extreme is to annihilate them and struggle to persist amidst impoverished things and places stripped of their generative nourishing autopoietic character.

Heidegger has accordingly shifted from the primacy of the projective constitutive and still anthropocentric subject, elucidated as the ekstatic being-in-the-world of *Dasein* in *Being and Time*, to the priority of the thing in encountering it. It is not consciousness or the subject, even as embodied, enactive, and extended, but rather things that constitute and orient a place. It is the thing that is formative of world. The event of the thing can be described as the thingly worldly other-constitution of moment, place, and sensibility. Things are not merely "there-for-me"; I am fundamentally dependent on and enmeshed with things and their places in their emptiness and materiality. These characteristics are underemphasized in the idealistic tendencies of classical phenomenology and contemporary discourses that conceal them in the embodiment, enactment, and extension of what remains—and much earlier than in the final analysis—a constitutive subject. It is not phenomenology as driven by the subject (whether conceived as consciousness or the body) that sets the measure, but things themselves in their myriad ways of being (thinging). The transcendental paradigm of the constitutive subject, even when naturalized and pragmatized, underemphasizes how the transcendental is inevitably ensnared and mediated in concrete historical life. The philosophy of the subject occludes the thing in totalizing the subject's perspective. They are incapable of recognizing other-constitution of the self through the "other-power" in things, places, mountains and rivers, environments, and open autopoietic ecological systems.[27] It is not abstracted matter, space, or unmediated objectness that forms orienting localities where mortals abide, work, play, and linger; it is specific concrete things that form them.

Inasmuch as the language of modern Occidental philosophy prioritizes the subject and identity, an insight expressed in distinctive ways by Heidegger and his critics Adorno and Levinas, other ways of speaking and philosophizing are vital. This concern informs the language of radical non-identity and the priority of the object in Adorno's confrontation with identity-thinking. He regards identity-thinking as repressing contradictions and differences that need intensification rather than dialectical consonance, while Levinas addresses ethical alterity and priority of the other in opposition to totality. Heidegger's later reorientation toward the thing, drawing on the "poetic thinking" of Daoists, poets, and thinkers, means turning to forms of poetic saying that are mindfully attentive and responsive to the particularities of the thing. Poetic letting and releasing, in which things are kept safe as the things that they are, consequently form "the higher clarity that allows things to appear in their own ways and grants mortals their measure" (GA 13: 215).

Heidegger's later poetics of the thing would speak with things more directly and intimately than subject-oriented phenomenology. Here, time and space are not absolute containers in which things occur; nor are they forms of intuition (as in Kant) or correlational intentional consciousness (as in Husserl) through which things are constituted in experience. Time and space occur and are encountered vis-à-vis the temporalizing and spatializing of things. This dynamic is world-formative and full of the world in which it is concealed: hiding the thing in the world, to adjust a statement from the *Zhuangzi* often construed—following Guo Xiang—as abiding undisturbed in the pure immanence of transformation, while the thing hides in and from the world.[28]

III. Complications with Things

10. The Thing as Resistance, Complexly Mediated, and Withdrawing

In this concluding section, the discussion is widened as three sets of questions about the thing, the thing in itself, and the possibility of an ethics of things are posed in ways that set the stage for Part One's subsequent chapters that focus on the emptiness, uselessness, and a comportment of care and nurturing the life of things in which the thing irreducibly exceeds pragmatically positioned raw material.

Heidegger remarked in the artwork essay how thinking seems to face the greatest opposition from the thing in its thingness as the inconspicuous non-appearing thing unyieldingly draws away from it (GA 5: 16–17). A difficulty concerning understanding the thing is that its apparent givenness, simplicity, and unity hide that which resists and escapes perception and conception of the thing, and the complex formation of the senses and meaning that allow a thing to be merely perceived. The thing resists, escapes, and furthermore can—depending on the thing—endanger those who approach it.

There are three ways of describing the thing's inaccessibility from Heidegger's historical situation and reception that contextualize, complicate, and potentially challenge his later philosophy of the thing.

First, the thing has been characterized as that which resists and stands over and against (*Gegen-stand*) the perceiver as a facticity irreducible to the subject, thus constituting its sense of facticity and external reality. Wilhelm Dilthey identified the thing with force, resistance, and restraint, qualities that form the subject's sense of external reality, in his 1890 work "The Origin of Our Belief in the Reality of the External World and Its Justification." According to a later note, "[t]he thing is the correlate of sensation, and the feeling of resistance is its condition" as the categories of life are formed in relation to the forces and things that compel and resist the subject hardening its sense of the facticity of reality (Dilthey 2004).

Second, the complexity of the thing seems to demand an archaeology in which it disappears instead of a phenomenology of its appearing. The neo-vitalist Hans Driesch argued against the direct phenomenological seeing of the thing as the lived experience of the thing, regarding its appearance of "being-there" to be a complexly mediated formation of sense, meaning, and the construction of experiential order (Driesch 1938: 136). More radical is the elimination of the thing in the emerging logical empiricist program of Rudolf Carnap in the 1920s. He analyzed the thing as a complex interpretive fiction, formed from basic experiential and logical elements into which it can be dissolved and reconstructed (Carnap 1924: 130). The thing consists of projection based on matter, sensation, and abstraction.

Third, the reality of the thing outstrips the experientially, linguistically, and conceptually mediated thing, or the symbolic thing, as in Lacan's differentiation of thing as signified and as beyond signification. There is something of the thing that inevitably withdraws, as Heidegger puts it, and escapes, as Derrida points out: "Contrary to what phenomenology—which is always phenomenology of perception—has tried to make us believe, contrary to what our desire cannot fail to be tempted into believing, the thing itself always escapes" (Derrida 1989: 9).

The thing has identity and unity over time and space vis-à-vis intentional consciousness. To be fair, Husserl himself recognized in his phenomenology of the thing the shading and appearing/non-appearing of the thing in the figure/ground relation, and the potentially infinite variation through which the self-appearing thing is perceived as a unity in its open and indeterminate horizon (Husserl 2003: 6, 114–15). The hiddenness of the thing in the perception of the thing is a non-accidental facet of the thing rather than the basis of an objection that would refute its being and meaning.

The hiddenness, potential dangerousness, and uncanniness of the thing call for humility in the face of the depth and manifoldness of the thing and an openness to appropriately adapt to the flowing, transforming patterns of things. The thing calls for its own forms of "leaping-ahead," as Heidegger described in a crucial passage in the 1937–38 lecture-course *Basic Questions of Philosophy*: it is not a coercive knowing as mastering from which the thing *qua* thing necessarily withdraws and escapes. Philosophy is not a scientific knowledge of things and their essence; nor is it purely the inventing, forming, and imposing of concepts.

What then is philosophy? Evoking the traditional Aristotelian definition of philosophy as the science of the essence of things while revising it in a quasi-Daoistic fashion, Heidegger defines philosophy as a useless opening knowing in anticipatory leaping-ahead of the self-concealing essencing of things (GA 45: 3, 29). It is here that the openness of the thing *as* thing begins to surface as distinct from the thing as available and useful for human existence (GA 45: 19–20). Intending the thing, and hence representation, already presupposes its openness (GA 45: 24). Knowing requires this openness of the thing and the opening making place for the thing in its appearing and non-appearing; Heidegger analyzed this as its unconcealment and self-concealment (*das Sichverbergen*). The self-reflexive or self-relational "self" or "itself," expressed in the German third-person reflexive pronoun "*sich*," indicates that it is an aspect of the thing itself and not purely a failure of experience and conception that is at stake.

11. The Question of the "Thing in Itself"

Let us continue to question the thing. A crucial facet of the thing is the thing's self-withdrawal, self-concealment, and its arising and functioning from nothingness that early Lao-Zhuang sources address. They do so without bifurcating the thing into the appearing thing and the thing in itself in Kant's *Critique of Pure Reason* or the signified symbolically ordered thing and the thing as alien, uncanny, and real beyond signification in Lacan's thing-theory.[29]

In Heidegger's interpretations of Kant's appearing and non-appearing thing during the 1920s and 1930s, Kant's thing-in-itself is a distinctive way of relating to the thing, another perspective on it (GA 3: 33; GA 25: 99). It is an unusual relation to or perspective on the thing, such as God as the ultimate most distant thing, since it is removed from all attestation and unavailable in every way to human knowledge (GA 41: 5, 130). Neither God nor things are interpreted as unconditional otherness or Lacanian monstrousness.

As described earlier, Heidegger does have a sense of the uncanniness and violence of nature as *phúsis* that he celebrated as creative in the mid-1930s. The uncanniness of the thing appears in Heidegger in the breakdown of its usefulness, its missing absence, and its technological annihilation. In addressing the thing's otherness, it is characteristically described more in the sense of awe, wonder, and the sublime than in the sense of the alien monstrousness of Lacan's reimagining of Freud's thing (Lacan 1992: 43–5, 62–3).

The thing's self-occurring and self-concealing (self in the sense of "*zi*" and "*sich*") require a transition from the phenomenology of (1) what appears to intentional or embodied consciousness and appearances as describable and graspable, to (2) what appears as resisting, escaping, and withdrawing in the self-concealment of the thing, to (3) what does not appear at all while being at work in the self-naturing of the thing (i.e., nothingness and emptiness). This free and easy shifting through manifold perspectives, equalizing the myriad things, and undoing fixation and bifurcation, is necessary for an appropriate encountering of and dwelling with the thing in the freedom of its own becoming.

This perspective of the freedom of the thing entails a different *ethos* or way of dwelling that recognizes their self-becoming as well as their anthropocentrically demarcated use. It contrasts with the demand for the domination of nature expressed in the early Chinese context in Xunzi's criticisms of Zhuangzi that external and internal nature must be actively controlled and forcefully reshaped; we see these in the Baconian vision of the mastery of nature analyzed in Horkheimer and Adorno's *Dialectic of Enlightenment*, or in Hegel's *Phenomenology of Spirit* that deems the freedom of the thing as self-contradictory and asserts that every free thing without a master must be turned into controlled and useful property (Hegel 1986: 318). But in forgetting and obscuring the life of things, the domination of nature does not lead to the freedom of spirit from nature over which it rules, as Hegel proposed. It is, rather, human enslavement as a piece of dominated nature, as Adorno and Horkheimer diagnosed.[30]

"Nature" and things as free from the ostensive necessity of domination, sacrifice and usefulness appear improbable amidst the prevailing devastation and plight that is more than ecological. Yet, as Heidegger reiterates from Hölderlin, "where there is danger, that which saves grows also."[31] That is to say, there is resistance where there is coercion, and the danger brings forth its response. The plight itself demands and animates the freedom of nature as—to think with and beyond Heidegger to question the present—an exemplary image, an orienting bearing and comportment, a responsive releasement and awaiting, a prophetic calling, and a critical social and environmental model.

12. Questioning the *Ethos* of Things

The prospect of this other *ethos* and voice entails conceptual and existential questions that will be considered in a preliminary way here and more fully addressed in Chapter 5. In addition to the questions of the reality and fictiveness, fullness and poverty, of the thing as appearing and non-appearing, there are difficulties concerning the *ethos* of nurturing life or, to recall Okakura's description, the way and art of being-in-the-world as dwelling with and amidst things. Two questions, informed by the critical readings of Heidegger conveyed by Levinas and Adorno, could be posed at this juncture.

First, is it possible to be responsive to things in free and easy mimetic and correlational relationships (which undo fixations) as opposed to slavish and fearful ones (which establish fixations instead of shifting through them), and without fetishism and idolatry? The former is requisite to confront the degradation of living and nonliving things even as the latter worry—expressed by Levinas in his 1961 essay "Heidegger, Gagarin, and Us" (Levinas 1990: 231-4)—must be genuinely addressed and avoided. Secondly, does a change in the culture and way of inhabiting the earth require a correlated transformation in economic and social conditions? Heidegger admittedly inadequately interrogates material relations of production, exchange, and consumption under existing capitalist structures and, according to his contemporary Adorno, obscures and mystifies them.[32]

The critical interrogations of Adorno and Levinas, as polemical yet observant readers of Heidegger's rural agrarian imaginary, indicate missing corners of the square: the importance of not neglecting interhuman relations and the material and political-economic circumstances of human existence. Nonetheless, despite trenchant philosophical and social-political problems in Heidegger's thought, confronting the ongoing alienation, commodification, and reification of human existence calls for contesting what has become of things and environments as well as persons in order to encounter them with ecophronesis in a more appropriate and receptive way, as having self-generating patterns, processes, and permutations of their own.[33]

Reconstructing and reimagining Heidegger's later Daoist-informed philosophy of the thing offers a significant formal indication, critical model, and guiding thread for confronting the contemporary degradation of things and environments precisely in insisting on (1) nonpurposive and non-pragmatic doing and letting, and (2) poetic listening to and saying thing and world as the fundamental capacity for human dwelling.[34] Heidegger's later conception does not speak of creative violent assertion for the sake of instituting new worlds and ways of being in which being more authentically and coercively holds sway. In the turn toward the thing, the poetic signifies attending to and learning from things and the environing world and adopting the appropriate exemplary words in interthingly and interworldly interpolation with them.

13. Buber and Heidegger as Thinkers of the Thing

I wish to conclude this chapter by insisting on Buber's historical and philosophical importance. Literature on Heidegger has distinct reasons for ignoring Buber's writings, even as they intersect with and inspired some of Heidegger's conceptual usage and linguistic play. Intriguingly, given his repeated references and debts to Buber's rendition of the *Zhuangzi*, Heidegger is not the first to draw connections between Daoism, modern technology, and different prospects of interacting with things.[35] Buber clarified these interconnections and the significance of Daoist *wuwei* as a response to the pathologies of technological modernity in his 1928 lecture "China and Us" (Buber 203: 285–9). Buber insisted on the ethical implications of early Daoist sources. Instead of rejecting modernity, the liberating ideas of 1789, and the Enlightenment, Buber's vision of Daoism allows for a reorientation away from domination, power, and the struggle for existence toward a genuine being-with-others, nurturing creatures, and co-creating the world.

Buber was an early decisive source for Heidegger's interpretation of Daoism. Buber is known for privileging I-thou over I-it relationships. But, at the same time, he elucidated alternative ways of relating to the "it," drawing from Daoist discourses of the thing and its mystery in the 1910s and 1920s in ways that intersect with Heidegger. Buber remarked in a 1924 lecture "The Religious World-Conception," given a few months after his August Ascona lectures on the *Daodejing*, "to view things without their mystery means to make them imaginary, it means to live with ghosts" rather than with genuine things.[36] We forget the thing as our names fail to grasp them and their mystery (Buber 2013: 228). The thing is altered into a mere object of desire and use, as described for instance in Hegel's *Phenomenology* (Hegel 1986: 318), when it is broken from the encounter and taken out of the fullness of its relational context (Buber 2013: 232). Still, there is more to the thing than use, exchange, and consumption. It is this corner of the square, the life and mystery of the thing articulated in Buber and Heidegger that constitutes the primary focus of Part One of the present book.

What then of the Daoist thing and Heidegger's thing that has begun to emerge in the first two chapters? Is it a contingent accident that Heidegger's turn toward the thing in its priority as world-formative, and no longer worldlessly at-hand, coincided with his intensive engagement with the *Daodejing* and the *Zhuangzi* during 1943–1951? This intercultural entangled nexus is elucidated in the next chapters on the empty and the useless unnecessary thing, with an eye toward other ways of dwelling and encountering—in-the-world with and amidst things in the expansive sense of their own ways of being.

3

Heidegger and Laozi's *Daodejing*:
The Gathering Emptiness of Thing and Place

I. *Dao* with and without Image and Word

1. Heidegger and the German Reception of Daoism

There is a long tradition of skepticism concerning Heidegger's Daoist affinities. Karl Löwith, a student and subsequent critic of Heidegger who taught in Japan from 1936 to 1941, noticed Heidegger's Daoist-sounding language and doubted its genuineness. He questioned in his 1960 essay "Remarks on the Difference between Orient and Occident" whether Heidegger's releasement could overcome Occidental subjectivity and that, with Heidegger's earlier purposive for-the-sake-of-which and dictates of being, it could truly come near to the non-differentiation of subject and object in the originary unity of being-in-the-world of acting without action (*wuwei*) (Löwith 1983: 600).

Measured according to the standpoint of Löwith's claim, Heidegger offers at best a flawed misappropriation of Daoism that cannot approach its truth. Of course, Heidegger never presented himself as an advocate or scholar of Daoism, and his later philosophy of the thing does not merely copy or plagiarize statements from the *Daodejing* but rather reimagines them in his own philosophical discourse. Nonetheless, Heidegger is a thinker of way and being-underway even more than being or meaning.[1] He states multiple times that "way" (*Weg*) is the elemental word and that the step (*Schritt*) between being and beings and the movement of the way (*be-wegen*) is the summation of his thinking (GA 98: 57). His commonly misinterpreted quasi-Daoist (in the ziranist sense) turn toward the thing (i.e., the thing as indicating much more than a pragmatic worldless entity) in the 1940s is intertwined with his multiple imperfect yet provocative engagements with the Daoist thing as articulated in the *Daodejing* and the *Zhuangzi*.[2] This interculturally mediated modern encounter with ancient sources is without doubt a reimagining and adaptation of Daoist imagery and strategies in Heidegger's distinctive philosophical scene, formed by its own presuppositions, purposes, and stakes.

The problems of German modernity shaped Heidegger's response to Daoism, much as they did those of his contemporaries. Alfred Döblin's remarkable 1916 modernist-Daoist novel *The Three Leaps of Wang Lun* (*Die drei Sprünge des Wang-lun*) began with Döblin "sacrificing" the work in dedication to the Daoist sage Liezi

(Döblin 2013: 8), a figure known for freely riding the wind. Faber and Wilhelm both translated the *Liezi*, and it was a familiar text to German language audiences. Döblin's novel contemplated the interconnections between *wuwei*, social-political oppression, and revolutionary violence through a fictionalized account of the eighteenth-century Shandong White Lotus rebel leader Wang Lun 王倫 (Detering 2008: 45–54). This novel helped inspire the engagement with Chinese thought in Marxist writers such as Bertolt Brecht and Anna Seghers. Brecht's mid-1930s reflections in the unpublished *Book of Twists and Turns* (*Buch der Wendungen*), voiced through a fictionalized version of the non-Daoist moral philosopher Me Ti (Mo Di 墨翟, c. 470–391 BCE), addressed Chinese philosophy, Marxist dialectics, and contemporary politics with the question of how to appropriately intervene in the flow and transitions of things.[3] Ernst Bloch's reflections on Daoism likewise concerned utopian political questions. Buber appealed in 1928 to *wuwei* against the Occidental fetishizing of power in "China and us," while Count von Keyserling pondered in 1919 Butcher Ding's effortless ox-cutting as an image of nourishing life while observing the mechanized death of the Chicago stockyards.[4]

Heidegger's interpretive encounter with these early Daoist sources in translation, which intriguingly intersects with other Weimar-era explications of Daoism, from Ludwig Klages on the political right to Buber and Bloch on the left, oscillates around his concerns with the thing and the word in relation to his own hermeneutical situation. This situation is informed by (1) technological modernity that, as an enframing world-picture, has neutralized words of their sense and devastated nonliving and living things; and, as traced in the previous chapter, (2) the failures—that Heidegger thematizes, albeit insufficiently answers—of his own philosophical and political thinking of the self-assertion of the will and creative sacrifice through the work during the 1930s.[5]

2. Chinese and German Images of Gathering and Emptiness

We might consider here connections between gathering and emptiness prior to Heidegger. According to the *Daodejing*, the *dao* has neither image nor name, and yet it evokes and resonates in the image and in the word. The primary imageless image to be pursued in this chapter is that of gathering in emptiness, which Heidegger finds in Lao-Zhuang sources. This imagery in the German context is not new, even as Heidegger reimagines it in his own style of thinking. The gathering empty valley, empty ground, and the groundless abyss are longstanding images of *dao* in Chinese sources and their German language reception.

Joseph von Görres pioneered the study of mythology in Germany. He wrote in his 1810 *History of the Myths of the Asiatic World* that "Dao is life, an abyss of all perfections, contains all beings, is itself decree and exemplar, but (for the creature) is unfathomable" (Görres 1810: 184). For Strauss in his 1870 edition of the *Daodejing*, *dao* is the empty abyss from which all things arise and return (Strauss 1870: 188). According to Rudolf Dvořák's 1895 book on Chinese religions, the empty *dao* is a bottomless abyss (*bodenloser Abgrund*) in which all the waters of the earth can flow and gather without ever being filled (Dvořák 1895: 42). The *dao* generates and nourishes; it also gathers and disperses. This gathering function is seen in a variety of

German translations and interpretations that continue to resonate in Heidegger's ways of speaking.

"Gathering" is a guiding word in Heidegger's terminology, as he interpreted the root meaning of saying (*lógos*) as gathering. The early Greek gathering in saying and the emptying of the soul of German mysticism undoubtedly play significant roles in his thinking. Nonetheless, there is a specific emptiness of things and words in Daoist (and, as seen in Part Two, Buddhist) sources from which Heidegger draws and rarely explicitly mentions. His emphasis on gathering in emptiness speaks to an interpretive model linked with Laozi, as he recurrently evokes Daoist forms of gathering in his descriptions of the fourfold, the thing, language, and emptiness.

An image that reappears in classic Lao-Zhuang texts is that emptiness draws together and enfolds, establishing places and forms of coming together. The *dao* is the empty hollow (*chong* 沖) that is filled and vacated by swirling waters and the filling and pouring out of the empty vessel in *Daodejing* 4 and 11 (Lou 1980: 10, 27). The valley is an image of the empty yet fecund open where waters gather. Aperture (*kong* 孔) is another Daoist thought-image of emptiness (Lou 1980: 52). Nothingness (*wu*) also functions as emptiness in the figure of the empty vessel (Lou 1980: 26–7). Klages, a figure dismissed by Heidegger as a popular philosopher (GA 29/30: 105), takes this, in his discussion of *Daodejing* 11 in *Spirit as Adversary of the Soul*, to imply that Daoist nothingness signifies emptiness, linking it with the Buddhist dharma and the symbolism of the zero.[6]

Another term for emptiness occurs in the *Daodejing* and in a well-known passage from the *Zhuangzi*. It states that the "fasting of the heart-mind" (*xinzhai* 心齋) is an awaiting of things in stillness and emptiness (*xuer daiwu* 虛而待物), which Heidegger calls to mind in the third *Country Path Conversation*, as the *dao* gathers only in emptiness (*weidao jixu* 唯道集虛). This expression for emptiness (*xu* 虛) is often linked with meditative or biospiritual states in which the heart-mind is emptied and can receive the world. *Xu* as enacting emptiness refers in the *Daodejing* to a practice interlinked with other practices of simplifying, stilling, and becoming tasteless, plain, and bland. Comparable to the Hebrew word "hevel" (empty, vapor) in the Ketuvim Book of Qohelet (Ecclesiastes), it can also signify vanity, futility, and falseness.

The translations of Victor von Strauss (1870), Martin Buber (1910), and Richard Wilhelm (1911, 1912), with which Heidegger was familiar, gave readers a sense of the prominence of emptiness in the texts ascribed to Laozi and Zhuangzi. Wilhelm translated this passage as "the soul becomes empty and becomes capable of receiving the world in itself. And it is the SENSE [*SINN*, as he translated *dao*, noting its archaic senses] that fills this emptiness. This being-empty is the fasting of the heart" (Wilhelm 1912: 29). Adopting a model of mysticism, Buber translates the heart-mind's emptiness as a state of the soul's detachment (*Ablösung*) in which the *dao* dwells (Buber 2013: 60). Further, Misch, a philosopher with whom Heidegger interacted in the 1920s and whose work Heidegger knew, explored this *Zhuangzi* passage at length in "The Way into Philosophy," a 1926 study of the heterogeneous origins of philosophy in breakthrough (*Durchbruch*) and life-reflection (*Lebensbesinnung*). Misch depicts the pouring (*ergießen*) into and out of the *dao*'s stillness and emptiness in the self's emptiness and detachment (*Loslösung*) (Misch 1926: 267).

The links between thing, gathering, and emptiness in Heidegger's *Gelassenheit*, as a form of dwelling, are indicative of a Daoist configuration; in particular, in how it prioritizes gathering and dispersing movement in emptiness (as in Misch) and openness to receiving the world (as in Wilhelm). How Heidegger engaged with the Daoist language of emptiness will be traced in the current chapter on the emptiness of the thing as well as in Part Two that concerns nothingness and emptiness.

The second part will delineate the interaction of Occidental, Daoist, and Buddhist varieties of nothingness and emptiness in Heidegger and his early East Asian reception. In the latter part, to glimpse ahead, we consider the extent to which emptiness is the site of gathering in "From a Dialogue on Language" in which the absence of the friend, Kuki Shūzō 九鬼周造 (1888–1941), in reminiscence is the gathering of that which endures (namely, the memory of the friend). Likewise, the dialogue discloses how the emptiness of language is the gathering of words; the emptiness (now using a Buddhist informed image) of sky allows for the gathering of color and form. In the current chapter, it is the emptiness of the thing as the site of the gathering of world that is in question.

3. *Dao* as Guiding-Word

The present work centers around a Chinese word. It appears in the title of the Chinese text, the *Daodejing*, most frequently mentioned and evoked in Heidegger's corpus. The most frequently mentioned East Asian (indeed, non-Occidental) word appearing in his works is *dao* 道. *Dao* signifies way. It can also mean discourse, principle, teaching, saying, and guiding, as Wilhelm points out (Wilhelm 1911: XV). Its cognate *dao* 導 means to guide or direct. The originary guiding word *dao*, which Heidegger describes as a mystery, resonates with his own basic originary word *Weg* (way) with which he stylizes his own journey in thinking.

This has a larger hermeneutical context worth considering. Heidegger's ways of speaking recall earlier German language interpretations of *dao* that inform Heidegger's linguistic community, while being distinctive from them.[7] The art historian and collector Otto Fischer wrote, for example, in his popular 1923 book on Chinese landscape painting: "The Chinese designated [the sense of nature and the essence of life] with the ancient mystery word *dao*. Long before Laozi and Confucius, *dao*, the sense and the way, is the deepest word in which all anticipation and all knowledge are hidden" (Fischer 1923: 165). According to Fischer, *dao* is not force (*Kraft*) but the opposite of force; imageless, it encompasses all images; groundless and abyssal yet containing all beings. *Dao* signals the emptiness, the zero point, the pivot, and the mystery of being. Chinese art enacts the nature it depicts, following and embodying the *dao* of the thing and the scene.[8]

Misch critiqued the phenomenology of Husserl and Heidegger in 1930 from the perspective of Dilthey's hermeneutical life philosophy, a work that Husserl and Heidegger mention. In it, Misch described the force of originary speech and how *lógos*, as the root word of the beginnings of Occidental philosophy and the science of logic, correlated with *dao* and *brahma* as the primordial words of the East.[9] Primordial words such as *dao* were depicted by Misch as a completing or perfecting holding sway (*vollkommenen Walten*) that stand between myth and philosophical breakthrough and enlightenment (Misch 1950: 311–12). Misch's arguments for the multiple global origins of philosophy in 1926 and 1930 led Husserl and Heidegger to repeatedly reiterate its exclusively Greek origins and Occidental character.[10] At the same time, Heidegger recognized the elemental world-formative force of words such as *lógos* and *dao*, but without mentioning an Indic primary word such as *brahma* or *dharma*.

What is *dao* as a primordial word? Prior to Misch and Heidegger, Buber noted that the first word is already a disintegration from the *dao* that it fails to name, relying on the paradox of names in the *Daodejing* itself (Buber 2013: 111). Fischer described *dao* as "the deep primordial lived-experience of the whole [Chinese] culture, and the primordial word of all their thinking and perceiving" (Fischer 1920: 168). Oswald Spengler also called *dao* a primordial word (*Urwort*), without mentioning other ones, and defined *dao* as the essential conflict and tension between the primal forces of *yin* and *yang* (Spengler 1922: 352). Heidegger focuses on a different point than these other examples: untranslatability. He mentions in several places how the originary elemental word *dao* evades translation (GA 11: 45; GA 12: 187); the question of untranslatability and the need for respectful hesitancy is at the heart of "From a Dialogue on Language" that will be considered later in Part Two.

The early Heidegger expresses a sense of the thing in the formation of the word. Original words express the encounter with that which is encountered in the early Heidegger: "The original word is a to-be-called, not a mere naming; it is much more something that addresses what is encountered in the world as it is encountered."[11] Despite such phenomenological moments in which the thing's life is glimpsed, language appears to center on human existence in his thinking in the later 1920s. In his subsequent reflections on poetic thinking and Daoist sources, the word again resonates with that which is encountered and is called and addressed. Originary words are formed in the address and interpolation of things. How then can such world-forming words be related and translated?

II. The Way, the Mystery, and the Emptiness of the Thing

4. The Way and the Mystery

Heidegger remarked in "The Principle of Identity" that his own originary singular verbal word *Ereignis* (being's appropriating event) is "as little translatable as the guiding Greek word *logos* and the Chinese *dao* [...]. It is now used as a *singulare tantum*."[12] *Ereignis* signifies event in ordinary German. It is for Heidegger, in its concealment and unconcealment and its history, the appropriating or enowning (*er-eignen*) temporalizing-historicizing non-ontic event of being.

In a passage that is conceptually closely affiliated with his 1962 *Zhuangzi* interpretation discussed in Chapter 4, the *dao* appears to function more radically than the Greek word *lógos* as the inaccessible, sustaining, primordial emptying and filling groundless ground of things. He asserts the significance of *dao* as way in a remarkable passage in *On the Way to Language*:

> The elemental word in Laozi's poetic thinking is *dao*, which "properly speaking" means way. But because we are prone to think of "way" superficially, as a stretch connecting two places, our word "way" has all too rashly been considered unfit to name what *dao* says. *Dao* is then translated as reason, mind, *raison*, meaning, *logos*. Yet *dao* could be the way that gives all ways, the very source of our power to think what reason, mind, meaning, logos properly mean to say-properly, by their proper nature.[13]

Heidegger then turns to a Daoist phrase that occurs in other reflections in conjunction with the releasement of things (GA 16: 528):

> Perhaps the mystery of all mysteries [*Geheimnis aller Geheimnisse*] of thoughtful saying conceals itself in the word "way," *dao*, if only we will let these names return to what they leave unspoken, if only we are capable of this, to allow them to do so.[14]

This passage, directly engaging expressions from the translated *Daodejing*, appears to embrace a Daoist elucidation of the relation of saying and the unsaid that reflects an ongoing concern of Heidegger's philosophical pathway that has its own reversals and turns.

In what ways? Way, mystery, and reversion to the silent evoke the language of the *Daodejing* in translated forms. Heidegger proposes in this passage linking *dao* with—no doubt in terms of his own understanding—the German word for way (*Weg*). Letting or allowing names to revert or return to what they leave unspoken (which the mysterious learning philosopher Wang Bi specifies as nothingness) refers (via translation) to *fan* 反 as the very motility (*be-wegen*) of *dao* that stirs in its stillness and moves through reversal. Way and the movement of way are among the most fundamental hermeneutical categories of his thinking, through which the key concepts of being, meaning, and human existence are interpreted. Heidegger interpreted *dao* repeatedly as way and being-underway in relation to his own pathfinding and wayfaring through dead-ends, reversals, and twisting turns. Hence, for instance, he described *dao* in a 1947 letter as "bringing on the way (movement)."[15] This interpretation is not due to the Chinese etymology of *dao*, which has nothing to do with movement per se. It is due to the description of *dao* in the *Daodejing* as reversal, opposition, and return (*fan*), which is defined as its fundamental transformative movement.[16]

Being underway, without a fixed and limiting determinate goal, in reversal and turning, signifies incessant transformation and a comportment that accords with it. It can also signify the acceptance of finitude and mortality in arising and dissolution. The stirring of nothingness is somethingness in the "Book of the Yellow Emperor" (*Huangdi shu* 黃帝書) chapter of the *Liezi*. As shape brings about shadow, and sound forms echo, by the nature of what it is, nothingness—without either movement or birth—stirs and births being; and being must, in the repetition of the patterns of things, return (*fu* 复) to nothingness as finite forms revert to the formless.[17]

Heidegger's "mystery of all mysteries" ("Geheimnis aller Geheimnisse") is a reference to the first chapter of the *Daodejing* (*xuan zhi you xuan* 玄之又玄) (Lou 1980: 2). The word *xuan* 玄 can be translated into English as mystery, profundity, or darkness. It is a recurring expression in the *Daodejing* and the *Zhuangzi*, and a key expression for

Wei-Jin-era teachings of "mysterious learning" (*xuanxue* 玄學), sometimes designated Neo-Daoism, and the Tang-era teaching of the "twofold mystery" (*chongxuan* 重玄).[18] With Heidegger's expression "mystery of all mysteries," the German could be translated as "secret of all secrets." This differs from Wilhelm's translation of the last lines of chapter one of the *Daodejing* that speak of a yet even deeper mystery of the mystery as the *dao*'s gateway or portal: "In its unity, it is called the mystery. The deeper mystery of the mystery is the gateway through which all wonders emerge."[19]

Mystery is a gateway or a site of passage in the *Daodejing*. Intriguingly, to reference a source mentioned by Heidegger and presumably familiar to him, Schelling emphasizes the image of the gateway (*men* 門) or portal (*Pforte*) in his Neo-Platonic interpretation of the *Daodejing* in *The Philosophy of Mythology*: "Dao means gateway, the dao-teaching is the teaching of the great gateway in being, of non-being, of that which is able to be, through which all finite being enters into actual being" (Schelling 1857: 564).

5. Uncut Blocks, Empty Vessels, and Inauspicious Devices

Before turning to Heidegger's readings of the empty jug, what is the broader historical situation of *Daodejing* 11? What is the vessel that is in question? There are three characteristics of the Chinese word in question that need to be adequately clarified.

Qi 器 primarily signifies utensil, instrument, or device, including the vessel and the weapon in the *Daodejing*. It has multiple intriguing roles in this text that are reflected in various English and German translations. First, in *Daodejing* 28, it refers to what is produced from unfashioned material or that which is scattered and differentiated from simplicity.[20] This image reoccurs in the *Zhuangzi*'s "Horses Hooves" (*mati* 馬蹄) outer chapter: it is the fault of the craftsperson and sage that deficient and broken simplicity produces devices (殘樸以為器). Wang Bi comments that when simplicity and genuineness are scattered in countless directions, devices are born and officials arise, and sages respond to the fragmented by bringing about reversion to simplicity.[21]

A significant facet of the *Daodejing* is the exemplary model of sustaining and reverting to simplicity (*pu* 樸) that is correlated with retaining and returning to emptiness (*xu* 虛) and stillness (*jing* 靜). The exemplary sages and sage-kings are said to retain and enact the unbroken simplicity of *dao* amidst the brokenness and differentiation of the world, perceiving the simplicity operative in differentiated things. In chapter 37, nameless simplicity is described as lacking purposiveness and desiring, which are limiting forms of conditioning, such that the world determines itself (天下將自定) and, to draw on chapter 57, people simplify themselves (民自樸).

The guiding image of simplicity is the naturally occurring uncarved block. It is also praised as plainness and blandness. Simplicity as a form of comportment is an attunement with the self-occurring of things and persons, which are not separated by an abyss in ziranist or (in an expansive unrestricted sense) naturalist early Daoist discourses. Chapter 16 speaks of enacting emptiness to the utmost and safeguarding stillness (致虛極, 守靜篤). Simplicity is correlated with emptiness and stillness in the nineteenth chapter. Such simplicity comes to signify a biospiritual comportment and practice in multiple Daoist transmissions, an aesthetic comportment and style in East Asian art and poetry, and an ontological-cosmological condition.[22]

Second, *qi* signifies vessel in passages in chapters 11, 29, 41, and 67, where it serves as an image of emptiness, openness, receiving, and *dao*. The word *qi* also designates the empty thing and vessel. In addition to chapter 11, *qi* is used to describe the world as spirit-vessel in *Daodejing* 29 (天下神器). Translations sometimes render this as spiritual thing or device. According to Wang Bi, as spirit has neither form nor fragrance, and devices are formed through amalgamations of form, the great intangible vessel of the world has no shape or form to fit and condition it.[23]

The *dao* is the longest forming and lasting great vessel (大器晚成) in chapter 41. Wang Bi comments on how the *dao* as the great vessel generates the world, without holding onto anything in it, and thus is enduring.[24] In chapter 67, it is the sage who becomes an open and receptive vessel, an empty and thus beneficial device for the world, and endures by stepping aside and benefiting the flourishing of things and people.[25] The empty vessel image refers in these lines to the openness and beneficial nourishment of the thing, the world, and the sage.

Third, *qi* means device or instrument in passages in chapters 31, 36, 57, and 80 where it concerns use and profit, power and war, not using and deploying implements and persons. The thing-implement is broken from simplicity. It is itself and can be used because of its emptiness, and its use as instrumental device can be inauspicious and destructive. *Qi* can accordingly refer to inauspicious and dangerous devices that should not be utilized.

In chapter 31, weapons are exposed as inauspicious instruments, destructive to things, and not to be used by those who enact *dao* except, with mourning, out of necessity. In chapter 36 it is said that the sharp (military and punitive) weapons and devices of the state should not be shown to the people, a statement of wisdom that the sage should not exhibit to the world, according to the *Zhuangzi* chapter *Quqie* 胠篋. The title is an image of human striving as it ironically means to coercively force open an already open bag. Several Chinese interpretations informed by the Huanglao and "legalist" models, such as the *Heshanggong*, take this to mean that instruments are most effective when used while being concealed.

Wang Bi likewise explicates this chapter to mean using yet not showing instruments. He adds the ziranist point that external coercion and punishment are to be avoided in order to act in accordance with the nature (*xing*) of people.[26] The *xing* 性 character is composed of the heart and life radicals. It is semantically unrelated yet conceptually linked with great nature (*da ziran*). It designates the characteristics and temperament that typically make a human what it is. It is a disputed concept in early Chinese philosophy that does not appear in the *Daodejing*. Wang Bi explains that deliberate coercive action and use ruin things in the world and persons in society (Lou 1980: 196; Lynn 1999: 33).

In *Daodejing* 57, it is claimed that the more devices and profits the state produces and pursues, the greater the disorder and poverty that will result. Although this has been interpreted as rejecting "legalist" administrative procedures, a philosophy that accentuates the uses of tactics and techniques (*shu* 術), the *Yulao* 喻老 and *Neichu shuo xia* 內儲說下 chapters of the *Hanfeizi* offer a legalistic interpretation that the two handles of reward and punishment (*shangfa* 賞罰) are the weapons of the state to be wielded in concealment by the sovereign. The *Heshanggong* commentary also takes governing to be about concealment of use rather than nonuse.

Wang Bi contends that the *Daodejing* concerns an emptied and thus impartial comportment, commenting that all devices utilized out of self-interest belong to the category of "sharp weapons" (*liqi* 利器) to be shunned as the people are allowed to follow their natures.[27] In chapter 80, a smaller and simpler state that does not use peoples and devices is said to be preferable, existing in an agrarian plainness and ordinariness that might have appealed to Heidegger (presumably in contrast to large states that mobilize and consume all things). The *Heshanggong* commentary takes this as the difference between promoting the devices of farming that nourish and those of war that destroy people.[28]

6. Chinese Interpretations of the Empty Vessel

What then of the image of the empty vessel to which Heidegger repeatedly returned? Chinese interpretations indicate some key facets of this image. One paradigmatic Chinese reading is found in the Han-era *Heshanggong* commentary. The emptiness of the wheel, vessel, and room are guiding images for biospiritual and biopolitical practice. How can nothingness and emptiness become keywords in explaining the workings of the self, the natural world, and society? They indicate a disposition of being able to receive and accordingly use all things. The emptied body and emptied kingdom can, by clearing away conditioning passions and desires, become the host for and receive spirit and blessing.

A second paradigmatic Chinese reading from the Wei-Jin period suggests that links between Laozi's emptiness and Zhuangzi's uselessness and imperfectionism can be deployed to assess Heidegger's interpretive strategy. The fundamental emptying of the thing serves as an example of *wuwei* in the commentaries of mysterious learning philosopher Wang Bi from the Wei-Jin era.

Wang Bi interprets "not" as "the nothing" from which action, being, and use arise. *Wuwei* is consequently not "not action." It is rather an acting (*wei*) and functioning/using (*yong* 用) of and from out of nothingness (*wu*). *Wuneng* 無能 is not "not able"; it is the capacity to receive and accept all things in nothingness (無能受物之故). Uselessness (*wuyong* 無用) is the use/functioning from out of nothingness. When it is in nothingness, the being of the vessel becomes useful (當其無, 有器之用). Being (*you* 有) is then a using or functioning (*yong*) from nothingness.[29]

Wang Bi's prioritization of nothingness, relative to being, signifies the formation of the emptiness and openness that allows each being and thing to enact its own nature. This priority was rejected in Guo Xiang's *Zhuangzi* commentary. It criticized the prioritizing of nothingness over being as a reification of the nothing into a first ground or cause. Guo Xiang equalized and relativized both being and nothing, concluding that there are only singular things in their own self-generation and self-determination. From the distinctive perspectives of generative nothingness in Wang Bi—and self-emptiness (*śūnyatā*, *kong*) in early Wei-Jin-era Buddhists such as Zhi Dun—Guo Xiang's radicalization of the ziranist strategy entails the closure of the fluid transformative functioning of nothingness in the hypostatization and fatalism of the thing. To modify Heidegger's language, Wang Bi introduces a meontological difference between beings and the nothingness of being that preserves the open clearing in which beings stand.

Wang Bi's primordial formless and substanceless nothingness is non-negational, not derivative of a negation of an assertion. It is not separated as a first principle or cause from things, as Guo Xiang appears to suggest. Nothingness is expressed in the patterning principle (*li*) and reciprocation immanent to things themselves in their self-generation and self-occurring. As Wang Bi remarked concerning the first line of *Daodejing* 5: heaven-and-earth trusts the self-occurring (of things) and not moralistic benevolence, there is no coercive intervening action or creation, only the myriad things in their self-reciprocating self-patterning.[30] Nothingness (*wu*), and not *dao*, is the ultimate guiding word indicating the nameless. Wang Bi's commentary on the *Book of Changes* clarifies his prioritization of the nothing as functioning through *dao*, the forces of *yin* and *yang*, and the myriad things:

> The reciprocal processes of *yin* and *yang* are designated *dao*. What is this *dao*? It is a name for nothingness; it is that which pervades everything; and it is that from which all things arise. As an equivalent, we designate it *dao*. As it operates silently and without substance, it is impossible to form images for it. Only when the functioning of being reaches its apex do the merits of nonbeing become manifest.[31]

The merits of nothingness and emptiness will be explored further in Part Two. It already should be noted how emptiness and the empty vessel are linked with humility that echoes in Heidegger's mindful attentiveness and humility in encountering things.

This modesty toward things and affairs is ubiquitous in early Chinese teachings concerning enacting emptiness (*xu*) as a biospiritual or ethical practice. We might, for a moment, consider two paradigmatic examples that link emptiness and humility in which the empty vessel signifies the capacity to welcome and receive. First, the *Book of Changes* states that the exemplary person receives others in emptiness and the enactment of emptying is movement toward the good.[32] It prescribes a comportment of emptiness and humbleness specifically in moments of increase and plenitude. Second, the late Han-era eclectic Confucian Xu Gan 徐幹 (171–218 CE) composed a chapter on "emptying *dao*" or the "*dao* of humility" (*xudao* 虛道) in his *Balanced Discourses* (*Zhong Lun* 中論). The empty vessel serves here as an exemplary ethical model of virtue. The exemplary person is said to empty the heart-mind of ambitions, thereby becoming humble, receptive, and able to appropriately respond to the situation.[33] It is unclear if Heidegger was familiar with Wilhelm's well-known *Book of Changes* edition. His language more closely matches the *Daodejing*. His interlinking of emptiness, silence, reticence, and humility, the explicit association with the releasement of things and the emptiness of the vessel, indicates Heidegger's specific use of Daoist sources even as they evoke aspects of teachings linked with the *Book of Changes*.

7. The Empty Vessel in Strauss, Wilhelm, and Heidegger (1870, 1911, 1943)

Keeping in view early ziranist readings of the vessel and thing, particularly in Wang Bi, this chapter now turns to tracing how Heidegger repeatedly returns to the movement of *dao*, the openness of the mystery, and the releasement and emptiness of the thing. This is paradigmatically expressed in the image of the empty vessel in *Daodejing* 11.

This reference reoccurs in "The Uniqueness of the Poet" in 1943 (GA 75: 43), the first of the *Country Path Conversations* in 1944 (GA 77: 133-8), the 1949 Bremen lecture on the thing (GA 79: 11-13), and "The Thing" in 1950 (GA 7: 173).

Instead of the poetic reiteration of *phúsis* of the work-in-the-thing that was emphasized in "The Origin of the Work of Art," it is its emptiness that allows the formed vessel to function and flourish as what it is. The vessel, serving as an image of the thing, is filled and emptied, gathering and releasing world through its emptiness. This breath-like flow of the emptying and filling of the thing is possible because of its emptiness, such that it cannot be separated or isolated from its environing world.

It is not accidental that Heidegger's initial reflections on *Daodejing* 11 occur in the context of the poet Hölderlin and the task of a poetic philosophizing, or since philosophy is limited as metaphysics and onto-theology, a poetic thinking. As in the early essay on the artwork, Heidegger seeks to establish the uniqueness, the autonomy, of the work. The uniqueness of the poetic word is, Heidegger writes in 1939, an existential moment in the history and disclosure of being "in which a fundamental shaking of all metaphysical and thus also the 'religious' and 'aesthetic' and 'political' truth of beings begins" (GA 75: 5).

In the 1943 essay, Heidegger turns to the *Daodejing* through a reflection on the experience of learning mindful attentiveness (*Achtsamkeit*) through "glimpsing inconspicuous simplicity, appropriating it ever more originally, and becoming ever more respectfully reserved before it" (GA 75: 42-3). Wilhelm's translation of *Daodejing* 15 speaks of being hesitant and careful, reserved and reticent like a guest, simple like an unworked thing, still in the midst of duration, abiding in incompletion and imperfection, and safeguarding *dao*. Heidegger discussed this chapter with the visiting Chinese scholar Paul Shih-yi Hsiao and quoted it in letters to Siegfried Bröse and Erhart Kästner to describe the cautious reserve and stillness operative in movement.[34] The poet's mindful and respectfully reserved encounter with the inconspicuous and modest simplicity of simple things leads back and returns to the ontological difference between beings and being, and not to *dao* as in *Daodejing* 15.

Heidegger claims at this point that "being" in this specific difference is referred to if not named in *Daodejing* 11. Informed by the thinking of being, which seeks to mindfully encounter the simplicity of things, his translation diverges in significant ways from those of Strauss and Wilhelm. The Chinese text uses "nothing" (*wu*) to speak of the empty center of the wheel, the vessel, and the room. This nothing makes their function and use possible.[35] Wilhelm takes this to refer to spatial emptiness, while Wang Bi elucidates it as the generative enactment of nothingness itself. *Wu* is rendered as nonbeing in Strauss, as nothing and (in its final appearance) nonbeing in Wilhelm, and as emptiness and (in its final occurrence) nonbeings in Heidegger.[36]

The distinctive characteristics of Heidegger's rendition in comparison with Strauss and Wilhelm are (1) its use of emptiness for *wu*; (2) the introduction of the "being of" the wheel, vessel, and room, bringing to the fore the use of being (*you* 有) in the chapter, whereas Strauss and Wilhelm refer only to the thing; and (3) how usefulness refers to being and being is bestowed or granted (*gewährt*) in emptiness.

There is a threefold relation in all three German translations that each gives its own distinctive form and content. Strauss elucidates the relation between nonbeing, thing, and use as one of accordance and effecting; Wilhelm of the relation between nothing, thing, and usability as resting and touching on and giving; and Heidegger of the granting of use through being and being through emptiness. Heidegger is neither purely intuiting truths nor imposing his own presuppositions; he is engaging the text within his own interpretive context. This is particularly true of his collaboration with Xiao who published an Italian translation of the *Daodejing* in 1941. He attended Heidegger's courses and collaborated with him in 1943–1944 in translating chapters of the *Daodejing* into German.[37]

8. The Implications of Emptiness (1943)

"The Uniqueness of the Poet" relates to the emptiness and nonbeing that safeguard being, on the one hand, and the usability of beings, on the other. Heidegger elucidates, in his revealing translation of this passage, the association between the empty nothing (*wu* 無) and the possibility and constitution of use and the useful (*yong* 用) in the context of a formulation of the ontological difference between beings and being: whereas beings (*Seiende*) produce usability, nonbeing (*Nicht-Seiende*) grants being (*Sein*). It is the empty (*Leere*) that grants and safeguards things such as the wheel, the vase and the house, and their appropriate usage (*Gebrauch* in Strauss's rendition of *Daodejing* 11) in contrast with mere instrumental gain (*Gewinn* in Strauss).[38] Words such as *Brauch* and *Gebrauch* are used in related senses in Heidegger's later writings: they do not signify a mere customary *habitus*, but a respectful, sharing, and attuned using and situated working with things. Exemplary illustrations of such a free co-responsive attunement are found throughout Daoist and later Chan Buddhist sources.

Heidegger's interpretation of *Daodejing* 11 in the context of an interpretation of Hölderlin expresses themes that are further unfolded over the course of the 1940s and 1950s. He finds an indicative clue in its translated words: "the hint rests on that which, as the in-between, holds everything open in itself and expands into the expanse of the duration [of the awhile] and the region that appears to us all too easily and frequently as nothing" (GA 75: 43). As traced later in Part Two, and despite his reputation as a philosopher of nothingness that is explored in chapter 8, this idea, the in-between of the openness and emptiness of being, increasingly alters Heidegger's earlier conception of nothingness. It is Heidegger who cites and adopts the *Daodejing* in this context, allowing the reconstruction of Daoist elements in his dialogues and lectures that deploy this same language.

Emptiness is not a spatial vacuum, as Heidegger later notes, nor is it air pushed out by liquid (GA 77: 131–2). It opens an elucidation of thing, place, and the temporality and spatiality of human existence. Instead of accentuating anxiety in face of the nothing, the emptiness of the in-between signifies the temporalizing meanwhile and the spatializing middle. It is elucidated as an in-between of the encountered duration of the awhile and the abiding awhile of the region. Place and space as well as the momentary instant and time are constituted amidst this gathering and dispersal. It is the emptiness of things and places that allows gathering and dispersion to occur (GA 75: 43).

Humans do not abide with things in neutral uniform space-time. They dwell between earth and world in the continuing meanwhile, the nearness of the in-the-midst in which persons and things are welcomed, and the thoughtful remembrance of the absent. Mortals abide and linger in these moments and places that can, for instance, recall the departed missing friend in a conversation on language decades later. It is in this expansiveness, the "inner" and the "empty," that humans receive their ways of essencing and from which the metaphysical representation of life, spirit, and soul derives (GA 75: 44).

III. Emptiness and the Thing between Releasement and Enframing

9. The Empty Jug, the Thing, and Releasement (1944–1945)

The question of pragmatic usefulness has a long history in Heidegger's writings, occupying a crucial role in the form of pragmatic readiness-to-hand in the first division of *Being and Time* and emphasized in pragmatist reconstructions of Heidegger's philosophy. Heidegger is concerned in his later lectures and lecture-courses concerning the thing with distinguishing things from their instrumental use and their technological enframing (*Gestell*).

Heidegger, as with other German intellectuals in the first half of the twentieth century (notably, Buber, Keyserling, and Wilhelm, among others), associates these ancient Chinese sources with the modern problematic of technology through notions of thingness, usefulness, and usability.[39] The first of the 1944–1945 *Country Path Conversations* brings up the empty jug (*Krug*, the same word used in Okakura, Fischer, and Klages) and the thing in the context of *tékhnē* and technological modernity.[40] As previously shown, the *Daodejing* and related texts are concerned with their own questions of craft, technique, suspending the will, waiting, and responsiveness to the thing as it is of itself such that Heidegger's country-path interlocutors evoke the conceptual constellation of this ancient Chinese text without invoking it.

Heidegger once again poses the question of the thing, of how to illumine the thing *qua* thing instead of as represented object, in the context of *tékhnē*. The initial approach recalls his 1935 essay on the artwork as the thing arises from earth. The thing in the form of the jug not only consists of earth: it is only standing (*stehen*) on earth through its consisting (*bestehen*) (GA 77: 126). This relational coming-to-stand is sedimented as the standing-reserve (*Bestand*) in which things are mere raw materials and resources for human use. The thing as uselessly itself does not consist only of the formed matter articulated in its classical definition; nor is it defined principally by its instrumental readiness and theoretical objective presence, as in *Being and Time*.

Recalling his earlier translation and interpretation of *Daodejing* 11, it is the emptiness of it as a vessel (*Gefäß*) that makes the jug (*Krug*) what it is. The emptiness between the sides, the bottom, and the edges is the holding of the vessel as that which holds ("das Fassende des Gefäßes") such that the jug, as a vessel standing in itself, is not only comprised of what compromises it, the shaped earth, but of emptiness.

This emptiness (*Leere*) and nothingness (*Nichts*) of the jug is in reality what the jug is. And this emptiness, as that which is ungraspable (*unfasslich*), cannot itself be held and grasped (GA 77: 130). How can the vessel's reality rest in an empty nothing? The vessel is not a pure nothingness, as the craftsperson shapes emptiness with the clay to form it.

Heidegger proceeds to referentially interrelate the thing, encountering (*gegnen* in its archaic sense) the counterpart (*entgegnen*), and the releasement in which the thing is recognized as "enregioned" (*vergegnet*) in a local region (*Gegend*). This description of the varieties of the counterpart and region is even more differentiated than Buber's earlier usage—in his early writings on Daoism, Hassidism, and dialogical ethics—of *begegnen* as encounter, *entgegnen* as opposition, *vergegnen* as mis-encounter, *Ereignis* as the event of meeting, and *Gegend* as environment.[41] Heidegger is not describing the interethical relationship, which encompasses meeting with things as well as God in Buber. This is the relation between the thing, the openness of interthingly interaction (that Heidegger elsewhere calls *Geding*, world as the gathering of things), and place that characterizes locality and consequently human dwelling.[42]

Heidegger's initial elucidation of releasement in the first *Country Path Conversation* does not refer to a state of mind such as serenity; nor does it refer to the constellation of soul, nothingness, and God of German mysticism. This is an inquiry inspired—via a long and complex interculturally mediated journey—by the text attributed to Laozi as mediated by Wilhelm and others. Heidegger draws on and incorporates Daoist elements—which operate as examples for reflective poetic thinking—in three ways: (1) he appears to evoke while reworking in his own philosophical context the language of German language translations and interpretations; (2) he assembles interpretive strategies that align with and can be interpreted according to the models of releasement-self-naturing (*wuwei-ziran*), resonance-responsiveness (*ganying* 感應), and *dao* as the movement of reversal, opposition, and return (*fan* 反); and (3) thinking the thing is depicted in a Lao-Zhuang style as a releasement to it in its specific essencing as a thing in its own moment and place by patiently encountering, abiding, waiting, and not-willing (GA 77: 133).

10. Heidegger's *Wuwei* and *Ziran*

Can Heidegger's thought be interpreted or reimagined as a thinking of *wuwei* and *ziran*? No doubt, at least in part. Heidegger's interpretive strategy historically reflects his earlier discussion of the *Daodejing* and conceptually correlates with *wuwei* and *ziran*; action (*wei*) and inaction (*wuwei*) are interpreted in the German reception of the *Daodejing* as willing and not-willing, and a number of texts describe Daoism as a philosophy of not-willing and willlessness.[43] In the nineteenth-century German philosophical scene, Arthur Schopenhauer and Eduard von Hartmann already conceived of Daoism as entailing the suspension of the individual will.[44] In a work Heidegger dismissively mentioned in 1929, Klages contended in his 1929 *Spirit as Adversary of the Soul* that Nietzsche's critique of not-willing cannot be applied to Daoism.[45]

Heidegger states that this thing is not a "thing in itself" but rather a "thing for itself" (GA 77: 133, 139). Hegel's *Phenomenology of Spirit* denies that there can be a thing for itself that is free from a master (Hegel 1986: 318). Heidegger echoes no doubt Meister Eckhart's language with which he was long familiar (GA 1: 218; GA 60: 316-17) and to whom the conversation directly refers precisely to deny that his releasement and Eckhart's releasement are the same (GA 77: 109). The mystical discourse of things lets things be while aiming at suspending things for the sake of the detachment of the soul, freeing it from sin and for union with God. Heidegger's language of releasement is distinctive. First, it is closer to skepticism in suspending the very compulsion for assertion, affirmation, and positivity that consume enthusiastic mystical absorption and speculative dialectics. Second, it is detached from monotheism and its atheistic negation without, however, embracing the "negative pantheism" of the pessimistic negation of the will. Heidegger could not see beyond Nietzsche's polemical critique of Schopenhauer and von Hartmann, who Nietzsche condemned as Schopenhauer's meager impoverished ape.[46]

If not Eckhart or Schopenhauer, much less their epigones, can the *Daodejing* with its humility before things be interpreted as offering a guiding thread for thinking the freedom toward and of worldly beings? Heidegger's European sources are insufficient, and he directly and indirectly draws on Daoist language. The thinking of the thing for itself, the thing in its own essencing, and the thing as that which it is of itself in Heidegger's first *Country Path Conversation* is indicative of the *ziran* of the *Daodejing*. This tendency is evident in its German reception and translation that asserts the freedom and the being of itself of the thing. Strauss translated *ziran* as freedom (*frei, freiwillig, Freiheit*), according to nature (*naturgemäß*), and measure of itself (*Richtmaß sein Selbst*).[47] Wilhelm translated it as independent (*selbständig*), "of itself" (*von selber*), self-exemplary (*sich selber zum Vorbild*), and the natural course of things (*natürlichen Lauf der Dinge*).[48] Strauss describes in his comments on chapter 11 how human freedom is only found in the "freedom of being" (Strauss 1870: 120). Wilhelm expresses the *ziran* of the myriad things as follows: "All creatures by themselves shape themselves" (Wilhelm 1911: 39).

The typical ways in which the thing is represented and explained as object rushes over the thing and neglects it as it is of itself. The thing is lost in its reduction to the pragmatically useful and theoretically posited elements that compose it. Encountering the thing in its own locality does not require more activity and willing on the part of the subject. Another comportment is called for that the first and third *Country Path Conversations* designate waiting. Waiting, as seen in the next chapter on Heidegger's third conversation and the *Zhuangzi*, occurs in the fasting and emptying of the heart-mind that is freed to encounter the thing.

Stepping back from the subject and the will occurs in Heidegger in waiting attentively and mindfully for the thing's essencing in its own constitutive openness. The thing is encountered temporally as abiding in the moment of its own "awhile" and spatially as enregioning in its place (GA 77: 133). The thing is not statically given invariably all at once, but in its movement, reversal, and counter-partnering, and in its gathering awhile and environing region in which it abides. Pure or exemplary waiting does not prescribe and dictate the nature of the thing to it. It does not seek to subsume it under a worldview or theoretical picture. It releases the thing to its own way and timing of being itself.

The thing's abiding in the duration of its moment and in its environing locality can also be referred to threads found in the *Daodejing*, and related sources, in which the generational life of the thing is recognized and acknowledged in its own moment and place. Early Daoism is often said to be ahistorical: yet the category of living generations is crucial to it. Early Daoist sources suggest nourishing the living and letting go of the dead, as only fixations, residues, and shadows remain of their former traces. It does not annihilate or suppress all traces of what has been before. It releases the past to itself. Heidegger appears to strike a different tone—although one that resonates with East Asian poetics of ruins, fading life, and mourning—in thoughtful remembrance of the absences that still address us: the abandoned tools and overgrown ruins along the country path, the faded ghostly figure in a worn photograph, or (in "From a Dialogue on Language") the long-departed friend invoked in the gathering of conversation. In Heidegger's thoughtful remembrance of the absent friend, it is not mere presence but the emptying that gathers and releases.

Heidegger's pursuit of "modern archaics" (to adopt an interpretive term from Wu 2014), a strategy directed toward recuperating the past and the archaic that has been shaped by the paradoxes of modernity, has been derided as anachronistic, melancholic, nostalgic, provincial, and rustic.[49] Such complaints are not without warrant, albeit incomplete, and in need of complication. First, it is accurate insofar as there is a tone of lament and loss that, nonetheless, should not be too quickly dismissed as a reactive, provincial, and—in Jean-François Lyotard's words, perhaps referring to a fairytale by the Brothers Grimm—that of a small-time, little, and crafty peasant (Lyotard 1994: 113). But, unlike the fairytale "The Peasant and the Devil," the crafty peasant was in this case tricked by the devil and left only with stubble. Heidegger appears naive, opportunistic, and ideologically deluded in 1933. Bloch has noted the reactive and revolutionary dynamics that inform Hebel and other rural peasant authors who appealed to Heidegger (Bloch 1984: 365–84). Adorno has observed how each perspective can have ideological and critical functions. These points are applicable to Heidegger's case: even if he is taken as an ideologue, which he is typically not, that ideology and its critique are indicative of alternative moments. Rather than signifying a merely reactionary fixation on what has been lost, as Heidegger's critics insist, his conception of the relation to the past can be interpreted—in its best moments—as its releasement in which memories and past things gather. This would signify a genuine non-coercive remembrance with respect to the past and that which is fading into the forgotten.

Secondly, the claim is one-sided. Heidegger's articulation of the moment and locality of the thing in his later thinking still has the threefold structure of temporality in altered form. There is a threefold nexus of the past in thoughtful remembrance (*andenken*), the present in the current moment of encounter or its absence, and the future in simple or pure waiting (emptied of anticipation and projection) in determining that which makes the thing what it is in its own free self-essencing and self-naturing.

11. Drinking from the Empty Vessel and Sojourning in the Expanse

The empty jug is not indeterminate emptiness as such. It is empty of drink. The availability and usefulness of the drink for the drinker, however, no longer characterize the jug's own way of being. As a being (*Seiende*) grants its use (GA 75: 43), the jug is a being that grants drinking yet is not solely determined by its use by the drinker. In an interpretive maneuver that clearly evokes the *Zhuangzi*, its own emptiness safeguards the thing from pure instrumentality. Emptiness holds the drink, preserving and safekeeping it (GA 77: 134).

The empty jug is not merely ready-to-hand for use as in *Being and Time*. It grants and allows the receiving and drinking of wine. Accordingly, by extension, the empty wheel grants and allows the cart to be drawn along the road, and the empty room grants and allows people and things to gather and dwell within it. Emptiness is the condition of the thing's self-naturing, a uselessness that grants the variety of its uses. It grants receiving and gathering, and what is formed in receiving and gathering can be used. Emptiness is, as a result, the prerequisite of the use and usefulness of the being of the thing.

The drink is not simply used even if it appears so in the haste of consumption. The drink draws from and abides in the wine and in the elemental: in the branches, in the earth, in the sunshine and rain, in the gifts of heaven. The emptiness of the jug abides in the expansiveness drawing from nourishing heaven and earth that are the primary exemplars of nourishing life in the *Daodejing*: they are long in duration because they live for the myriad things rather than themselves (Lou 1980: 19). Parallel to the *Daodejing*'s *dao*, Heidegger's expanse is limitless and unbounded; it also abides in the jug as it moves and returns to itself evoking the *dao*'s way of moving. Accordingly, Heidegger's interlocutors recognize how the jug is itself only because it rests in this expanse and in the elemental in vine, water, and sunshine. Heidegger delineates further how the thing is an abiding and sojourning (*verweilen*) in and returning (*Rückkehr*) to itself. The empty jug, he states, abides in itself and returns to itself in the moment of the while in which it tarries through expansiveness (GA 77: 135). This signals how the *dao* is wide and all-encompassing, sustaining and fostering, and moves through self-reverting and returning, in Wilhelm's edition of the *Daodejing*.

Another word has an interesting role in the German language reception of the *Daodejing* and the *Zhuangzi*. The verb *verweilen* signifies a temporal abiding, lingering, tarrying, and sojourning. The different senses of (1) abiding as appropriate moment and (2) lingering as overstaying led to two different sets of uses in the German context. First, it intimates the generational life of the thing and the art of freely abiding, inhabiting, sojourning, and wandering amidst the world. Indeed, several works deploy this expression in unfolding the way as freely and aptly tarrying in a place and moment.[50] Strauss accordingly explains in his comments how the sages abide and tarry (*verweilen*) for the moment in a place and, without fixation, they do not remain when the moment is done (Strauss 1870: 349). Heidegger's emphasis on appropriately abiding in a moment and place reflects this sense of *verweilen*, in contrast with the haste and hurrying (*übereilen*) that misses encountering (*Begegnung*) and responding to (*Entgegnung*) the thing as resonant counterpart (*Gegnen*) and its environing locality (*Gegend*).

Secondly, the verb signifies what is to be avoided in some interpretations. August Pfizmaier and Hertha Federmann use *verweilen* in the sense of inappropriately remaining and overstaying one's moment.[51] The sages in her translation consequently do not abide or linger (*verweilen*). They do not fixate the moment or place, and they depart once their work is done. The variability and ambiguity of *verweilen* are shown in Wilhelm's various contrary uses. He utilized *verweilen* in the sense of the appropriate moment in his 1911 *Daodejing* translation (Wilhelm 1911: 104) and in the sense of inappropriate overstaying in his 1925 book on Laozi (Wilhelm 1925: 49).

What then is the appropriate moment and locality of the wine-jug? Heidegger states that it is drinking in celebration, as the jug is something festive in the expansive vastness in which people, things, earth, and heaven abide and sojourn (GA 77: 136). This wide expansiveness is where relationships between thing and counterpart, counterpart and releasement, releasement and being human transpire. The simple is disclosed amidst this seemingly complex relational nexus. The simple is a mysterious puzzle ("das Rätselhafte des Einfachen") as it is gathered in that which is designated the counterpart (GA 77: 138).

How should we interpret the "counterpart" in the encounter? *Gegnen* in its archaic sense signifies encountering the counterpart as well as facing against what is opposed. The counterparting (*gegnen*) in its enregioning (*vergegnen*) is not, however, a horizon of our comportment of releasement (as in mysticism) nor of things as objects for us (as in instrumentalism). Quite the reverse, it is things as themselves and for themselves (GA 77: 139). *Gelassenheit* is defined as a letting-counterparting of being's event (GA 82: 551). This event concerns recalling and safeguarding things and their sense. Heidegger's prioritization of the thing, which his contemporary Adorno echoed in the freedom toward and primacy of the object, is a reversal of the pragmatic instrumentality, objectified theoretical presence, and fundamental worldlessness of the thing in the late 1920s. Heidegger's Daoist, early Pre-Socratic, and German poetic sources best account for this reversal, given the direct and indirect idealism of his philosophical training and milieu.

There is in Heidegger's first conversation the wide expansiveness that encompasses things, the puzzling, mysterious secret glimpsed in the simplicity of things, and our releasement through the self-releasement of things in their own way of being themselves, that evoke and offer a poetic-philosophical reimagining of the way (*dao*), movement (*fan*), mystery (*xuan*), and being of itself (*ziran*).

This configuration of words and their uses is more than a coincidence given Heidegger's focused engagement with the *Daodejing* and the *Zhuangzi* in the closing years of the Second World War and the opening years of its aftermath. It makes sense given his long-term engagement with reading various translations of these texts and discussing them with Chinese and Japanese interlocutors from 1919 to the conclusion of his life; despite their exclusion from academic philosophy, his own definition of philosophy as principally Greek-German, and his anxieties about not knowing Chinese. This semi-Daoist ziranist interpretive constellation is rethought and redescribed subsequently in the *Bremen Lectures* and "The Thing" as the thinging of the thing that is also the worlding of world in which mortals fittingly or unfittingly abide and sojourn in their building, dwelling, and saying.

12. The Priority of the Thing (1949–1950)

The four 1949 *Bremen Lectures*, entitled "Insight into What Is," inquire into the thing, enframing positionality, the danger, and the turn. They offer a diagnosis, and hence indicate a critical model, of the suppression and destruction of the thing.

Evoking possibly Nietzsche's critique of an all-viewing and all-consuming historical consciousness in which nothing can be alien in the second *Untimely Meditation*, Heidegger begins these lectures with a description of the present situation in which there is a diminishment of all distances and intervals of time and space. This is not only a matter of consciousness; it concerns the contemporary configuration of reality that threatens beings and their meaning formative sense.

Places and things can be interpreted as a relational continuum of singulars in which each event—in its own hiatus—gathers and discloses world. They lose their interval spacing as nearness and distance are lost in limiting fixed presence. All becomes available, in Heidegger's depiction, through travel and technological reproduction, and media such as newspapers, radio, film, and television. Places and things are endangered as such by forgetfulness of things and the prospect of nuclear war and the devastation it would bring (GA 7: 168; GA 79: 3). Places and things without interval and spacing appear to bring universal availability, a characteristic of the pragmatic ready-to-hand in *Being and Time*. Yet pure undifferentiated and unspaced presence cannot bring genuine nearness and proximity to a specific place or thing that—when freed from mere givenness and positivity (a positivism that characterizes the metaphysical and onto-theological tradition) into its own openness—calls for its responsive attentiveness.

The thing looks as if it is adjacent and ready-to-hand in being used and used up, but it fails to appear as thing in such an instrumental referential nexus. It is still distant and un-encountered in its thingliness when experienced through availability and usefulness and represented as a merely objectively present object. Its thingliness does not consist in its instrumental use and objectified representation as object, in which it is obscured and forgotten. Nor can it be defined in terms of the objectness, the over-againstness, of the object to the subject, as the thing stands in itself and has its own barely acknowledged independence.

The thing demands to be thought in and from its own sense, its own independent thingly self-so to recall the *Daodejing*. The rejection of idealism in the priority of the thing does not presuppose the avowal of a naive dogmatic realism, since it recognizes the formation, mediation, and relationality of the thing as elemental to its own event and way of being. Idealism is not overcome, Heidegger notes, through mere realism but by stepping out of the confines of this metaphysical opposition and its presuppositions (GA 12: 100; GA 15: 293-4; GA 87: 148). Whereas idealism is ensnared in the constitutive subject, realism is captured in ontic beings. Once again in "The Thing" Heidegger is concerned not with the primacy of the subject, as constitutive of meaning, or the object, as the abstract matter into which the thing and its elemental reality are eliminated, but with the thing in the event of its own being and in its interthingly nexus.

Heidegger's reflections on the thing as self-standing in its emptiness, uselessness, and consequent availability and usability are informed by a crucial chapter in the *Daodejing*. In *Daodejing* chapter 11, the exemplary thing is the empty vessel and thus its *ziran* is of a produced and not a naturally occurring thing, undoing the distinction between the natural and the artificial that some accounts ascribe to early Daoism. Heidegger describes how Plato and, as a result, Occidental metaphysics tend to distinguish between produced artifacts and natural things. It then measures the thing according to the model of creation, production, and the idea. Heidegger follows a different track here, suggestive of a distinctively early Daoist source. The probable implicit interlocutor of this reflection shows that the thing's self-naturing as thing is primary and not its natural formation or human production. Even the produced thing concerns first and foremost the thing and its truth.

The jug is a vessel that holds formed through the artisan's working with earth (GA 7: 168; GA 79: 5). However, it is not only the earthly material elements and the subjectivity and work of the artisan that form the jug. The jug is an emptiness that holds and its being as holding emptiness is what brings it into being by means of earth and artist. The paradigm of production and instrumental usefulness casts its net over things. It thereby obscures the thing, the self-standing of which elicits human desire, effort, and consumption. The Daoist *ziran* of the thing, Heidegger's self-standing of the thing, is indicative of an alternative *ethos*, poetics, and critical model of dwelling in the plight and needfulness of the present situation, a situation in which humans, things, interthingly bonds, and the adaptive self-regulating auto- or eco-poiesis of ecological systems have been interrupted.

IV. Between Emptiness and Annihilation

13. Holding Emptiness

A standard view maintains that nihilism deploys nothingness and emptiness to destroy sense and value, leaving humanity bereft in a cruel and indifferent cosmos. The crises of modernity call for a renewed human or divine subject that provides meaning to human striving. One can arrive at a different diagnosis drawing from the *Daodejing*, in which nothingness (*wu*) generates and nourishes life, emptiness (*xu*) unfixes, simplifies, and opens the heart-mind, and darkness (*hei* 黑) preserves the seeds that emerge and sprout in the light and revitalizes the sleeping. The projected lighting and framing of meaning and value are pervasive and do not answer the dangers of the current situation. What is needed is a return to the life of things themselves in their own myriad ways of dwelling and one best relates to multiplicity through simplicity.

Daodejing 28 recommends practicing virtuosity while remaining childlike. It says, "[K]now light and preserve darkness" (知其白, 守其黑). Wang Bi comments that there is no need to seek either light or darkness, as things naturally arise and return of themselves (Lou 1980: 74). Strauss translated this as follows: "Those who know their light wrap themselves in their darkness."[52] Buber quotes Strauss's translation in the afterword to his *Zhuangzi* edition and interprets this phrase as expressing an image of birth and growth in hiddenness (*Verborgenheit*).[53] Heidegger mentions this sentence in the 1930 Bremen version of "The Essence of Truth" where he interpreted it as concealment and unconcealment in the context of letting beings be and the mystery (GA 80.1: 370). He refers to and quotes Strauss's rendition several times over decades. Heidegger elucidates this line, with Thales of Miletus in mind, differently in *Identity and Difference* than in "The Essence of Truth." He states: "To this we join the truth that all know and of which few are capable: Mortal thought must sink into the darkness of the depths of the well to see the star by day" (GA 11: 138: GA 79: 93). Hiddenness and darkness must be preserved and safeguarded for that which emerges, just as in *Gelassenheit* the mystery of simplicity safeguards and nourishes the thing.

What of the emptiness of the vessel? It is not its solidity that does the holding. The empty space, this nothingness of the jug, is what the jug is comprised of as the holding, containing vessel. When the jug is filled, the pouring that fills it flows into its emptiness. The empty grants the vessel's holding. The emptiness and nothingness that belong to and constitute the vessel is what the vessel is as a holding container that holds and contains. The thingliness of the container does not then rest in the materiality from which it is made. It rests in the emptiness that holds and contains.

The jug is that which holds through its emptiness. It is produced (*herstellen*) to stand forth (*Herstand*) as *this* holding vessel. First, standing forth means to sprout and emerge from darkness, whether this occurs as self-making or being formed by others. Secondly, it means the produced thing's standing forth transpires in the unconcealment of that which is already present (GA 7: 170; GA 79: 7). Emptiness is therefore the precondition of materiality and production, as the vessel's thingness does not consist in the material of which it is compromised, but in the emptiness that enacts its holding.

The jug was previously associated with the festival. Here, it is linked with religious ritual and sacrifice in which the gods approach. This is not the violent rhetoric of *pólemos* and sacrifice of the mid-1930s. It is now set in the context of generosity, gifting, and granting. The empty vessel gathers and gifts not only water and wine but mortals, gods, earth, and heaven. The jug's mold (*Guss*) and the pour (*Giessen*) are etymologically related to Indo-Germanic sacrificing and gifting (*ghu*) as a dwelling with the divine and in the enfolding simplicity (*Einfalt*) of the fourfold (GA 7: 174; GA 79: 12). Illustrating Heidegger's point, the Sanskrit word *juhóti* encompasses the semantic range of to pour, offer, sacrifice, and worship.

Intriguingly, Wilhelm entitled *Daodejing* 28 as the return or reversion to simplicity (*Einfalt*). He rendered the sentence translated by Strauss and quoted by Heidegger as "Who recognizes the light and nonetheless lingers in the dark is the exemplary model of the world" (Wilhelm 1911: 30). If this enfolding, encompassing simplicity is scattered, then the uncarved is carved into vessels and people are carved into the useable. How can the thing and the person retain or return to its uncarved darkness and simplicity amidst being carved and used? That would be the great forming that requires no cutting or, to recall Butcher Ding in the *Zhuangzi*, the carving of emptiness that serves as an image of nurturing rather than of scattering life (Wilhelm 1911: 30).

The Daoist context of an enfolding four-cornered world without cutting edges was delineated in the previous chapter. The fourfold appears in Heidegger's lecture as the interval of things. It is concealed in enframing positionality and the collapse of all distances and intervals between things in their availability, usability, and positioning in standing-reserve that will be further analyzed in the next two chapters.

14. Shapers of Emptiness and Annihilation

Heidegger continues stating that the artisan does not create or produce the jug *qua* jug in working and shaping its bottom, sides, and edges. The artisan holds onto and shapes the emptiness, in which the thingliness of the vessel arises and stands, bringing it forth as the containing vessel to be filled and poured. The jug's emptiness is that which determines the artisan's handling and, if this instance can be extended, human production. This entails a dramatic consequence that Heidegger insufficiently clarifies. It is not nature as abstract matter or useful raw material that forms the basis of human processes of production. It is nature as the encompassing fourfold and as the self-so of things and their world-formative interthingly relations (*Ge-ding*) that forms the basis of human action and inaction.

The fourfold is thought of as an enfolding, gathering simplicity. Heaven and earth form the interval and place of human dwelling, suggestive of the classical Chinese conception of *tianrendi* 天人地. Earth signifies in Heidegger's lecture the elemental as it forms, bears, and fruits, nourishing waters, rocks, plants, and animals. Heaven is depicted as the elemental of sun, moon, and stars; the alteration of the seasons and of daylight and the darkness of night; it is hospitable and inhospitable weather, atmosphere, and—an image of Buddhist emptiness considered in "From a Dialogue on Language"—clouds that form and dissipate in the empty blue depth of the aether. The gods beckon from and withdraw into the hidden holding sway of the divine (GA 7: 180; GA 79: 17).

What then of mortals and their activities? Mortals are those beings aware of their own death, and hence they do not include stones and animals that belong to the earth. To this extent, Heidegger does not fully break with the anthropocentric paradigm of *Being and Time* here or in the 1946 "Letter on Humanism." The abyssal affinity and difference between the animal and the human in the latter text improve on his earlier account of their separating abyss (GA 29/30: 384). Its language still indicates the limits of this confrontation with anthropocentric humanism (GA 9: 326). It is humans who presuppose, rely on, and intervene in an interthingly world consisting of things, their relations, and the places they gather and grant. They are no longer lords and masters ruling over being, yet they still retain a special status in saying, safeguarding, and shepherding beings. Humans, in the *Bremen Lectures*, are the workers, shapers, and builders of emptiness and annihilation, as they are the medium and work through which things can be formed, used, and destroyed.

Heidegger's discussion of nuclear annihilation resonates with J. Robert Oppenheimer's allusion to Kṛṣṇa's words in *Bhagavad Gītā* 11.32: "Now I [time, in the original text] have become death, the destroyer of worlds" (Monk 2014: 430) and the nuclear fears of the era. Heidegger's analysis is distinctive in focusing on the obliteration of localities and things in addition to human lives. Annihilation is world-destruction targeting things, in his 1949 lecture, their interthingly nexus, and the places that they gather. This indicates in a preliminary way an environmental questioning of the consumption and destruction of things and localities. Such destruction does not only occur with the use of weapons of mass obliteration, as they confirm for Heidegger the already existing tendency toward annihilating and reducing the thing to a naught.

Here the differences should be noted between Daoist emptiness and nothingness that nurture and preserve things and the coercive decomposition to nonbeing revealed not only in human economic and military activities. In such an enframing configuration of reality, the thing's concealed essencing cannot come into the light, its word cannot be heard, and the thingness of the thing remains concealed and forgotten. However, the thing is preserved in its hiddenness and darkness even as it is consumed and annihilated in its usefulness and light. It is therefore its darkness, silence, and uselessness that protect the thing and allow it to be itself. In a strategy strongly evocative of the reversal of perspectives in the *Zhuangzi*, humans can only commence to approach the thing *as* thing by shifting their limiting perspective and entering into the thing's own region (or "en-regioning") such as the joyful fish in a non-anthropocentric form of being-with.

The thing's annihilation enacts a double deception for Heidegger: first, the supremacy and exceptionality of science that marginalizes and excludes other varieties of encountering the real in its reality; secondly, the misconception that things are nonetheless still things in their enframed positionality and the tacit presupposition that they were and could potentially be the things that they are once again. Heidegger concludes, this has not happened yet in thinking. Does he mean all thinking, Occidental thinking (*abendländisches Denken*), or philosophical thinking? The answer is uncertain here. It is contradictory in other texts that either appeal to or hesitate before South and East Asian forms of thinking and other prospective ways of dwelling-within-the-world. Heidegger suspects that Occidental discourses concerning China and India are more reflective of their own presuppositions and representations than any genuine encounter (GA 99: 138). This is a salient and helpful suspicion if it is deployed to interrogate rather than hamper intercultural thinking.

Early ziranist Daoist sources express that the thing should be encountered through the letting of *wuwei* in its moment, receptively observed and followed in its fluctuations, and let go of its demise. Heidegger, in contrast, notes that the thing has yet to be genuinely encountered as thing. He states in "The Thing" that if things had already shown themselves *qua* things in their thingness, then the thing's thingness would have become manifest and laid claim to thinking. The thing *qua* thing remains proscribed, nil, and in that sense is prepared for annihilation. These processes have transpired and continue to transpire so fundamentally that things are no longer permitted to occur as themselves in a nexus of coercive action and intervention (the *wei* in early Chinese contexts that *wuwei* suspends). Furthermore, in their concealment in pragmatic use and objectifying representation, they have not yet even begun to appear as things *qua* things. This conclusion is either pessimistic, if it is a matter that can be answered by thought, or indicative of an encounter yet to occur that serves as an exemplar of waiting and a formal indicative model or guiding thread for the encounter.

15. World between Asia and Europe

How can such enframing and eradication of thing and world be thought much less contested and transformed? The modern global situation makes it difficult if not impossible, for Heidegger. According to Petzet, Heidegger once revealingly joked: "Mao Tse? That is the *Ge-Stell* (the enframing) of Lao-tse" (Petzet 1993: 212). It appears

Laozi's insight no longer speaks or is heard in the modern Chinese world, just as the words of pre-Socratic thinkers and poets echo without being heard in the modern Occident. And in the posthumously published "Spiegel Interview," he states both that (1) we cannot overlook the possibility that a thinking born from more primordial transmissions might arise in Russia and China that could enable a free relationship with technology, which—given his agrarian utopian tendencies—probably refers to images of archaic agrarian communities, and (2) no Zen Buddhist or other Eastern experiences can assist Europe from its own specific devastating plight.[54]

This much later observation is clarified in his June 1950 *Black Notebooks* where he states that technology forms a different constellation and takes on a different problematic in China, Europe, and Russia. Each—and in this passage, he speaks of Europe, East Asia, and India—calls for their own distinctive forms of confrontation (*Auseinandersetzung*) that cannot begin to be answered by mere borrowing and adopting (*übernehmen*) from the other (GA 98: 368). This signifies that Europeanization and technologization have become planetary, as he frequently remarks elsewhere, and yet the responses to this global situation are formed relative to things, local enregioning places, and guiding indicative words.

Heidegger's own intercultural situation reveals the complexity of such a response and—in contrast to the essentialism of an identical people—the need for a formally indicative democratic and pluralistic cross-cultural thinking of the local and the global, as opposed to the fixated identities of localist, folkish, or nationalist particularism, and homogenizing universalism, which both fail in significant ways to appropriately recognize the interactive participatory singular in others and things. Whereas it operates as a pivotal expression for Heidegger in the 1930s, which he attempted to interpret ontologically rather than anthropologically racially, he explicitly rejected folkish (*völkisch*) and nationalistic principles in the mid-1940s while remaining suspicious of the global as "inter" or "over" national that remains informed by it. He designated the latter condition in 1969, responding to Tsujimura Kōichi 辻村公一 (1922–2010), "world-civilization" in which the ascendency of administrative-instrumental economy, politics, and technology has reduced everything else not merely to a secondary superstructure but a crumbling annex, and in which human existence finds itself homeless, whether in Europe or Asia (GA 16: 711–13).

Heidegger's assessment might appear overly one-sided and should be resituated in the context of critical social analysis. Modernity is diagnosed in Heidegger as administrative-bureaucratic (which he confronted in the form of planning and the disintegration of human existence into "human resources") and instrumental-technological (which he conceived through enframing positionality and standing-reserve). This critical confrontation with modernity is developed in distinctive ways by a range of German intellectuals: Max Weber, Buber, Spengler, and German irrationalist worldview philosophies, "Western Marxism" and the Frankfurt school, as well as Heidegger. Heidegger elucidates, beginning particularly in 1943 as he twists free from the paradigm of subject and will, a unique and still apposite response to modern crisis-tendencies, which are not due to a "mistake" but a formative destiny to be confronted (GA 45: 24), through the priority of thing in place and world.

The devastation of place and the plight of homelessness identified in his later thought are not simply theoretical or technical questions. It concerns questioning, building, and dwelling for which ziranist discourses indicate suggestive thought-images and models. Such elemental questioning and the prospect of a more appropriate ecophronetic building and dwelling with things in the present world will be traced in the following chapters.

4

Heidegger and the *Zhuangzi*:
The Uselessness and Unnecessariness of Things

I. Heidegger's Pathways with Zhuangzi

1. Heidegger in Bremen

We will consider a few examples in this chapter that lead to insights into the historical context and conceptual significance of Heidegger's adaptation of the *Zhuangzi* and a Zhuangzian interpretation of Heidegger.

Heidegger seems to more eagerly communicate his interests in Daoist sources and East Asian art and culture during his visits to Bremen. There he discussed and drew on the *Daodejing* and the *Zhuangzi* in lectures and conversations, in 1930, 1949, 1951, and 1960. Heidegger's cosmopolitan intercultural engagements in this culturally open Hanseatic trading city were due in part to his shared East Asian interests with his Bremen friend, the writer Heinrich Wiegand Petzet. According to Petzet's biographical *Encounters and Dialogues with Martin Heidegger, 1929–1976*, a cornerstone for the study of Heidegger's East Asian entanglements, Heidegger shared his fascination with East Asian art, culture, and philosophy. His portrayal of Heidegger's recitation and interpretation of the joy of fish from the *Zhuangzi* at a 1930 evening gathering was discussed earlier in the introduction to Chapter 1 (Petzet 1993: 18). To briefly sketch a sampling of these Daoist references, which are discussed at greater detail elsewhere in the present book, Heidegger mentioned the *Daodejing* 28 passage on light and darkness during his 1930 lecture, the empty vessel of *Daodejing* 11 in his 1949 lectures, and the woodcarver from the *Zhuangzi* in his 1960 lecture "Image and Word" ("Bild und Wort").

The Bremen author Hans Jürgen Seekamp, best known for his work on the poet Stefan George, noted Heidegger's engagement with Daoism and reflections on the meaning of *dao* during his lecture given on May 4, 1951, on *Lógos*, in Bremen—where, he adds, people have "a cultivated sense for Asia"—in a short 1960 article published in the Indian publication *United Asia*.[1] He notes that Europe has not yet genuinely comprehended or built a bridge with Asia, despite the poetic and philosophical inspirations of the East in the Occident and the German poets and intellectuals who have actively embraced it.[2]

In speaking of potentially building a genuine bridge in the future, Seekamp introduces Heidegger and his hesitation concerning whether genuine understanding across distinctive languages is possible. Seekamp concludes his essay by quoting from Heidegger's talk: "We do not know what really is meant when we hear people say 'Tao,' since we do not think the word in its native language, nor can we at all imitate such a thought."[3] Heidegger is fundamentally a philosopher of the way and its motility. Parallel to early Daoist sources, he speaks of the way of being, nothing, things, existence, and his own specific way, yet *dao* remains to an extent incommensurable with his way. The *dao* speaks no doubt to the Occident that does not have ears to comprehend it. Heidegger might hear it to some extent yet is reticent to speak of it. Perhaps he is following the advice of *Daodejing* 56 that those who speak do not know and those who know do not speak.[4]

2. Heidegger between *Pólemos* and *Gelassenheit*

Respectful reticence and reserve safeguard what is hidden for Heidegger. His public reticence does not negate his extended history of attentiveness to the *Laozi* and *Zhuangzi*. This attention seemingly disappears between 1931 and 1942, an era in his thought of the primacy of the will. His attention resumes and takes an intriguing and more visible turn in 1943 with "The Uniqueness of the Poet." This initiates a period in which he seriously studies the Daoist classics and critically reevaluates, even if inadequately for his critics, the disastrous catastrophe of National Socialism. He reassesses his own philosophy and the dangers of his own previous discourse of decision, self-assertion, creative conflict and violent confrontation (*pólemos*), and the primacy of the will. He systematically relied on this discursive configuration in his early advocacy, as rector of the University of Freiburg during 1933–1935, on behalf of the new National Socialist regime's coercive fusion and coordination (*Gleichschaltung*) of all aspects of university life and German existence, with devastating consequences.[5] In the postwar period, he described this as "the greatest stupidity of his life," although he never adequately publicly confronted this past.[6]

Heidegger repeatedly claimed after the war that he broke with National Socialism in 1934 when he resigned as rector and refused to participate in the handover of power to the new rector (GA 16: 400; GA 102: 30). The issue is more complicated. As Lyotard remarked, Heidegger was aware from the beginning that National Socialism was nonsense and consciously and intentionally chose to join the movement to attempt to influence its direction (Lyotard 1994: 113). Hannah Arendt and Elisabeth Blochmann felt particularly betrayed by his opportunism to be on the seemingly "winning" side of history. Moreover, Heidegger's vision of "ontological revolution" and poetic renewal was peripheral to the movement's main motivations and themes. He is not a thinker of the totalitarian racial state but of a poeticizing people. He avoids key facets of National Socialism such as its Aryanism and repeatedly criticizes its biological, value, and worldview commitments as vulgar.[7] Heidegger likewise decried the populist elements of the movement, complaining that it preferred boxing, cars, and radio to Hölderlin's poetry. Accordingly, Heidegger is better classified as a conservative elitist literati-intellectual (Habermas speaks of "German mandarins") and compromised follower

(*Mitläufer*) rather than as a Nazi activist, ideologue, officeholder, or—to speak from the standpoint of our own situation—a rightwing populist.[8] As Arendt and others have analyzed, Heidegger lacked any serious engagement in and reflection on state-power that can be checked by the self-ordering of a flourishing public sphere, open political deliberation and participation, and legally secured individual rights. Authoritarian sentiments, fascistic aesthetic experimentalism and expressionism, and charismatic romanticism infused his thinking of the 1930s, as is evident in his account of artworks and poetry.[9] At the same time, the diverse abundance of Heidegger's thought should not be reductively condensed to this moment.

How then did Heidegger's thinking transition from an apologetic and ideologically driven sacrificial and violent ethics of *pólemos* and work, toward the freedom of letting releasement (*lassen*)? From the creative violent holding sway of being as *phúsis* toward the generative self-ordering of things and world in the holding sway of being? We should call this an anticipatory shifting toward *dao*, while never arriving there, given the distance and hesitation between Europe and Asia in Heidegger's thinking. One source of this shift is the *Zhuangzi*. This text reports repeated refusals of coercive political participation and coordination. Zhuangzi is depicted in the "Autumn Floods" chapter as preferring the life of a turtle freely and uselessly meandering on the muddy riverbank instead of serving usefully, and embalmed and fixated, in the prince's court. People, things, and words freely rambling from their stratified instrumental positionality are perceived as chaotic anarchic threats to disciplinary order. In the anti-politics of the *Zhuangzi*, political service is likened to a turtle being killed, prepared, and put on display, in contrast to it uselessly and freely enjoying its water and mud by itself. Other passages intimate a different social form of anti-politics. There is also an agrarian politics of egalitarian simplicity without distinctions between ruler and ruled. This idea is expressed in passages of the *Zhuangzi*, the *Liezi*, and negatively in Ge Hong's "Interrogating Bao" (*Jie Bao* 詰鮑) chapter of the *Baopuzi*, where this anarchic "Lao-Zhuang" social-political ziranist tendency is condemned in Ge Hong's legitimation of an authoritarian and hierarchical Confucian-legalist political order.[10]

Several Chinese and intercultural transmissions interpret Daoism as a philosophy of freedom. Early Daoist sources have been repeatedly linked with individual liberty from the coercion of state and society in the Chinese and European imagination. We should consider a few contextualizing historical examples once again. The idea of a free and equal self-generative and self-ordering politics was linked with anarchistic socialism in Julius Hart and Martin Buber in fin-de-siècle Germany. In Hart's poetic utopian vision, *dao* is an anarchy in which unforced harmony is born from the conflict and cacophony of things (Hart 1905: 51–2). The *Zhuangzi* was allied with anarchism and individualism in its early twentieth-century German reception. Richard Wilhelm described this tendency as expressing an anarchistic ideal of a golden age without rulers (Wilhelm 1929: 40). Liang Chiang (Liang Qiang 梁强), in a 1938 German language Jena dissertation on Chinese economics and society, described Chinese history as a dialectic between authoritarian communalism and anarchistic individualism, beginning with Laozi and Zhuangzi (Chiang 1938: 69). Hans and Sophie Scholl and the White Rose student resistance appealed to Laozi's conception of flourishing, spontaneous, self-ordering society against the abuses of the Nazi state (Cantor 2023).

Unlike these brave students in Munich, Heidegger had failed to see in the 1930s the crucial differences between people, state, and charismatic leadership. The exiled German Sinologist Werner Eichhorn illuminated Zhuangzian freedom against the background of Nazi totalitarianism (Eichhorn 1942: 140–62). While authoritarian and conservative readings have stressed the apolitical aesthetic and subjective character of Zhuangzi's freedom, thereby depoliticizing it, Eichhorn understood that it operates within the nexus of things and social-political relations with transformative political repercussions.

Daoism offered models of worldly relational freedom in contrast to the freedom of atomistic self-interested selves or totalitarian collective subjects legitimating the power of the state. The German understanding of Daoist freedom, with its complex historical transmissions, is operative in Heidegger's reflections during the closing years of the Second World War. Although one should beware of overstating the importance of the *Zhuangzi* and its sense of freedom for Heidegger, his Zhuangzian inspired reflections on letting, waiting, and uselessness in a defeated, occupied Germany in "Evening Conversation: In a Prisoner of War Camp in Russia, between a Younger and an Older Man" (1945), published in *Country Path Conversations*, implement a radically different *ethos* of releasement (*Gelassenheit*) and variations on letting (*lassen*) with reference to the *Zhuangzi*. The focus on the thing (in the expansive sense) rather than God and soul points toward more than the *Gelassenheit* familiar from earlier German sources to the modern paradigm of comparative mysticism.

Heidegger was, according to Löwith's analysis of *Being and Time*, a philosopher of usefulness, the purposive for-the-sake-of which, the thing-in-the-work, and the event of being that are the opposite of Daoism (Löwith 1983: 600). How did Heidegger become a thinker who evoked and addressed Lao-Zhuang forms of uselessness, freedom from purposiveness, and letting the thing be in its own way of being? Löwith's suspicions are partly right. Heidegger's semi-Daoist reflections from 1943 to 1950 are delimited by his cultural, philosophical, and political concerns and his interpretive situation.

Heidegger's reflections disclose considerable Daoist-related elements in his post-1943 thinking. His postwar "thought-poems" and notebooks speak of turning between being and nothingness, releasement while remaining oneself in transforming and wandering, and being freely underway (his own version of Zhuangzian calm and carefree wandering) that is complete in its own movement without goal or purpose (GA 81: 352; GA 101: 162). He also describes the waiting in which one becomes one's own and people and things are granted their return to stillness.[11] Several of his thought-poems and previously unpublished notes are evocative of an interculturally mediated Daoist "imaginary" and *ethos* from which Heidegger drew in juxtaposition with his overshadowing early Greek and German sources.

The Daoist motifs adopted by Heidegger cannot be said to constitute a "Daoist turn" as such. Still, they are symptomatic of an encounter and engagement. These traces and touches are not accidental or contingent facets of Heidegger's later thinking. These facets reveal different prospects for an *ethos* of letting and releasing things and persons and concern other vital motifs of his mature philosophy: usefulness and uselessness, the thing, technology, poetic thinking, dwelling, world-disclosive elemental words, and—as analyzed in Part Two—emptiness and nothingness.

3. Words, Images, and Guiding Threads

Heidegger refers more frequently to words and images associated with the *Laozi*, as evident in the 1949 *Bremen Lectures* and in multiple discussions of the thing. He does express, directly and indirectly, familiarity with the German language *Zhuangzi* editions of Buber (1910) and Wilhelm (1912). Confirming this persistent attention to the *Zhuangzi*, Heidegger evokes it throughout the 1944–1945 third *Country Path Conversation*. He cited Buber's selections from the *Zhuangzi* in the 1960 Bremen lecture "Image and Word."[12] Image and word are themes in early Daoist texts that deploy thought-images and suggestive and paradoxical words to indicate the great imageless image and wordless word expressed in *Daodejing* 41.[13] Another chapter, *Daodejing* 14, speaks of seeing what cannot be seen, hearing what cannot be heard, the formless forms, and the thread running through the way (Lou 1980: 31–2).

Heidegger refers in this lecture to mostly Occidental examples (Augustine, Klee, Heraclitus) except for the instructive portrayal of the artisan of the holy "bell-stand" from Buber's rendition of *Zhuangzi* chapter 19, "Fulfilling Life" (*dasheng* 達生). Once again, a Daoist text shows how the point is inaction in the sense of the "great carving" that does not hack and fracture; instead, it accords with the thing and its spirit while participating in its transformation. This functions as an exemplary thought-image of nurturing and fulfilling life in the *Zhuangzi*. It serves as a guiding thread (*Leitfaden*) for the direction of the way for Heidegger (GA 74: 185, 187). A thread is part of a web of threads that veil and reveal in their veiling the imagelessness of the wordless.[14] Heidegger notes how the gathering of texts and words calls for a readiness and preparation for the mysteriousness of things and their interthingly relations that approach in conversation.[15] He once again not only mentions or invokes Lao-Zhuang sources in this lecture. Heidegger positions their words and thought-images as elements of his own way of thinking. This is indicative of a deeper engagement. It might be called a quasi-Daoistic shift in view of Heidegger's undeniable differences from Chinese varieties of Daoism and in his selective integration of specific ziranist elements and thought-images.

In this narrative, a non-instrumental artistry serves as a thought-image for how to interact with things. The wooden bell-stand (*Glockenspielstande*) emerges, as if it were the tree itself expressed through the work of spirits, as it is shaped through a responsive artistry born of the "fasting that calms the heart-mind" (*zhai yi jing xin* 齋以靜心) without dependence on purposive pragmatic technique, skill, or calculation.[16] This is a making and using that follows and is in accord with the thing and its transformations. This understanding leads to the question of to what extent technology could be an adaptation to instead of a projecting and dominating of things and places.

Heidegger addresses the uselessness of things and words through the "necessity of the unnecessary" and the "usefulness of uselessness" (*wuyong zhiyong* 無用之用) in the *Zhuangzi* in the third of the *Country Path Conversations* and in his 1962 lecture "Transmitted and Technological Language" in which he ponders the "languaging" (the "it speaks") of language. The connection between spontaneity and calculation, usefulness and uselessness, appears in Heidegger's 1945 and 1962 references to Wilhelm's translation of the *Zhuangzi* that is the primary focus of the present chapter.

The Zhuangzian "useful uselessness," exhibited in a series of narratives in which the useless thing (in the expansive sense of stone, tree, person, and so on) flourishes, while the useful thing is destroyed in being used, and becomes the condition of use, in contrast with the thing being principally characterized by its ready-to-hand pragmatic availability and usability. Instrumental usefulness suppresses and forgets, while presupposing the thing in the functioning (*zhiyong*) of its nonuse (*wuyong*) and self-so-ing of itself.

Several passages help contextualize the notion of the thing and use in the *Zhuangzi*. In the *Zhuangzi* outer chapter "Knowledge's Northern Rambling" (*zhibeiyou* 知北遊), it is noted that "what things the thing is not itself the thing" (物物者非物) and in the outer chapter "Mountain Tree" (*shanmu* 山木) that the genuine person lets "things thing without being thinged by things" (物物而不物於物).[17] This need not entail a rejection of thing *qua* thing if it signifies undoing the fixation of self and thing and, by implication in the modern situation, subject and object through the recognition of their emptiness. It is its own emptiness or nothingness and self-naturing (i.e., the thinglessness of things) that things (gathers) the thing. The exemplary attunement with things is one of uselessness and non-purposiveness. This lets things thing, as they are of themselves, while remaining in a comportment that is free, at ease, and undetermined (un-thinged) by the thinging of things.[18] Zhuangzian freedom perspectively shifts the self who is sojourning with and amidst beings, earth, and sky.

Heidegger's later reflections concerning uselessness diverge from its senses in the texts of the mid-1930s. It is an expression that Heidegger recurrently revisits in his later works, typically without either directly or indirectly referring to the *Zhuangzi*, where it is coordinated with the letting go of *Gelassenheit* that steps back from coercive creating and willing as well as instrumental calculation and usage. It would be overly simplistic to describe Heidegger's trajectory as leading from decisionist voluntarism to fatalistic passivism. It is also insufficient to identify his thinking of releasement solely with either medieval German mysticism or early Lao-Zhuang Daoism. Its Daoist inheritance is clearly strong, however, as Heidegger depicts, through exemplary thought-images and illustrative models, a way of being-in-the-world and dwelling with and amidst things, mortals, and gods between heaven and earth. It is underappreciated the extent to which there is a Daoist bent at work in his language of the fourfold, comprised of mortals and immortals, heaven and earth. Likewise, his letting releasement does not signify either an otherworldly mystical unification of the soul with God or a fixed contemplative passivity.[19] Heidegger repeatedly denies that his thought is a form of mysticism (GA 77: 109, 185). As Pöggeler describes Heidegger's last conversations with Bernhard Welte, Heidegger's study of Eckhart and mysticism led him not to God and the soul but to the things that form way and place: "God was only God in the 'unspoken' language of the 'things' by the country path" (Pöggeler 1987: 47). Heidegger's mature discourse of things and pathways is directly connected with his interpretation of Daoist texts.

Letting releasement, with its clear Eckhartian roots, acquires a less monotheistic and quasi-Daoistic tonality and style in Heidegger's thinking. His releasement functions in significant ways like *wuwei*. Its intercultural journey already associated it with letting (*laissez* from old Germanic *lazan*) and even *laissez-faire* in François Quesnay's physiocracy that advocated government by *phúsis* interpreted as according with natural simplicity, unfettering the self-productivity of the earth and the people, and *laissez faire et laissez passer*. *Wuwei* is not an economic policy in early Daoist texts. Nor is it a mystical retreat into the interiority of the inner self. Acting and attuning from nonaction (*wei wuwei*) is an intra-worldly art of being-in-the-world that empties, quiets, and simplifies the self, desire, and will with humility while releasing things to themselves and their own essencing. This can be interpreted as a Heideggerian instance of self-so-ness.

This ziranist bent of Heidegger's thinking is individual oriented in the 1920s and thing oriented after 1943. In Heidegger's early thought, from approximately 1919 to 1930, an anarchic or libertarian *laissez-faire*-like moment (perhaps informed in part by Okakura's account of Daoist *wuwei* and *ziran*) is operative in notions of returning to one's own singular self-essencing and being-with, as the solicitude making room for and helping the individuation of others. In 1929, Heidegger can speak of co-existentially dwelling with the thing while prioritizing Dasein and the freedom of its own self-happening. The thing here is the phenomenological correlational matter to be encountered and thought. There is also the use of *ziran*-like self-happening of the truth of being, concealing and unconcealing itself, in his 1930 Bremen lecture that draws on Buber's *Zhuangzi*. Heidegger repeatedly speaks of "helping" without producing effects, once again evoking the Daoist sage who is described as helping and nurturing without interventionist or coercive acting.[20] In the first of the *Country Path Conversations*, letting releasement is described as helping without assertively willing and effecting (GA 77: 108). This quasi-Daoist or ziranist proclivity appears more strongly in Heidegger's thinking after 1943. The *ziran*-oriented moment occurs in recognizing the self-essencing not only of Dasein (as in 1929) but of entities, earth, and sky. Heidegger's earlier and later ziranist moments give the impression of being entangled with the *Laozi* and the *Zhuangzi*.

Heidegger's Daoist entanglements become clearer beginning around 1943. First, releasement is not about turning away and withdrawing into tranquility or serenity of mind, as in Stoic *ataraxia*. This does not let things approach and become near in silence, Heidegger notes around 1942/43, during a period of heightened engagement with the *Daodejing* (GA 97: 33). It is not about the silencing enacted by the self but hearing into the silent: "the silence of nature and the simplicity of all things" (GA 97: 23). Nature exists not only through human activity and projection but through the letting emerge and worlding of earth (GA 99: 53). What is inadequately called "nature," insofar as nature signifies objective presence (GA 102: 44), is not heard in acting, willing, or anti-willing that are necessarily obstructions. It is in inaction (*Nicht-Handeln*)—which is not a mere doing nothing (*Nichts-tun*)—that the playful open space of the clearing of being is prepared (GA 97: 23).

Second, amidst these same reflections, Heidegger articulates a statement that links with his other discussions related to Wilhelm's translation of the *Zhuangzi*: "the most necessary is the unnecessary and the useful is the necessary" (GA 97: 30). The unnecessariness or uselessness of the thing is a moment of its freedom and self-naturing in the *Zhuangzi*, as the translations of Buber and Wilhelm accentuate. Releasement is articulated in the 1940s in ways that intersect with thought-images and moments from the *Zhuangzi*. It is expressed as a worldly attunement and comportment of free receptivity and responsiveness to and the safeguarding of things and world in their own *ziran*-like self-happening.²¹

This is not all. Some of Heidegger's reflections during this period mirror in significant ways ideas expressed in the *Zhuangzi* editions of Buber and Wilhelm that were familiar reading to Heidegger since the Weimar Republic. The list is extensive: the emptying of the heart-mind, the unfettering letting releasement, the resonant-responsiveness, the usefulness of the uselessness, the perfection of imperfection, the shifting of perspectives toward the thing's own way of being, freely and easily becoming oneself in sojourning and wandering, and the nourishing of the life of the myriad things.

II. Emptiness, Uselessness, and Waiting

4. Letting and Healing in the *Country Path Conversations*

There are three dialogues in *Country Path Conversations*: A Three-way Conversation on a Country Path between a Scientist, a Scholar, and a Guide (*Weisen*) delineated in the last chapter; The Teacher Meets the Tower Warden at the Door to the Tower Stairway; and Evening Conversation: In a Prisoner of War Camp in Russia, between a Younger and an Older Man. While the first dialogue raises issues and themes analogous to "The Uniqueness of the Poet" (1943) and "The Thing" (1950), the "Evening Conversation" is unique among Heidegger's works in significant ways and several of its themes are not explicitly taken up in subsequent reflections.

It is already atypical in revolving around the *Zhuangzi* instead of the more typically featured *Laozi* text. It is portrayed as taking place in a Soviet prisoner of war camp in the vast Siberian forests between a younger captured German soldier and an older one. It is geopolitical in that it is dated May 7, 1945, the date of the unconditional capitulation of Nazi Germany, and engages in a dialogical reflection on the "German disaster." This refers not only to the crisis of modernity, as is more emblematic of Heidegger's later discourse, even while it relates the Nazi calamity that has befallen the German people to a fundamental loss of being itself.

The conversation commences with the younger soldier encountering "what is healing" (*das Heilsame*), which Heidegger elucidates in the "Letter on Humanism" three years later.²² He encounters it in the vast expansiveness, a thought-image (yet not a symbol) of the cosmos in the earlier conversation of the vast forest that enwraps the unwholesomeness of the camp while remaining unattainable from within these confines.²³ Otherwise than in his discourse of the mid-1930s, this encounter is explicitly described as not deriving from a choice, decision, or the assertion of the will, whether individual, collective, or conceived of as happening through being. It occurs through being "let into [*eingelassen*] what heals," "of the letting of its happening [*Veranlassung*]."²⁴ This dialogue is shaped by its play on the various senses of letting, allowing, and releasing related to the stem-word "*lassen*" and the complexities of therapeutic healing, possibly evoking early Daoist responsive attunement and nurturing things in a situation of devastation in which nothing is permitted to grow, be nurtured, and healed. Healing concerns other- rather than self-power.

How then does the mystery of this letting occur in Heidegger? How can such letting be thought, given the realities of injury and harm? The conversation is haunted by the specter of the unwholesome as that which cannot heal (*das Unheilsame*), a question taken up in the 1948 diagnosis of the pathologies of modernity in the "Letter on Humanism" discussed in the next chapter, and the inability of deep wounds to heal: "And what is not all wounded and torn apart in us?—us, for whom a blinded leading-astray of our own people is too deplorable to permit wasting a complaint on, despite the devastation that covers our native soil and its helplessly perplexed [*ratlose*] humans." This situation of covering and perplexity leading to devastation is depicted by the older man in reference to the phenomenon of evil. Evil is interpreted in reference to fury and malice: the "devastation of the earth and the annihilation of the human essence that goes with it are somehow evil [*das Böse*]."[25]

The conversation continues by positioning the desolation and desertification of National Socialism and the Second World War in relation to a more originary devastation of earth and humanity. The older man states: "Devastation [*Verwüstung*] means for us, after all, that everything—the world, the human, and the earth—will be transformed into a desert [*Wüste*]."[26] This desolation is "of the earth and of human existence."[27] It has left a deserted wasteland behind: "the deserted [*verlassene*] expanse of the abandonment [*Verlassenheit*] of all life."[28] Heidegger defined the desert in a later letter as "the area where there is no growth" wherein "nothing is let grown" (GA 16: 563). As the *Zhuangzi* critiques the calculative and purposive nurturing of life for life's free self-nourishing, Heidegger depicts the modern condition as one where "growing life" is obstructed and replaced by a totalizing administrative, technological regime of calculative planning.[29] The *Zhuangzi* text and Heidegger reveal key facets of the problematic of nurturing life in the face of purposive regimes of instrumental usefulness, even if they don't appropriately express the spontaneous public and political self-ordering that is indispensable for contesting and limiting the coercive powers of party, state, or market.[30]

What then of the political circumstances of this conversation about devastation and healing? Heidegger does not directly confront the banality of systematized evil or his own complicity during the 1930s.[31] Nonetheless, Heidegger can be understood as "condemning" National Socialism in this way in this and other works of this era. He does so, however, in the *Black Notebooks* not by itself on its own terms or by appealing to standard criticisms. He explains it as part of a larger process that he controversially perceives to be expressed in Americanism, communism, and globalizing modernity itself, of which National Socialism is insufficiently confronted as another flawed and disastrous instance.[32] As for the *Black Notebooks* themselves, which are mostly philosophical instead of directly political, they document the transformations in his thinking from the ascendancy of national self-assertion through the consequent devastation to a refusal of both the national and assertion for the sake of reticence and releasement.

This transformation through devastation appears in the dialogue of the two interlocutors. Given the devastation of the earth, and their own ravaged essence, what then can these two useless imprisoned men do, and what can the German people do? In an extended conversation concerned with waiting, that echoes the emptied heart-mind that waits upon things in the *Zhuangzi*, the conversants differentiate a waiting for "something" that is structured by anticipation and expectation (*auf etwas warten, Erwarten*) and a "pure waiting" (*reines Warten*), without anticipation and projection, in which one waits upon nothing (*das Nichts*).[33] This waiting on nothing cannot be an awaiting of or for the nothing; otherwise it could not be pure: it awaits and clings to neither being nor nothing, but "waits on that which answers pure waiting," the "echo of pure coming," evoking the Zhuangzian fasting of the heart-mind as awaiting things in emptiness.[34] Without beginning or ending, in chapter 20, there is only waiting.

The received *Zhuangzi* text refers to waiting numerous times. There is no reason to wait and depend on others' opinions or what will take place or be correct in the future. There is an awaiting for the revolutions of the heavens and seasons. There is the waiting for the true or genuine person (*zhenren*) and genuine knowing (*zhenzhi* 真知) in the first section of Chapter 6. In a crucial *Zhuangzi* passage, vital energy is depicted as (in Ziporyn's 2009 translation) "an emptiness, a waiting for the presence of beings. The way alone is what gathers in this emptiness. And it is this emptiness that is the fasting of the mind."[35] There is the pure waiting of the heart-mind in emptiness as beings, or that which comes to presence, gather in emptiness.

Early Chinese philosophies emphasized varieties of forceful intervening action (*wei* 為), the minimization of coercive action (*wuwei*), or their alternation depending on circumstances in the *Book of Changes*. Döblin and Brecht were concerned in their encounters with Chinese thinking with questions of how to transformatively intervene in and dialectically navigate the flowing transition of beings. Informed by the *Daodejing* and the *Zhuangzi*, Buber and Heidegger questioned the very notion of action. Heidegger discovered a different model of action and inaction in the *Zhuangzi* that guided his reflections in the *Country Path Conversations* and the "Letter on Humanism." This was the transformation of acting in awaiting, in contrast with acting in intervening and its maximization or minimization. Heidegger's depictions of waiting, emptiness, and gathering closely evoke this and other passages from the *Zhuangzi*. Waiting is described by Heidegger in this 1945 conversation as a "letting come," or letting arrive, and a "safeguarding" (evoking Daoist nurturing and preserving) that is not an expectation concerning a predicted or unpredicted future. It is instead, like Zhuangzi's self-emptying heart-mind, a waiting that empties the mind of any expectation of what is to come. Without expectation and protections, it is things that gather. The emptiness that gathers is to this extent the opposite of nihilistic annihilation that destroys things and obscures world with devastating technologies of war and the paradigm of all-pervasive pragmatic usefulness. It is at this moment of the conversation that Zhuangzian themes begin to emerge that will be sealed by the direct quotation in the conclusion.

The enactment of letting that Heidegger has in mind appears in the form of the useless and unnecessary. It is activity and willing that appear as and set the measure of the useful and necessary. Here there is an interpretive reversal against the instrumentalist paradigm that presupposes and invokes Wilhelm's translation of the *Zhuangzi*: "Only one who has learned to know the necessity of the unnecessary … " and "the unnecessary remains at all times the most necessary of all."[36]

5. Heidegger's Reliance on Richard Wilhelm's *Zhuangzi*

The denial of the *Zhuangzi*'s impact on Heidegger's thinking would be easier to make if Heidegger's language did not rely on idiosyncrasies in Wilhelm's translations. Wilhelm was a prolific translator. His editions of the Chinese classics were a crucial means for German readers of Heidegger's generation to access Chinese texts, including classical and religious Daoist sources. In addition to his translations of the *Book of Changes* and several Confucian classics, Wilhelm translated into German the *Liezi* 列子 and *The Secret* [or Mystery] *of the Golden Flower* (*Taiyi Jinhua Zongzhi* 太乙金華宗旨), a work of inner alchemy (*neidan* 內丹) meditative techniques that contains an introduction written by his friend Carl G. Jung.[37]

Despite Wilhelm's prolific quantity of translations and his Sinological expertise and authority, Heidegger explicitly addresses solely the *Laozi* and *Zhuangzi* texts and does not necessarily follow Wilhelm's translations and commentaries even as he is at points reacting to them. For example, Wilhelm rendered the title of his 1911 translation as *The Book of the Old Master on Sense and Life* (*Das Buch des alten Meisters vom Sinn und Leben*). *Daode* 道德 signifies for Wilhelm the "sense of life." Heidegger does not employ Wilhelm's life-philosophical translations of *dao* as sense or meaning (*Sinn*) and *de* 德 as life (*Leben*) or life-force (*Lebenskraft*). Nor would Heidegger accept the Kantian and life-philosophical conceptual registers that Wilhelm deploys to introduce the *Daodejing* and the *Zhuangzi* to German linguistic audiences. Wilhelm would portray the *Zhuangzi*, particularly chapter two, as a Chinese "critique of pure reason," contending that the paradoxes of chapter two constituted a critique of reason that refuted skepticism for the sake of life's unity.[38] This is partially appropriate insofar as the *Zhuangzi* text should be read as skeptically undermining Huizi's skepticism, akin to Wittgenstein's skeptical critique of dogmatic skepticism as presupposing language-games and forms and practices of life in his *On Certainty* (Wittgenstein 1969). However, a totalizing transperspectival unity and its view from nowhere are neither the only nor the best way to interpret this text. Zhuangzi is portrayed in it as a free shifting participant co-transitioning through conditions, discourses, perspectives, and worlds. He escapes the confines of the world by immanently and freely encountering the world in its variations and transformations. Thus, according to Guo Xiang's commentary, Zhuangzi's equalizing oneness is not a mere unity. It signifies how Zhuangzian freedom anarchically embraces each thing as singularly itself, self-ordering in its own way, and following its own generativity (*ziran*).

Relying on the ubiquitous system of classification of forms of philosophy during this period between naturalism, subjective idealism, and objective idealism, Wilhelm classified Zhuangzi's philosophy as a type of objective idealism that shared family resemblances with the discourses of Heraclitus and Spinoza and promoted a *Gelassenheit* not afflicted by life's suffering.[39] The *Zhuangzi*'s objective idealism accordingly offers an impersonal objective overview of the whole of existence in which all is equalized from the perspective of eternity (Wilhelm 1912: xiii). The balancing between heaven and earth is described as a condition that is still, tasteless, released; that is concentrated, empty, and not riveted to being and acting (Wilhelm 1912: 116).

It is worth noting that Wilhelm and Buber utilized the words *Gelassenheit* (as a condition of letting) and *lassen* (to let) in translations familiar to Heidegger. Buber could deploy Daoist terms of a non-indifferent and non-attached resonance with things in order to describe the I/thou relationship to God, in his 1923 work *I and Thou* (*Ich und Du*): the relationship, he writes, has a "*Gelassenheit* to all things and a sensibility that helps them" ("die Gelassenheit zu allen Dingen und die Berührung, die ihnen hilft").[40] "Helping things" is Buber's construal of Daoist nourishing things. Earlier German language authors described *dao* "as the primordial ground, the sustainer and nourisher of all things" (Rotermund 1874: 12). This facet of early Daoism is taken up into Heidegger's language of "safeguarding" and "healing."

There are numerous differences between Wilhelm and Heidegger. Wilhelm categorizes Zhuangzi's Daoism as a form of active immanent mysticism that embraces and unites with rather than flees from life and its forces. Pantheism and mysticism are modern Occidental homogenizing categories. Heidegger consistently rejected the adequacy of these concepts, even as some elements of his thinking, precisely those that have been examined with regard to Meister Eckhart and Daoism, were identified with them by various interpreters and critics.[41]

Heidegger expressed skepticism concerning such categorizations and the worldview philosophies that promoted them. Wilhelm specifies the fundamental thought of the *Zhuangzi* to be "sovereign freedom," in which the genuine person is at one with life in an active and this-worldly form of mysticism as opposed to its passive and other-worldly forms.[42] Zhuangzi is a this-worldly mystic in Wilhelm's depiction who uplifts by embracing life rather than sinking away from it in self-absorption. This indicates that the Daoist suspension of the self is world-affirming, as Klages claimed in his 1929 response to Nietzsche's critique of the renunciation of the will as necessarily entailing ascetic world-denial.[43]

There are significant departures between how Heidegger and Wilhelm construe basic Daoist words and concepts. Notwithstanding the clear conceptual differences between Wilhelm and Heidegger, their interpretations are entwined in Heidegger's reliance on Wilhelm's translations. Heidegger's semi-Daoist ways of speaking draw on Wilhelm's poetic expressions (as illustrated in Chapter 3). It is therefore worthwhile to trace Wilhelm's uses of uselessness and the "necessity of the unnecessary" to consider why Heidegger adopted his translation in this case.

In the 1945 "Evening Conversation," Heidegger does not refer to Wilhelm's translation of *wuyong zhiyong* 無用之用 from the concluding passage of chapter four (*Renjian shi* 人間世, which Wilhelm translates as "In der Menschenwelt" / "In the Human World") in the *Inner Chapters*.[44] Heidegger does not refer here to the concluding section of chapter one that he cites and discusses at length in the 1962 Comburg lecture "Transmitted Language and Technological Language." This lecture once more connects usefulness and uselessness to questions concerning language and things in the epoch of the technological world-picture, which obstructs the kinds of responsiveness and saying illustrated in the thought-images of the *Zhuangzi*.

The "Evening Conversation" refers to a different passage from Wilhelm's *Zhuangzi*. "Die Notwendigkeit des Unnötigen" is Wilhelm's title for the dialogue between Zhuangzi and his skeptical sophist friend Huizi in chapter 26 (*Waiwu* 外物 as "External Things"

[*Außendinge*]) of the *Miscellaneous Chapters*.⁴⁵ Wilhelm's expression "the necessity of the unnecessary" ("die Notwendigkeit des Unnötigen"), adopted by Heidegger, is a rendition of one possible meaning of the phrase in comparison with the more typically used terms of usefulness and uselessness. This dialogue in Wilhelm's rendition is cited in the conclusion of Heidegger's "Evening Conversation" without naming these two early Chinese philosophers. Bret Davis's translation into English states:

> The one said: "You are talking about the unnecessary."
> The other said: "A person must first have recognized the unnecessary before one can talk with him about the necessary. The earth is wide and large, and yet, in order to stand, the human needs only enough space to be able to put his foot down. But if directly next to his foot a crevice were to open up that dropped down into the underworld, then would the space where he stands still be of use to him?"
> The one said: "It would be of no more use to him."
> The other said: "From this the necessity of the unnecessary is clearly apparent."⁴⁶

It has been argued that Wilhelm's translation of *yong* as necessity is infelicitous. Even if this assessment is accepted, as it indicates one possible sense of this idea, given Wilhelm's hermeneutical situation, one could well ask what is the specific difference between the first expression from chapter four (*wuyong zhi yong* 無用之用) and the second from chapter 26 (*wuyong zhi wei yong* 無用之為用) and their contexts that led Wilhelm to translate one in terms of usefulness of uselessness and the other in terms of the necessity of the unnecessary? Why did Wilhelm mark a difference between these two expressions when most German and English translations do not? Both phrases are typically interpreted as the usefulness of the useless, while Wilhelm and Heidegger mark a difference and deploy both use and necessity. It still leaves the question of why Heidegger made the second expression the leitmotif of the "Evening Conversation."

6. Letting, Waiting, and Releasement

The unnecessary is explicitly juxtaposed with the instrumental and technical character of reason as *ratio* and modern rationality in this text, as well as with the Occidental essence of thinking that does not allow itself to wait and let.⁴⁷ Heidegger raises an issue that will be taken up in the "Letter on Humanism," as he reflects on "action" and its adequacy as a measure of the human with its presuppositions identifying reason as *ratio* and the human being as the rational animal. These constructions are inadequate to the human essence understood as the being that waits and remains attentive and responsive in that which they belong.

In the patience of waiting, Heidegger remarked, we (and we should consider who this "we" is) are the inlet or letting in (*Einlass*) for that which is coming: "We are in such a manner as though we were to first come to ourselves, in letting in [*einlassend*] the coming, as those who are themselves only by abandoning themselves—this, however, by means of waiting toward [*entgegenwarten*] the coming."⁴⁸ Playing on the German word for the present moment, *Gegenwart*, he interprets the word according to its two components: as a "present moment" (Gegenwart) understood in a verbal sense as a "waiting-toward" (gegen-warten).⁴⁹ The genuine present transpires as a pure waiting (warten) toward (gegen, which can mean "in the direction of" or "against") that which is to come. This pure (i.e., unnecessary and useless) waiting does not await something; it waits without anticipations, expectations, or that which is deemed necessary and useful.

What does patient waiting signify in this setting? Is this the emptied heart-mind that awaits things in emptiness of the *Zhuangzi*? Waiting is delineated elsewhere in Heidegger as essentially a letting. It is not a product of willing and acting, and the silent emptiness in which the echo can be heard (GA 81: 170). In waiting, in the third of the *Country Path Conversations*, we "let ourselves into, namely into that in which we belong"; namely, "by letting things rest in their own repose," which occurs in an emptiness that cannot be filled.⁵⁰ This letting things be themselves in their releasement occurs through emptiness and signifies an anarchic freedom: "Freedom rests in being able to let [*Lassenkönnen*], not in ordering and dominating."⁵¹ Discarding restrictive ways of controlling and ordering things and allowing them to pursue their own course is a fundamentally Zhuangzian point that other contemporary readers construed along anarchistic and libertarian lines. These modern adaptations are possible because Daoist freedom does not belong to the monadic self, nor is it the command and will of the subject, which better define power. Genuine freedom arises in worldly relations with others and things in which they have room for their own freedom. Heidegger adopts Daoist freedom to an extent in his own conception of freedom as a return to one's own self-essencing: freedom toward oneself and the open groundless ground that has no fixed foundations.⁵²

It has been argued that Heidegger's sense of letting here might have inspirational sources in Meister Eckhart, Böhme, and Schelling, without any need to mention Laozi or Zhuangzi.⁵³ However, we might recall Wilhelm's interpretation of the *Zhuangzi* as teaching a sovereign freedom and *Gelassenheit* amidst life. Moreover, it is Heidegger who evokes and employs Daoist thought-images throughout this text. Heidegger's direct references and his circumlocutions prompt the question of the extent to which he appropriated a range of Daoist concepts from the editions of Buber and Wilhelm. These include *wuwei* (which is linked with letting and waiting in Chinese and German sources), *ziran* (as a non-instrumentalized naturalness happening in and for itself), and the wandering freedom and releasement of things. Does it vindicate speaking of a "Daoist turn" in Heidegger or more modestly of transformative Lao-Zhuang traces and spurs that are marked, for example, in the alteration of tone and semantic content between the 1939–1941 (GA 96) and the 1942–1948 (GA 97) *Black Notebooks*? The language of waiting, letting, and *Gelassenheit* barely appears in the former text that is ensnared in geopolitical issues of will, power, and conflict. It plays an increasingly notable role in the latter, as the will becomes the counter-image rather than the expression and work of *phúsis*, indicating an adjustment in his thinking that correlates with his intensified attention to Laozi and Zhuangzi.

7. The Unnecessary, the Useless, and an Unnecessary and Useless People

It is striking that Heidegger has his two interlocutors intriguingly rejecting the notion of nations and nationalisms in the "Evening Conversation," including what he deems its internationalized form. In the context of rejecting nationalism, the concluding pages articulate how the German people, a "useless," "unnecessary" people, must learn the necessity of the unnecessary and become a people of pure waiting, letting and releasing things precisely in order to release themselves. Human letting is only possible because of being's letting be of things: "We learn letting go only in the letting be of being" (GA 97: 153). In the Daoist context, *ziran* is the condition of *wuwei*.

Heidegger's deployment of *Gelassenheit* reverberates with the word's linguistic heritage from Eckhart through Schelling.[54] Still, Heidegger states that his thinking of releasement is not akin to Eckhart's turning away from the sinful earthly will to the divine will.[55] His releasement does not concern, as Böhme portrays, the worldly detachment of *Gelassenheit*, suspending the sinful selfness (*Selbstheit*) and temptations of earthly temporal things that hinder the soul's intimacy with the eternal and divine (Böhme 1732: 50, 123). This difference intersects with the *Zhuangzi* in which there is no suspension of the self's will for a divine will nor the condemnation of creatures as sinful and evil (Böhme 1732: 115). The thing is dependent on its own self-generative co-creative ways of being rather than divine creation or idealist projection. The unfettered self can transition through restrictive one-dimensional perspectives and shift with the myriad things following their own self-naturing.

Heidegger's letting releasement occurs much more along the lines of the German reception of the *Zhuangzi* and its sense of liberation as precisely being in and with the world, and nourishing, safeguarding, and healing the life of things. It is in this sense an *ethos* instead of a mystical state. "Nourishing life" (*yangsheng* 養生) in the *Zhuangzi* can be interpreted in relation to immanently cultivating life and therapeutically healing life from what afflicts it. This resonates in Heidegger's description in the third *Country Path Conversation* of the letting and waiting that heals and nurtures.[56] Letting releases both things and humans into that which heals (*das Heilsame*). In this passage, healing is called for in answer to an affliction: it is a way for a people that had been misled by "false leaders" and their aims posited as "necessary" and is confronted by its own uselessness and unnecessariness.

Heidegger accordingly has reasons for speaking of the necessity of the unnecessary. First, it appears that for Heidegger, the useful is identifiable with the necessary according to the instrumental paradigm that equates the two, and which is challenged by the unnecessary that promises a unique way of dwelling and modality of being. Secondly, the expressions *das Notwendige* and *die Notwendigkeit* do not signify the necessary as that which must be the case or the compulsion of logical implication, although it does signify a fateful compulsion (GA 77: 237–8).

The necessary in Heidegger's reflections is what is urgent and needful (*nötig*) in answering distress in a situation of need and emergency (*Not*). It is the unnecessary that responds to this situation of needfulness, "learning to know the need [*Not*] in which everywhere the unnecessary [*das Unnötige*] must still persevere."[57] It would be dubious to project Heidegger's elucidation of necessity onto Wilhelm's initial rendering. Still, it appears that his translation also presupposes a wider field of meanings for "necessity" (i.e., the Chinese word *yong* and the German word *Notwendigkeit*) than a form of logical compulsion.

Heidegger's "Evening Conversation" ends with the confirmation of its Zhuangzian context by explicitly quoting chapter 26 of the *Zhuangzi* in which Huizi and Zhuangzi debate the meanings of the necessary and unnecessary (useful and useless), a conversation that has reverberated throughout the conversation of the old and young men imprisoned in a Soviet prisoner of war camp. It is evident in this conversation that Heidegger did not appropriate Daoism to legitimate or excuse National Socialism, but rather to confront what he now considered its destructive malice that had left desolation and ruins in its wake.

Heidegger's historically delimited confrontations with the destructiveness of National Socialism, and his own initial complicity, take place here and in other postwar reflections, as in his personal reflections of the *Black Notebooks* published in GA 98. These criticisms refer to the history of being and technological modernity in which Weimar and Nazi-era fears of a chaotic and fallen public sphere and communist threat have been substituted with suspicions that democracy operates as another more masked form of technological domination without perceiving its formally indicative self-organizing propensities. There are multifarious problems with dysfunctional and systematically distorted existing democracies. Heidegger, to briefly contemplate his political thought, failed to sufficiently consider the normative and critical functions of the public and private realms, elementary republics and democratic participation, and personal rights, points incisively articulated by Arendt, no doubt with her former teacher in mind (Arendt 1976; Arendt 2018). Heidegger's later political reflections express missed opportunities for a more genuine confrontation with his own past and questions of freedom and authority. They do not refer to the anarchic spontaneity and self-organizing tendencies of Daoist political discourses that fascinated Buber in his 1924 Ascona lectures on the *Daodejing*.[58] Nor do they ponder Arendt's powerful analyses of an irreducibly plural and unrestricted public sphere, civil society, and democratic participation with guaranteed rights safeguarding individual, interpersonal, and interbodily life; nor do they consider—to use Habermas's language—the colonization of the lifeworld and public sphere by the systems of the state and the market.[59]

III. Heidegger and the German Reception of the *Zhuangzi*

8. Uselessness, Saying, and the Very Sense of Things

The *Zhuangzi* was enthusiastically received during the Weimar Republic due to its spirit of freedom, breaking barriers, naturalness, and transformation. Heidegger's continuing attentiveness to the *Zhuangzi* is revealed in his later lectures held in Bremen in 1960 (already discussed above) and Comburg in 1962. Each addresses topics at the heart of his later thinking: of twisting free from technological enframing to genuinely encounter images, words, and the thing in its openness, mystery, and self-thingness.

Heidegger returned to the *Zhuangzi* and the problematic of usefulness and uselessness in a lecture given on July 18, 1962, on "Transmitted Language and Technological Language." In this discussion of learning, the limits of language, and the appropriate words for things, Heidegger quotes at length Wilhelm's translation of "The Useless Tree" (*Der unnütze Baum*) containing the conversation between Zhuangzi and Huizi that concludes chapter one of the *Zhuangzi*. Heidegger cited the entirety of Wilhelm's translation of the passage that is included with the Chinese text in the endnote; it also reappears as a whole in a discussion of philosophy vis-à-vis poetic thinking in the first volume of Jean Beaufret's *Dialogue with Heidegger*.[60] It is clear in Beaufret that this passage of the *Zhuangzi* is indicative and thought-provoking for thinking, even if distinct from the restraints of philosophy as seen in Plato's systematic conceptualizing of being (Beaufret 1968: 15). The image of Zhuangzi's useless tree appears in other writings of Heidegger, such as his late 1950s discussion of letting as an originary doing and saying as a letting shine forth of the self-concealing clearing (GA 101: 47).

Why might have Heidegger concentrated his attention on this passage? Given the criticisms his philosophy of being received, Heidegger might well have identified with Huizi's accusation against Zhuangzi of using fantastic, grandiose, and useless words, and responding with indications transgressing the limits of the useful. Heidegger appeals to the *Zhuangzi*, as mediated by Wilhelm's translation, to diagnose the modern administrative technological epoch, and to ponder possibilities of reawakening a sense of speaking with and encountering things through a form of meditative reflection (*Besinnung*) that involves awakening a sensibility for the useless.[61]

Directly prior to quoting the *Zhuangzi*, Heidegger introduces the necessity of uselessness that is found in the very sense of things. He describes this sense of the useless as the most necessary and needful (*das Nötigste*) for encountering "the sense of things" (*der Sinn der Dinge*) and as constituting the very sense and usefulness of the useful (*das Nützliche*).[62] The sense of things as things is presupposed and obscured by the instrumentalization of things. It is the pivot and point of departure for genuine saying and thinking that moves toward the things that address and lay claim to them. Zhuangzi's way of "being-with" stands open to encountering the gourd, the tree, or the fish in their uselessness and playfulness outside of "anthropological" (i.e., anthropocentric) usefulness.

The repeated conversations between Huizi and Zhuangzi about uselessness, which encompass gourds and trees, reveal in Heidegger's portrayal the precariousness of the inversion that makes the useful the measure of usefulness, as it is under the dominion of the modern technological world-picture. This imposition of the measure of the useful misses the determining power of the useless, which is not made and out of which nothing can be made, as it is "the sense of things" disclosing themselves (GA 80.2: 1177).

Heeding the thing's own sense shifts the perspective from anthropological instrumentality to the barely heard thing. It is not incidental that Heidegger recognizes uselessness and the "useless" sense-forming thing itself as the locus of sense. This thread runs throughout Heidegger's engagement with early Daoist sources and his own later ziranist-inflected thinking of the thing. Heidegger deploys this Zhuangzian-inspired conception of the useless sense of things, correlating uselessness (*wuyong*) with self-so-ness (*ziran*, inadequately translated into and conceived in English as "nature"). He does so to counter the instrumentalist reduction of things to technique and a pedagogy aiming at the reduction of language to information, and to challenge the mastery and calculation of things as useful, and the compulsion to achieve successful pragmatic results according to the restrictive parameters of what counts as success. Learning is, however, not imposing a measure of use on those who learn and their objects of study; it is attending to the unspoken measure in things themselves.

Heidegger construes learning along the lines of *wuwei* as a non-coercive "letting be learned" (*lernenlassen*). Letting be learned emerges through "transmitted language" that is too often dismissed as merely natural prescientific ways of speaking. Nonetheless, transmitted language is the language of quotidian life and encountering and dwelling with others and things. To lose this contact and relationship with things is to lose what it is to be essentially human as a worldly being. The "essentially human" does not signify for Heidegger the anthropocentric and humanistic separation of the human from the world, which he interrogated in the semi-Daoistic-inflected "Letter on Humanism." It is a dwelling with and being in the thick of the life of things.

A nontechnically reduced and impoverished language—as illustrated in poetic saying and thinking, which the sayings attributed to Laozi and Zhuangzi express in thought-images and turning phrases—happens as spoken and unspoken saying. Saying is a showing and letting-appear of what is present and absent, of reality in the widest sense.[63] Such saying does not obscure things and hide world, as technical language does in its pursuit of the domination of nature and the mastery of things as merely "useful" and "useless."[64] Contesting the self-alienating and self-destructive domination of things is insufficient if it does not entail cultivating an ethics and culture of responsive co-appropriating and collaborating with others, things, and places.

Saying stays open to encountering what is unsaid and unsayable: "the nearness of the unspoken and unspeakable."[65] This wording reformulates Heidegger's remark regarding Laozi in *On the Way to Language*: "the mystery of mysteries of thoughtful saying conceals itself in the word 'way,' *dao*, if only we will let these names return to what they leave unspoken, if only we are capable of this, to allow them to do so."[66] Heidegger's refusal of pragmatist and technocratic forms of confining and impoverishing ways of speaking and thinking in this short lecture draws on the *Zhuangzi*. It remains still too pertinent in the current danger of the ecological devastation of earth and living and nonliving things.

9. The Hermeneutical Situation of Heidegger's Zhuangzi

The *Zhuangzi* plays an intriguing role in Heidegger's thinking in the texts "Image and Word" and "Transmitted Language and Technological Language," even if it is insufficient to speak of a Daoist turn to characterize Heidegger's later thinking. These two texts reintroduce once again the thematic of uselessness and the sense of things that steps beyond Heidegger's Occidental sources of Meister Eckhart, Schelling, and Hölderlin.[67] The intrinsic "self-so-ing" sense of things is a Zhuangzian perspectival shift: not only phenomenologically showing themselves from themselves but being themselves. In addition, for comparative and intercultural philosophers of contemporary thought, there are partial family resemblances between tendencies in both discourses, and Heidegger has a significant role both in the contemporary Occidental and East Asian philosophical reception of Lao-Zhuang discourses.

We have seen in the previous section how Heidegger is concerned in this lecture with a learning that undoes linguistic and conceptual fixations and allows for encountering things themselves in their uselessness and their own significance. Zhuangzi and Heidegger are not merely critics of linguistic reification; they illuminate destructuring therapeutic strategies for unfixing the fixated construction and experience of thing and world.[68] Heidegger could accordingly uncover in this ancient text teachings that resonated with his own thinking, that endeavored to unfix and loosen the modern administrative technological framework for the sake of freely dwelling in the thick of things and abiding amidst the world.

Heidegger's appropriative encounter and reimagining of this Chinese text, relying on the editions of Buber and Wilhelm, occurred in a historical situation of an increasing attentiveness to the *Zhuangzi* and other East Asian sources. The writer Hermann Hesse, who praised the translations of the *Zhuangzi* of both Buber and Wilhelm, wrote of Wilhelm's edition in 1912: "Zhuangzi is the greatest and most brilliant poet among Chinese thinkers" and "Of all the books of Chinese thinkers that I know, the *Zhuangzi* has the most appeal and melody."[69]

It is worth noting that the appreciation of the *Zhuangzi* expressed in Buber, Heidegger, and Georg Misch was not universal among Heidegger's philosophical community. Karl Jaspers, in his postwar work on the "great philosophers" that encompasses Confucius, the Buddha, Laozi, and Nāgārjuna, does not focus on the point of the *Zhuangzi*'s playful placing into question of fixations, its linguistic strategies of liberating human dispositions that offer a radical model of the existential openness of communication that Jaspers endeavors to articulate. Instead, he claims (no doubt because of the apparently disrespectful treatment of Confucius): "The atmosphere in [Laozi] is peaceful; in [Zhuangzi] it is polemical, full of arrogance, mockery, contempt."[70]

Among Heidegger's philosophical contemporaries, two appear especially relevant. Although figures like Klages engaged the *Daodejing* in ways that Heidegger might have registered given his repeated dismissive references to his 1929 work, Buber and Misch have the most extensive and productive philosophical relation with the *Zhuangzi*. Buber translated and commented on the work as discussed previously above. Buber also extensively engaged with the *Daodejing* in ways that influenced the I-it and I-thou encounters (in those moments when stones, trees, and cats break through their mere "it-ness") and relationships of *I and Thou*.[71] Further, Buber was the only one of these philosophers to engage with the magical and preternatural forms of Daoism that he perceived to be operative in popular literature, such as the *Strange Tales from a Chinese Studio* (*Liaozhai zhiyi* 聊齋誌異) of the Qing era author Pu Songling 蒲松齡 (1640–1715) which he translated from English into German in 1911 as *Chinese Ghost and Love Stories*.[72] Just as Hasidic stories reflected its religiosity for Buber, these stories reflected the interpenetration of the material and spiritual worlds.

10. Heidegger, Misch, and the Question of Occidental Philosophy

At this point, to conclude this chapter with an additional historical clue, it is important to emphasize that another compelling approach to the multiplicity of philosophy was available during the Weimar Republic. Heidegger and Husserl were reacting against this discourse when they insisted in the 1930s that philosophy is and can only be Greek-

European. Misch is best known as the student, son-in-law, and editor of the collected works of the hermeneutical life-philosopher Wilhelm Dilthey. He is furthermore an underappreciated yet significant early twentieth-century intercultural philosopher, revealing in his underrecognized 1926 work *The Way into Philosophy* (*Der Weg in die Philosophie*) how the *Zhuangzi*, in "Autumn Floods" among other chapters, not only gestures at but radically enacts the interruptive breakdown of one's own limited fixed viewpoint and "breakthrough" (*Durchbruch*)—from the everyday pre-reflective natural attitude—that characterizes philosophy and the multiplicity of its origins in diverse cultural milieus.

Misch equates the autumn floods, in which the great river recognizes its own smallness, and the barriers and fixations of its limited self-conception are dismantled by entering the sea that signifies the infinite, with Plato's allegory of the cave as narratives of philosophical transformation. Occidental philosophy is confronted with its limited self-conception in entering the great sea of questioning and self-reflection. Misch only contemplates three passages from the *Zhuangzi*: autumn floods in chapter seventeen, the fasting of the heart-mind in chapter four, and the paradox of categories on beginning and not beginning, being and nonbeing, and this and that in the second chapter on equalizing things. Notwithstanding his problematic characterization of Zhuangzi as a pantheistic mystic, a category that privileges homogenizing identity and Occidental religiosity, Misch recognizes and embraces the philosophical significance of the *Zhuangzi*. His broader conclusion is that the variety of arguments, dialogues, and illustrative stories expressed in the *Zhuangzi* are indicative of a radical self-reflective breakthrough and can therefore be considered genuinely philosophical.

Misch's point in this work is that philosophy as critical self-reflection (*Selbst-Besinnung*) on life and its senses has multiple origins and transmissions, of which Occidental metaphysics and science are only one historical configuration. Husserl and Heidegger's denial of such a claim gives the impression of having Misch's thesis in mind when they contend that philosophy as science (Husserl in the *Crisis*) or as metaphysics (Heidegger in *Identity and Difference* and *What Is Called Thinking?*) is intrinsically Greek-Occidental.[73] Husserl and Heidegger made, in essence, the same statement and meant it in two different ways. While Husserl praised the Buddha in the 1920s as coming close to Socrates and philosophy, Buddhism lacked in his view the universal systematic scientific character that could free it from myth. Ernst Cassirer likewise in *The Philosophy of Symbolic Forms*, in contrast to Misch's insight into original self-reflection, construed Buddhism and Daoism as opposed varieties of myth and mysticism, one negating and the other embracing temporality (Cassirer 1955: 124–6). Heidegger also did not incorporate them into the category of philosophy.[74] But he did increasingly contest this narrow category with a poetic thinking that could potentially interact with—in respectful reserve—a greater variety of teachings.

Heidegger's analysis of the Occidental formation of philosophy has a critical point, as the history and legacy of philosophy as metaphysics and onto-theology is to be confronted and contested rather than embraced. Further, he mentions how ancient Chinese or Aztec thought are not engaged with as matters to be thought through mindful questioning but only as objects of universal world-historical comparative representation (GA 8: 169–70). As early as 1926 Heidegger articulated the kind of suspicions about Orientalist enthusiasm for Eastern philosophy and occultism as a reflection of one's own spiritual impoverishment that would inform his subsequent doubts about the Occidental adaptation of Zen Buddhism and Eastern world-experiences (GA 16: 50, 679). Nevertheless, despite his own extensive reading of and familiarity with East Asian sources, Heidegger hesitates to take the next step of more genuinely and thoroughly engaging them precisely as matters to be questioned and thought while retaining the reserve and respect owed to different configurations and modalities of thinking.

This occurs in a historically mediated nexus. We can articulate from the philosophical engagements of Buber and Misch, the translations of Buber and Wilhelm, and their contexts a sense of the rich and complex reception of the *Zhuangzi* in early twentieth-century intercultural discourses in German speaking countries from which Heidegger's Daoist-inspired reflections draw.[75]

Heidegger's ziranist-informed turning in the mid- and late 1940s transpires in the crisis conditions of National Socialism, the German defeat, and the administrative-technocratic regime of the necessity of the useful that increasingly characterizes modernity. This Zhuangzian turning to that which is useless and unnecessary opened alternative possibilities and retrievals in Heidegger's thinking in the postwar period. Let us consider further in the next chapter what roles they played in Heidegger's endeavors to elucidate an appropriate manner of being-in-the-world and *ethos* of dwelling in confrontation with the mechanisms of the enframing positioning of persons and things as raw materials. This is instituted under the sway of administrative technological modernity that systematically reproduces damaged life.[76] Stepping beyond Heidegger, the transformation of ethical and poetic dwelling also needs participatory public realms and pluralistic political processes—the spontaneity of which philosophers and theorists can at best only anticipate and not conceptually dictate—if we are to confront our contemporary social-ecological predicament more appropriately.

5

Heidegger's Dao amidst Thing and World

I. The Way and the Releasement of Things

1. Heidegger's Dao

Heidegger's multifaceted journey guided him—via in part his mediated encounter with the "ziranist" sources the *Daodejing* and *Zhuangzi*—to defining the openness and mystery of the self-essencing (the thinging and worlding) of thing and world.[1] Heidegger's emergent prioritization of the thing in the mid- and late 1940s is informed to an extent (as shown in the previous chapters) by his interaction with *ziran*-oriented Daoist texts in translation that he directly mentions and indirectly uses and evokes. Heidegger's proximity to the idea of acting from responsive attunement (*wei wuwei*) in emptiness, simplicity, and stillness with the thing in its ongoing transforming (*hua*) and self-so-naturing is intimated in several of his expressions and discursive strategies. His pathway toward the thing is opened in a formalizing and emptying that allows oneself to be addressed by the thing in its own ways of being. This ziranist moment intersects with his later more robust manner of addressing the thing's life on its own terms.

The subject is reconceived as being-there and being-in-the-world in Heidegger's early philosophy. It remains ensnared (as Adorno and Heidegger himself perceived) in constitutive idealism and transcendental philosophy, which it struggles yet arguably fails to overcome, according to his later self-critiques.[2] It is only radically transformed in the recognition of what can be elucidated as the "other-constitution," occurring through things and world that Heidegger articulated in the 1949 *Bremen Lectures* and other works. Heidegger's engagement with translated ziranist texts, in conjunction with early Pre-Socratic Greek thinking and the poet of poets Hölderlin, offers one documented source and conceivably the best explanation for this dramatic shift toward recognizing the mystery, namelessness, and irreducibility of things as they are in and of themselves and, further, toward sensing their own priority, which—a prospect Heidegger observed in the *Zhuangzi*—liberates them from the constructed artificial necessity of pragmatic usefulness. Given this context, Heidegger can well be said to intimate an *ethos* (thought more originally as a way of worldly dwelling and formative way-making) and a *dao* of responsive releasement and attunement with things and the environing worlds, moments, and places that they form.

It would be an overstatement to portray Heidegger's thinking as a variety of Daoism. Still, it is without doubt "wayist" in a European form in giving priority to the way instead of to a rigid structure or content. This thinking of way and its movements evokes and is at times entangled with Daoist and Chinese conceptions of *dao*, while being distinct from them. This intertwinement has notable consequences for how Heidegger's philosophical wayfaring is to be understood. The present chapter outlines a ziranist elucidation of Heidegger's philosophy or, more modestly stated, its "ziranist" dimension, expressed in at least one albeit not all corners of his thought. The initial sections of this chapter will draw further conclusions about the Daoist background of Heidegger's thinking of the way, releasement, and the thing. The later sections of the chapter examine how this interpretive situation informs his later reflections on *ethos*, action, habitation, and letting.

2. Heidegger's Thinking of the Way

Heidegger is known as the philosopher of being who relentlessly pursued this one question throughout his life's work. His philosophical pathway is, nonetheless, characterized less by the question of being, the constitution of meaning, truth as unconcealment, or the appropriating event of being, than it is by the question of the way.[3] These guiding words are repeatedly reconstituted by Heidegger along his pathway. More noteworthy, according to Heidegger, is the way, being underway, following darkened forest and meandering country paths, making one's way by being and going underway (GA 98: 390; GA 100: 41), and consequently the question and changing locus of the happening of the event on the way: human existence as Dasein, nothingness, being, thing, and saying word. The appropriative or enowning event (*Ereignis*) as *er-eignen* does not signify making its own as in owning, mastering, and taking possession; it means, on the contrary, if interpreted according to early Daoist experiences of *ziran*, the becoming its own, the self-essencing, and the self-naturing of the matter itself: being (*Sein*) in its historical concealments and manifestations.[4] What do essence and event mean in Heidegger's discourse? Essencing (*Wesen*) does not signify *quidditas*, whatness, and identity: it refers to verbally understood presencing, worldliness, and the whiling of the while in which space and time are referred back to the nexus of moment and place.[5] In the 1930s Heidegger elaborated the being-historical (*Seinsgeschichtliche*) thinking of the appropriating or enowning ontological happening (*er-eignen*) of being, that is, being in its self-ownness, as an attempt to think the letting of being in which being essences as itself and time names the unconcealing self-essencing of being.[6]

Taken by themselves, without their own relational and verbal specificity in his discourse, "being" and "meaning" are stagnant ways to interpret Heidegger's thought. Being, Heidegger notes, is always "being *of*" (in the sense of the double genitive); beings are always "beings *as*" (GA 98: 193). The "of" and "as" are encountered through the way. Heidegger repeatedly stated that his collected works should be defined as ways rather than works. Expressions such as "way" and "being under way" are not merely rhetorical. They indicate a philosophical method (if taken in a wide sense not limited to technique). Heidegger's critique of method emerged from his reflections on it as he sought a "method," which would not be limited to method as technique and would open concrete singular phenomena instead of obfuscating them. This was the case from his early confrontations with Husserl's categorical intuition and Dilthey's interpretive understanding, his articulation of formal indication and destructuring in the 1920s, to his later conception of thinking as way.

In his previously unpublished reflections from 1952 to 1957 (GA 100), he recurrently returns to the priority and significance of the way for his thinking of being and mortal human existence. Heidegger proposes that the minimal demand of thinking is to persist on the selfsame (*selben*) way without remaining in the identically same (*gleichen*) place.[7] As the *Zhuangzi* portrays shifting through myriad perspectives without fixating on one perspective, and freely wandering without one final purposive goal, Heidegger's way is similarly a wandering through field and forest without a prearranged goal or teleological purpose (GA 100: 169, 208). Heidegger elucidates thinking as traversing a course without being trapped in one location. The selfsame can be understood as the self-occurring way in contrast to the repetition of the identical that would occur without movement, individuation, and difference (GA 100: 9). The step back from thinking as representation to thinking as moving-way (*be-wegen*, an expression he deployed earlier to explicate Laozi's "reversal" [*fan*] as the way's movement) is designated in one reflection as the summation of his thinking: it steps back, not to a previous thinking that once was but to where thinking sojourns and abides (GA 98: 57).

Heidegger defines his way as one of preliminary "preparatory thinking" (GA 100: 12). This way does not signify "the way," echoing the statement that the posited fixated way is not the way, in *Daodejing* 1, but a movement underway and a forming of the way.[8] Preparatory thinking does not posit a beginning or project a conclusion. It arises within the movement of the way back ("Be-Wegung des Rückweges"), a way back that encompasses (among other elements) hearing and hearkening to stillness, the unsayable that is the basis of saying, and responding in a saying moved by the releasement into stillness (GA 100: 12–13, 30, 32). The Daoist connection between emptying and safeguarding and stillness and movement in Heidegger's thought is confirmed in his references to *Daodejing* 15 in several letters that accentuate a disposition of gentle reserve and stillness in activity and movement (Hsiao 1987: 103; GA 16: 618; Petzet 1986: 58).

Emptying the heart-mind, reverting to stillness, and allowing the world to gather and depart are well-known Lao-Zhuang thought-images. Returning to the releasing freedom of stillness occupies a key role in Heidegger's postwar reflections, as he describes genuine thinking as an ear for and hearkening toward the stillness of the world in which hearing attends to the gathering of the unpretentious and humble voices of earth and thing (GA 98: 18–19). There is a sounding with the ground-tone of things in the voicing of silent stillness, and a gathering in the stilling of stillness (GA 97: 347, 354–5). This silent stillness is said to speak as saying responds to its addressing claim. The way back and the reversal are not then toward a proximate or first cause, a static content, or a set origin, as in the "philosophy of origins" (*Ursprungsphilosophie*), whether that origin is being or meaning, attributed to Heidegger.

The returning back movement in Heidegger's meditations is a moving toward the source rather than to that which is past. Heidegger's reversing movement and stepping back on the path toward being parallels reversal (*fan*) as the movement of *dao*, which he himself interrelated, as examined in Chapter 3. This source is depicted as a Daoist-like empty stillness and darkness wherein things gather world, are heard, and answered in saying (GA 98: 404). Heidegger relies on a Daoist-informed register when the origin is defined not only as abyssal and groundless (a vocabulary derived from German mysticism and Schelling) but as still, simple, mysterious, empty, and dark and calling for responsive worldly attunement. These are expressions extended throughout the *Daodejing*, the *Zhuangzi*, and Heidegger's late- and postwar reflections.

Two distinct elements can therefore be disentangled in Heidegger's articulation of stepping and moving back. First, the "way back" through the epochs of being and its history signifies a confrontation with Pre-Socratic thinking and the history of Occidental metaphysics. Yet, thought of as "reversing movement," the language deployed here is also entangled with his reading of the way (*dao*) as a way of reversal (*fan*) in the *Daodejing*. This way back, doubling back, and returning movement, as when one reaches a dead end on a path, is directed toward truth in its own reserved hiddenness (GA 100: 14). The originary ontological event of truth is its own self-occurring concealing-unconcealing, prior to *légein*, *lógos*, and representational cognition. Thinking is a preparation for the disclosure of truth rather than dogmatically positing it. The happening of truth, amidst which we can encounter and think truth, calls for responsive hearkening and respectful reticence to it *as* truth. Philosophy should become more poetic, not by writing poetry but by enacting this responsiveness in its own way and thus becoming a thinking of the thing and matter to be thought.

As thinking is a moving underway, it is essentially preliminary, preparatory. As it arrives at dead ends and turns that require tracking back, thinking is inexorably confronted by the need for self-critique and sincerity amidst transformation. The question of being is itself a preliminary, preparatory questioning and movement in the course of this questioning (GA 100: 60). Heidegger states accordingly that his way of thinking has been misunderstood insofar as (1) his thinking attempts to be provisional in each place and time and (2) originary self-criticism is anchored in the recognition of the provisional character of thinking.[9] His path of thinking is not systematic and not a metaphysical system of being that is necessarily a repetition of the forgetting of being. It is a course of questioning (GA 100: 56).

The ways of thinking and questioning are indeterminate in the sense of being free and unfixed. They are not arbitrary. Thinking and conversation, possibly as glimpsed in the conversations between Huizi and Zhuangzi, call for setting out and going on a path, without any preordained measure or criteria that would keep one secure from journeying on byways, deserted solitary pathways, and ways that lead seemingly nowhere (GA 100: 190). These useless paths, however, are places in which truth becomes recognized, in contrast to the disciplinary paradigm of useful results in which movement and journeying in truth and error are precluded and thoughtful dialogical conversation cannot even begin. Encountering truth, which transpires as un-concealment and un-error, necessitates encountering concealment and error from which mindful thinking can begin to ponder and question not only others but more fundamentally itself. Genuine thoughtful reflection (*Besinnung*) is consequently therapeutic self-critique as a step that releases the next step underway:

Every thoughtful criticism of what has already been thought is self-criticism. It concerns not only what precedes it but a way-formative mindful reflection that is underway: the endeavor to indwell in the unsaid of the joining.[10]

Originary thinking is a letting be learned (GA 98: 395). It does not dictate but follows the course of the questioning to thinking that which is to be thought: the matters and things of themselves. These matters and things are no longer merely the correlates of the intentional consciousness analyzed in classical phenomenology. They are to be addressed with reserve as appearing and speaking from their own self-essencing. Heidegger's mature thinking preserves a phenomenological moment that has been transformed into a ziranist thinking directed toward the primacy of the thing in its own self-naturing. This self-naturing is not a conceptual definition of the thing. Nor should it be construed as a natural determination or a sole determination if these are interpreted as a form of natural necessity that negates the thing's freedom and mystery.[11] Self-naturing signals openness and responsiveness toward the question-worthy mystery of the thing. It is the thing that calls forth practices of observation, listening, mindful reflection, and releasement.

Releasement has become a way of being open to entities and the world in Heidegger, indicating an affinity with Daoist discourses that confirm *ziran* as the archetypal model of *dao*, as expressed in the conclusion of *Daodejing* chapter 25: *dao* models its self-generative ownness or self-so-ing (*dao fa ziran* 道法自然). Such releasement into "naturalness" does not consist of a state of ecstatic mystical absorption or a self-absorbed calm serenity of mind. Entering into stillness and releasing things concerns a comportment enacted and lived in being-in-the-world, in the thick of and in reply to them. As in his Daoist sources, releasement is above all a reserved reverent resonance with things in the fourfold. Heidegger clarifies accordingly how it is an intra-worldly preparation in and for the encounter, and that which presents itself in the encounter and its "transcendence" is directed toward enregioning entities and interfolding earth and sky rather than toward what is beyond or outside of them. Releasement is not a form of explanation at all; nor is it a search for either proximate or first causes such as God (GA 100: 83). It is, in affinity with *wuwei*, a way of being disposed toward, attuned with, and having a "sense for" thing and world.

3. The *Daodejing*'s Darkness and the *Zhuangzi*'s Errancy

An orienting attunement does not determine the path or its destination. It has no predetermined and fixed purpose or goal. As the way is preliminary, preparatory, and formed in its very movement, thinking cannot predict or avoid the myriad "detour paths, side-paths, wrong paths, forest paths, field paths" it takes as part of its journey.[12] Errancy (*Irre*) and reversal are not only elements of movement. They are, as he argued in the 1930 Daoist-influenced "The Essence of Truth," elements of concealing/unconcealing truth itself.[13]

Heidegger stated in the 1960s that this lecture was the decisive expression of his later thinking that in fact aims at what is earliest (GA 102: 94). The recently published 1930 lecture version directly and indirectly engages with Daoist thought-images.

Quoting a favorite passage from *Daodejing* 28 concerning concealment, darkness, and mystery, Heidegger directly proceeds to analyze how human existence already stands in errancy (GA 80.1: 397). This passage, no longer preceded by any direct reference to the *Daodejing* in its final published version, is frequently quoted and examined in literature regarding Heidegger without any inkling of its initial Daoist-informed context (GA 9: 196). Errancy is not simply an accidental defect. It is determinate for the constitution of historical existence itself, as people are driven away from the mystery to what appears usefully practicable (*Gangbaren*), and it recurrently forgets and misses itself within the twists and turns of what appears immediately given and available. Truth does not characteristically essence as itself in insistent and unreceptive human existence, as it operates in forgetfulness, and the question arises: how then can existence, if at all, prepare for and enter into the essencing of truth?

Freedom is the essencing of truth unconcealed in the letting of being.[14] The freedom of the essencing of truth consists of an expanding receptiveness to mystery: "knowing lightness, one wraps oneself in darkness" (GA 80.1: 396–7). *Geheimnis* (mystery, secret), as delineated in earlier chapters, is a common German translation of *xuan* (mystery). Its Daoist dimension in Heidegger occurs not only in the 1930 lecture on truth but in his later reflections on mystery and letting releasement. Heidegger's shifts through constitutive concealment and errancy can be given a ziranist interpretation. His reflections on the un-essencing to the essencing of truth in expansive receptivity, openness, and the letting of being appears as if it were a commentary on the *Daodejing*'s twofold mystery, in which un-essencing and essencing are forms of self-essencing, and concealment and unconcealment are forms of truth.

There is a two fold functioning of the un-essencing of truth in the 1930 lecture. Human existence is confronted with and called to truth from within this fundamental constitutive: (1) concealment (hiddenness) and (2) errancy that arises within it. Truth is in essence the opposite of untruth and error that is to be constantly excised, in Occidental thought. As in the *Zhuangzi*, the supposed great way (*dadao* 大道) is not a way at all as the byway discloses the genuine great way. As indicated in the dialogues and stories of the *Zhuangzi* translated by Buber and Wilhelm, the claim to truth of one perspective and position proves itself to be falsity, and the presumed falsity (such as the animal, the criminal, the crippled, the rural recluse, and the ecstatic shamanistic wanderer) excluded by the philosophical schools (Confucian, legalist, Mohist, and so on) reveals itself as a reorienting perspective. Accordingly, for instance, the infinite is revealed in the finite and mundane in reorienting perspective-switching tales of exemplary Daoist and Zen masters of old in the *Zhuangzi*, in Wei-Jin era mysterious learning sources, and in the Tang era Chan Buddhism associated with Linji Yixuan 臨濟義玄 (?–866 CE) and other iconoclastic figures. Such writings mobilize imagery of the infinitesimal, the disfigured and imperfect, and the erroneous as sites of uselessness and illumination.

In Heidegger's 1930 lectures on truth, the clearing occurs, and truth transpires, within errancy itself. This Daoist connection continues to resonate in his later discussions of concealment, darkness, and mystery. Once again returning to a thought-image expressed in the *Daodejing*, explicitly mentioned in the context of mystery in these early lecture versions of "The Essence of Truth" (GA 80.1: 370), it is the darkest darkness that safeguards and discloses the clearing in these reflections of the 1950s (GA 100: 92). This Daoist sense of nurturing darkness reoccurs in the mid-1950s. Heidegger continues in *Identity and Difference* to ponder *Daodejing* 28 in conjunction with Hölderlin in a discussion of how the locus of thinking is hidden in darkness. He describes how this darkness is not mere absence or lack. As in the *Daodejing*, it is the secretive mystery (*Geheimnis*) that preserves. In Heidegger's formulation, darkness is the mystery of the clearing (*Lichtung*) as it holds and preserves the brightness (*Lichte*) within itself (GA 11: 138). In a reflection in his notebooks on this theme of darkness as the mystery of light, he concludes that darkening itself frees, clears, and lights the way (GA 100: 119).

4. Three Strategies to Elucidate the Thing

What then of the thing's mystery? The thing occupies a crucial and distinctive position in Heidegger's sojourn in errancy and truth, that only gradually arrives at the ziranist mystery of things. The first four chapters delineated how Heidegger's thing-philosophy transitions through several intermediary positions from which three moments have been underscored in part one of the present work: (1) the thing as instrumental, objectively present, and worldless in regard to human existence as the ekstatic world-opening of being-there (late 1920s); (2) the thing-in-the-work as ensnared in the creativity and violence of the work and as offered to being (mid-1930s); and (3) the event of the "it things" as the durational gathering of the world in the thing that conditions (*be-dingen*) a unique moment and environing local region (after the mid-1940s). The present book has traced Heidegger's transition from the self-world of human existence and the worldlessness of the thing to the essencing (Heidegger's *Wesen*) and self-naturing (Lao-Zhuang *ziran*) of the thing *as* thing. The first strategy, unfolded particularly in the late 1920s, remains overly anthropocentric and subjectivistic, as Heidegger noted in his own auto-critiques of the project of *Being and Time*, as the thing continues to be an object of use and theorizing separated from animal and human life. There are glimpses of another truth of animals and things that was underdeveloped in his early philosophy and remains insufficiently articulated in his later thinking. The second strategy of the mid-1930s overly emphasizes the self-generating event of being and the being-historical deeds, works, and mission of creative *poiesis*. Formative violent artists, poets, thinkers, and lawgivers sacrifice things to give shape to new worlds and ways of dwelling. A more adequate understanding of the ecopoiesis of the interthingly nexus requires breaking with Heidegger's conception of *poiesis* during the 1930s, due to it being bound up with a coercive collectivist ideology of the people and their homeland. The third strategy, particularly prominent between 1943 and 1951, promises to unveil the thing's world-generative event, as the thing things of itself, and the needfulness of recognizing the thing's releasement, in its own way of being itself, in relation to human existence and to being as such.

This third strategy has substantive implications. The ontic of the ontic-ontological difference, the beings dissolved into being, according to Heidegger's critics like Adorno, is renewed in the altered conception of the thing as having its own sense that addresses human saying. It is not the sway of sovereign being but the shift to the worlding thing, and the prospect of reworlding the world through the self-naturing of things. This insight into the thing radicalizes Heidegger's critique of anthropological and anthropocentric humanism. This is the case even while he still differentiates and accentuates the human being as self-aware finite mortal, being's shepherd, and the one who says and safeguards the thing. The thing shifts from instrumental equipmentality, the isolated separation, and neutral worldlessness of mere presence (*Präsenz*), to formative gathering and worlding. It transitions from the periphery of his early phenomenology to the center of his confrontation with the environmental and existential destructiveness of administrative and technical modernity. The essencing thing is no longer the conditioned appearance for consciousness or human existence, as it gathers and conditions mortals in their essencing (GA 98: 120). Making place for things is to make place for ourselves. It is things that gather and constitute sites in which humans can dwell and wander. This formation of place could be demarcated—in view of the *Zhuangzi*—as the openness and equilibrium of an autopoietically self-transforming, interthingly relational nexus. This nexus in its openness and transformability differs from and can be positioned to contest the purposive systems of systems theory, which Heidegger questioned in the form of automated cybernetics in his late reflections (GA 102), from the enframing systematic totalizing of metaphysics, or from the fixated nexus of instrumental usefulness that forget the singularity of being-there and the thing. The pragmatic instrumental nexus of availability and usefulness analyzed in *Being and Time* is revealed in Heidegger's later thought to presuppose the thingly or interthingly formation of place and world in which mortal human existence finds itself, dwells, and builds in ways that nourish or fail to nourish things and the conditions of life.

The thing is no longer either a pragmatically ready-to-hand or a posited-represented object. It has come forth as that which "conditions" (*be-dingen*, as grounding, standing-over-from, and object) while—in a part of a thought-poem that echoes the *Zhuangzi*—we "wander quietly in that which constantly changes."[15] Heidegger deploys a thought-model from the *Zhuangzi*: as mortals are determined by ceaselessly transforming things and their natural conditions, freedom means to spontaneously and responsively wander and sojourn with and amidst things and their shifting perspectives in emptiness, simplicity and stillness, without dependence and fixation.

Heidegger's most revolutionary thinking of the thing is conveyed throughout his writings after 1943. They indicate a critical template for confronting the forgetting, reification, and domination of things, in which they become through pragmatically justified coercion merely useful and useless things, to the detriment of places and human dwelling. However, there are moments in his later works that this ziranist moment is not sustained and anthropocentric humanism, which deems things as mere things, reasserts itself. At times, the thing, such as the stone or the table, becomes once again a mere ontic phenomenon distinguished from the ontological-ontic being of human existence and the ontology of being (GA 89: 7–8). Such moments, when the reassertion of anthropocentrism and the denigration of things recur, are typically in later expositions of the themes of *Being and Time* in which his own intervening shifts and self-criticisms (such as in GA 82) are unmentioned.

II. Rethinking *Ethos*

5. *Dao* and *Ethos*

The *Daodejing*, the *Zhuangzi*, and related texts teach nourishing the life of things without appealing to laws and prescriptive moral principles and rules that are criticized as a loss and falling away from *dao* and the self-so-ness of the myriad things. There are no fixed and fixating rules yet there are exemplary indicative models to emulate and enact. The people emulate the sages who emulate in turn the elemental. Like heaven, earth, and water in *Daodejing* 7 and 8, the exemplary sages assist and benefit things without purposive striving or calculative technique.

Sages do not follow the prescriptions and rules of the philosophical schools: neither the legalistic strategies and methods of maximizing sovereign power that is more *virtù* than virtue, nor the universal moral principles and calculation of Mo Di and the Mohist school (*Mojia* 墨家), and not the moralizing benevolence and righteousness (*renyi* 仁義) associated with Confucius and the "Confucian" or "erudite school" (*rujia* 儒家) that existed before and after its greatest master and teacher Confucius. Like the so-called egoists and skeptical sophists, who are predominantly known through polemical argumentation against them, early ziranist texts contest conventional rule-based morality as prejudicial and deleterious. Unlike the egoists and sophists, whose thoughts are variously incorporated into the ziranist *Zhuangzi* and *Liezi*, they do so for what might well be described as an *ethos* of enacting *dao* in everyday existence.

Dao indicates that which is more primordial than any morality, ethics, or originary *ethos*. At the same time, its expressions and traces are exemplary for how all things sojourn and abide: people emulate and model themselves upon the sage-kings and sages, the sages emulate heaven and earth, heaven and earth emulate *dao*, and the *dao* emulates its own self-naturing.[16] The ziranist language of echoing, emulating, learning, mirroring, modeling, resonating, and responding is indicative of an attuning comportment with and amidst things and world as they follow their own changes. Indeed, this language is also adopted in varieties of Chinese and East Asian Buddhism such as Chan/Zen.

Such responsive attunement is delineated in a variety of ways in a philosophical arrangement that adopts and modifies existing religious imagery. First, informed by models of biospiritual meditation that are also at work in the meditative "art of the heart-mind" chapters of the *Huainanzi* and *Guanzi*, the *Daodejing* stresses the value of quietly staying within oneself in the simplicity of one's own room and local place, as in *Daodejing* 47, which Heidegger approvingly quoted in a 1965 letter to Ernst Jünger (Heidegger-Jünger 2016: 32).

Secondly, employing the shamanistic language and imagery of biospiritual far-roaming (*yuanyou* 遠遊), the *Zhuangzi* accentuates the free transformative sojourning and wandering of the unfixated self with and amidst the transformation of things. The unfixated self is at home in homelessness, argumentative and perspectival shifts (chapter two), and dream-like landscapes of the sublime and the uncanny (chapters one and seven). As several early twentieth-century German language writers (Hesse) and Sinologists (Eichhorn) discerned, the *Zhuangzi* points toward exemplary instances and models of a mutable self that is freely attuning without reification and alienation from the relational nexus of itself and its world.

6. *Ethos*, Ethics, and Morality between Laozi and Heidegger

What is *ethos*, and can this Greek word be used to express elements of early Chinese thinking? No doubt it designates something specifically Greek and untranslatable, as with each elemental word. Yet, at the same time, the work of translation adopts what was once specifically Greek or Chinese into modern German, English, and other discourses. Then the question becomes the appropriateness of *ethos* in contrast with other words such as ethics, morality, and virtue.

"*Ethos*" refers to custom, habit, and character in its modern usage and thus would appear to be in no better position than these other expressions. Its older etymological meaning is not "fixed ingrained character" (as in the Latin *habitus*). It is one's way of being and abiding in an accustomed place. *Ethos* denotes in this setting an abiding moment in an enreigioning local place and how one dwells within it, that is the nexus in which character, virtue, and their absence are enacted. It is this sense of *ethos* that Heidegger explicates as a more—if still not fully—originary ethics.

The Greek conception of *ethos* is helpful, if applied with appropriate caveats, given the distinctiveness of early Chinese and Greek thinking and keeping in mind that *dao* is more primordial than any *ethos* or way of life. It aids explication of the attunement of *dao* that is prior to and simpler than virtue-ethics (and any ingrained or customary moral skill or *habitus*) and any rule-based system of moral principles and calculations, as evident in its critiques of Confucianism and Mohism. Lao-Zhuang virtuosity (*de* 德) was construed in its early German reception variously as a form of virtue (*Tugend* in the title of von Plaenckner's 1870 translation), a morally indifferent practice of mysticism, an anti-moralistic ethic akin to anarchistic or Nietzsche's critiques of ethics, or an *ethos* and sense (Wilhelm's "*Sinn*"). Victor von Strauss described Daoist virtuosity in the 1870s as an *ethos* and comportment of doing and non-doing.[17] Non-doing can also be interpreted affirmatively, as in Dilthey's depiction of the moral ideal of the *Daodejing* as a profound and sublime teaching of the virtues of humility, frugality, and compassion; Karl Jaspers' portrayal of non-doing as the origin of Laozi's *ethos*; or in Ernst Bloch's interpretation of *dao* as an orientational bearing of simplicity and life- and world-tactfulness.[18]

Bloch's point deserves further attention, as both he and Heidegger recognize a teaching of free worldly attunement in early Daoist sources. "Orientation," in the Latin sense of *orīrī*, signifies positioning and aligning oneself according to the rise and movement of the sun. Kant articulated in a 1786 essay the orientational directionality of sensibility and thought that, as in his example of the sense of right and left, could not be derived from the external world. But Bloch can speak of dao as a sensible "tact" with worldly things, such that sensibility and exteriority cannot be separated, as orientation in the Daoist context points toward adaptive relational positioning with the worldly self-patterning of things. That is, orientation is not a positioning by the subject or a point within abstract space; it is an ongoing process of attunement with the changing configurations of things that the later Heidegger calls world. To this degree, it is not incorrect to speak of this form of Daoism as comprising a this-worldly and life-embracing orientation, ethos, attunement, and life-praxis enacted in an ensemble of practices of emptying.

Early Daoism was frequently defined as an art of life (*Lebenskunst*), and the German edition of Okakura elucidated *dao* as an "art of being-in-the-world" as seen in Chapter 1 above (Okakura 1919: 29). The *dao* is likewise described as gathering and dwelling—in their pre- or non-Heideggerian senses—in both the heart-mind and in the land. Water, as an image of the highest good in *Daodejing* chapter 8, is depicted as disclosing and forming the goodness of earth (Strauss) and place (Wilhelm) by its dwelling there (Strauss 1870: 38; Wilhelm 1911: 10). These threads indicate a linguistic web that intersects with Heidegger's language that has its own specific configuration as well as partaking in a generational linguistic community.

Heidegger's critical suspicion toward ethics and moral theory is another point of intersection with early Daoism, in its critiques of conventional morality as the decline of the way, as interpreted in its German language reception. Heidegger rejected, often dismissively, standard forms of moral and value theory and repeatedly denied that his philosophy contained an ethics as a theory of moral values, worldviews, rules, principles, or axioms. Such categories for him are external and coercive to the matter itself of the ethical: relationship and comportment. The exceptions are those moments when Heidegger addressed the prospect of an originary ethics, or that which is more originary than ethics, which enacts a way of being-in-the-world, being-there, and *ethos* as abiding, dwelling, and sojourning in a hermeneutical situation and specific moment and place.

Heidegger already engaged with the question of *ethos* in contrast with ethics in his lecture-courses after the First World War, particularly in his confrontations with Aristotle's practical and life philosophy.[19] The shifting of the sense of *ethos* can be traced from his initial to his later interpretations. First, *ethos* emerges in the more existentially oriented thinking of the 1920s as the way in which a being exists or, more hermeneutically speaking, as an individuated art of existing in an interpretive situation. As Heidegger outlines in a 1930 assessment of Kant, ethics fails in actual practical moral situations in which specific decisions are demanded (GA 31: 79). It operates, to deploy the language of *Being and Time*, as a dominating leaping-in, in that it coerces others, obscuring their possibilities instead of being an emancipatory leaping-ahead that opens and releases their own plural possibilities for individuation (GA 2: 122). Heidegger accordingly emphasizes prospects for authenticity and individuation and not the virtues, rules, and principles that dominate customary moral theory and misses the plurality and complexity of ethical life.

"Ethics" is a questionable category insofar as it is a decayed and fallen version of what the ethical genuinely concerns, which Heidegger variously designated as an originary ethics, *ethos*, and dwelling.[20] In the phases of Heidegger's trajectory, the philosophical category of "ethics" remains in doubt while he attempts to articulate an alternative to it called *ethos* or that which is more elemental than any *ethos*. In 1935, *ethos* is described as having lost its intimate bonds with *phúsis*, as morality has abbreviated it to an ought without being and that which is merely ethical (GA 40: 18).

In contrast to Heidegger's earlier destructuring criticisms of ethics, *ethos* emerges more lucidly in his postwar writings. In the "Letter on Humanism," *ethos* is the "originary ethics" of the character and way wherein humans can dwell in answering attunement with their environing place and world. Ethics, "in keeping with the basic meaning of the word *ethos*," is to "ponder the human abode" (GA 9: 354). This abode is the opening region where finite conditional mortals abide between heaven and earth. The open enregioning, which acts as a crossing and intersecting gathering and jointure, is a relational contextual site that withdraws from and resists—if only in its traces and tracks which are ever more erased and concealed—being thoroughly enclosed, ordered, and determined as an enframed systematic totality in which each thing has its use and value. In such a totality each thing, environing enregioning or localizing place, and (by extension) ecosystem is defined by and positioned according to a fixating and coercive criterion of usefulness. In 1946–1947, *ethos* signifies abode, dwelling place, and the open region where humans come to their own appropriate self-essencing (GA 9: 354).

In Occidental onto-theology only God can actually be self-essencing and it is the absolute that self-presences to itself, according to Hegel (GA 5: 129). Genuine essencing is understood in a quasi-ziranist manner in Heidegger as a self-generative essencing and self-presencing through the turnings, reversals, and alterations that make something come forth and conceal itself as what it is. Heidegger contests and reinterprets the metaphysical discourse of essence and presence to indicate that which it yet fails to signify: the things themselves *as* things necessitate openness and releasement toward the mystery of their own manner of being.

Heidegger's later thinking of the thing does and does not apply to human existence. Humans still have a particular role in the adventure and household of being as Heidegger contests anthropocentric humanism. This contestation is carried out without fixating on a pure biocentrism that forgets humans. Humans need to be ecologically motivated through a culture of the cultivation and nourishing of nature; they would remain merely ontic in reductively misconstruing beings as mere biological objects. It is in this context that Heidegger speaks of ethics in his later writings. Ethics is first and foremost a relation between finite mortal beings who say and safeguard thing and world. The distinctive ways in which humans, things, and world generatively presence (*an-wesen* as distinguished from *Präsenz*) is the originary sense of ethics, according to Heidegger in his *Zollikon Seminars* with the Swiss psychoanalytic psychiatrist Medard Boss: "Standing in the demand of that which presences is the greatest demand made upon humans. It is 'ethics.'"[21] Ethics concerns and inadequately expresses the ways in which human beings stand in self-presencing toward each other. This interhuman orientation does not rule out distinctive performative enactments of *ethos* in human relations with thing and world, that generatively presence in their own ways according to their own self-essencing.

"Presencing" (*Anwesen*) does not denote the stagnant givenness or a substantializing of others, things, and the world. It is much more indicative of a fluctuating self-presencing that makes an addressing claim and demand which can be heard and unheard in propinquity and distance. Heidegger wants to think such presencing in confrontation with and departure from the Occidental metaphysics of presence and essence that ignores the communicative interval between self-naturing things. In paradigmatic Occidental onto-theological metaphysics only God and the absolute are genuinely self-presencing. It is early Daoist discourses that hint at an alternative by teaching not the Godhood or absoluteness in things, as in forms of mysticism or pantheism that conflate and reify God and world, but the freedom of their self-happening.[22] The demand to be receptive and respond to self-presencing is what Heidegger entitled originary ethics, *ethos*, or a relationality more fundamental than such expressions can appropriately indicate: "More important than all ethics is *ethos*. More important than *ethos* is to consider its essencing as the mortal abode in relation to the mystery."[23]

What does it signify when Heidegger rejects using the term "ethics" except as an *ethos* or an "originary ethics" (*ursprüngliche Ethik*) (GA 9: 356)? It necessitates thinking the ethics of being in ways that no longer limit the ethical to the agency, subjectivity, and willing that obscure the moment and place where they occur. Ethics (as the theoretically oriented positing of norms and values) inhibits such encounters from transpiring, in contrast with an ethics of being and the nurturing of the art of existence. This art as *poiesis* cannot be purely an art of the self and its cultivation. It concerns the disclosive encounters in which I and others exist in care and carelessness, responsibility and irresponsibility. Ethics, in Heidegger's analysis, is akin to the loss of *dao* in the intensification of benevolence and righteousness diagnosed in the *Daodejing*, resulting in the absence of what it intends. The reversal or step back is toward openness and releasement in the mystery of the interthingly interrelationality wherein each thing essences as itself.

7. Heidegger's Transversal: From Embracing to Contesting the Will to Power

According to the underappreciated Berlin philosopher Katharina Kanthack, Heidegger is a philosopher of relationality and ethos (Kanthack 1958 and 1964). Following her interpretation, the question of what *ethos* signifies does not concern mere relationality; it is about the ways in which relations are decided, deliberated, enacted, and practiced. What then of acting in a responsive attunement with things? Relation (*Ver-Hältnis*) emerges in a comportment (*Verhalten*) of reservedness (*Verhaltenheit*) that allows something to relate in its own manner of being.[24] How did Heidegger arrive at this sense of reservedness, which already began to emerge in the 1935 *Contributions to Philosophy* (GA 65: 489–90), and the releasement into world and mystery of his later thinking? It is already intimated in 1930 and reemerges around 1943. Let us step back to consider the intervening period that prepared the way for Heidegger's 1940s encounters with Laozi and Zhuangzi.

Heidegger's early project in *Being and Time* articulates a leaping-ahead for the other that enables individuation and self-individuation through a confrontation with one's own finitude and mortality. The latter is frequently construed as decisionistic, and his early philosophy can be interpreted as oscillating between letting (other) and willing (self).[25] This oscillation occurs in the 1930 lectures on truth, consequently complicating and placing in doubt the thesis that Heidegger's pathway advances from activist decisionism to National Socialism to passive resignation.[26] Despite Heidegger's

Daoist moments in 1930, he does not return to considering the Lao-Zhuang path of *wuwei* and *ziran* until 1943, embracing and then endeavoring to extricate himself with varying degrees of success from a thinking of *pólemos*, assertion, power, and will that was entangled with the politics of National Socialist Germany and the philosophy of Nietzsche. Heidegger would retrospectively describe this 1930s entanglement as breaking him.[27]

This interpretive situation is revealed in Heidegger's depiction of *ethos*. In a later development of his destructuring interpretive strategy, he uncovers in the 1935 *Introduction to Metaphysics* how "*ethos* has been degraded to the ethical," in which the good becomes mere value and the fullness of ethical life becomes the empty formula of mere morality, just as *phúsis*—the upsurge and sway of being—is narrowed to *tékhnē*, the instrumental and technical manipulation and control of things (GA 40: 13, 134). Being is perceived as and devalued into another meager value and a ghostly "ought" and thereby separated from that which is (GA 40: 151; GA 55: 84).

The positing and affirmation of "values" and "oughts," even in a sweeping Nietzschean form without and against previous morality and religion, cannot save beings from becoming mere instrumental means, as value-thinking is intrinsically fixating, restricting, and instrumentalizing with respect to what it intends. Valuing and value-thinking are inevitably calculative and reductive to that which the will posits as useful (GA 6.2: 205). This extends to the will itself that is lost in the very creation and positing of it as a value. Despite Heidegger's decisionistic language in the early National Socialist era, he gradually contested the discourse of decision and will—which he linked with Nietzsche—during the late 1930s (GA 47 and 48). This created for him a decisive turning point toward the 1943 quasi-Daoistic turn as acting from responsive attunement (as in *wei wuwei*) displaces an acting out of coercive assertion (as in *wei*). This critique of decisionist action, which corrects his own earlier thinking and not merely its misinterpretation as he would have it, is extended to Jean-Paul Sartre's conception of existence preceding essence and the essence of the human construed as freely chosen existence, in the "Letter on Humanism" (GA 9: 329–30).

Marxist postwar polemics associated Heidegger's anti-humanism with Klages's biocentrism as reactionary expressions of decaying bourgeois life.[28] Klages in his 1929 book, advocating vitalistic life-philosophy, had already critiqued anthropocentrism, humanism, and logocentrism (as the fixation and priority of the word over action and thing) for the sake of biocentrism (the primacy of the biological) during the Weimar Republic. Heidegger resists interpreting human existence solely according to ontic discourses of anthropology, biology, or psychology regardless of whether these are construed mechanistically or "vitalistically." The question of humanism and anti-humanism has its own unique dynamic in Heidegger's postwar thought as it does not justify or draw on the primacy of either the biological or the anthropological, as becomes evident in his confrontations with German interpretations of Nietzsche in the late 1930s. This context, which informs his subsequent 1942–1944 Daoist turning, deserves further attention.

Heidegger's engagement with Nietzsche, beginning with the 1936/37 lecture-courses (published in GA 43 and 44), is simultaneously a confrontation with his own previous voluntarist thinking as well as with Klages's psycho-biological thought (which

Klages designated "anti-logocentric" and "biocentric"), Alfred Baeumler's political-ideologically driven "heroic realism," and other National Socialist anthropological racial appropriations of Nietzsche. Heidegger explicitly critiqued these in 1941 as the "Berlin interpretation of Nietzsche."[29] Notwithstanding his initial enthusiastic support for the National Socialist movement within the context of the *Gleichschaltung* of the university and the postwar condemnation of him as a member and follower (*Mitläufer*) of the party, it is evident that Heidegger did not accept and explicitly rejected several cornerstones of its ideology from the beginning. Heidegger's polemical critics often downplay—ironically, as in the recent work of Richard Wolin, relativizing the horrors of National Socialism in an attempt to classify Heidegger as so much worse—how he had systematically rejected the assumptions of biologism and psychologism in both their mechanistic scientific and organicist vitalistic forms in *Being and Time* and his works of the 1930s, even as he became ensnared in the Nazi "conservative revolution" and attempted to appropriate and justify it in his own philosophical terms.

Heidegger's reservations continued throughout the Nazi era which was dominated by biological organicist modes of thinking that he opposed initially in favor of a deeply problematic existentially decisive collective will of the people (*Volk*) in the early and mid-1930s and then in a more radical turn—in dialogue with Daoist images of worldly freedom—toward the opening of being and the thing. Heidegger fatefully fell prey in the early 1930s to the totalizing idea of a collective autopoietic people, suppressing the plural autopoiesis of myriad relationally interactive singulars that leads to anarchic and democratic self-organization. Heidegger would not adopt this social-political direction expressed in ziranist moments in the *Zhuangzi* and the *Liezi*. In such moments in the latter two texts, the interactive and transformative autopoiesis of the cacophony, chaos, and self-movement of the myriad things entails relational individuals going through their own changes and forming shifting self-ordering patterns. The closed totalizing autopoiesis of destined and fated nature (as in limiting hypostatizing appropriations of Daoist *ziran*), or a collective entity such as the totalitarian nation-state or Heidegger's self-poeticizing *Volk*, or systems of deterministic power or society (as in systems theory) are varieties of reification that forget and suppress the self-naturing of the myriad things and the self-reflexive participation of intrinsically plural individuals.

Still, it is inaccurate to categorize Heidegger's position during this period as vitalistic racism. Organicist tendencies of the 1930s were based on the vitalist-oriented philosophies of Nietzsche, Hans Driesch (despite his own pacifist and anti-fascist position), Klages and Spengler, and popularized in a directly racialized form by the in-house party philosopher-ideologists Alfred Baeumler and Alfred Rosenberg.[30] Heidegger's letting of being represented a reversal of Nietzsche's overcoming of pessimism and nihilism through action for Nazi ideologues; they accused him of fostering fearful anxiety, unheroic despair, and anti-Germanic nihilism. Heidegger was aware of such accusations (GA 82: 277). To briefly consider an example, according to Ernst Krieck, a leading Nazi education theorist, Heidegger's ontology, pacificism, psychoanalysis, and the theory of relativity, all shared a common nihilism of supposedly Jewish origins (Krieck 1934: 23–4). He decried Heidegger's "crusade of nothingness" as undoing the effectivity of time and history that necessitates the natural ground of race for its completion (Krieck 1943: 127). Krieck repeatedly returns in his writings to the vital creativity of the moment that embraces nature (identified as race) and that rejects the disintegrative weakness of anxiety (*Angst*), care (*Sorge*), boredom (*Langeweile*), disquiet (*Unruhe*), and limitation (*Begrenzung*). Race, inadequately expressed for Krieck in Heidegger's ostensible existential nihilism, grounds the demand for ordering and policing people and things, which has no time for useless existential moods and poetic words. Radical conservative suspicions of the modernism of Heideggerian existential anxiety continued after the war. The anti-modern modernist poet Gottfried Benn, who like Heidegger abandoned active support for the movement after initial enthusiasm for its assumption of power, could write a poem in the postwar period decrying the self-concern of unreligious and anti-humanist existential anxiety and thrownness. This philosophy failed to genuinely defend the traditional Occident, God's beautiful land of the middle (Benn 1951: 35, 37).

Both uncritical apologists and polemical detractors fail to recognize the complexity of Heidegger's position in the early years of the regime. He criticized Nazi biological and anthropological racial discourse, questioned its populist appeals to the masses, and ignored its militarism. Yet Heidegger was more willing to advocate other very questionable elements of Nazi ideology, such as its charismatic authoritarian "leadership principle," its demand for one collective German identity, and its coercive coordination (*Gleichschaltung*) of every aspect of German life that he promoted as rector of the University of Freiburg during 1933–1934.[31] After the loss of his rectorship, and growing disfavor in the party, he heightened his objections. Heidegger interrogated what he designated the "zoology of the will" and the fateful configuration of biological life, the primacy of the will, and heroic-tragic voluntarist activism prevalent in popular life-philosophy and the German reception of Nietzsche. He increasingly maintained, against Nietzsche's philosophy of value and the primacy of will, that affirming and willing values and meanings cannot overcome the nihilistic predicament of the self-devaluing of values. Nietzsche's strategy signifies, on the contrary, nihilism's consummation as all of being becomes a means for willing. The will-to-power becomes a self-consuming end for itself. The very need for will, action, and creating values is itself the primary problem posed by Nietzsche's "inverted Platonism" and still all too metaphysical project, according to Heidegger's diagnosis. The question concerning whether willing is a monistic unity or a multiplicity of forces, raised by Deleuze, does not address the problematic character of reducing being and reality to will and value, fixating the subject instead of freeing it, and in this manner consummating rather than overcoming nihilism.[32]

Heidegger's intensive confrontation with Nietzsche's philosophy of the will to power and value in the late 1930s preceded his turn toward early Daoism in which things and the world are freely affirmed without will, power, or values. Such a prospect is not unique to Heidegger. It was raised earlier in the late Weimar Republic by Buber who confronted the Nietzschean *conatus* and will-to-power with Daoist *wuwei* (Buber 2013: 285–9). It was negatively proposed yet not pursued in sufficient detail in Klages's 1929 *Spirit as Adversary of the Soul* (Klages 1981: 342, 496). It is articulated in a new form in Heidegger's Daoist-inflected reflections of the 1940s on releasement and the thing in which Heidegger perceived the necessity of rethinking action itself and stepping out of the dilemma of affirming (as in Nietzsche) or negating (as in Schopenhauer) the will.

Both positions, and nineteenth-century optimism and pessimism in general, remain explicitly or implicitly committed to the paradigm of the will's supremacy.

The rejoinder to the crisis of nihilism, as a consequence of the "abandonment of being" (*Seinsverlassenheit*), unfolded in his works of the 1930s (GA 65: 119), is no longer to be sought through the affirmation or negation of the will, value, idea, and action (GA 7: 89–90, 97). It is thought after the 1943 turn toward *Gelassenheit* through figures of thought such as the "releasement of letting beings be,"[33] the releasement of stillness in regard to things (GA 53: 68), the stillness of movement/waying (*be-wegen*) (Hsiao 1987: 103; GA 16: 618; Petzet 1986: 58), letting be as calling forth the thing to world and releasing the worlding-thing (GA 98: 16); it occurs also in the releasement of mortal habitation between sky and earth, and—in the namelessness of beginning prior to and without moralism, humanism, and anthropomorphism—the releasement of the letting be of the granting provided by binding or joining-together (*fügend-gönnenden*) (GA 81: 142). Heidegger's language of gathering (*Sammlung*) and fugue/jointure (*Fuge*) indicates the specific coming together of moment and place formed by interthingly and intraworldly interactions. It is in such places where human beings find themselves and potentially attune and dispose themselves toward them in receiving and dwelling.

Heidegger's question-provoking thought-models offer traces and indications of other ways of being-in-the-world and dwelling with things. These models are often taken to express a need for mythopoetic re-enchantment and rediscovering wonder in disenchanted and desolate modernity. They can be accorded a more heuristic and minimalist interpretation and positioned as critical models to question and confront the paradigm of mastery, domination, and control that is intertwined with the impoverishment and subjugation of humans and the decimation of localities, environments, and ecosystems.[34] On the one hand, the constitutive subject converts all into mere objects, including itself in mere objectness, and humans increasingly become mere instrumental administrative-technical resources compelled by constructs of usefulness and uselessness. On the other hand, gathering things and places, as well as self-generative environments and ecosystems, are not only left deficient in "meaning," which remains an all too idealistic category, but also in their self-generative autopoietic functioning, which forms their sense for humans that demands recultivation. It is difficult to discover and fashion meaning and value when things and places have lost their own self-patterning sympoietic sense.

If this is the case, mortals (as Heidegger later designates finite human existence) do not need more willing, assertion, and activity for the sake of posited and constructed values and purposes, since these merely reproduce the projected order of administrative-technical deworlding positionality in which the autopoietic self-determination of humans and things is enclosed, obstructed, and inevitably thereby diminished. This questioning analysis of modernity intersects with the critical social analysis of Adorno and the Frankfurt School that can be deployed to reimagine leaping-ahead for things—in their own distances, moments, and places—with a more explicitly critical and emancipatory orientation.[35] Mortals are called to shift perspectives from thinking of themselves as "masters of being" exercising dominion over things—a mastery in which they have reified, enslaved, and alienated their own self-naturing—to being "shepherds of being" in the sense of guiding, fostering, and safeguarding (GA 9: 342; GA 82: 569). Heidegger expresses in two versions of a thought-poem concerning releasement, which cannot be fixed as a rule or a virtue, how granting and safeguarding are enacted through waiting and releasement: "Only in waiting do we become our own, granting and safeguarding humans and things a return to calm" (GA 81: 57; GA 81: 73).

Silence allows the other to speak and be heard. How might stillness help safeguard the thing? Such stillness is not merely an aesthetic predilection; it is a condition of genuine hearing and hearkening toward others and things. Responsive co-relating saying, Heidegger notes, is only possible from listening. Such receptivity to the thing in listening brings the thing to world by letting it come to and be as itself, the thing to thing and the world to world, and in this manner potentially safeguarding it. Not only persons, who should not be disregarded, but things and their environing localities need to have space and be allowed to flourish.

Heidegger's language of shepherding and safeguarding is illustrative and indicative of an altered conception of human agency as participating in sense-forming place and being called to responsively and ecomimetically build. As described in the 1951 lecture "Building Dwelling Thinking," building (*bauen*) has a twofold meaning: (1) erecting (*errichten*) and producing (*herstellen*) structures; (2) and guarding (*hüten*), cherishing (*hegen*), and nourishing (*pflegen*) earth, field, and life.[36] *Bauen* in the latter sense is that which preserves, nurtures, and safeguards, as is etymologically indicated by the Gothic *wunian* and Old Saxon *wuon* (GA 7: 150). It is this second semantic and experiential range of meanings that Heidegger calls to contemplate once more.

III. Resituating the Subject

8. Interrogating Humanism and Naturalism

As Heidegger noted in his 1944 *Heraclitus* lecture-course, "humans are those living beings who have and are distinguished by *ethos*" (GA 55: 223). The question of *ethos* leads into what it signifies to be human. These considerations regarding *ethos* led to core issues of the 1947 "Letter on Humanism." It was composed in reply to questions about Sartre, existentialism, and humanism posed by Jean Beaufret in late 1946. This short essay seeks to break from metaphysical and what we would now designate anthropocentric humanism without, as he says, abandoning the human in the inhuman ("un-menschlich, 'inhuman'") that is outside of its own self-essencing ("außerhalb seines Wesens") (GA 9: 319).

Fascism is notorious for its racialized hierarchy of ostensibly over- and under-humans. Heidegger's essay contests the exclusion of any humans based on a fixed conception of the human, evoking his earlier criticisms of anthropological and biological definitions of human existence. Traditional paradigmatic humanism, with its valuing of Roman *humanitas*, civilized as properly human and diminishing of the other as barbarian and less than normatively human, obstructs the human, in its belonging to being, from being comprehended from out of itself. As specified in the *Zhuangzi*, there is no recognition of the human without forgetting the human and recognizing the human in the natural.³⁷ Recognizing the self-naturing of the human entails recognizing how it abides within the world (the natural) in its own ways of dwelling and being itself (the human). The question for Heidegger concerns how to recognize the belongingness of humans to being, without absorbing the human into being, and dissolving reified subjectness while disclosing being-there for oneself (GA 82: 569). This thematic signifies an intersection with Daoist ziranist "naturalism," in which "nature" needs to be elucidated as fundamentally self-generative and autopoietic, in the subtext of Heidegger's later writings and their intercultural reception.

Is such an intersection justified? Lao-Zhuang Daoist sources are not directly and openly mentioned in Heidegger's "Letter on Humanism." Encouraged by Beaufret's queries, the "Letter on Humanism" addresses Sartre's proposition that existentialism is a humanism centered on human subjectivity and calling for committed political action. Heidegger's letter adopts a critical stance toward action, agency, humanism, and subjectivity that can be interpreted without hermeneutical violence, according to the *wuwei-ziran* model of reverberating attunement and self-naturing actuality.

Although the letter does not expressly refer to Daoist sources, Laozi and Zhuangzi linger in its background as it was composed after his intensive engagement with the *Daodejing* and *Zhuangzi*. The essay appears akin to a Daoist reflection in its interrogation of action and letting, humanism and naturalism, living and nonliving things. Early interpreters connected Heidegger's anti-humanism with Daoism, foreshadowing the extensively discussed topic of anti-humanism and dwelling-in-nature in ensuing Heidegger scholarship and comparative and cross-cultural philosophy.³⁸

Fritz Dehn, best known for his writings on Rilke, condemned Heidegger's anti-humanism in a 1948 work defending religious humanism. In "Of Humanity in Humans," he associated Heidegger's philosophy of existence and a "renewed Daoism" as varieties of an inhuman and inhumane "godless mysticism," lacking love and humanity, which replaced God's personal creation from love with an impersonal and anonymous nothingness.³⁹ Dehn, Klaus Mann, and other critics categorized Heidegger as a "Daoist," no doubt as an insult. Less polemically, and with more familiarity with Daoist sources, the art historian Hans Gerhard Evers remarked that Heidegger might be finally reaching his goal by a "dangerous path" that eventually arrived at a poetic and naturalistic sensibility "not distant from East Asian *dao*" (Evers 1951: 147). The sense of nature and "naturalism" (bracketing its typical reductive meaning of one theoretical explanation of nature in preference for naturing itself) conveyed in these remarks, informed by modern intercultural readings of Laozi and Zen Buddhism, indicates the fullness of the thing with its counterparts and region. These hint at its autopoietic self-naturing, not restricted by a fixed use, purpose, or principle, which is suppressed in reductive forms of naturalism that neglect the thing's specific essencing in its own moment and place and, hence, human ekstatic essencing as well.

9. Reimagining and Releasing Action and Agency

The "Letter on Humanism" can be interpreted through another Daoist perspective insofar as it reimagines action and inaction in ways that correlate with coercive action and noncoercive action. The opening lines of the letter announce: "We are still far from decisively thinking the nature of action. Acting is only recognized as the bringing about of an effect, the reality of which is valued according to its use. Yet the essence of action is completion (*Vollbringen*). That is, to unfold something into the fullness of its essencing" (GA 9: 313).

"The Letter on Humanism" calls for a rethinking of action in confrontation with the traditional teleological and modern instrumentalist paradigms that truncate the fullness of acting and letting to instrumental means for intended and purposive results. Heidegger critiques the fixation on action, due to its enframed and instrumentalized character. Action is envisioned as altering the condition of the world, yet it cannot genuinely do so. Instead, it merely repeats and reinforces (compare GA 7: 97). Heidegger argues that his critique of action and activism does not entail a mere inactivity or a passive resignation. Acting is no longer presumed to be an instrumental effecting or producing for the sake of a projected product or purpose. This conclusion is perhaps informed by Zhuangzi, which is arguably the most radical illustration of questioning conventional ways of conceiving action according to the coercive measure of usefulness, to the extent that the early Confucian thinker Xunzi 荀子 accused Zhuangzi of neglecting the human for the sake of the natural.[40]

Heidegger's notebooks from this period further clarify his remarks in the letter. They also reveal how they are interconnected with concepts that are interwoven with his reading of the *Daodejing* and the *Zhuangzi*. In his self-reflections on the "Letter on Humanism," he notes that it does not justify a position but a way (GA 82: 566) and its very purpose is "to protect the puzzling mystery" ("das Rätsel zu schützen") (GA 82: 565). He states in another revealing passage that doing is to be thought as the essence of a *poiesis* that turns toward—once again using language familiar from Daoism—"the worldly freedom of stillness."[41] From what form of *poiesis* does this "turning toward" turn away from? *Poiesis* is no longer bound to the creative assertion and violence of individuals and peoples, as it was in his writings of the 1930s. Creative violence is not legitimated, and creative and poetic formation need not engage in violence for the sake of breaking the violence of nature, as Heidegger held in the mid-1930s.[42] Heidegger perhaps learned from his extensive engagement with the *Daodejing* in the 1940s that *dao* requires and demands no force, power, or violence, and that these in reality entail its loss. The poetic is consequently rethought during this period as a doing, creating, and building from stillness, emptiness, and calm. It is in such circumstances that things are recognized to be formative of the moments and places, of environment and world, in which humans—in Levinas's language—elementally dwell and live from.

Heidegger proposed the necessity of rethinking the very category of action, at the beginning of the "Letter on Humanism." Agency itself is rethought in view of the poetic in his subsequent reflections during the 1950s. Humans are construed as being and acting through their *ethos* and *poiesis* of moment and place in his later writings. *Poiesis* and poetic saying are not limited to aesthetic phenomena or to creative agency and production. They are an expression of embodied being-there and dwelling in the world that calls and brings forth world. As intimated in disclosive poetic words, the poetic is not only an aesthetic phenomenon. It is also a disclosure of human comportment and dwelling. More than this, in the 1951 lecture "Poetically Humans Dwell," Heidegger describes the poetic as "the basic capacity for human dwelling" such that the poetic is essential to human dwelling (GA 7: 206–7).

What sense of the poetic is operative here? First, it ought to be noted that the German word *Dichtung* has a wider range of meanings than the English word *poetry* and Heidegger elucidates the poem in its verbal enactive sense of "to poetize" (*dichten*). Heidegger's later articulation of the poetic is not as the creative originary violence of the "Origin of the Work of Art." Poeticizing is described, in a 1937 essay on Hölderlin, as a "formative designating of gods and the essencing of things" and poetic dwelling as the presence of gods and the nearness of the essencing of things.[43] This continuing emphasis on human doing and speaking in his 1937 account is redirected toward an acting and saying from thing and world in his 1951 essay in which poeticizing and agency are thought from out of the genuine temporality of moment and spatiality of place, rather than from an individual or collective subject, such as individual Dasein in *Being and Time* or the collective German people during the Nazi era.

Poeticizing now consists primarily of a responsive encountering and being-with the elemental, thing, and the world in moment and place, such that the human shaping and building of homes can occur. This sense of the poetic, which is more than receptive-expressive as conceived through the will, is existentially prior to human creative and formative powers celebrated in the 1930s. It is also prior to the instrumental availability of things as means in *Being and Time*. Pragmatic usefulness/uselessness can be set and fixated as the calculative measure of others and things only because humans already dwell poetically between the open measure of earth and sky. The poetic does not force itself on the thing to rip away its secrets. It allows the thing to set its own measure to which human dwelling and building can answer or fail to answer back.

The poetic is exemplary for dwelling and thinking, which fails to be genuinely poetic by being drawn away from thought-images to bare concepts, as the poetic is the site where language as patient listening occurs, and with it reserved unforced anticipation, and the free readiness to respond carefully and attentively. Heidegger strikes an altered tone in contrast to the priority of the self-assertive will in the 1930s. He now accentuates the generosity, gentleness, and kindness of being that comes forth in a bearing of respectful reserve and mindful attentiveness. The thing emerges as that which calls forth a reticence and respect in its being encountered and thought.

10. Acting from the Way and Its Mystery

It is not coincidental that Heidegger's references to Laozi and Zhuangzi often occur in the context of discussions of Hölderlin and Pre-Socratic thinkers. Heidegger engaged early Daoist sources as offering illuminating exemplars of poetic thinking and poetic thought-images and models that intimate other ways of inhabiting and being-in-the-world. They might even be at times guiding, given how they work their way into his writings. Describing the *Daodejing*, or the *Zhuangzi*, as expressing forms of poetic thinking seems inadequate to its philosophical content (GA 12: 187). However, poetic thinking and going on a way are higher than philosophy, which Heidegger portrays as not thinking and having lost its way. Moreover, this expression does capture the imagistic, playful, and transformative uses of language found in these two works and the formative role that they played in East Asian aesthetics, poetics, and *ethos*.[44] Heidegger's deployment of Daoism is not unfamiliar to Chinese cultural history.

It evokes the eclectic Daoism operative in Wei-Jin-era mysterious learning literati and Tang-era poets rather than the Daoism of ascetic hermits and religious practitioners.[45]

Daoist correlated elements are discernibly at play in Heidegger's later thinking. He continues to adopt the Zhuangzian-informed language of uselessness and the unnecessary in his notebooks. This language is also utilized to rethink action. Evoking the *Zhuangzi*, as illustrated in Chapter 4, he describes how the necessary actions of the necessary world are useless to change worldly conditions, in contrast to the superfluous and useless which would signify its potential actual transformation. In this context, the essencing of what humans are genuinely capable of must be thought as formed independently of the paradigm of acting and doing (GA 97: 43). Doing and freedom are no longer conceived as attributes of a self-assertive, essentially worldless subject and "use" and its necessity are resituated in this context of encounter and engagement through releasement. Doing is the coming to completion of situations and things. It is therefore enacted beyond and cannot be fittingly conceived through the concepts of willing, projecting, planning, calculating, and asserting of a constitutive or self-contained subject.[46] As Heidegger learned from the failure of his analytic of Dasein in *Being and Time*, the fundamentally problematic nature of the unitary self and idealistic subject remains unresolved even if it is redescribed as worldly being-there. This problem endures in recent accounts maintaining the priority of the subject, as promoted in the new phenomenology, in which the constitutive or transcendental subject is unquestioned while being reconstrued as embodied, embedded, enacted, and extended.

What is the alternative to the paradigm of the will and the subject that explicitly and implicitly continued to inform Heidegger's thinking of human existence in the 1920s and 1930s and from which he sought to twist free? It is only in 1943 that a more definitive alternative begins to emerge as the constitutive and acting subject is radically rethought from its situatedness with things, place, and world. The *ethos* of releasement is crucial to this transfigured perspective. In his postwar reflections (such as GA 98 and GA 99), letting is not a privation or negation of action. It is not merely a subjective attitude or sensibility but a responsive attunement with the event and worlding of the thing (GA 99: 40–1). Letting functions as a precondition of appropriately understanding action, and of enacting genuine action, modeled as responsive to situated place and as steps in movement on a pathway. Genuine action requires the recognition of stillness. Such stillness and inaction need not entail quietist world-denial or negation; it is the condition of the responsiveness of world-encounter and participation. That is, stillness allows an attuned and resonant bearing of inactive action to be practiced.

In letting and its corresponding saying, an action is not to be interpreted as a discrete isolated moment of exertion nor taken as the expression of a coercive and fixating identity or totality. Action does not follow from one's own decision or reflection, as it might appear to do in the more existential moments of *Being and Time*. It is an expression of one's comportment, *ethos*, and being-in-the-world. *Ethos*, or that which is more original than *ethos*, in Heidegger's explication of it cannot be limited to a static form of character or habit that predetermines action, since action is to be understood as belonging to a going, moving, and wayfaring, as making a way and forming moment and place in mindful or unmindful interaction with things. The mobility and freedom of the way cannot be predetermined and do not preclude—as discussed earlier above—errancy, false and closed pathways, reversals, and the step back to walk a different path. Such action does not belong to an individual or collective subjective, as action is an event encompassing the subject. Acting is then a continuity on a pathway and altered as different pathways are encountered and taken. Acting is being on and enacting a way. It is a way, he states in the letter, of bringing things to their plenitude (GA 9: 313).

The reflections on action and inaction in Heidegger and Daoist sources do more than co-illuminate one another as Heidegger's words evoke them. Acting without acting is a co-responding and completing-with thing and world as they unfold in their own essencing and presencing (in Heidegger's discourse) or their own generative self-naturing (in Daoist discourses). Heidegger's description of acting as unfolding something into the fullness of its essencing, and participating in completion, correlates with passages attributed to Laozi. *Daodejing* 41 states that *dao* is hidden, nameless, and brings all things to completion. Chapter 51 says that *dao* exercises no control over things while bringing them into their maturity. This is called the mysterious. The exemplary sages participate in the *dao*'s mystery, namelessness, and stillness, thereby nourishing, maturing, and completing things.

The *Daodejing* portrays how the actions of sages are attuned with the *dao*'s mystery, namelessness, and stillness. All three expressions have notable roles in Heidegger's rethinking of action and the human in relation to being. If humans are to find their way into being again, he notes, then they must first learn to exist in namelessness (GA 9: 316). Being is an unforced force operative in stillness without any effort or compulsion, and stillness is the "mystery of the world" and the essencing of language that co-relationally indicates and expresses the mystery without cognitively mastering it (GA 98: 277, 288). It is the poetic word that responds to the mystery, the nameless, and the silent. Poetic thinking and saying are not arbitrary and subjective expressions. They are directed at encountering things in the happening of their own truth as they themselves interact and interpolate. In this, they are forming the interthingly nexus of the whiling moment and enregioning place in which acting as way-making and building takes place.

11. Between Enframing and Self-so-ness

The current chapter has sketched how Heidegger's thinking of action and *ethos* can be given a ziranist elucidation. *Ziran* should not be construed through modern Occidental conceptions of nature; naturalness should be instead reinterpreted through an orienting *ethos* and exemplary model of the *ziran* receptive to the metamorphosis of things themselves. This "naturalness" is not the reductive variety that, Heidegger remarks, remains a tenacious obstacle to genuinely encountering and mindfully thinking from world and thing (GA 97: 252). The thing is no longer a thing when it is only perceived as a readily available means in pragmatic use. The thing is also more than what is objectively conceived as presence: once the thing is explained to be a construct or product of energy, idea, force, matter, or some other principle, it is not the thing *qua* thing, but an object positioned according to the enframing world-picture of instrumental utility. A more fitting *ethos* of nourishing, making space for, and caring for, things, in Heidegger's later thinking, guided if not solely determined by Lao-Zhuang models of *wuwei-ziran* and releasement-self-presencing, is indispensable to begin to sincerely encounter things and interthingly environments and respond to the current ecological disaster. This is the case even if—given the complexity and enormity of this crisis for humans and other species facing extinction—no single element is sufficient by itself.[47]

What then is a thing? It is best to ask it and observe the tracks and traces of its self-patterning path. Part One of the present work endeavored to demonstrate the tangible scope to which there are robust ziranist tendencies effective in Heidegger's thinking of the thing and dwelling. This has two significant consequences. First, these elements can in turn be deployed to reimagine and reconstruct Heidegger's thought-images, pathways, and models through the Lao-Zhuang philosophy of resonant attunement, with the self-naturing or spontaneous nonpurposive self-generation of things for the sake of a nonpurposive and non-instrumentalized nourishing of life (*yangsheng*).[48] Second, despite its philosophical and political problems, Heidegger's thinking offers (1) formally indicative—to employ Adorno's expression once again—critical models to question the ongoing administrative and technical positioning and domination of the environing and human world and (2) other ways of bearing and dwelling that leap ahead, make room for, and release others, things, and environments from the bonds of constitutive-enframing subjects and enclosing systems.

While Heidegger's thinking of the thing became entangled with two books credited to Laozi and Zhuangzi, Heidegger's thinking of nothingness and emptiness also intersected with Buddhist and Japanese sources and interlocutors. This work now turns from the convergent mutually illuminating priority of the thing in ziranist Daoism and Heidegger's later thinking, and the innumerable senses of the thing's mystery and self-so-ness, to nothingness and emptiness and their senses, in the second part.

Part Two

Nothingness, Emptiness, and the Clearing

6

Daoist Nothingness, Buddhist Emptiness, and the Myth of "Oriental Nothingness"

I. Preliminary Indications

1. Introduction to Part Two

Part One has its point of departure in the thing, and Part Two in the nothing. The present chapter, akin to chapter 1 earlier, provides a preparatory introduction of Daoist and Buddhist sources that facilitate interculturally resituating and critically exceeding Heidegger's thinking. Before we trace the unfolding of an elemental nonderivative nothingness in the early and later writings of Heidegger in Chapter 7, we should accordingly consider the Daoist and Buddhist encounters with and conceptions of nothingness with which it is recurrently interconnected in discourses of comparative philosophy. A number of those explorations reductively apply Occidental concepts of nothingness adopted from G. W. F. Hegel or even Heidegger, or project Orientalist ideological and mythologized ideas of "Oriental nothingness" and nihilism (popularized in nineteenth-century Europe) onto these conceptions. They take insufficient notice of the multiplicity and singularity of diverse transmissions, teachings, and their historical confrontations and entanglements.

This interculturally mediated hermeneutical situation requires respectful caution and patient reserve, so that the matter to be thought can begin to be encountered and speak. Heidegger himself calls for this in his postwar hermeneutics of European and East Asian forms of thinking. Such respectful reservedness needs to make room for and risk the encounter with the other while not precluding its possibilities for mutual understanding. Heidegger's intercultural reflections in "From a Dialogue on Language" point the way in insisting that spaces be opened for encountering the other in their own sense, while at the same time limiting the way by positing and reifying an incommensurable experiential and linguistic abyss between the "Occident" and the "Orient." To think with and contrary to Heidegger once again, as Heidegger demanded perhaps more than his critics do, this fixed border can be loosened through the anarchic openness and emptiness that such a boundary would limit.

Heidegger does not propose or rely on a problematic conception of "Oriental nothingness" developed by earlier philosophers such as Hegel and embraced in East Asian philosophical discourses in response to Occidental critiques.[1] He does not dismiss or reject, but wavers in the face of identifying his own thinking of nothingness and emptiness with Japanese notions of nothingness and emptiness in "From a Dialogue on Language." His thought is intertwined not only with Daoist but also Buddhist and modern East Asian philosophies of nothingness and emptiness, as will be traced throughout Part Two.

What then are the functions of nothingness and emptiness in paradigmatic Daoist and Buddhist contexts? First, the early images of nature, in what is now called China, are not the nothingness of *creatio ex nihilo* or the nonbeing of Parmenides and Plato. This nothingness is, rather, generative watery chaos (perceived either as self-stirring or as stirred by heaven), the dragon of the *Book of Changes* that slumbers within the hidden depths of mountain lakes and whose ascension brings forth nourishing rain and life, and maternal tenderness and nurturing.[2] These images became linked in the formation of the *Daodejing* and related sources with an emerging conception of nothingness developed through a logic of negativity. Heidegger would be mistaken, and Rudolf Carnap would be correct, if Heidegger were understood as denying that nothingness becomes perceptible and conceivable through negativity and negation. However, Carnap and the positivists are incorrect insofar as Heidegger proceeded from Dasein to negativity during this period (GA 91: 119); that is, from a phenomenology of existential negativity, which is encountered prior to and shapes our understanding of conceptual negation, to the (supposed) "non-sense" of nothingness, which emerges as something more and other than negation and as that which makes it possible. Absence and negativity belong to Dasein and are not yet thought more primordially as elements of the openness/hiddenness in which Dasein exists, as notes from the early 1930s make clear (GA 91: 119, 122). As will be considered in the final chapters, Heidegger's thinking of nothingness might appear too positivistic when analyzed in the contexts of Daoist generative nothingness, Buddhist emptiness, or the absolute nothingness of Nishida Kitarō and the Kyōto School.

Nothingness as death and distance from God in Christian onto-theology, the groundless abyss and anxiety of existentialism, the generative nothingness glimpsed in the *Daodejing* and its reception, and the emptiness of early Buddhist discourses are each distinctive and to an extent incommensurable. Their distinctiveness demands hermeneutical respect rather than reductive totalizing speculation. Nonetheless, Daoist and Buddhist sources reveal an intersecting movement from experiential and linguistic negativity to an affirmative sense of the "not" and a more primordial formative nothingness or emptiness. This interpretive situation requires a tentative three fold distinction: (1) the existential negativity of the Buddhist therapeutic analysis of suffering, illness, and death or of existential limit-situations and disorienting conditions such as radical anxiety and boredom; (2) the linguistic and logical negativity of negation that is typically construed in Occidental philosophy as secondary and derivative to positive assertions about beings; and (3) a radical nothingness or emptiness, as that which is in some way other or more than and irreducible to the existential and logical negativity through which it is encountered and glimpsed. Such radical forms of nothingness are perceived in a variety of ways: as the terrifying groundless abyss; as the nihilistic absurd and contingent undermining all meaning and value; as an openness in which things arise and depart; and as the primordial concealed, womblike nourishing darkness from which the myriad things arise and return.[3]

In Chapter 6, we will address nothingness and emptiness as presented in paradigmatic Daoist and Buddhist discourses so as to reassess, in Chapter 7, Heidegger's early existentially oriented philosophy of nothingness in the late 1920s and its subsequent shifts. We will then follow Heidegger's interpretive transitions from the language of existential negativity and nothingness as abyss, to a more generative conception of nothingness and the emptiness of the clearing and opening, that appears to evoke Daoist and Buddhist discourses. This resonance is usually unspoken and indirect, yet there are texts in which Heidegger directly reveals his interest in the nothingness and emptiness of East Asian sources. Chapter 8 will then examine the intercultural entanglements of Heidegger's thinking of nothingness in its early reception in the 1930s and 1940s by East Asian philosophers and intellectuals. The conclusion briefly outlines the work as a whole and addresses several social-political dilemmas concerning the modern discourse of nothingness, in which I outline its critical potential despite dubious political appropriations which require the ideological enchantment and fixation of identity that reduce dynamic relational things in their communicative exchange and interval to homogeneity.

II. Daoism, Negativity, and Generative Nothingness

2. Negation and Nothingness in Early Chinese Philosophy

Chinese and East Asian philosophies as a whole cannot be simply identified with nothingness and emptiness as portrayed in Hegel's myth of "Oriental nothingness." Hegel's misunderstanding is due to (1) his interests in prioritizing European spirit, as exceptionally rational and free, and (2) his lack of radicality in conceiving negativity and the nothing (a critique made by Adorno and Heidegger). It is also attributable to (3) his want of historical understanding. Nothingness is not the essence of "Oriental mind" imprisoned in abstract negativity. It emerges from specific Daoist and Buddhist discourses that play a formative role in broader aesthetic, cultural, practical, and intellectual tendencies. In the early formation of the Chinese language and thought, including the background sources of the *Daodejing*, concrete natural phenomena and elements like water, earth, and sky play a more fundamental role than negation or nothingness, which presuppose various abstract conceptual developments and their radical critique.[4] Both the *Daodejing* and *Zhuangzi* engage in a therapeutic destructuring of fixating concepts, perspectives, and positions that must have already existed to be overcome.

What is the context of negativity and nothingness in early Chinese philosophy? Early Confucian texts such as the *Book of Rites* (*Liji* 禮記) or the *Mencius* (*Mengzi* 孟子) illustrate the ordinary early Chinese usage of expressions that (literally translated) signify no-thing (*wuwu* 無物), nonbeing (*wuyou* 無有), and even doubled "no-no" to signify never (*wuwu* 無無). In the first Gaozi 告子 chapter of the *Mencius*, phrases such as "nothing will not grow" (無物不長) and "nothing will be lost" (無物不消) signify that all things will grow and flourish. "No being" means that no person is without a propensity toward goodness (人無有不善), just as no water lacks a propensity toward moving downward (水無有不下). The rare doubled not (無無) in early texts occurs twice in the *Book of Rites* in the sense of "never be without" in proper ritual activities. It is revealing that the earliest strata of the *Book of Changes*, which would develop into a paradigmatic source for subsequent Chinese philosophical reflection, do not emphasize negativity and nothingness. These will become central to its later expositions and uses, particularly in Wang Bi's paradigmatic commentaries. His interpretation integrates concepts, strategies, and thought-images from the *Book of Changes* and the *Daodejing*, extending them into an expansive philosophy of nothingness that is at most only implicit in the earlier strata of these works.[5]

The negational "not" and the nothing that signifies no things or entities, to the extent that it is derived from it, have conventional negational senses in early Chinese sources that presuppose the priority of things and beings as present. Beings encompass natural entities and systems as well as ghosts and spirits that are only visible to human perception through their tracks and traces. There are two discursive families (*jia* 家) in which negation and nothingness begin to take on other meanings, indicating different ways of pondering the not and the nothing. The first is the school of names (*mingjia* 名家). It mobilizes paradoxical conceptual constructions that lead to what is often described in Occidental terms as nominalist, sophistical, and skeptical contradictions. These strategies guide Zhuangzi's frequent skeptical interlocutor, Hui Shi (惠施; Huizi 惠子), famous for formulating paradoxes, and inform crucial passages of chapter two of the *Zhuangzi* anthology. The second is the lineage of the way (*daojia* 道家) that was identified with the *Daodejing* in antiquity and linked with either the Yellow Emperor (Huangdi 黃帝) in practically directed Huanglao 黃老 teachings or with the *Zhuangzi*. The expression *daojia* 道家 was used by the early Han-era historian Sima Qian to explain these varieties of Daoism.[6] Religious Daoist movements (*daojiao* 道教) which link elemental forces with spiritual forms (gods, spirits, and immortals) and accentuate practices of biospiritual self-transformation (inner training and inner alchemy) emerged in the late and post-Han period.[7]

The paradoxical and mysterious expressions of the *Daodejing*, a mystery that is to be doubled rather than resolved, lead to a radical insight into the nature of things and exemplary comportments instead of skeptical doubt or suspension of belief. They open into the abyss beyond concepts instead of merely skeptically doubting and questioning concepts (compare Buber 2017: 535). The not and the nothing do not only function in negational and paradoxical expressions in the *Daodejing* and *Zhuangzi* collections. Two other semantic registers are involved here. The not-x indicates forms of practice and attunement such as in the "action without action" of *wei wuwei* 為無為, the non-knowing of *wuzhi* 無知, the non-desiring of *wuyu* 無欲, the emptied heart-mind of the *Zhuangzi*'s *wuxin* 無心 that is also used in Chan Buddhist discourses, and the non-entanglement in affairs of *wushi* 無事. The "non-" (*wu*) signifies a transformation of action, desire and knowing, rather than a mere negation. These transformative practices are already linked with enacting emptiness, simplicity, and stillness. They point toward an attunement or an accord with *dao* of heaven and earth, the elements, and the myriad things, as a primordial occurring of nothingness.

Such practices and operative states of nothingness are linked with early forms of biospiritual and meditative practices, which form part of the background of the formation of religious Daoism, and conditions of emptiness expressed through a variety of terms. *Xu* 虛 means a hollow space. It operates negatively as absence or lack in *Daodejing* 53. It designates a practice of emptying in *Daodejing* chapters 3 and 16 where it is associated with silence and simplicity. *Chong* 沖 refers to emptiness as washed away, filling up, and pouring forth. *Kong* 孔, meaning aperture or hole, refers to emptying virtuosity (*kongde* 孔德) as the functioning of the *dao* in *Daodejing* 21. The *Zhuangzi* text also uses *kong* 空, signifying empty and hollow, which is later adopted to translate Sanskrit *śūnya* (emptiness).[8] In the *Daodejing*, the *Zhuangzi*, and related sources, nonbeing, no-thing, and nothingness emerge as portending more and other than the "not" of negation and skeptical contradiction.

In the earlier oracle bone script, the homophonic *mu* 母 (mother) was loaned to express negation and later distinguished as *wu* 毋. The early pictogram that became *wu* 無 (at that time pronounced *ma*) pictured a shamanic person dancing, which would later be borrowed to signify "not." This loan-process was based on their homophonous sound rather than meaning. The primordial sense of nothingness was not contained in or immediately related to the *wu*-character as maintained in anachronistic and speculative etymologies. It became linked with this character through a historical linguistic and interpretive process that formed and drew on the resonances established between "not" and the loan-characters—which were primarily loaned due to sound—for mother and the shamanic dance. Possibly they associated nothingness with qualities of maternal nurturing and shamanic insight, which inform the background of the *Daodejing* and the *Zhuangzi*.

The *wu* character appears throughout the *Daodejing*, most often in the negational grammatical form of not-x that attests to its conventional common usage. The double not or nothing (*wuwu* 無無), which is not a negation of nothingness but its functioning in the *Zhuangzi*, does not occur in the *Daodejing*.[9] "Nonbeing" (*wuyou*) has two occurrences in the *Daodejing*. It means conventional not being in chapter 19. In chapter 43, it is said that "acting without acting" emulates the water-like permeability, softness, and fluidity of *dao*, as that which has no being can enter even into that which has no entrance (無有入無間). There are several historical reasons, based on transmitted and excavated texts, to suspect that the darkness and fecundity of water and the nurturing maternal womb are older images of *dao* than the nothingness that became its dominant image in subsequent Chinese discourses. These include Han-era and Song-Ming-era Confucians who adopted elements from Daoist and Buddhist philosophy, while polemically rejecting them overall.

3. The "no-thing" and the Generative Primordiality of Nothingness

The "not-" expressions in the *Daodejing* occur in the form of not-x in which x is to be perceived as an altered perspective. Only later sources isolate the not or double it (*wuwu*) as nothingness per se. There are, however, indications of radical nothingness in the nonbeing and no-thing of chapters 43 and 14.

In chapter 43, that which is without being can enter into that which is without entrance and is sealed. Responsively attuned acting without acting emulates this nonbeing (*wuyou*). Analogous to water, which is a thought-image as well as a natural phenomenon, it freely flows with the changing myriad things without obstruction. Being like nonbeing could mean, in a minimalistic reading, to exist like, or as if, nothing, in the conventional sense of that which is not; thus, it would evade barriers and conditions. If *Daodejing* chapter 43 is read in conjunction with other chapters, it is clear there is more to nothingness than mere negational not being. The commentarial transmission, including the *Heshanggong* and Wang Bi commentaries, construes nonbeing to signify a more primordial self-stirring, generative nothingness.

Nothingness is completely empty yet full of generative potentiality and promise in the notion of returning to the empty pole (*wuji* 無極), expressed in *Daodejing* chapter 28 (復歸於無極). The *Heshanggong* commentary identifies abiding in the empty pole of nothingness, along with the fullness of virtuosity and longevity of life associated with purposive Daoist self-cultivation and biospiritual practices. In his commentary on *Daodejing* chapter 55, and in a more ziranist and Zhuangzian spirit, Wang Bi contrasts the freedom of residing in the empty pole with purposive practices and techniques deemed restrictive and coercive. Wang Bi remarks that the heart-mind (*xin* 心) should be without contention, desire, and intentional purpose, letting itself reside in nonbeing, such that the vital forces (*qi*) are not coerced by striving for virtuosity and longevity.[10] They are only in accord with *dao*, according to his commentary about chapter 21, in embracing them through emptiness.

Wang Bi does not reject practice to idly speculate about nothingness, as critics contend. As also seen in sections of the *Zhuangzi* that destructure practices of nurturing life (*yangsheng*), Wang Bi distinguishes the purposive skills and techniques of nourishing life that undermine what they seek, from nonpurposive practices of emptying, and an art of existence from nothingness as the empty generative source. Appropriate use/functioning transpires only in nonpurposive and non-coerced alignment with the use/functioning of nothingness.[11] The former might be described as the enactment of dispositional emptiness and the latter as ontological or onto-cosmological nothingness.

Wang Bi's expression for nothingness (literally, no-thing: *wuwu* 無物) occurs only twice in the *Daodejing*, in chapter 14, that offers a portrait of practicing *dao* as an according with it in its formless and nameless nothingness:

> Looking without seeing, it is called level; listening without hearing, it is called rare; grasping without obtaining, it is called minute. These three cannot be examined, and are hence blended into one. Above it is not bright; below it is not obscure. Measureless and nameless, it is returning to no-thing (*wuwu*). It is form without form, the image of no-thing (*wuwu*), indistinct and faint. Welcoming it without perceiving its beginning; following it without perceiving its ending. Holding on to the ancient way is to exist in the present. Knowing the ancient origin is to practice *dao* [in the present].[12]

The *Daodejing* contains, according to Wang Bi's ziranist elucidation, a radical therapeutic potential for the present. It provides this through emptying and unfixing the forces of life from limiting practices and techniques and through linguistic-conceptual strategies of destructuring and emptying words and concepts. The realization of free nonpurposiveness is styled and signaled, yet not named or defined, through indicative orientating concepts such as emptiness (*xu*), nothingness, and uselessness (*buyong* 不用 and *wuyong* 無用). These imply releasing ourselves and the myriad things from reifying fixations of practice and language into the generativity of nothingness.[13]

The philosophy of nothingness is elevated into the principal teaching of the *Daodejing* in the post-Han-era mysterious learning (*xuanxue* 玄學) movement.[14] Wang Bi does not only play a key role in its Chinese reception. The German translations that Heidegger relied on were based on the Wang Bi *Daodejing* edition and commentary. Wang Bi and later exegetists do not interpret the no-, non-, or not- (*wu-x*) phrases of the *Daodejing* as mere negations. The no- expressions are a manner of speaking and styling showing that which otherwise could not be shown. The "not"- operates as an indication of the functioning of and acting according to nothingness. In this way, *wuwei* is understood as acting from out of nothingness. It is emptied in not being an acting from a particular something, and in emptiness can be attuned by nothingness itself. Purposive action (*wei*) is acting from out of a conditional, fixating, and limiting something. The *wuwei* of the exemplary person (*junzi* 君子) is an "acting out of nothing" that responsively accords with the functioning of nothingness itself.[15] Similarly, *wuzhi* is knowing from nothingness; *wuyu* is desiring from nothingness.

The "non-" in the *Daodejing*, according to the commentary of Wang Bi, reverses and points toward the flowing functioning of the shapeless (*wuzhuang* 無狀), formless (*wuxing* 無形), and nameless (*wuming* 無名) way (*dao* 道) itself. The use (*yong* 用) in no-use or no-function (*wuyong*) of *Daodejing* chapter 11 and the *Zhuangzi* was a Daoist thematic to which Heidegger repeatedly returned in his thinking of appropriate use (*Gebrauch*) and uselessness (*Nutzlosigkeit*); it is interpreted as the primordial using/functioning/operating (*yong*) of nothingness in Wang Bi such that "uselessness" is a using from nothingness rather than somethingness. In his exegesis of the *Daodejing*, *dao* and its associated generative and maternal qualities, through a tracing from the mystery, point toward the functioning of primordial nothingness from which all things arise and to which they all return. Early Daoist primordial nothingness is not the indeterminate and unmediated abstraction criticized by Hegel. It is rather, in *Daodejing* 40, the pivot that enacts and is enacted through all movement, arising, and reversal (i.e., in Hegel's language, mediation). And, in *Daodejing* 43, it is described as flowing without resistance through both the hardest and emptiest of things.

The movement of reversal and return between incipient nothingness and emergent fullness expressed in *Daodejing* 40 is similarly articulated in Wang Bi's commentaries on the *Book of Changes*. That movement is elucidated through a philosophy of nothingness in ways that would mold subsequent Chinese speculative discourses that cannot be described in detail here. Most revealing perhaps is the incorporation of nothingness in late Warring States and eclectic Han-era Confucianism as well as its systematic elaboration in Song-Ming-era Neo-Confucianism.

To succinctly describe why some modern interpretations incorporated Confucianism into "Oriental nothingness," the primary reason is early European missionaries. They depicted Neo-Confucian literati as practicing sitting in emptiness and conceptualizing nothingness. This Neo-Confucian discourse of "nothingness" concerns the empty pole (*wuji* 無極), an expression whose earliest extant uses are found in *Daodejing* 28 and the *Zhuangzi* before entering into the commentarial transmission of the *Book of Changes* and Confucian cosmological discourses. *Wuji* signifies in Zhu Xi 朱熹 the raw chaotic unformed potentiality and promise that goes on to become the ordered realization and interfused fullness of patterning principle (*li* 理) and vital energy (*qi* 氣) in the great ultimate pole (*taiji* 太極).[16] Nothingness could accordingly be retrospectively construed in East Asian contexts as a key shared teaching of the Buddha, Confucius, and Laozi and in modern Occidental discourses as "Oriental nothingness," which was in philosophy criticized by Hegel, and embraced as a relative nothingness opposed to the world of will and representation by Schopenhauer.[17]

III. Buddhism and Self-Emptiness

4. The Buddha's Emptiness

Siddhārtha Gautama meditated under the bodhi tree in stillness. He responded to speculative questions with silence. After his awakening, the Buddha taught that there is no substantially fixed form of the self (*anātman*) or things as they causally dependently arise in becoming. He did not teach nothingness and was never regarded as a teacher of nothingness in early and classical Indian and South Asian depictions. "Buddhist nothingness" is predominantly a modern construction shaped and reshaped in cross-cultural exchanges. The modern European reception of the Buddhist dharma emphasized how it is a cult and teaching of nothingness, an impression that still influences contemporary criticisms of Buddhist teachings. Hegel's critique of what he conceived to be Buddhist nothingness, Nietzsche's worries about Buddhist and European nihilism, and Heidegger's repetition of Nietzsche's remarks are exemplary instances of European suspicions regarding the consequences of Buddhist emptiness (*śūnyatā*). Such suspicions arose despite the fact that emptiness was not stressed in the discourses attributed to the historical Buddha in the Theravāda Pāli canon and was rarely used to designate nonbeing or nothingness in premodern Buddhist transmissions. On the contrary, being and nonbeing are both described as empty of essence.

European philosophers have systematically misinterpreted Buddhist emptiness. Hegel is a primary source of such confusion. According to his assessment in the *Science of Logic*, drawing on missionary accounts of this nihilistic "cult of nothingness," Buddhism preeminently typifies the nihilism of Oriental nothingness in which "nothingness, the empty void, is the absolute principle" (Hegel 1986c: 84). Hegel's misunderstanding of Buddhism as an undifferentiated universal nihilation of anything positive reverberates in later German discourses (as in Adorno, GS 3: 40). In its European reception, Buddhist emptiness has been and continues to be systematically misconstrued as a destructive nihilating nothingness. The vitalist Ludwig Klages could describe the "nihilistic morality of Buddhism" in the 1940s as a paradoxical abyss, a morality of flight from the world, an unwillingness to live, and the suicide of thought (Klages 1944: 465). The European accentuation of "Buddhist nothingness" systematically distorts its development and roles in Buddhist sources. There are several reasons why the nothingness ascribed to Buddhism in Hegel's narrative and its early European reception is erroneous. We can momentarily consider here select paradigmatic elements and phases of the history of Buddhist emptiness to help situate it relative to nothingness in Hegel and Heidegger.

First, śūnyatā was not counted among the primary teachings of the Buddha in the oldest discourses, as recorded in the Pāli canon or other extent canons. It is not systematically emphasized by the Buddha at all in these works. Emptiness emerges over time as a way to systematically explain his primary teachings of dependent origination (paṭiccasamuppāda) and the three marks of existence: impermanence (aniccā), existential suffering (duḥkha), and non-self (anattā).

Secondly, suñña (empty, void, zero) is frequently used in Pāli Sutta literature to convey the conventional sense of empty rooms and places where meditative practices occur, thereby giving it a less negative valence. It is also used—along with expressions such as ritta (blank, vacant), tuccha (deserted, vain), and asāra (insubstantial, worthless)—to negatively signify insubstantial hollowness, transience, and vanity. In this way, it is used to explain the notion of "no-self" as an emptiness of enduring substantial selfhood (as in *Samyutta Nikaya* 35.85), and as a specific form of meditative concentration and practice, as in the "Division on Emptiness" (Suññatavagga) collection in the *Middle Length Discourses* (*Majjhima Nikaya*).[18]

Thirdly, in the context of Mahāyāna philosophy, the analysis of emptiness occurs alongside discourses of mind and the *tathāgatagarbha* (the primordial womb, embryo, or matrix of Buddhahood) or buddha-nature. In later kataphatic discourses of buddha-nature (initially the potentiality for awakening occurring in a fraction of beings and progressively in all things), emptiness did not designate a quintessential teaching.[19] These tendencies are much more prevalent in East Asian varieties of the Buddhist dharma than the apophatic emptiness deployed in Madhyamika. It is a heuristic, a useful means, and a provisional teaching in many early and later forms and schools of the Buddha dharma. Emptiness operates in these contexts as a means of meditatively and linguistically destructuring fixating attachments and illusions to allow the suchness of reality to disclose itself.

Fourthly, Madhyamaka is the teaching of the middle that there is no self-nature, only emptiness. Along with other Buddhist teachings that prioritized emptiness as a definitive teaching, Madhyamaka accentuated determinate practices of linguistic destructuring and meditative emptying. They did not understand it to signify an absolute or indeterminate generalized nothingness, contrary to Hegel's influential narrative. Emptiness is linked in Nāgārjuna's *Fundamental Verses of the Middle Way* (*Mūlamadhyamakakārikā*) with the determinate negation of substantiality and, is always, a determinate emptiness *of* form, mind, self, things, dharmas, as elemental constituents, or even emptiness itself.

What then of emptiness? Its early senses and uses also indicate how emptiness is not the fundamental expression or experience for early forms of Buddhism, not to mention subsequent forms that classified emptiness as a preliminary heuristic in prioritizing mind or buddha-nature. The word has an extensive and complex development in Indian and Buddhist thought. Śūnya derives from the root śvi: hollow, barren, and vain. It is etymologically related to the Latin word *cavus*. Its earliest meanings are no doubt principally conventional and negative: emptiness signifies the illusory and ephemeral, the barrenness and vanity of the self and its world in early Buddhist discourses, as recorded in the three baskets (*tipiṭaka*) of the Theravāda Pāli canon.

Given such senses of the illusory and transitory in early Buddhism, how did emptiness take on a more affirmative resonance and become one of the central Buddhist teachings? The threefold sense of emptiness, as ordinary conventional space and absence, as hollow transient vanity, and as a path of liberation, is made explicit in the Theravāda commentarial tradition. The two non-systematic uses of "emptiness" in its conventional and negative senses are still apparent in Buddhaghosa's comprehensive fifth-century commentarial treatise *The Path of Purification* (*Visuddhimagga*). Its later chapters on wisdom reveal a more radical conception of emptiness: the text equates meditation on non-self with meditation on emptiness, as the Buddha already is said to have done, and delineates the systematic relation between emptiness as an emptying meditative modality, ultimate emancipatory awakening, and *nibbāna* (*nirvāṇa*) as signless, desireless, and empty (Buddhaghosa 2010: 697, 726).

5. The Emptying Emptiness of the Middle Path (Madhyamaka)

Emptiness has multiple senses in Buddhist discourses. Most basically, it can operate either as a heuristic provisional teaching and skillful means (*upāya, fangbian* 方便), leading to the purity of suchness (*tathātā, zhenru* 真如), luminous mind (*prabhāsvara, guangmingxin* 光明心), or buddha-reality or nature (*buddhadhātu, foxing* 佛性), as being empty of afflictions and defilements (*kleśa*). Or, as in the paradigmatic works of Madhyamaka philosophy and perfection of wisdom (*prajñāpāramitā*) sūtra literature, it can operate as fundamentally constitutive of the path of awakening and liberation in the teachings of the greater vehicle. There is no intrinsic or independent self-nature (*svabhāva, zixing* 自性), only emptiness as the determinate self-emptiness of things.

Madhyamaka prioritized emptiness as that which is middle-most between being and nothingness. It contests hypostatized substantialism and nihilistic annihilationism, which it dismantles through the self-contradictory consequences of affirmation and denial. Nāgārjuna (c. 150 CE–250 CE) was one of the final "great philosophers" discussed by Karl Jaspers in his work of this name in the 1950s (Jaspers 1966). Heidegger probably knew little directly of Nāgārjuna or Madhyamaka, which offered one of the most striking and influential interpretations of Buddhist emptiness. Nāgārjuna articulated emptiness as the implication of dependent origination that can then be deployed to systematically dismantle all (including other Buddhist) conceptions and discourses. The opening lines of *Fundamental Verses of the Middle Way* express a *via negativa* that would undo both "self-nature" (or self-essence) and "other-nature" (or other-essence, *parābhava*): "Not from itself, not from another, not from both, nor without cause [that is, not from neither]. Never in any way is there any existing thing that has arisen."[20] No adequate noncontradictory distinctions can be made between self- and other-nature, self- and other-caused, such that all events and phenomena are empty of such posited and constructed elements.

Emptiness is shown through Nāgārjuna's classic analysis to be a determinate "emptiness of," demonstrated by logically reducing each proposed position and viewpoint about beings and nothingness to self-contradiction. While earlier Buddhist discourses thematized practicing the correct view (*samyak-dṛuṣṭi*) as the first step in the eightfold path, Nāgārjuna articulates the "relinquishment of all views" (MKK 27:30). The analysis of views enacts liberation from fixating and limiting views: "emptiness is the relinquishing of all views. For whomever emptiness becomes a view that one will accomplish nothing" (MKK 13:8).

The determinate negativity of emptiness undermines views through their contradictions without arriving at an affirmative view or perspective of being or nothingness. Emptiness is accordingly not a view and is itself without any intrinsic self-nature in the emptiness of emptiness. The Buddha did not offer a teaching but a therapeutic strategy of emptying and undoing *samāropa*. This expression can be translated as fixation, hypostatization, reification, or erroneous affirmation: "No Dharma whatsoever was ever taught by the Buddha to anyone" (MKK 25.24). The primary teaching is then not a teaching but the enactment of emptiness: "since all existents are empty, views such as eternalism, annihilationism, etc.—where will they occur, to whom will they occur, which of them will occur, and for what reason will they occur?" (MKK 27.29).

The logical deconstruction of views (*prasaṅga*) through their inherent contradictions and the apophatic negative therapeutic character of Madhyamaka is emphasized in the commentarial transmission of Candrakīrti (c. 600–650). The Buddha's teachings heuristically negate each and all views: "This is the meaning of the Sūtra, and this meaning is exhausted in its negation of any other agent," such that one will cling to neither object nor subject, form (*rūpa*) nor mind (*citta*), nor to their emptiness (*śūnyatā*).

IV. Daoist-Buddhist Differences and Entanglements

6. Conflicts and Mediations between Buddhist Emptiness and Daoist Nothingness

Chinese Madhyamaka continued to wield emptiness to disassemble views and fixations. This deployment is evident in the nothingness of Daoist-Buddhist discourses in the "Treatise on Emptiness as Nonsubstantiality" (*Bu Zhenkong Lun* 不真空論) composed by the Jin dynasty philosopher and monk Sengzhao 僧肇 (384–414 CE). This treatise dismantled reifying substantialist depictions of emptiness in terms of being or nonbeing. Buddhist emptiness of form was perceived to be the realization of the free and easy wandering (*xiaoyao you*) promised by Zhuangzi in an elemental emptiness that cannot be limited to either being or nonbeing. He articulated a central correlation between enacting emptying and emptiness: as the mind becomes emptier, practice becomes more extensive.[21]

Later Sinicized Buddhist lineages increasingly classified emptiness as a preliminary meditative heuristic that clears away obstructions and opens the buddha-nature (originary awakening) in beings as a more advanced and perfected teaching. Huayan is the most radical vision of relational holism that preserves each singular event. In Huayan, overly succinctly put, each singularly unique event encompasses each and every other event without obstruction or reduction. In Tiantai 天台 emptiness and form, mind and reality mutually encompass one another. During the mid- and late Tang dynasty era, in the universal buddha-nature teachings of the Tiantai philosopher Zhanran 湛然 and in the antinomian and iconoclastic Chan rhetoric and practice of Mazu Daoyi 馬祖道一 (709–788 CE) and Linji Yixuan, all sentient and non-sentient natural phenomena, the ordinary everyday mind (*pingchang xin* 平常心), and impure objects such as excrement are respectively specified as expressing and partaking in the emptiness of all distinctions (including those between the sacred and the profane) and buddha-nature as the intrinsic capacity for illumination and awakening. The thought-image of the empty sky discussed by Heidegger can signify in Buddhist discourses elemental emptiness and the clarity and luminosity of the one mind or buddha-nature.[22] This is the nature that is directly perceived through enacting emptiness in meditative practices that developed into meditation on the transformation inducing paradoxes and "great doubt" of the kōan (*gong'an* 公案).

Heidegger's thinking of nothingness and emptiness as the highest expressions of being has an analogous structure to the emptiness of nature in East Asian Buddhist sources and their appropriation in modern Japanese philosophy, as discussed in the following chapters. Let us first conclude this section by briefly reviewing a late Tang dynasty–era discourse on emptiness and nothingness, before turning to this thematic in Heidegger and then subsequently, in Chapter 7, the entanglements between Heidegger's nothingness and modern Japanese thought.

The ninth-century Chan and Huayan teacher Guifeng Zongmi, for example, counterpoised them in his account of the three teachings of Buddhism, Confucianism, and Daoism in his highly influential *Inquiry into the Origin of Humanity* (*Yuanren lun* 原人論).[23] Zongmi's hermeneutical approach in this work and in his writings on competing forms of Chan Buddhism influenced the development of Korean and Japanese Chan.[24] The *Origin of Humanity* was important for its classificatory hermeneutics of non-Buddhist and Buddhist teachings in the subsequent history of East Asian Buddhist dharma. It is a pivotal work for modern Buddhist studies and was already extensively discussed and translated twice into German during the first half of the twentieth century.[25]

Emptiness is not an abstract, indeterminate, generalized nothingness, as in Hegel's influential portrayal that lingers in Heidegger's 1930s impressions of Buddhism. Zongmi critiques various one-sided forms of emptiness, including Mazu's Chan in the *Chan Prolegomenon* (*Chanyuan zhuquanji duxu* 禪源諸卷集都序): for Zongmi, emptiness is determinate of forms and existents. It is the emptiness *of* form in Buddhism, as he understands it, and form is entangled with immediate and mediated karmic determinations, such that the path of liberation comes from destructuring and emptying karma, delusion, and underlying forms of "storehouse" consciousness (*ālayavijñāna*; *alai yeshi* 阿賴耶識). The emptiness *of* emptiness still requires the correlation of the emptying of emptied form that is expressed in the "of." But, for Zongmi, all possibilities are contained in and self-generated as naturally self-so from the empty state of nothingness to which they revert in the teaching of Laozi. Zongmi concludes that Daoist nothingness and natural spontaneity do not offer an adequate analysis and explanation of determinate and karmic causal conditions and thus cannot provide an appropriate diagnosis and pathway for their therapeutic cure that can transition through emptiness to the self-awareness of the buddha-nature (Gregory 1995: 80–104).

The emptiness of things and the world itself entails that they infinitely arise and dissipate without end, yet the essence of *dao* is not Laozi's nothingness (which Zongmi dismisses as arbitrary and incoherent) as thing and world have a determinate non-spontaneous source, becoming, and outcome. The consummate teaching reveals "nature," deploying the more fixed notion of inherent nature (*xing* 性) rather than *ziran*, which he critiqued as random without causal and karmic conditioning. The emptiness of the selfless essence is the tranquil illumination of the concealed womb and embryo of Buddhahood.[26] Zongmi proposed that the Buddha "taught that all is empty" (i.e., of any fixed intrinsic nature) for the sake of disclosing "the pure, numinous, and awakened genuine mind, which is absolutely identical with that of the buddhas" (i.e., of genuine nature).[27]

7. Transition to Chapter 7

Nothingness is neither a mere derivative negation nor a hidden something or substance. It constitutes the very dynamic of reality and being. Heidegger's nothingness appears to deeply resonate with Daoist and Buddhist conceptions of nothingness even as he had limited exposure to the full variation considered in this chapter, which has set the stage for elucidating Heidegger's nothing in view of the luminous clarity of Buddhist emptiness and the dark mystery of Daoist nothingness.

To recapitulate, Buddhist emptiness, as linked with the causal matrix of dependent origination, or the implicit buddha-nature operative in sentient beings (in the paradigmatic Huayan of Fazang 法藏), or all things (in Zhanran's Tiantai), is seen as either excluding or encompassing Daoist nothingness as a lower teaching of humans and gods in orthodox Tang-era Buddhist discourses.[28] The history of Buddhist-Daoist interactions, which contributed to their European reception and the idea of "Oriental" nothingness, is not only one of competition and critique. Intersections between Buddhist emptiness and Daoist nothingness began with the introduction of the Buddhist dharma into China during the late Han period and early Chinese Buddhist thinkers such as Zhi Dun, Dao'an, and Sengzhao trained in ziranist Daoist and mysterious learning discourses. It continued to resonate in Chan and Zen practices and teachings that embraced the freedom of *ziran* to interrupt conventional boundaries and karmic attachments and fixations, including the reification of merit and sacredness in Buddhist discourses that overlook their own emptiness. The emptiness of buddha-nature expressed in all natural phenomena was associated with the generative nothingness operative in nature in Tang-era calligraphy, painting, poetry, and meditative practices. The notion of a naturalistic (in the expansive generative sense) art of existence and aesthetic of the Tang became paradigmatic in several modern Occidental and East Asian texts read by Heidegger and others influenced by him.

The identification of these distinctive conceptions of nothingness and emptiness developed further with synthesizing projects that maintained the shared identify of the "three teachings" (*sanjiao* 三教) as an attempt to resolve their philosophical and practical conflicts. Their intersections are at play in Heidegger's encounters and entanglements with East Asian philosophy, particularly as mediated through modern interpretations of Zen Buddhism that were introduced to Heidegger already in 1919 in the gift of Itō Kichinosuke and in a 1930 letter by Ohe Seiichi. However, the existential and discursive interpretive situations that make nothingness or emptiness significant in these divergent contexts are potentially incommensurable and unbridgeable, and at least call for respectful hesitancy and reserve, as Heidegger notes in "From a Dialogue on Language." This reservedness has been criticized as an impediment to pursuing intercultural philosophy. Yet Heidegger describes this hesitation as a necessary hermeneutical preparation for a less superficial and more originary communication across radically distinctive languages and ways of thinking.

Nothingness, Emptiness, and the Clearing: An Intercultural Interpretation

I. Nothingness and Emptiness in Heidegger and His Context

1. Heidegger, Negativity, and Nothingness

Heidegger remarked in his 1938–1939 reflections on Hegel that Hegel's negativity is not genuine negativity, since the "not" and nihilation already presuppose positivity and are positioned as absorbable into the yes and the affirmative.[1] Negative philosophy is not negative enough as it presumes and reverts to positivity. Negativity in Hegel must continually be put to work in the "labor of the negative," which results in affirmation according to an identity-driven dialectic that sublimates all difference and resistance. In his logic, indeterminate nothingness must be determinately superseded in becoming; Hegel is unable to think negativity otherwise than from a fundamentally insubordinate nothingness. This has significant consequences for his confrontation with Asian conceptions of nothingness that he perceives as a threat to proper dialectical thought.

Hegel's historically influential narrative of "Oriental nothingness," construed as an empty, idle, and static abstraction, misconstrues the senses and functions of Buddhist emptiness and Daoist nothingness. These are relational and holistic without requiring assimilation into an abstract systematizing identity. Hegel's influential exposition misses their determinate specificity: the relational interdependent "of" character of emptiness, the generativity and fluidity of nothingness, but also their distinctive therapeutical deployments to undo the hypostatization of mind and world, and the fixations that hinder the plural self-generative dynamics of autopoietic life.[2]

It is still the case, however, that Buddhist and Daoist discourses reveal different existential concerns and possibilities than the histories of nothingness in Occidental philosophy.[3] Parmenides stated: "It is necessary to speak and to think what is; for being is, but nothing is not" (B 6.1–2). An extensive line of diverse thinkers from Parmenides and Plato to Bergson and Carnap, among others, have sought to eliminate nothingness as an impossible, contradictory, and meaningless expression or, as in Hegel's dialectic, bring it under the dominion of the affirmative. In this Occidental context, in which the nothing is a mere not and cannot be properly thought, Heidegger's elucidation of nothingness in his 1929 Freiburg inaugural lecture "What is Metaphysics?" appears distinct and radical. It promised to traverse the abyss between "East" and "West" for several early readers and drew intense condemnation from his early critics.

Heidegger elicited this intercultural attention by giving nothingness its own determinate specificity that could not be reduced to either the dialectical negativity of Hegel or the logical negation of positivism. His existential analysis of nothingness in 1929 did not directly concern Buddhist emptiness or Daoist nothingness. It did share intersecting elements that would only be intensified in Heidegger's subsequent reflections on nothingness as the emptiness and openness in which the releasement of things transpires. Let us now contemplate how emptiness and nothingness unfold in his early and later thought and their intercultural entanglements.

2. Emptiness, Formal Indication, and Destruction in the Early Heidegger

Heidegger's later thinking of emptiness as openness reconnects, as is noted in "From a Dialogue on Language," with his early hermeneutics (GA 11: 90–4). Heidegger describes hermeneutics as a practice of formal indication (*formale Anzeige*) in the 1920–1922 lecture-courses *Phenomenology of Religious Life* and *Phenomenological Interpretations of Aristotle*. Its key method is the dismantling, formalizing, and emptying of commitments and prejudices. This includes the unquestioning commitment to universality and the theoretical stance (GA 60: 59), bound to and absorbed in a particular context with its specific content in order to encounter phenomena in their own concrete character.

Heidegger methodologically proceeded from the fixated givenness of mere facticity to the categorial, existential character of the facticity of the interpretive situation through formal indication (GA 61: 20). Formal indication, for which formal logic fails to be sufficiently formal (GA 61: 20, 33), is analyzed as disclosing that which is concrete through formalization and emptying (GA 61: 33). Formal indication suspends complete and final understanding so as to open access to and free the encounter with the matter in question (GA 60: 67). This enactment of emptying prioritizes encountering object and the thing, even though it does not yet lead Heidegger to embrace the thing's ownness and priority.

The emptying of indicative-opening formalization in the early 1920s proceeds through destructuring (*Destruktion*) historically stratified transmissions and the absorbed fixated situation, thus allowing the situation to be genuinely encountered in its own historicity as an event. This process of destructuring and emptying, which shares features of Buddhist discursive and meditative practices of negation and emptying, opens the encounter with beings in their concreteness and one's own being-there in-the-world.[4] This hermeneutical strategy remains operative in *Being and Time*. In the opening pages the question of the sense of being appears as the most abstract, empty, and formal question. It is at the same time the most decisive and concrete question for the individuation of "being-there" (Dasein) in its own concrete singular situation (GA 2: 39).

3. Nothingness as the Temporalizing of Factical Life

Heidegger's earliest philosophical discussions of nothingness addressed it as a non-real conceptual object in the works of Alexius Meinong in 1912 and as nominal in

Duns Scotus (in fact, Thomas of Erfurt) in 1916 (GA 1: 27; GA 1: 549). These earlier studies indicate how nothingness and negation can be meaningful and operative even if they do not name really existing objects. An object is that which has a characteristic, regardless of whether it actually exists (such as fictional objects), and even if its characteristics are only negative limiting ones. Heidegger's thinking of nothingness in the 1920s could be interpreted as meaningful through a Meinongian understanding of beingless and negative objects.[5] This strategy is inadequate because Heidegger's discourse need not assume nonexisting objects and extends beyond issues of nominal irreal objects. Likewise, his analysis departs from the schema of a relative, negative, privative nothingness (*nihil privativum*) and impossible absolute nothingness (*nihil simpliciter*) proposed by the late medieval Modist speculative grammarians.

Heidegger's reflections on nothingness in the 1920s concern (1) the existential dynamics of negativity and nothingness disclosed in ruination and radical anxiety, boredom, and being-towards-death; and (2) how the nothingness in question is prior to the "not" of negation and the "is" of affirmation and to the absence and presence of (real or irreal) objects. Heidegger's confrontation with more elemental types of nothingness began in the early 1920s.

A key early confrontation with nothingness occurred in Heidegger's lecture-course held during 1922. In this work, emptiness is its possibility of movement (GA 61: 131). Nullity is the possibility of finite factical life, to which ruination (*Ruinanz*) returns it. The nothing appears as the whither or whereto (*wohin*) of the ruination and sudden falling (*Sturzen*) of the factical life of human existence. "Factical" refers here to the embedded, entangled, resistant, and situated nature of existence. The tendency of factical life toward self-overturning and downfall is not an alien fate that befalls it. This propensity is a constitutive elemental feature of its very character (GA 61: 145).

Nothingness, as other and more than the mere "not something" of pragmatic unavailability of things and linguistic negation, is disclosed in situations of uneventfulness, unsuccessfulness, pointlessness, and hopelessness (GA 61: 146). Heidegger would later describe these through radical anxiety and profound boredom. This nothingness is not revealed by a particular absence or lack in which possibilities remain, such as an empty space that can be filled or a missing object that can be returned. It is rather a radical non-occurring and impossibility that can consume concerned life. Nothingness in these early lecture-courses is arrived at through the emptying of sedimented content, allowing the concrete to be encountered. In emptying, nothingness is formally indicated as characterizing the factical situation and co-temporalizing of concerned life itself. The nothingness constitutively at the core of human existence is not a negative relation to an absent object, nor mere emptiness or indeterminateness. It temporalizes fundamentally as nullification or annihilation (*Vernichtung*) (GA 61: 147).

It is interesting that the expression *Vernichtung* was commonly used in nineteenth-century discussions of Buddhist *nirvāṇa*, construed as the extinction of the individual soul or, more expansively, as the annihilation of the life-principle or of being itself. This reception deployed it mostly negatively, as nihilistic. Still, it was positively interpreted as an emancipation from the existential negativity of suffering in German pessimism from Schopenhauer to Philipp Mainländer. Schopenhauer maintained a relative instead of an absolute nothingness in describing his own and Buddhist conceptions of nothingness. His critic Nietzsche recognized this, but his other critics did not. The Neo-Kantian philosopher Wilhelm Windelband, and others, in their polemics against disintegrative pessimism portrayed Schopenhauer as an advocate of the bliss of absolute annihilation, linking him and Buddhism with an absolute atheistic nothingness.[6]

Heidegger's theological, Neo-Kantian, and phenomenological teachers had rejected and polemicized against pessimism. Heidegger himself initially reveals little familiarity with or interest in the historical entanglements of German nothingness and Buddhist emptiness (expressed in Hegel, Schopenhauer, and Nietzsche), except for a few remarks distancing his thinking from Buddhism (GA 65: 171) and in reference to Nietzsche's critique of nihilism. His articulation of the self-forming ruination and fallenness of life occurs in the context of his phenomenological analysis of Christian life and the problematic of atheism. Nonetheless, analogously to Schopenhauer a century earlier, he arrives at a constitutive existential negativity and nothingness that can neither be logically relativized nor dialectically controlled and sublimated. Unlike Schopenhauer, the existential negativity of suffering life (that he identified with *saṃsāra*) is not overcome through the annihilation that suspends it (*nirvāṇa*) but through individuating life in the face of its uncertainty, uncanniness, and nothingness. Heidegger's early indifference toward Buddhism and general disinterest toward Schopenhauer could not prevent his thought from being entangled and linked with both in its intercultural reception, as Heidegger was accused of promoting yet another variation of pessimistic nihilism.

4. Nothingness and Individuation or Emptiness and the Singular

Nothingness and annihilation, understood relatively from the conditional perspective of will and representation, were linked in Schopenhauer with overcoming the suffering self through suspending the will and de-individuation. Heidegger interpreted nothingness in contrast, in 1922, as the structural impossibility of factical life that compelled its individuation. They are still intertwined in *Being and Time*, in which Heidegger asks: "What could be more foreign to the they-self, lost in the worried disparate 'world,' than the self who is individuated to itself in uncanniness and thrownness into nothingness?" (GA 2: 277).

In *Being and Time*, it is radical comprehensive existential anxiety (*Angst*), grasping and trembling one's very existence in its thrownness as a whole, which discloses and individuates being as being-possible and being-free for (GA 2: 187–8). Instead of being simply meaning-constituting and projective, Dasein is thrown into the event of the "it" and the "there," that is, into a world that it can encounter in anxiety, boredom, and solitude as uncannily other and as nothingness. The familiar everyday being-at-home-in-the-world falls away in uncanniness, immanently arising from the character of existence itself (GA 2: 189). In the inexorable interruptive disrelational potentiality of its own death, the self is thrown into the nothingness of itself and the world (GA 2: 276–7, 308). Anxiety compels yet opens existence in and to its possibility as that which it can only be from itself, as singular and individuated (GA 2: 249).

This nothing strikes through negativity by placing existence as such into question, yet it is not merely external or negative, as it allows existence to freely become and be itself. It is here that Heidegger coincides with Schopenhauer to the extent that the nothing is not purely external, arriving from the outside, and is not only a negativity to be dialectically overcome. At the same time, evoking the model of the dark night of the soul, this existential nothingness appears disrelational yet relative to the individual self that is thrown into question. Nothingness and the constitutive lack of orientation and bearing (as described in GA 27: 354) are not alien but the very condition of human existence. They indicate the freedom and self-transformative transcendence of ekstatic human existence as individuated to its being-there and being-in-the-world.[7]

Nothingness is simultaneously existential fear and trembling, a familiar thematic from Christian and existentialist discourses, and openness and possibility. When nothingness as openness is shifted from human existence to being, it is no longer purely relative to the subject and the prospect of a radical nothingness emerges. Nothingness as the radical openness of being is unusual in Occidental philosophical and religious discourses. These characteristically denigrate nothingness as a derivative secondary negation of existents or as a fallen distance from being, God, or positivity. In addition to polemical accusations of Schopenhauerian pessimism and Buddhist nihilism made against Heidegger, which stressed the nothingness of being-towards-death, it was nothingness as empty openness, and the potential generativity of its possibilities for being, in Heidegger's writings of the late 1920s, that inspired Buddhist and Daoist interpretations among European and Asian readers, including Kitayama Junyū 北山淳友 (1902–1962), as examined in the next chapter.

Are such identifications utterly erroneous? Let us look at two examples of Buddhist emptiness to indicate a preliminary orientation through which this question might be answered: the Indo-Chinese perfection of wisdom (*Prajñāpāramitā*) sūtra literature and classical Tang-era Huayan. The *Heart Sūtra* (*Xinjing* 心經) notably states: "Form (*rūpa*) is emptiness (*śūnyatā*), emptiness is form."[8] Heidegger is mindful of this popular expression of the key idea of Mahāyāna Buddhism since he discusses it in his dialogue with a Japanese interlocutor. Heidegger's nothingness as empty formless openness co-resonates with the *Prajñāpāramitā* understanding of emptiness as the condition of form, in which form is likewise the condition of emptiness, or it is the correlation of emptiness (*kong* 空) as principle (*li* 理) and form (*se* 色) as singular event (*shi* 事) in Fazang's interpretation of Huayan.[9]

It might be assumed that Heidegger's Dasein is concerned with the self, the Buddhist dharma with the denial of the self, and that therefore they are incompatible. The situation is more complex. Heidegger insists that the analytic of Dasein concerns Dasein in its possibility and individuation rather than the egotistical self (GA 29/30: 8). Heidegger's "Dasein" is not a substantive naturally or metaphysically determined self or subject. It is determined by its way of existing in its possibilities, in nothingness, and in openness. Possibility, nothingness and the not, and openness indicate perspectives on how it comes to be itself, in its own manner of being, in its relations and disruptive disrelations. Dasein's being-there is a being held-in-nothingness (GA 9: 115); its essence rests in its ek-sistence in the openness of the "there" (GA 9: 189). Accordingly, its genuine possibilities are awakened in the concreteness of its thereness, which opens onto the nothing that is shaped by the elemental not and the free open region that occurs through things. As will be tracked throughout this chapter, this elemental "not" is more primordial than both the "not" of negation and the "is" of assertion, and the no of Schopenhauer and the yes of Nietzsche.[10] Because he does not appropriately enter into the not-like of being, Nietzsche's strategy of affirmation repeats and deepens the problematic of modern nihilism instead of "overcoming" it, as "European Buddhism."[11]

In contrast to Heidegger, early Buddhist teachings of no-essential-self (*anātman*) indicate practices of undoing hypostatizing attachments of the self by analyzing its causal constitution, dependent origination, and emptiness.[12] The self is broken down into its conditional formation (*saṅkhāra*) and constituent elements (*dharmas*). The Buddhist dismantling of fixated formations and self-conceptions of the self has a different task than Heidegger's contestation of the reified self. Still, it intersects at points as a questioning of the self that leads to a different sense and culture of the self, one that is open to singularity without self-absorbed egoism. The self's destructuring need not entail its absorption into an identity or totality in either context. As articulated by Fazang during the Tang era, for instance, meditatively destructuring the fixated self discloses the singular as relational (as each interpenetrates and encompasses all) and singularly itself in its own positionality relative to the whole. We will return to the anarchic, equalizing, participatory implications of Huayan interactive pluralism in the conclusion.

II. The German Contexts of Buddhist "Nothingness"

5. Buddhism and Nothingness in German Thought

The challenge of nothingness is that it is neither a mere naught nor something that can be said to be. Still, the question of nothingness is even more forgotten than the question of being that begins *Being and Time*. Briefly put, God creates being from nothingness that does not operate as a primal source, as in Daoist thought, but becomes an empty lifeless distance from God, responsible, in Augustinian onto-theology, for error and sin in creatures. Nothingness has been predominantly denigrated in and excluded from occidental philosophy, from Parmenides to Carnap. There are a few exceptions, however, as in Leibniz's interpretation of nothingness and the zero as constitutive elements of the nature of reality and mathematics or in Schopenhauer's articulation of the constitutive character of nothingness. Despite such exceptional moments in the history of European philosophy, which to an extent inform Heidegger's distinctive strategy, nothingness continues to be constrained and limited by the logic of affirmation and positivity in modern European thought.

Given the relentless demand for beings as useful and representable objects in their availability, positivity, and presence, nothingness is either construed as a moment of negativity to be dialectically subsumed (as in Hegel's dialectic that begins with being and concludes with absolute affirmation) or a false substantialization of negation that only denies qualities or existence itself to objects and nothing more, as in Bergson's

1907 *Creative Evolution* or Carnap's 1931 polemic against Heidegger. For Hegel as much as Carnap, being and nothingness concern affirmation and negation, presupposing a conceptualization and logic of being and what can be said. That is, dialectical and logical negativity are meaningful as derivative and secondary to the presence and positivity of being. Philosophical affirmations of presence and the positivity of the real, the undialectical moment in Hegel and the unempirical moment in Bergson and Carnap, suppress rather than resolve questions of empty formlessness, radical negativity, and elemental nothingness.

First, the situation is more complicated. Presence and availability are not the only, and not necessarily the primary, attributes of what can be expressed in language. Words do not constitute and determine things but let them presence (GA 12: 220). Presence signifies the concealing and unconcealing presencing and absencing of beings and being; it is always presencing "of" and not the static enframed presence as availability. Words can accordingly express and indicate derivative and elemental absence, emptiness, and nothingness in a variety of ways, which can signify and make sense in appropriate discursive-practical contexts. Secondly, negativity and nothingness take on at times a more constitutive role in episodes in the history of European philosophy: for instance, in Leibniz and Schopenhauer. Heidegger was intrigued by Leibniz's argumentation that led beyond nothingness as merely derivative negation and privation to an elemental presupposed and constitutive nothingness in the very nature of things. The larger context of Leibniz's reflections is his incorporation of constitutive nothingness into the image of creation, the very nature and perfection of things, and of the zero into mathematics, which he used to interpret the transformative dyadic logic of the *Book of Changes*.[13]

Heidegger barely acknowledged Schopenhauer in his writings and lecture-courses. His few references throughout his life are dismissive. He criticized Schopenhauer's rejection of university philosophy, and his trivialization of Schelling and Hegel, and described him as a "literary writer" (*Schriftsteller*) who had a disastrous impact on Nietzsche and nineteenth-century philosophy.[14] But Schopenhauer's significance should not be denied, as he rejected the possibility of absolutizing the nothingness related to logical negation as self-contradictory, while at the same time articulating the positivity of negativity in existential and constitutive forms of negativity and nothingness. Three kinds of negativity, and correlated approaches to nothingness, can be distinguished in this context: logical negativity related to negation, existential negativity related to woe and death, and a constitutive generative negativity that structures the character of being itself.[15]

Heidegger regularly returned to the role of the nothing and negativity in Leibniz, Hegel and Nietzsche while disregarding the pertinent discourses and controversies unfolded in nineteenth-century German controversies over pessimism, from Schopenhauer through Philipp Mainländer and Eduard von Hartmann to Nietzsche.[16] These authors, along with Richard Wagner and other literati and artists, pursued questions concerning Buddhist nothingness and the value of life. This discourse was entangled with disputes over the pessimistic and nihilistic character of Buddhist "nothingness" ("das Nichts," as *śūnyatā* was rendered) and "annihilation" (*Vernichtung*, as *nirvāṇa* was typically translated into German).

Discourses concerning European Buddhism were not, of course, exclusively about annihilation, negativity, and nothingness. The Buddhist dharma was also a source for ideas of embracing the ethical value of nature and creatures. The history of European Buddhism informed visions of a new ethics that affirmed animal and vegetative life in Ludwig Klages's notion of "biocentrism" and in the Halle theologian and pastor Fritz Jahr's formulation of "bioethics." Jahr's 1926 and 1927 essays introduced the expression "bioethics" and called for a bioethical imperative to respect all and not only human life. He appealed to an ethics of relational life in which humans are seen to be interconnected with all animals and plants in the Buddha, Schopenhauer, Wagner, von Hartmann, and other figures (Jahr 1926; Jahr 1927). Jahr describes the Buddha's rebirths in animal and human forms from the Pāli Canon's *Jātakas* (narratives of the past lives of the Buddha) and von Hartmann's depiction of the suffering of flowers. According to Jahr, appealing to Buddhist and Christian teachings, love cannot be limited by party, nation, or species, and compassion and duties toward animals and plants cannot diminish those toward other humans. Jahr publicly advocated democratization, liberalization, and the freedom of thought during the closing years of the Weimar Republic (Jahr 1930; Jahr 1933). The idea of embracing interwoven nature had both reactionary (Klages) and liberal (Jahr) deployments during the Weimar Republic. The organicist vitalist and democratic pacifist Hans Driesch was a vocal public opponent of militarism, nationalism, and National Socialism. Adorno provides the most differentiated analysis of these tendencies in distinguishing the identity-promoting ideological functions of archaic images (which he associated with Wagner, Klages, Jung, and Heidegger) and the critical potential of dialectical images of nature and animal suffering.[17]

European Buddhism accordingly played several different roles in the cultural life of the Weimar Republic. Heidegger's hermeneutical situation encompassed philosophical contemporaries (Max Scheler, Misch, Husserl, Jaspers, among others), public intellectuals (Klages, Theodor Lessing, Oswald Spengler), while Alfred Döblin, Hermann Hesse, and other authors engaged South Asian Buddhist themes during that period.[18] The popular imagination often concerned Buddhist asceticism and the relationship with nature. Whereas Döblin perceived Buddhist negativity and asceticism as a purifying means to a free activity at one with nature (Döblin 1921), Hesse narrated how his version of Siddhartha rejected following the Buddha's ascetic path for one embracing nature in his powerful novel *Siddhartha* (Hesse 1922). Even as "Buddhist nothingness" is much more extensively discussed than Daoism in German cultural and philosophical contexts, there is much less evidence of its significance for Heidegger, except for his later discussions of Zen with Japanese interlocutors such as Nishitani Keiji 西谷啓治 (1900–1990) in 1938 or D. T. Suzuki 鈴木大拙 (1870–1966) and Hisamatsu Shin'ichi 久松真一 (1889–1980) in the postwar era.[19]

Are there earlier hints? Okakura Kakuzō's *Book of Tea*, which Heidegger seems to be familiar with at an early date, as discussed in Part One, briefly mentions the negativity of Indian Buddhism and Nāgārjuna as one side of Zen Buddhism and then associates Zen with Daoism in promoting a distinctively East Asian life-attitude and aesthetics of emptiness, naturalness, plainness, and simplicity (Okakura 1919: 31–3, 44). These are aspects of Zen that Heidegger appears attracted to in comments in later years, particularly in conversations with Japanese visitors. One might suspect that there were relevant conversations with Japanese interlocutors during the Weimar Republic given their frequency (Yusa 1998: 45–71) and as recollections of his early friendship and conversations with Kuki Shūzō center the conversations on language, nothingness, and emptiness found in "From a Dialogue on Language." Zen Buddhism was without doubt part of Heidegger's linguistic community and intellectual context, yet, unlike the *Daodejing* and the *Zhuangzi*, there is little direct historical evidence of engagement with South Asian or East Asian varieties of Buddhism during the Weimar Republic era. What does this short decisive text itself reveal?

6. The Very Question of Nothingness

After the succinct, pivotal discussions of nothingness in *Being and Time*, his 1929 inaugural lecture "What is Metaphysics?" addressed nothingness as logical and existential negativity and as constitutive of openness and possibility. This is an interculturally entangled journey if we follow the early reception of this lecture, Heidegger's subsequent tendency to increasingly emphasize the integral emptiness of being instead of the existential fear and trembling of abyssal ungroundable nothingness, and the connections he himself establishes between nothingness, emptiness, and being in his conversations with actual and fictionalized Japanese interlocutors.

"Occidental thinking," insofar as one can speak of such a generalized category, tends to reify the not and nothingness as mere negation that is secondary and derivative of the affirmation, presence, and positivity of that which is. In Heidegger's analysis, however, logical negation cannot be primary, as it presupposes an elemental naught. Logical negation is rooted in a more originary existential encounter with the negativity of the abyss and lack of ground of the nothingness disclosed in disorienting experiences such as the anticipation of one's own death, radical anxiety, and profound boredom.

Heidegger's positivistic critics construe his expression that "the nothing nothings" (*das Nichts nichtet*) as a substantializing and potentially nihilistic reification of negation. There are several reasons why this is not the case. First, it expresses the verbal enactive character (*nichten*) of the nothing (*das Nichts*). Secondly, verbally understood nothingness is a functioning and not an entity. It is neither the affirmation of existence nor a something—and accordingly not the logical reification criticized by Carnap—nor is it a meaningless null. "Nothing" is not a substantive form or idea since it is a formally indicative or hermeneutical concept, what Heidegger later describes as a way. "Nothing," as a formal indication, hermeneutically anticipates and opens the experiential and performative condition of the not-ness and negativity that makes possible acting and thinking—including logical negation and consequently logic and science.

Heidegger's interpretive strategy need not entail a repudiation of science or logic, as Carnap fears (Carnap 1931). It is a reflection calling for encountering the not-ness in which beings and any thinking about beings as present or absent, existing or not-existing, transpires. This is the open clearing that the space of reasons as a space presupposes. The constitutive character of elemental nothingness becomes evident in Heidegger's reflections on Leibniz's nothingness, which serves as a necessary element for the creation and enactment of nature and spirit.

7. Leibniz's Question and Elemental Nothingness

It is not inadvertent that Heidegger's essay circles around Leibniz's question: why is there something rather than nothing? Nothingness has been largely marginalized in the history of occidental thought. At the beginnings of Greek philosophy, Parmenides asserted that we cannot properly think nothing, as it is not. Plato explained negation as difference, refusing to recognize more primal forms of negativity and nothingness. Augustine and subsequent Christian philosophy tended to see nothingness as the absence of God or, in negative theologies and dialectical philosophy, as a negative step on the way to the absolute. Modern philosophy has likewise been hostile to nothingness. For Husserl, thinking is inherently a thinking of something. In conventional philosophy, from positivists like Carnap to vitalists like Bergson, "nothingness" signals an illusory nullity. It is at best understandable through negation as a secondary derivative denial of that which is. These suspicions of nothingness permeate modern European criticisms, from Hegel to Nietzsche, of Buddhism, Daoism, and "Oriental nothingness" as fundamentally nihilistic.

Given the Occidental restraints on thinking nothingness, how is it that Heidegger could begin to thoroughly rethink nothingness in ways that intersect with Buddhist and Daoist discourses? Heidegger ignored Schopenhauer and criticized negative theology and Hegel's dialectics for lacking sufficiently radical notions of negativity and nothingness. It is Leibniz who points the way toward a more primordial nothingness prior to all beings. Revealingly, the Leibniz and Heidegger scholar Katharina Kanthack noted the constitutive role of negativity in Heidegger, in contrast to Scheler and phenomenology, remarking: "Heidegger, in his mysteriously encrypted works, exposed the 'primordial negativism' [*Urnegativismus*] of human existence" (Kanthack 1948: 42).

In the 1949 introduction to "What Is Metaphysics?" Heidegger discussed the question of being and nothingness posed by Leibniz. Leibniz had asked, as the point of departure of his proof of God's existence: "why is there something rather than nothing?" (Leibniz 1842: 409). Since nothingness is the simplest possibility, being requires a sufficient reason to justify it. Leibniz answered that both terms, being and nothing, could only be justified and explained through a third term, God, which is external to and provides the ground for both. According to Leibniz's proof in the 1714 work *Principles of Nature and Grace founded in Reason*, if there were no God, there would be no sufficient reason for existence over nonexistence, and the world would not exist, never arising from primordial nothingness. Since the world exists, its sufficient reason (namely, God) must exist.

In Heidegger's elucidation, rather than being or God, it is the nothing appearing in Leibniz's argument that provokes the greatest perplexity. Heidegger notes that the question of why there is something rather than nothing is the most baffling of questions. It is already perplexing in its own terms of something (beings) and nothing, even before considering Leibniz's further recourse to God as an external transcendent third term that explains the movement from nothingness to being.

Heidegger describes how Leibniz's question must be posed in a fundamentally different sense. Leibniz's statement that "nothing is simpler and easier than something" (Leibniz 1842: 409) gives nothingness an elemental sense, in which beings in their presence and positivity potentially become derivative to that which is not. Heidegger recognizes how Leibniz's question departs from the strategy of beginning with beings and proceeding to their first cause, God, by beginning instead with the nothingness that is not being and that is easier and simpler than being (GA 9: 382). In Leibniz's demonstration, this "not-being" functions as unlimited and infinite possibility from which God creates this specific determinate order of things.

Heidegger perceives how Leibniz's entire argumentation presupposes a primordial nonderivative sense of nothingness in the very nature of actuality. Leibniz's account of *creatio ex nihilo* presumes a naught prior to existence and the derivative privation and negation of existence. Leibniz recognizes this naught when he concludes that nothingness enters into the very constitution of things, just as the zero in the zero-one dyad is constitutive in mathematics and serves as an image of creation itself in its possibility and actuality, emptiness and fullness. Leibniz perceived this same logic of nothingness and creation to be at work in the *Book of Changes* (Leibniz 1703: 85–9). The *Book of Changes* offers a model of the alternation between nothingness and being in Chinese traditions as well, as is evident in Wang Bi's classic commentary (Lynn 1994). Heidegger is once again drawing on a philosophical problematic that has an intercultural history in German philosophy that he does not directly engage. Still, it would be difficult not to notice how reflections on Chinese conceptions of nothingness and the zero based on the *Book of Changes* are discussed at length by Leibniz and Hegel, just as Buddhist nothingness is a contested topic between Hegel, Schopenhauer, and Nietzsche.[20]

The mathematical notion and use of zero (*śūnya*), negative numbers, and infinity (*ananta*), often supposed to be characteristic of modern European conceptual thinking, were initially developed by Indian mathematicians like Brahmagupta (598–668 CE) in relation to the philosophy of emptiness (*śūnya* is used for emptiness and the zero) and eventually transferred to Europe through Islamic mathematics. These notions, which Descartes had still refused to utilize on the principle that the nothing is naught and only God can be infinite, revolutionized mathematics in Leibniz and his era. Heidegger identified the application of the new mathematical paradigm in Leibniz, in which all being and nonbeing becomes subject to mathematical projection and construction, as a crucial element in the formation of technological modernity, but he did so without sufficiently attending to its interculturally transmitted Indian and Arabic sources.[21]

Leibniz systematically applied the zero and infinity throughout his mathematical and philosophical works. He linked the mathematical zero with nothingness, which assumes three roles: mathematical, ontological-cosmological, and theological. Being and all things are constituted from nothingness and God, the zero and the one, from which its essential finitude results and its possibilities for self-ruination in error, fallenness, and sinfulness emerge. They arise due to finitude, the nothingness within things, and not directly from God, who has by his very idea no limits or imperfections. Nothingness accordingly has a double function in Leibniz's philosophical system: elemental nothingness is pure empty and open possibility that in its actualization becomes limiting and finite in beings. This is what creates the conditions of the privative nothingness of the Augustinian onto-theological discourse shared by the rationalists Descartes and Leibniz. Heidegger repeatedly returns to Leibniz's question and the proposed simplicity, ease and priority of the nothing. He returns not only to the question itself but to Leibniz's strategy and model, which reveals how nothingness is constitutive in the elemental core of being and existence.[22]

We can now begin to disentangle in Heidegger's thinking the different senses and roles of the nothing: (1) existentially and negatively in affliction, disrelation, and limitation; (2) constitutively of possibility; and (3) elementally in openness and clearing. Heidegger's discourse of nothingness thus cuts across and encompasses a range of meanings: generative abyssal hiddenness and mystery; freedom in openness to an infinite plenitude one cannot encompass or master; the vast empty fullness of potentiality; existential negativity in anxiety, misery, and death; logical and dialectical negation; and the nihilistic denial of being and sense.

8. Buddhism, Nothingness, and Nihilism in Nietzsche and Heidegger

Heidegger's thinking of nihilism is determined by his confrontation with Nietzsche. He consequently presupposes, even if he avoids adequately engaging, Nietzsche's interpretation of Buddhism as a primary exemplary vehicle of nihilism that has been reincarnated in European modernity. Nietzsche asked in the preface of *On the Genealogy of Morals* whether Europe is heading "towards a new Buddhism? Toward a European Buddhism?" The expression "European Buddhism" reappears in his notes for the never-completed *Will to Power* on which Heidegger lectured at length in the late 1930s and early 1940s. The issue of modern European nihilism is consequently interconnected with the notion of Buddhist nihilism in Nietzsche's argumentation. Nietzsche demands an active nihilism in reaction to "European Buddhism," an affirmative pessimism, and a "Buddhism of the deed" (Nelson 2022b: 83–96).

This is the complex setting in which Heidegger's sparse early references to Buddhism occur, including the remark in *Contributions to Philosophy* that his being-historical thinking is the reverse of Buddhism: "The less humans are as beings-as-entity, the less frozen they are toward the being-as-entity [*das Seiende*] in which they find themselves, and the closer they come to being [*Sein*]. (No Buddhism! The opposite)" (GA 65: 171). Despite their sparseness, Buddhist emptiness in these early references informs the context in which Heidegger's later thinking of emptiness unfolds.

Before turning to his postwar thought, why does the transition from beings and beingness to being itself evoke Buddhism and require its denial in the situation of the 1930s? The very next paragraph turns to the history of philosophy as a uniquely Occidental affair. This historical reason does not seem sufficient, since the passage itself does not mention this history and Heidegger specifically stressed here the transition from beings as entities to being itself. Elsewhere he characterizes this as the "not" of the ontological difference that is nonidentically the same as the "not" of nothingness (GA 9: 123). Heidegger might have in mind here criticisms of his thought, including by National Socialist ideologues, as advancing a new form of nihilist pessimism through death and the nothing. For his critics, this does not lead from beings to being but rather to mere nothingness. Buddhism destructures beings-as-entities and leaves them hanging in nothingness, whereas Heidegger turns toward being. First, the nihilistic interpretation of Buddhism misses the determinate functioning of emptiness in Buddhist discourses and practices. Secondly, the nihilistic indictment presented against Heidegger often evokes European imaginings of Buddhism and Daoism.

Another motivation for this negative reference to Buddhism might be Heidegger's own understanding of Buddhism, which he perceives to be sufficiently proximate to his own thinking to call for a denial. Given Nietzsche's analysis of Buddhism, it might be that it remains in the transformational moment of the nothing as such (as German philosophers interpreted Buddhist emptiness), without realizing the nothingness of being and, also, not recognizing the many forms of Buddhist practice and discourse that lead through destructuring selflessness and emptiness to the very nature or buddha-nature of things. It is this last point that Heidegger's Japanese readers and interlocutors would note, and Heidegger himself in his dialogue with a Japanese interlocutor.

Heidegger's references to Buddhism in relation to nihilism in the 1930s are formed in response to Nietzsche. Heidegger quotes Nietzsche's identification of the teachings of the Buddha and Schopenhauer and his description of art as "anti-Christian, anti-Buddhist, [and] anti-nihilist par excellence" (GA 6.1: 71, 285; GA 44: 68). Yet Heidegger does not explicitly address the problematic of pessimism and Buddhism that Nietzsche inherited from Schopenhauer, which could have drawn him into controversies over Buddhism. At the same time, Heidegger's transmutation of the question of nihilism would lead to, if followed through to these debates, an altered conception. Heidegger rejects depicting nihilism as an issue of value or meaning. It concerns the history of being itself. According to Heidegger's analysis of technological modernity, nihilism concerns the modern organization of life itself. This enframing organizing of life is expressed in a fourfold dynamic of the abandonment of being in the modern technical worldview, understood as the latest stage of Occidental metaphysics: the destruction of the earth, the darkening of sky and world, the flight of the gods, and the massification of humans (GA 40: 29, 34; GA 65: 119).

Heidegger would subsequently more precisely differentiate the nothingness that nothings (*das nichtende Nichts*) from the nothingness that annihilates (*das vernichtende nichtige Nichts*). He did so not only to avoid associations with nihilism and pessimism but to confront Nietzsche's uncanniest guest of nihilistic nothingness with nothingness as disclosive clearing (*die Lichtung*) and free opening region (*das Freie*).[23] Such nothingness does not lead to the active nihilism of arbitrary self-assertion and self-willing, whether of an individual or collective subject, but—if we read Heidegger with Zhuangzi—to perspectively disassembling fixated subjects and identities in uncovering freedom and sense within the midst of things and world. That is, meaning is not constituted by the individual or collective subject and its identity and mastery. It is emptying-opening, generative, and born of freedom in care and being-with or, breaking with their earlier human-centered interpretation, contact and interdependence with others and things.[24]

III. The Nothingness and Emptiness of Being

9. Nothingness, Emptiness, and Openness

What then is the relationship between beings and being that evokes the specter of Buddhism? Heidegger makes two claims in the late 1930s regarding the relation between being and nothingness. The first proceeds from beings to nothing to being: "Beings are 'because' nothing is, and the nothing is 'because' being (*Seyn*) is" (GA 67: 27). Being is in this sense the highest word for what Heidegger seeks to communicate. The second is that being itself "is" the nothing.[25]

In what sense is being itself nothingness? This is not Hegel's assertion that they are identical in their empty abstraction. Nor is it the nihilistic definition of being as mere meaningless nothingness. Heidegger's delimitation of the nothingness of being has multiple functions that answer and offer an alternative to the previous discourses of nothingness that continue to dominate contemporary thinking: first, on the one hand, it signals the being-historical self-veiling and concealing of being. It indicates the epochal refusal and devastation of being that is interconnected with the question of modern nihilism (GA 67: 19, 143). Secondly, on the other hand, the abyssal nothing essences as the very clearing, openness, and absencing-presencing in which beings are.[26] While the first is used to delineate the problematic of nihilism, the latter intimates a response to the devastating nothingness of Occidental philosophy through the clearing, the open, and the releasing nothing.

Emptiness, clearing, and the openness of the middle and between increasingly become the key qualities through which the later Heidegger conveys the elemental senses of being, as emptiness and nothingness become the ultimate expressions for being. The nothingness of nihilism is not overcome by turning to forms of affirmation, presence and positivity that fixate and reify beings. It requires moving toward the abyssal nothingness of being in which affirmation and negation, absence and presence, concealment and unconcealment emerge and in which their varying historical configurations are fixated and hold sway.

Was Heidegger's sense of Buddhism only a negative Nietzschean informed one? Heidegger's postwar reflections and encounters suggest not. He appreciates the ziranist "self-so" moment of expansive open naturalness in Zen Buddhism in conversations with prominent Japanese proponents of Zen.[27] A conspicuous tendency of East Asian Buddhism states that formlessness and form are interwoven, as emptiness leads not to mere negativity and nothingness but to nature in its clarity and luminosity. Such tendencies in Daoism and Chan/Zen Buddhism informed an extensive naturalistic *ethos* in dwelling and aesthetic-cultural practices in painting and poetry that highlighted stillness, simplicity, plainness, and naturalness. This sense of nature, which he interprets through his own understanding of color and emptiness and earth and sky, appears to be at work in Heidegger's appropriation of East Asian thought-images and concepts.

Zen is not the only Buddhist transmission of significance in the context of Heidegger's thought and its reception. There are also moments in Heidegger that intersect with the Pure Land Buddhism that informed several Japanese interpretations of his thought within and outside the Kyōto school. Pure Land Buddhism encompasses a sense of religious devotion and a historical dimension that is thought to be lacking in Zen Buddhism. History is the history of the decay of the dharma and human receptivity to it until the point is reached at the "end of the dharma" (*mofa*; *mappō* 末法), when only the grace of the Bodhisattva, such as Amida Buddha (Amitābha, the buddha of infinite light) can save fallen humanity through the "other-power" of unrestricted compassion. These points co-reverberate with moments in Heidegger's later thinking and dialogues, concerning being as empty and open and the possibility of another beginning and saving power (*das Rettende*) arising precisely in the limit and the moment of maximum danger.

Could Heidegger's thought-image of the saving new gods to-come be imagined or reimagined in the Bodhisattvas who realize the emptiness and luminosity in each thing and enact unrestricted forgiveness and compassion? Such questions impel us beyond Heidegger into the metanoetics of Tanabe Hajime 田辺元 (1885–1962) who adopted images of other-power, infinite compassion, and other Pure Land Buddhist elements.

10. Gatherings in Emptiness

Hermeneutical co-resonances between Zen and Pure Land Buddhism and modern intercultural discourses are at play in Heidegger's East Asian reception, in his own responses to this reception, and in popular and academic discourses of intercultural philosophy.[28] A primary example of how Heidegger answers his East Asian entanglements and reception is found in "From a Dialogue on Language." The interpretation of the priority of the empty naught unfolded in this present chapter is confirmed by Heidegger's reflections on the emptiness of the thing in "The Thing" and of language in this dialogue.

This fictionalized and highly stylized dialogue is based in part on an actual one in March 1954 with the Germanist Tezuka Tomio 手塚富雄 (1903–1983).[29] The dialogue centers on the absent friend Kuki. In this conversational meditation on emptiness, we glimpse how absence, emptiness, and stillness allow the gathering of events, memories, things, and words. This gathering in emptiness is indicated in various ways, from the image of the Noh theater's empty stage to the silence that enables genuine listening and conversation, from the delight in the alluring stillness of *iki* to the emptiness that allows recollection of the absent departed one. These ways also include the emptiness in which form and color are configured and take shape, the open in which the mountain appears through the gathering gesture in a Noh play, or the open clearing of being. These senses of "nothingness" were more readily grasped by Japanese readers of "What Is Metaphysics?" (GA 12: 102–3), as emptiness, according to the Japanese interlocutor, operates as the highest name for being (GA 12: 103). This emptiness is not only rooted in Buddhist philosophical conceptions of *śūnyatā*, but in encounters and experiences with mountains and rivers, rocks and trees, and other things and places.

The dialogue enacts a hesitation and reticence on the side of the questioner (Heidegger) about using Occidental concepts to explain Eastern and Japanese concepts and experiences. This hesitation allows a dialogue to emerge, even as Heidegger in the figure of the inquirer conveys skepticism concerning the achievement of genuine intercultural understanding. The enquirer consequently expresses delight in hearing the words of his Japanese interlocutor, as well as reluctance to deploy Occidental categories such as aesthetics to elucidate *iki* 粋, being and nothingness to articulate emptiness, and language (*Sprache*) to explain *kotoba* 言葉.

First, Kuki's analysis of *iki* is discussed as expressing reserved hesitation and delight before alluring stillness (GA 12: 133), a motif unfolded throughout the dialogue. Secondly, with the Buddhist conception of emptiness and form in the background, *iro* 色 is said to signify color and *kū* 空 the boundless emptiness of the open sky (GA 12: 129). In their mutual interplay, there can be no *kū* without *iro*, and no *iro* without *kū* (GA 12: 97). This is drawn from the Buddhist philosophy of co-constitutive form, which is only emptiness, and emptiness which is only form (色即是空, 空即是色), as expressed in the *Heart Sūtra*.[30] *Iro* and *kū* together in their mutual interplay indicate the elemental source: the emptiness in which things appear and flourish. This is the event of the lightening conveyance of the graciousness that brings forth and holds sway over that which needs the nurturing shelter of that which flourishes and flowers.

Language itself is thematized as leaves or petals from *koto*: *koto* 言 (word) is cognate with *koto* 事 (thing, matter, and affair). This same character in Chinese Huayan Buddhism signifies the singular event or thing that encompasses the whole, and its emptiness means the interpenetration of each singular. Huayan's logic of multiplicity might suggest that there is in emptiness (principle) an interpenetration of all singular languages (particulars) without a common identity to be asserted or negated. Heidegger's dialogue remarks that there is not a common concept of language that can be automatically applied to each language. Each language's word for language offers a hint, pathway, and freeing word toward encountering what discloses itself in that language as a matter or affair to be thought. The Japanese expression for the nature or reality of events evoked in language is *kotoba* (GA 12: 134). *Ba* literally signifies leaves and petals; *koto* designates that which delights in a thing's event and shining forth. It is that which comes to radiant disclosure distinctively in each singular moment, in the fullness of its own gracefulness (GA 12: 134).

Language is a saying-encountering of the thing, such as the mountain, in vastness and stillness. Words are leaves gathering in emptiness in co-relation with things. There is an encounter in emptiness in the appearing of a mountain, in a beholding that is itself inapparent. Such emptiness then is said to be the same as nothingness. This is the elemental nothingness in which mountains are mountains, again playing on Buddhist imagery. This nothing is not a merely destructive nihilistic nothingness, as Heidegger's Japanese interlocutors recognize, but instead that which is other than and encompasses both presence and absence, positivity and negativity (GA 12: 103).

11. Elemental Nothingness

Heidegger is not primarily a thinker of presence or of a negation that coercively reverts to the identity of positivity and presence. The alleged givenness and positivity of mere presence cannot disclose the infinite, groundless movement of presence and absence in the clearing. Heidegger is not a philosopher of being as positively given presence. He is rather a thinker of "presencing" in absence, nothingness, and the empty clearing that lets potentialities surge forth, allows gathering to occur, and interthingly existence to be enacted. The promise and arrival of the hidden fullness of gathering can arise only within elemental absence (GA 7: 138, 227). As the pragmatic accessibility or theoretical representation of beings is placed in question through the ontological difference between beings and being, being as sheer presence is questioned through constitutive emptiness. Things come to be seen in emptiness; they come to word in the silence that can responsively listen. Absence, emptiness, and nothingness are not deployed as pure or mere indeterminate negativities. They are originary disclosive names for being and not contraries or opposites to be subsumed.

As in his source the *Daodejing*, absence, darkness, and mystery are in Heidegger's thinking that which preserve and nurture. In ways that evoke Buddhist formlessness and Daoist *ziran*, such expressions signify that that which is determinate is elemental, constitutive, and that it is what is at stake in undoing, releasement, and being exposed in the clearing, in which the emptying-gathering of that which is absent and present (*ab- und anwesen*) occurs. The clearing or opening of being is an emptiness in which things arise and disclose themselves from themselves and address humans, calling them in the stillness in which humans can begin to listen and respond.

Nothingness was still directly linked in "What Is Metaphysics?" with negativity in existential anxiety in which accessibility, presence, and representation are shaken. The original nonderivative "negativity" of nothingness is subsequently expressed by Heidegger as the elemental abyssal condition of ground (*Abgrund des Grundes*) that is the truth and event of being (GA 65: 33; GA 68: 47). It is also described as absence and emptiness and as the open clearing of being and the gathering of time, space, and thing. These words do not convey what is merely "negative," understood as inherently derivative denial and negation. Nothingness is accordingly not a mere nothing, a derivative negation of beings, an incident of negativity to be overcome and sublated; it indicates the generative, the elemental, and the freely occurring openness through which being is disclosed in its appropriating or enowning ontological event (*ereignende Ereignis*) and beings exist in their own ways of being.

Heidegger accordingly does not reduce ontic beings to ontological being in ontological totalization, as several of his critics have asserted. Being is the nothingness and clearing in which beings—through the "not" or nonidentity of the ontological difference between being and beings—can be themselves in accord with their own autopoietic self-naturing.[31] This becomes possible in the nonidentical sameness of the "not" of nothingness and the "not" of the ontological difference (GA 9: 123). The "not" of the between is the opening clearing of being, in which being (*Sein*) and beings (*Seiende*) can be encountered and thought in their distinctive difference.

Heidegger remarked in his reflections on Hegel on negativity, in which negativity resists Hegel's efforts to subdue it, that "[t]he not of being is the original nothing. The not 'of' being in the sense of a *genetivus subjectivus*. Being itself is not-like (*Nichthaft*), has nothing in itself" (GA 68: 29). Nothingness does not merely signify the nonexistent, it signifies the "essencing" (Heidegger's upsurgence-withdrawal and presencing-absencing of essence) of being itself as abyssal and abyss-like (GA 68: 47). Nothing is an elemental name for abyssal being rather than its opposite or negation. Being and nothingness cannot be dialectically opposed and subsumed, as the "not" and the nothing are primal elements of being and being of nothingness. Is the "not" then more characteristic of being than the "is"? Or, what if being in its event never was nor will be, if it neither departs nor arrives?

IV. The Not of Primordial Nothingness

12. The Priority of the Elemental Not

Heidegger commented in the *Contributions to Philosophy* that "[o]nly because being essences in a not-like way does it have nonbeing as its other. Because this other is the other of itself" (GA 65: 267). The "not" can be described as the pivot of the way in Heidegger and emptiness as encompassing actuality, possibility, and impossibility. Possibility is higher than actuality, according to *Being and Time* (GA 2: 38), and the not (from abyssal nothingness and empty possibilities to concrete absence, lack, and resistance) is greater than affirmation and negation, concerning that which is present and available (GA 65: 266).

The intertwined "not" and the nothing operate in multiple ways in Heidegger's discourse. The not functions as (1) ordinary linguistic, logical, and dialectical varieties of negation with which conventional philosophy begins and ends; (2) anxiety provoking lack, resistance, and nihilation, particularly the irresistible inescapability of death; (3) abyssal formlessness and darkness encountered as horror or—in a more Daoist vein—as safeguarding, healing, and nurturing; (4) generative elemental openness that allows dynamic arising, emergence, and holding sway (*phúsis*); (5) open space of the between in which beings gather and form places and localities; (6) the not in remembrance that allows the gathering of who and what has been lost, such as the absent passed friend who remains near in memory; and (7) the not-yet in awaiting without expectation or calculation, in which turning and metamorphosis transpire.

The latter two operations of the not (6 and 7) are also described as stretched between the recollection of what is no-more and the anticipation of what is not-yet through which Heidegger articulates the holy and the divine. In a 1950 letter to Hartmut Buchner concerning "The Thing," Heidegger could describe the absence that characterizes the divine (*das Göttliche*) as indicating both the no-more and the not-yet, the gods that were and the gods to come.[32] Correspondingly, in "From a Dialogue on Language," the absence indicated in farewell gathers that which endures; silence and the stillness of breath allow the fullness of saying; the emptiness of saying gathers words that permit things to communicate; the emptiness of things is the gathering of world in them.

Heidegger's thinking of the elemental "not" and not-like extends beyond the category of meontology, or a merely negative ontology, and breaks through the nihilism, of which he has been accused. Heidegger's thinking of this radical primordial "not" contests the logic of affirmation, presence, and positivity that dominates Occidental thought. It thereby intersects with specific facets of early Lao-Zhuang Daoist discourses of generative nothingness, Buddhist conceptions of emptiness and nature, the releasement and receptivity expressed in German mysticism and poetry, and even the nonidentity thinking of his polemical critic Adorno, while remaining irreducible to them and offering an alternative path. Hermeneutically contextualizing and interculturally situating Heidegger's thinking, as enacted in the chapters of the present book, has not limited Heidegger's thinking to mere historiography but has allowed us to better comprehend its own uniqueness, scope, and limits.[33]

13. Uncanny Guests and Other Beginnings

The present chapter undertook a twofold task. First, its philosophical task, unfolded through a series of historical contextualizations and interpretive redescriptions, outlined how the releasement into elemental nothingness and emptiness entails the undoing of fixations, and opening for encountering and responding to gathering beings and things, as such and as a whole. This can arguably be deployed as a responsive attunement and critical model in relation to contemporary social ecological crisis-tendencies.

Secondly, its historical interpretive undertaking was to reconstruct Heidegger's sojourn with nothingness and emptiness in intersection with ziranist "naturalistic" moments in Daoist and Buddhist sources. It is naturalistic only in the expansive sense of attending to and observing natural phenomena in their own self-naturing without reduction to a fixed epistemological or metaphysical model of nature and the thing. This is not nature as available, calculable, and ready for use. As Heidegger speaks of Hebel's *dao*-like naturalness, a facet of Hebel appreciated by Ernst Bloch (Bloch 1984): "The naturalness of nature is the rising and setting of the sun, the moon, the stars, which directly addresses humans in their dwelling in granting the mysteriousness of the world."[34] Naturalness enacts an interpolation of address (*ansprechen*) and granting and doing justice (*zusprechen*, literally "speaking to") between beings that is not restricted to intrahuman communication and an overly narrow anthropocentric *ethos*.

Heidegger's ambiguous understanding of the Buddhist dharma can be interpreted according to the *ziran* model. His texts reveal no interest in causal-karmic Buddhist discourses that were opposed to anarchic *ziran* by Zongmi and other orthodox Buddhist philosophers. His dialogues with Japanese interlocutors reveal affinities with discourses of the emptiness of buddha-nature as it is expressed through natural phenomena and poetic words, rather than in reference to redeeming bodhisattvas. Heidegger finds poetic and philosophical inspiration in his encounters with East Asian concepts, images, and words; he does not find religious or mystical enchantment that would lead to a direct embrace or conversion. Such an identification with Zen or other Eastern teachings is rejected in his interview with the *Spiegel* magazine (GA 16: 679).

One reason for this suspicion is expressed in the postwar *Bremen und Freiburg Lectures*, in which Heidegger asked (adopting Nietzsche's expression) whether the uncanniest guest of nihilism derives from the East or the West. He replies that both have opened the door to it and are equally incapable of responding to it (GA 79: 134). However, in the *Spiegel* interview, Heidegger also states that possibilities of renewal and a freer relationship with the technological world arising from archaic transmissions in China and Russia cannot be excluded (GA 16: 677). This remark appears to refer to agrarian utopian images of free self-organizing rural communities. In the case of

China, it is clear from related remarks elsewhere that he does not mean the idea of a Chinese authoritarian order, mentioned in his notes on Ernst Jünger (GA 90: 400, 406); nor does it refer to Maoism, which he perceived as another form of enframing positioning (Petzet 1993: 212). He is referring to Laozi's *dao*. In a late note, Heidegger explicitly relates Chinese self-determination and possible world-renewal with a return to the teaching of Laozi (GA 91: 667). This passage is followed by expressions that he recurrently deploys in relation to the *Daodejing*, once again revealing their interconnectedness in his thought: the stillest stillness, the unheard and inapparent "not-ing" of the nothing, meeting and encountering place, and a non-instrumentalizing appropriate enregioned and attuned practice (*Brauch*) (GA 91: 668).

Heidegger's "Daoist turn" is once again evident even if this turn must be a qualified one. It is limited to a specific reimagining of its *wuwei-ziran* tones and their continuing resonance in subsequent East Asian art, discourse, and practice. The genealogy of interculturally entangled nothingness articulated in Part Two of this work discloses how moments in Heidegger's journey correlate and resonate in significant ways with specific elements of Daoist generative nothingness and Buddhist emptiness of form and self-identity. This coalescence is in part contingent and in part due to Heidegger's entanglements with East Asian texts and interlocutors.

8

The Nothing, Nihilism, and Heidegger's East Asian Entanglements

I. The Question of the Nothing

1. Heidegger as a Thinker of Nothingness

Hegemonic forms of modern European philosophy, from Kant and Hegel to Bergson and Carnap, find genuine or radical nothingness to be incomprehensible, as nothingness ultimately must refer to the positivity of the being that it presupposes in negation. Heidegger's "the nothing nothings" ("das nichts nichtet") is among his most controversial statements. It has been repeatedly denounced as absurd, nonsensical, or nihilistic since its initial articulation in 1929. This negative reception led Heidegger to remark numerous times that he was completely misunderstood in Europe and that it was his Japanese readers who understood what he meant to say with nothingness (GA 11: 106; GA 12: 103; GA 15: 414): "The reaction to this writing in Europe was: nihilism and hostility to 'logic'. One found in it in the Far East an appropriately understood 'nothing' as a word for being" (GA 15: 414). Heidegger did not note on any of these occasions that several Japanese interpreters contended that his nothingness adhered to the Occidental prioritization of being and had failed to come near to absolute, genuine, or "Oriental" nothingness.

Before considering Heidegger's nothing and its early German-Japanese reception, what was the European situation in which he considered it misinterpreted? How did Heidegger become a philosopher identified with nihilism despite his frequent assertions to the contrary? This is a perceived consequence of his analyses of death and nothingness prior to his confrontations with Nietzsche's analysis of nihilism in the 1930s. Heidegger's *Being and Time* elucidated a primordial nullity at the heart of human existence as thrown into the world in being-toward-death: "The projection is not only determined as each time thrown by the nullity of its fundamental being, but as a projection it is itself essentially a nullity (*Nichtigkeit*)" (GA 2: 117). After the 1927 publication of *Being and Time*—with its analysis of existential anxiety and being-toward-death (*Sein-zum-Tode*)—and his 1929 Freiburg inaugural lecture "What Is Metaphysics?"—with its analysis of radical anxiety (*Angst*) in the face of the impersonal self-nihilating nothingness of "the nothing nothings," Heidegger's thought was identified with a nihilistic nothingness.

Multiple European and East Asian intellectuals described his thought as a "philosophy of nothingness" (*Philosophie des Nichts* or *Nichts-Philosophie*), a negative ontology or meontology (Wahl 1957: 154), a variety of nihilism (Meyer 1936: 86–9; Gürster 1938: 48), a European form of Buddhism (Anders 2001: 64), and a Daoist-like embrace of nothingness (Jordan 1932: 102; Mann 1949: 10). Three of his early critics negatively identify Heidegger, Buddhism, and Daoism as sharing a common nihilism. First, Günther Anders encapsulated these interpretative tendencies in a 1946 essay, "Nihilism and Existence," in which he criticized Heidegger's thinking as "in a certain sense" a modern European Buddhism that is both atheistic, skeptical, nihilistic, as well as conservative, ritualistic, and seeking redemption (Anders 2001: 64).

Secondly, the German linguist and literary theorist Leo Jordan, who had written about Voltaire and China in 1913, was one of the first scholars to link Heidegger with Daoism. In a work critiquing German abstract thinking and its confusions about nothingness, Jordan described Heidegger's "What Is Metaphysics?" as an attempt to renew Hegel's logic of negativity, but that fell into a German mystical and Daoist-like generative conception of nothingness from which all life is perceived as arising (Jordan 1932: 102, 147). Jordan noted a few pages earlier how the interconnection between heaven, emptiness, *dao*, nothingness, as well as between deception and concealment—which Heidegger might be thought to have reinvented in his recent lectures on nothingness and truth—is as ancient as the Chinese script (Jordan 1932: 97).

Third, the exiled writer Klaus Mann, in his final 1949 essay "Europe's Search for a New Credo," described Heidegger as a "mystic of Nothingness," an "idolater of the Nihil," a supporter of the "nihilistic revolution" of National Socialism, and a thinker who made a Daoist-like and unimaginable "absence" and "total nonexistence" the basis of philosophy (Mann 1949: 10). Anders, Jordan, and Mann identified Heidegger and Buddhism or Daoism as embracing nothingness and nihilism—without differentiation—in similar ways.

Heidegger's thinking of nothingness in *Being and Time* and "What Is Metaphysics?" was critiqued as meaningless in positivism, as bourgeois fascistic irrationalism in Marxism (e.g., Lukács 1951, 1955), for its depersonalizing impersonality in the name of the interpersonal other in Emmanuel Levinas, and for the sake of radical subjectivity in Jean-Paul Sartre (Levinas 1932; Sartre 1943; Levinas 1982). Rudolf Carnap condemned Heidegger's *Nichts-Philosophie* as reifying negation (which is inherently derivative and secondary to assertions about facts and their logical relations) into a meaningless pseudo-concept of nothingness and denied it even the expressive and evocative value of poetic words.[1] György Lukács contended in *Existentialism or Marxism?* that the prioritization of nothingness is a fetishization not of logic but of the despair and negativity of capitalist society. It provides an impersonal mythology for a crisis-ridden decaying social order and thereby obscures the productivity and potentiality of the human subject (Lukács 1951: 44–5).

Although absent in the 1932 essay "Martin Heidegger and Ontology," Levinas's 1935 work *On Escape* interrogated the impersonality of the "there is" (*il y a*) of being, murmuring in the abyss of nothingness from which we are compelled to escape, yet cannot. Sartre interprets Heidegger's being and nothingness as "reciprocal forces of expulsion" that constitute the real in his 1943 magnum opus *Being and Nothingness*

(Sartre 1943: 51). Sartre concurs with Heidegger's argument that negation presupposes the nothing, contrary to the positivist account of negation, and the constitutive role of nothingness in human existence (Sartre 1943: 52, 60). He contests, even so, the apparent impersonality of Heidegger's "nothing nothings" with the being (the for-itself of consciousness) that is self-nihilating in the face of the absurdity and superfluity (*de trop*) of being-in-itself. Nothingness is identified with the nothingness of the subject that constitutes its radical factical freedom that it cannot escape and is compelled to choose. Sartre intriguingly expressed the link between freedom and nothingness by interpreting humans as active creators of being and sense from out of their own nothingness. It is not accurate to interpret Sartre as reducing nothingness to subjectivity, as nothingness is the unfathomable gap and impersonal point of departure from which the dynamic of personal and interpersonal existence ensues in, for the most part, the inauthenticity and bad faith that does not recognize its own freedom.

Heidegger's thinking of the nothing reveals different tendencies over time, none of which constitute an existential or Sartrean self-creation from the nothingness of subjectivity. His "What Is Metaphysics?" showed how humans are exposed to and shaped through the nonderivative event of nothingness. In contrast, he states in 1934/35 that humans are witnesses of being in language, and that without language, as with stones, plants, and animals, there can be no nonbeing, nothingness, and emptiness, thereby giving it a derivative character (GA 39: 62; GA 40: 127). Seemingly drawing on the *Daodejing* and the *Zhuangzi*, Heidegger's postwar thinking depicts how humans await, witness, and say being, thing, and world in openness and emptiness.

The construal of Heidegger's thinking as promoting nihilism misses the complex history of his thinking of nothingness. Nearly from the beginning, Heidegger had to contest the growing local and international perception that he was destructively glorifying nothingness. A standard narrative states that his turn (*die Kehre*) was from the temporalizing formation of the world for human existence as being-there (Dasein) to the priority of being's event. Another narrative, evolving after the conclusion of the Second World War, confirmed earlier interpretations in claiming that Heidegger's turn consisted of a turn away from a "philosophy of nothingness" to a "thinking of being itself" (*Sein selbst*) (Naber 1947). This account is also questionable given Heidegger's pathway from existential nothingness to the emptiness of the clearing.

Heidegger maintained in his later 1943 postscript and 1949 introduction to "What Is Metaphysics?" that he had been systematically misinterpreted. He maintained that his discourse of nothingness contested rather than advocated nihilism. It did not conclude with the priority of a destructive but rather a generative nothingness. The nothingness encountered in attunements of radical anxiety and boredom is both a concealing veil and a disclosive encounter. The transition through nothingness shows being to be abyssal and groundless (*abgründig*). It suggests, more fundamentally, being as an illuminating, shining forth clearing (*Lichtung*), openness (*Offenheit*), and emptiness (*die Leere*). The clearing is an opening lighting center beyond beings. It encircles all that is like the barely known nothing (GA 5: 40; Heidegger 2002: 30).

Nevertheless, Heidegger can still state in the 1943 postscript: "One of the essential places of speechlessness is anxiety in the sense of the terror to which the abyss of the nothing attunes humans" (GA 9: 310; Heidegger 1998: 238). Nothingness continues to convey elements of existential horror and anxiety in relation to the abyss, as explicitly accentuated in his 1929 lecture and in the early overall reception of his thought, and not only in French existentialism. At the same time, Heidegger articulates dimensions of the abyss, which is "neither empty nothingness nor a dark confusion, but the event" (GA 79: 128).

There are dimensions of openness, associated in Kantian philosophy with the sublime, such as the emptying of the clearing and encountering being's calm, encompassing, inexhaustible expansiveness in releasement. This is found in, for instance, the emptiness (kū 空) in the 1953–1954 "From a Dialogue on Language," or as disclosed in the self-veiling expansiveness of the Siberian wilderness to the two prisoners of war in the 1944/45 "Evening Conversation in a Prison Camp in Russia."[2]

2. Heidegger's Entanglements with East Asian Philosophy

How did Heidegger's thinking of nothingness become entangled with East Asian philosophies? The question of nothingness and emptiness in Heidegger is an intriguing one on its own. This question is also at play in Heidegger's reception in Japanese philosophy and the emerging postwar field of so-called "comparative philosophy," as well as in Heidegger's reflections on the emptiness of the thing in "The Thing" and language in "From a Dialogue on Language."[3]

Heidegger's encounters with East Asian philosophy began as early as 1919, as described earlier in Chapter 1. He has been suspected of borrowing the expression being-in-the world ("in-der-welt-sein") from the 1919 German translation of Okakura Kakuzō, *The Book of Tea*, which he received as a gift in 1919 from Itō Kichinosuke. It states of the *Zhuangzi*: "Chinese historians have always spoken of Daoism as the 'art of being-in-the-world,' because it is about the present, about ourselves."[4] Heidegger's discourse of being-in-the-world no doubt reflects Lutheran discourses of the fallenness, sinfulness, and suffering of "being in the world" ("in der Welt sein" without hyphens) and yet potentially—as intimated in the *Zhuangzi*—also reflects a *poiesis* of immanently and ecomimetically dwelling with things within the world.

Heidegger noted repeatedly in the postwar period the special affiliation between the discourse of nothingness in "What Is Metaphysics?" and his dialogue with Japanese philosophy. His thinking shifts between an existential nothingness and an opening emptiness, with reference to the Japanese translation of "What Is Metaphysics?" in "From a Dialogue on Language" and in the 1969 *Dankansprache* in which he mentions that German and European philosophers had characterized this lecture as "nihilism," while its Japanese translator Yuasa Seinosuke 湯浅誠之助 had comprehended what it genuinely meant to indicate.[5]

Heidegger became increasingly aware of emerging comparisons in the 1930s and sought to differentiate his interpretation of nothingness and nonbeing (as being's event) from any form of Buddhism. This is evident in his 1935 declaration that his thinking is the opposite of Buddhism and his repetition of Nietzsche's critique of Buddhism and Schopenhauer in the lecture courses of the late 1930s.[6] Heidegger's gesture of refusal is not evident in the 1953/54 "Dialogue on Language" in which he acknowledges an affinity and distance in addressing Buddhist emptiness in a discussion of the Japanese understanding of *kū* (emptiness). His figure in the dialogue states that emptiness and nothingness are the same ("Die Leere ist dann dasselbe wie das Nichts") and the Japanese interlocutor responds that for the Japanese, "emptiness" is the highest word for what Europeans mean to say with the word "Being."[7] The dialogue does not enter into how, in East Asian Mahāyāna interpretive contexts, the identification of emptiness with being might imply that the emptiness of emptiness is not the highest Buddhist teaching but rather the disclosure of suchness or concealed nature, the originally awakened Buddha-nature (*tathāgatagarbha*) in beings, through emptiness.

Refusal and rejection are not manifest in his 1963 televised interview with the Thai Buddhist monk Bhikkhu Maha Mani. Denial is replaced with a mixture of acknowledgment and hesitation, as Heidegger recognizes an affinity in speaking of a nothingness that is not merely nothing, and of fundamental differences of language that once again appear to entail untranslatability and linguistic incommensurability (GA 16: 589–93). Heidegger's correspondence with his wife also confirms his interest and reticence in intercultural engagement. He wrote in 1955 that Indo-Germanic categories and grammar impede properly understanding the Japanese language and in 1966 that he avoided discussing Zen Buddhist sources since he lacked the linguistic background to appropriately engage them (Heidegger 2008: 248, 295). Critics of Heidegger's dearth of substantive engagement with Buddhist discourses in the postwar period conflate respectful reticence with refusal and rejection.

Heidegger's earlier negative assertions in the 1930s regarding Buddhism are a different matter. His early remarks appear mediated by the reception of Buddhism in Schopenhauer and Nietzsche. His postwar comments focusing on Zen Buddhism are mediated by his interaction with Japanese philosophers and the Japanese reception of his philosophy. Heidegger had frequent contacts and dialogues with Japanese intellectuals during the Weimar, National Socialist, and Federal Republic periods.

The Japanese reception of Heidegger's work began in the 1920s. The 1930 Japanese translation of "What Is Metaphysics?" was the earliest published translation of a text authored by Heidegger. His early Japanese reception emphasized this lecture's thinking of nothingness. Nonetheless, unlike the early European reception, the critical side of its Japanese reception stressed how this nothingness is still too beholden to being in contrast with Asian ("Oriental") conceptions and experiences of nothingness and emptiness. That is to say, the interculturally entangled modern European and Occidental discourses of nothingness, particularly those linked with Hegel and Heidegger, mediated modern Japanese appropriations of Buddhist emptiness (*śūnyatā*) as "Oriental" and "absolute" nothingness.[8]

II. Nothingness and Its Intercultural Entanglements

3. Daoist Nothingness and Buddhist Emptiness between Europe and Asia

This hermeneutical strategy is particularly evident in Nishida Kitarō, the founding philosopher of the Kyōto school. He distinguished an "Oriental" philosophy and logic of nothingness (as a predicate logic) from Occidental philosophy and its logic of being (as a subject logic).⁹ The concept of "Oriental nothingness" was centered on the Japanese understanding of *kū* (Buddhist *śūnyatā*). In the discourses of Asian and comparative philosophy of this era it could be extended in the geopolitics of Japanese Pan-Asianist discourses to assimilate and rank Asian forms of spirit in a quasi-Hegelian form of historical development.¹⁰ This however would no doubt extend beyond Nishida's own intentions, given his more ambiguous and moderate political position.

The notion of "Oriental nothingness" was formulated in response to the European dismissal of it by Hegel and other philosophers (Hegel 1986b: 210–11; Hegel 1986c: 84). The concept could be expanded to encompass several Indian Hindu and Buddhist forms of negativity. These include the "neti neti" of the *Bṛhadāraṇyaka Upaniṣad* and the Buddha's fourfold negation [*catuṣkoṭi*]; Daoist and mysterious learning (so-called "Neo-Daoist") *wu* 無 as well as varieties of East Asian Mahāyāna Buddhism; and the initial pole of nothingness (*wuji* 無極) in interplay with the great ultimate (*taiji* 太極) that developed in the *Book of Changes* commentarial transmission and Neo-Confucianism.

In the situation of Japanese-German relations during the National Socialist Era, Nishida's thought was introduced to German language audiences in a series of translations between 1936 (Nishida 1936, 1936b, 1939) and the more widely available 1943 translation *The Intelligible World: Three Philosophical Treatises*. Robert Schinzinger, a German student of Cassirer (PhD in 1922), helped introduce Nishida's thought to Germany in the early 1940s with his introduction to this translation and in other writings. Schinzinger distinguished Nishida and Heidegger in detail in the introduction, outlining Nishida's recognition of how being becomes manifest in Dasein's being held into nothingness in Heidegger, and the degree to which Heidegger accordingly remained captured in the Occidental metaphysical paradigm of the supremacy of being and its logic of assertion (Nishida 1943: 30–3).

Schinzinger was not alone in addressing the affinities and differences between Nishida and Heidegger regarding nothingness during this period. Kitayama Junyū lived in Germany from 1925 to 1944. He initially studied with Edmund Husserl in Freiburg before completing his dissertation on Vasubandhu's Yogācāra metaphysics in 1929 with Karl Jaspers in Heidelberg. In his book *Metaphysics of Buddhism* (*Metaphysik des Buddhismus*), published in 1934, he deployed the phenomenology of Husserl and Heidegger to ontologically reinterpret consciousness-oriented Yogācāra Buddhism.¹¹ A 1935 issue of *Kant Studien* noted that this dissertation attempted "to interpret and reveal Vasubandhu teachings in the language of contemporary German metaphysical theorists (Scheler, Husserl, and Heidegger)" (Brightwell 2015: 450).

Kitayama was conversant with Heidegger's thinking from his studies in Freiburg, thanking him in the preface to his dissertation, and extensively referring to his works (including "What Is Metaphysics?") and deploying them to phenomenologically interpret Vasubandhu's philosophy as an elucidation of karmic and samsaric Dasein. In his 1934 book, Yogācāra Buddhism does not offer a psychologistic philosophy of consciousness, as in standard portrayals of its ostensive idealism. It provides rather an existential "analytic of Dasein" of karmically thrown Dasein, its constitution and structures of being, and the possibility of redemption in "absolute nothingness" exemplified by the Buddha's path of awakening. In suffering, finitude, and mortality,

Dasein (he uses Heidegger's term) is a question to itself facing its existence toward inevitable death and thrown abandonment in terrifying nothingness (Kitayama 1934: 78). In the existential emptiness of thirst (taṇhā) and in encountering the disorienting questionability of relative nothingness, absolute nothingness (śūnyatā) is disclosed. It is construed in Heideggerian language: human existence as being-there annihilates itself in relation to its own fundamental groundlessness in the illumination of absolute nothingness (Kitayama 1934: 194–5). In such absolute nothingness, in the transpositional unknowing of the Buddha, freedom and creative life are disclosed as immanent ways of Dasein's bearing and comportment within its world.

The turn from radical nothingness to everyday life is also found in his subsequent expositions of Dōgen Zenji 道元禅師 (Kitayama 1940: 1–15) and Laozi 老子 (Kitayama 1942) in the early 1940s. As discussed below, Kitayama attributed Heidegger's expression "*das Nichts nichet*" to Laozi in his 1940/1942 work *West-Eastern Encounter: Japan's Culture and Tradition* (*West-östliche Begegnung: Japans Kultur und Tradition*). Kitayama's changed relation to Heidegger is more overtly stated in a 1943 article on Nishida published in *Kant Studien*. Kitayama maintained here that "Occidental spirit" is anthropomorphic and intellectualist. It fixates subject and object and neglects nothingness in prioritizing being (Kitayama 1943b: 268–9). "Oriental spirit," in contrast, is ostensibly cosmic, intuitive, and perceives natural and inter-human relations as its guide. It prioritizes absolute nothingness as encompassing things and discovering reality's self-identity in absolute contradiction. Nishida comprehends the reality of the world in its groundless nothingness through the unity of opposites in the self-identity of absolute contradiction.[12]

The anticipated presence and positivity of an absolute perspectiveless totalizing identity is more Hegelian (at least as widely understood) than Buddhist. Buddhist emptiness, more akin to therapeutic skepticism than metaphysical dogmatism, destructures rather than asserts the totalizing synthesis of identity and nonidentity that seeks to subjugate alterity and singularity through speculative dialectic and dialetheia.[13] First, a mere logic of nothingness misses its relational intimacy with the thing evident in *Daodejing* 11 and Heidegger's adaptation of the dynamic of thing and nothing. Second, identity is a condition of concepts and representations, after all, and not things and world. Classical Chinese Buddhism suggests an alternative to enforced identity and totalizing unity that compulsively seeks to destroy alterity and individuality. The relational interpenetration and resonant interpolation of particular things entail a logic of mutual pervasion and encompassing of all phenomena in Huayan, and of mind and reality in Tiantai, that together form the philosophical context of Zen Buddhism. Zen Buddhist practices of meditating on the kōan (*gong'an* 公案) resist resolving paradoxes into identities by heightening contradictoriness and paradoxicality into the "great doubt" (C. *dayi*, J. *taigi* 大疑).

What then of the uncanny guest of nihilism? In their depictions of the present state of Japanese philosophy in the 1940s, Schinzinger and Lüth caution against nihilistic interpretations of nothingness and overly sweeping readings of "absolute contradictoriness" in Nishida, restraining its philosophical boldness and distinctiveness vis-à-vis Occidental discourses about nothingness. They elucidate Nishida's nothingness as concretion, fullness, and determinacy. In this manner, they differentiate it from a vacant, abstract nothingness defined through negation, and from the genuine nothingness of the fullness and completion of reality itself (*dharmakāya*) and its Buddha-nature, which cannot be limited to being (Lüth 1944: 99–101; Nishida 1943: 30–2). However, this is misleading, insofar as such concepts are conceived as positing positive objects or subjects, and since Nishida maintains that nothingness is a predicate that cannot be reified into a subject.[14] Carnap likewise warned of the reification of negation, since it is derivative in relation to assertions about ultimately physical objects and their various relations. Nishida's predicate of nothingness indicates in contrast to Carnap's analysis the true emptiness of things in which they have—without the fixation of essence, self, or substance or the reification of nothingness—their own self-determination and concrete specificity (Taketi 1940: 285).

Nishida's genuine thinking emerges, according to Kitayama, as a radical philosophy of nothingness that reconceives Oriental nothingness through its confrontation with Occidental being and liberates us from the restrictions of Occidental conceptions of being. This claim encompasses Heidegger as its culmination:

That is why we call it "philosophy of nothingness" in contrast to the philosophy of being of the Occident from Plato to Heidegger. The nothingness that Nishida has reached as the ultimate of all being and of thought is the ancient inheritance of East Asian spirit. It occurs as a problem in both Buddhism and Daoism.

(Kitayama 1943b: 269)

The essential distinctiveness of Occidental and Oriental forms of nothingness is a key theme in the intercultural philosophy of figures related to the Kyōto School. In a 1940 German article by Taketi, the radical nihilism of "Oriental nothingness" affirms life, world, and the act from the abyss of the present rather than denying the present, as in Christianity and European nihilism (Taketi 1940: 278–9). In the paradigmatic account of the varieties of nothingness by Hisamatsu Shinichi, published in English in 1962, "Oriental nothingness" is irreducible to both logical negation and existential nothingness. It is also self-emptying, prior to the existential negativity and logical negation that, respectively, existentialism and positivism deploy to explain or discard nothingness.[15] Hisamatsu interpreted awakening as a return to the moments of everyday existence, in which (adopting an expression from the iconoclastic Tang dynasty Chan master Linji Yixuan, in turn, drawn from the *Zhuangzi*) the genuine person without positionality or rank (*wuwei zhenren* 無位真人) abides in non-abiding, dwelling without fixation (Hisamatsu 2002: 29–33).

Kyōto school and other Japanese intellectuals such as Kitayama deployed an interculturally reshaped Buddhist notion of emptiness as nothingness (linked with European ideas of nothingness and Chan-Zen Buddhist uses of *wu/mu* 無) to prove the inadequacy of nothingness in Heidegger. Nishida and Kitayama appreciated the impersonality (in contrast to the readings of Levinas and Sartre that stress the person and subjectivity) and verbal event character of nothingness in Heidegger. Yet this thinking of nothing as the way of encountering being (*Sein*) is just as limited as the negative mysticism and theology in which nothingness reveals God. Heidegger's nothingness was partial and limited in view of "absolute nothingness" (*zettaimu* 絶対無), which is the self-emptying locus or place (*basho* 場所) of all perspectives and positions. This was because it still referred and was bound to being and its implicit yet still too representational subject/object modeling of reality.

Nothingness primordially conditions the world as being stems from nothingness, such that subject logic alone is inadequate for grasping the dialectical totality of reality (Nishida 1936: 127). Far from being pessimistic or nihilistic in Nishida, the absolute nothingness at the heart of Oriental culture is the genuine locus of encountering concrete phenomena as they are in their suchness (*tathātā*) and thus world-affirmation.[16] In absolute nothingness, the mountain is precisely the mountain, water is water, and beings are just what they are (Nishida 1943: 119). Nishida is referring to the kōan ascribed to Qingyuan Weixin 青原惟信, a Tang Dynasty Linji Chan Master, which appears in Dōgen's *Mountains and Waters Sūtra* (*Sansui Kyō* 山水經).

After such early entanglements between Heidegger and Chinese and Japanese philosophy from the 1920s to 1940s, Heidegger's nihilating nothingness was increasingly perceived as a touchstone in the emerging field of comparative philosophy, not only in Germany and Japan but in international scholarship. Much of this literature was more willing than Kitayama, Lüth, or Schinzinger to accentuate the affinities between nothingness in Heidegger and Nishida or Buddhism. Takeuchi Yoshinori 武内義範, for instance, remarked: "A way of thinking akin to Nishida's is found in the recent development of Heidegger's philosophy, although there was no direct influence either way" (Takeuchi 2004: 203). Relying on Nishida's notion of nothingness as identity in complete contradiction, he states: "Heidegger's philosophy of Being meets with a philosophy of Nothingness—because Being and Nothingness are identical in their contradiction" (Takeuchi 2004: 204).

In an analogous fashion, multiple postwar authors linked Buddhist emptiness with Heidegger's nothingness. Here are a few instructive cases. First, the pragmatist Sydney Hook proclaimed Buddhist "emptiness is empty" to be as nonsensical as Heidegger's "nothingness nothings," a logical category mistake in every language (Hook 1959: 164). Second, less dismissively, Sarvepalli Radhakrishnan noted how Heidegger gave nothingness "an active function ('das Nichts nichtet'), which influences our being. He even makes it one with absolute being. One is reminded of the Buddhistic conception of the void (*śūnya*)" (Radhakrishnan 1953: 430). Third, Swan Liat Kwee noted in his 1953 Leiden dissertation on comparative philosophy how "the Void" has an active creative function in Heidegger's "das Nichts nichtet" (Kwee 1953: 184). The latter two statements concerning self-nihilating nothingness show how it is active, creative, and world-generative in South Asian Buddhist *śūnyatā* as much as with early Daoist *wu* 無. This is despite the differences between these two concepts that have been recurrently entangled and distinguished since the introduction of the Buddhist dharma into China, as delineated previously, at the beginning of Part Two.

The interpretive strategy of the later Heidegger appears closer to Daoist generative nothingness with its recognition of natality and mortality, the very naturalness of things, and of practices of emptying and letting as the myriad things gather and disperse. But Heidegger did not directly or explicitly (contrary to Jordan 1932: 102, 147) attribute generative or creative qualities to nihilating nothingness in his 1929

"What Is Metaphysics?" lecture. As the neo-orthodox theologian Karl Barth notes, Heidegger analyzes nothingness from the perspective of human existence in 1929, while it is Sartre who analyzes human existence in its freedom and facticity from the point of departure of fundamental nothingness.[17] Encountering nothingness in radical anguish and boredom places beings radically into question and, accordingly, the being of Dasein itself. Freedom as thrown transcendence into the world is disclosed in this existential questionability and uncanniness.

Despite the latent anthropocentric and Christian background of Heidegger's thinking of nothingness in 1929, in which the positivity of nothingness is not yet its full generativity, it already resonates to an extent with Buddhist and Daoist discourses, as is evident in its reception. His account of nothingness quickly became entangled with Asian philosophy in his early German and Japanese reception. Heidegger's thinking, which evokes and deploys Daoist nothingness and to a lesser degree Buddhist emptiness, became interculturally entwined in comparative philosophy with generative interpretations of nothingness. This is not without sources in Heidegger's own path of thinking, from an emphasis on existential nothingness to nothingness as the potentially generative and nourishing emptiness of the between and the clearing of being.

4. Nothingness, Emptiness, and the Spacing of Things

Numerous anecdotes by Heidegger and others testify that Heidegger engaged in conversations about Japanese thought and Zen Buddhism with visiting students and scholars from 1919 to the end of his life. Nishitani reported that he and Heidegger had extensive discussions about Zen Buddhism during his studies at the University of Freiburg from 1937 to 1939 and Heidegger is reported to have said after reading a book by D. T. Suzuki that "[i]f I understand this man correctly, this is what I have been trying to say in all my writings."[18] Heidegger mentions Zen Buddhist thought-images and kōans in conversations and correspondence after the Second World War. This includes referring, in the conclusion of his 1958 conversation on art with Hisamatsu (GA 16: 557), to the sound of one hand clapping and noting how it was a beloved kōan for the great Rinzai master Hakuin Ekaku 白隠慧鶴 (1686–1769), and corresponding with the Austrian intercultural haiku-poet Imma von Bodmershof over haiku and kōan (Pieger 2000: 98).

More conspicuously, Heidegger directly mentions a Zen Buddhist teaching in "From a Dialogue on Language," as Heidegger's fictionalized Japanese interlocutor states that the mountain appears in emptiness. This dialogue about emptiness and gathering raises several questions. What is the function of this use of emptiness in this dialogue? How are nothingness and emptiness said to be "the same" (*dasselbe*) and "other than all presence and absence" ("das Andere zu allem An- und Abwesenden") as specified in the questioner's answer (GA 12: 103)? What is the emptiness in respectful distancing and withdrawal (*Entziehen*), and in the stillness and silence (*die Stille*) that calls and in which one can listen?

The two interlocutors delineate and enact a kind of emptiness as figures of emptiness reoccur throughout their dialogue. Emptiness is seen as informing fundamental Japanese expressions. One primary example is *iki* 粋. It was popularized in modernity by Kuki (GA 12: 80–6) and became familiar to Heidegger through him.[19] The conversants note several images and expressions related to emptiness, such as how in the Noh theatre the empty stage allows the gathering of the scene to occur (GA 12: 101). Deploying familiar Buddhist imagery, *kū* is described as the limitless expansiveness, like that of the sky (GA 12: 129) and as the openness and emptiness of the sky (GA 12: 136). The clear transparent sky is the classic Buddhist image of the empty (*śūnya*). Clouds are images of forms (*rūpa*; the Chinese character *se* 色 also means color, as it does in this dialogue). Together they indicate the openness in which phenomena arise and disappear. The emptiness of hearing allows the gathering of words in language, and the dialogue concludes with the gathering of the enduring (GA 12: 143, 146).

Given Heidegger's mutating phenomenology of the thing, already examined in Part One, to what extent can emptiness be the gathering and constitution of things? Is there an emptiness, as Heidegger pursued in the 1935 *Contributions to Philosophy*, which signifies something other than the failure of anticipation and expectation, or the empty intentionality, which may or may not be fulfilled, of classical phenomenology (GA 65: 381–2)? Is there a more specific connection between the nothingness portrayed in 1929 and the emptiness of language and the thing in his postwar writings that helps illuminate his assertion that they are ultimately the same?

One contextual hint can be traced in Kitayama's works and their reception. They were widely cited in German discussions of Japanese thought during the National Socialist era. These include references by the geopolitical theorist Karl Haushofer and Paul Lüth, whose 1944 book *Die japanische Philosophie* relies on Kitayama's delineation of Nishida's philosophy of nothingness (Lüth 1944: 97–108). Kitayama's book *West-Eastern Encounter* was first published in 1940 and substantially revised in a second edition appearing in 1942.[20] Kitayama expounds in it an East Asian philosophy of nothingness inspired not only by Buddhist emptiness but also by Daoist nothingness (*wu* 無), the primordial ground of being, of Laozi (Kitayama 1942: 40). In his 1939 article Nishida critiqued the fixation and radicalization of nothingness in Daoism, contending that the teaching of absolute nothingness is only effectively achieved in Mahāyāna Buddhism.[21] Kitayama shares this assessment of Mahāyāna (Kitayama 1943: 3). He is, however, more willing to embrace Daoist teachings of nothingness and the thing, as he depicts them as shaping the formation of East Asian and Zen Buddhist culture and sensibility.

Lao-Zhuang Daoism was construed as a variety of naturalism by numerous early twentieth-century Japanese interpreters—such as Anesaki Masaharu 姉崎正治 (1915), Okakura (1919), and Kitayama (1942). They each emphasized its constitutive role in Chan Buddhism and the East Asian aesthetic that embraces naturalness through emptiness. Anesaki interprets Daoism as a harmonizing repose in nature and the great primordial mood of the way (Anesaki 1915: 55–6). Okakura understood it as a naturalistic this-worldly relativism and art of adoptively being-in-the-world (Okakura 1919: 27–32). Kitayama characterizes it as a "naturalistic nihilism" in which freedom is intuited in nothingness in stillness and non-acting action (Kitayama 1942: 40–1).

Nothingness is the generative beginning of heaven and earth; being is the womb of the myriad things (Kitayama 1942: 174). This nothingness is the groundless ground of beings, silent and wordless, unspeakable and unconceptualizable, and approachable only through an enacting of becoming empty and clear (Kitayama 1942: 24, 38–41). Speaking of the Tang dynasty poet and painter Wang Wei 王維 (792–761), Kitayama delineates how real space can be encountered in the emptiness of solitude and silence. Things in the fullness of their self-being communicate in this space to the poet and appear to the painter: "We translate this explication of space with the words of Laozi: 'The nothing nothings'" (Kitayama 1942: 160). It is space that is emptying through things. His exegesis evokes yet is distinctive from how Heidegger elucidates the same eleventh chapter of the *Daodejing* and the "emptying" of the thing.

Kitayama proposes that nothingness (*Nichts*) and the non-self (*Nicht-Ich*) form the essence and unity of East Asian culture (Kitayama 1942: 183). East Asian philosophical and aesthetic-poetic sensibilities in his account reflect the insight that "[t]he nihilation of the nothing (*das Nichten des Nichts*) is the activity of space that, from the human perspective, is given as form or appearance." Each reality is the appearing of a shadow in light and each thing, such as the mountain or the stone, is a throw (*Wurf*) through the nihilation of space (Kitayama 1942: 161). The expression "the nothing nothings," attributed to Laozi in reference to *Daodejing* 11, is a characteristic of the spatiality in which the thing appears as shadow and throw as a nihilation of the nothing. Kitayama analyzed the nihilating activity of nothingness as a primordial spatiality in which things arise. The expression *wuwu* 無無, which he seems to have in mind here, could be construed as "the nothing nothings" or the functioning of and arising from nothingness in Wang Bi's *Daodejing* commentary.[22] This expression is not found in the transmitted text of the *Daodejing* but only in subsequent Daoist and East Asian Buddhist sources, in which it is entangled with the emptiness of emptiness (*kongkong* 空空).

In classical Indian Theravāda and Mādhyamika teachings, emptiness means to be empty of substantial selfhood (*ātman*), self-nature (*svabhāva*), and form (*rūpa*) in dependent arising (*pratītyasamutpāda*). Emptiness operates as a world-constituting primordiality in *dharmadhatu*, *tathāgatagarbha* (recall the previous discussion of Zongmi), and Vajrayāna teachings. In these movements, it is given a generativity and creativity that continue to resonate in how Kitayama interprets, as we have seen, the "absolute" self-nihilating nothingness in the very different circumstances of Laozi and Nishida. Notwithstanding his father's status as a Pure Land Buddhist priest, and his studies of Yogācāra Buddhist philosophy, teachings in which *śūnyatā* does not play as all-pervasive a role as in Mādhyamika, Buddhist nothingness assumes a dominant cultural and social-political position in Kitayama's German writings of the 1930s and 1940s. These influential works in Nazi Germany covered Buddhism, Daoism, and—as with other Japanese nationalist intellectuals—Shintō and the "warrior's way" (*bushidō* 武士道) of the Samurai.

There are copious instances of the questionable social-political character of the philosophy of nothingness in Kitayama's writings. We can consider two of these publications here. First, in Kitayama's 1943 booklet *Sanctification of the State and Human Transfiguration: Buddhism and Japan* (*Heiligung des Staates und Verklärung des Menschen: Buddhismus und Japan*), Mahāyāna Buddhism occupies a crucial role for him in providing the Japanese people a universal geopolitical and georeligious teaching of compassionate world-redemption (Kitayama 1943; Kubota 2008: 622). It is specifically the Mahāyāna teaching of *nirvāṇa* (nothingness as sublime infinite generative source) that sanctifies and is embodied in the Japanese imperial state, replacing Hegel's Prussian state, which transfigures and liberates humanity through its world-historical purpose (Kitayama 1943: 31–2). As Hegel's world-spirit culminates in the "Germanic world" and the Prussian monarchic state, "Oriental spirit" culminates in Imperial Japan in the Pan-Asianist philosophy of history operative in the war-time discourses of Kanokogi, Kitayama, or Nishitani.

Secondly, a "heroic *ethos*" and warrior ethic of nothingness is unfolded in his 1944 book *Heroic Ethos* (*Heroisches Ethos*).[23] In his interpretation of the concluding fifth book on emptiness of *The Book of Five Rings* (*Gorin no Sho* 五輪書) by Miyamoto Musashi 宮本武蔵, an *ethos* without fixed principles or norms emerges in the spirit of this "real nullity" (*wirkliche Nichtigkeit*), in which there is nothing at all, no knowing and no evil, but only the good. While "relative nullity" counters the seduction of the false and illusory, real nullity is articulated as a spontaneous and detached comportment and *ethos* that exceeds the boundaries of skill and technique (1944: 110–11); this occurs by assimilating a long series of images of perfectly attuned action, from the *Zhuangzi*'s Butcher Ding nourishing life in cutting up the ox and Zen Buddhism to this heroic *ethos*.

Kitayama's philosophy of nothingness is problematic given its historical and social-political positionality—in the intersections of Japanese-German intellectual and ideological exchange in the 1930s and 1940s—and due to its commitment to the priority of an attitude of neutral detachment and indifference, rather than—as in the *ethos* of his Buddhist and Daoist sources—to an ethics of anarchic nurturing care and responsive compassion to others and things through nothingness.[24]

5. The Emptiness of Words and Things

The question of nothingness and emptiness is at play in Heidegger's discussions of the emptiness of the thing that, depending on the text, explicitly or implicitly refer to the empty vessel of *Daodejing* 11. As in the German edition of Okakura's *Book of Tea*, as well as in Fischer and Klages, Heidegger calls the vessel a jug (*Krug*; the English translation has pitcher). It is uncertain to what extent Heidegger is cognizant of the specificity of Japanese arguments and debates concerning his conception of nothingness beyond the general acknowledgment and gratitude that he noted in 1953/54 and 1969.

Heidegger was cognizant of Carnap's logical positivist and Sartre's existentialist responses to it. He denied their appropriateness while at the same time, due to shifts in his own thinking, transitioning from the existential nothingness of the late 1920s (which Kitayama categorized as relative) to nothingness as the generative clearing and emptiness of the "in-between" of beings (*Seiende*) and being (*Sein*). Heidegger's later thinking evokes Buddhist emptiness and Japanese discourses of absolute nothingness, while also having an unclear relation to them. For example, in his analysis of the *Daodejing*, Kitayama construed being as the womb of things arising from nothingness; Heidegger posited nothingness as the middle term between being and things. He stated in the late 1930s that nothingness is a saying of being more primordial than somethingness. Nothingness for Heidegger signifies not "not-beings" but "Being." It is an originary saying of Being, amidst which humans address and are addressed by things, and its immeasurable answerless ontological event.[25]

Heidegger repositions his argumentation in "What Is Metaphysics?" as a confrontation with and moment toward the potential overcoming of the "philosophy of nothingness" and the nihilism that he locates at the core of the modern subject. Nothingness is increasingly concomitant with the "not" of beings (*Seiende*) in Being (*Sein*). This is not merely negative or negational in the sense of a *nihil negativum*, and with the ontological difference: "Nothing is the 'not' of beings and hence being as experienced from beings" (GA 9: 123; Heidegger 1998: 97). To the extent that being (even as the Being that is not beings in the ontological difference) remains the epicenter of his thought, Heidegger remains beholden to the Occidental paradigm of being and has not yet arrived near the vicinity of Nishida's genuine locus of nothingness, as interpreted in Kitayama, Schinzinger, and Nishitani.[26] Nothingness is the perspective of beings on being; nothingness and emptiness are "the same"; still, at the same time, emptiness is potentially (since it is spoken by his dramatized Japanese interlocutor) the "highest name" for being (GA 12: 103). While Heidegger could comprehend the interlocutor's claim in his own discourse, as he too has thematized a kind of emptiness of being, the questioner responds by expressing reserve and stepping back from the identification of *kū* and *Sein*.

"From a Dialogue on Language" circles around the untranslatability of a language, as the questioner repeatedly withdraws and holds back from describing *iki* in the Occidental philosophical language of aesthetics, *kū* in the Western language of being, or *kotoba* 言葉 as *Sprache*. Such hesitation and reserve have been interpreted both as arrogance standing against communication and as humility and modesty toward others. It is presented in this dialogue as enacting an emptying and stillness that allows for a listening and entering into the other's saying instead of a mere talking about language and communication (GA 12: 147-9). The encounter transpires through the emptiness of language that undoes its fixations. It is not without language insofar as there can be no openness of beings, of that which is not a being (*Nichtseienden*), or of emptiness without language (GA 5: 61; Heidegger 2002: 46).

In what sense then can one attribute emptiness to being in Heidegger's discourse? He claimed in the 1951 version of "Overcoming Metaphysics" that the emptiness of beings (*Seiende*) is the distance and forgetting of being, while the emptiness of being in which beings arise can never be filled up with the fullness of beings (GA 7: 94). To return to the thing in an altered setting, Heidegger states in several versions of his thinking of the thing that emptiness does not only allow the gathering of things; it is the gathering (*Versammlung*) of the thing in empty openness that allows it to be as a thing. Heidegger's later elucidation of the thing appears to be mediated by his readings of the *Daodejing* and the *Zhuangzi*. It is distinctive from the hermeneutics of the emptiness and self-nihilation of space that Kitayama attributed to Laozi.

Whereas Kitayama construes the thing as a temporary transient throw, shadow, and fold arising through the activity of self-nihilating spatiality, Heidegger addresses emptiness as the gathering of elements, and the fourfold (*das Geviert*) of sky and earth, mortals and immortals, that allows the thing to be as what it is.[27] Hisamatsu remarked in a conversation with Heidegger on May 18, 1958, that the Occident apprehends the origin as being and Zen as empty formlessness in which there is freedom without restriction. Heidegger in response once again draws a connection between his own thinking and East Asian philosophy in concurring in his response that emptiness is neither a negative nothingness nor a lack. Spatial emptiness, which does not exhaust emptiness, is a clearing as granting (*das Einräumende*) the gathering of things (GA 16: 555).

The empty jug recipiently hosts, gathers, and offers wine (fusing imagery from Hölderlin and the *Daodejing*) precisely in its emptiness. What is the relationship between Heidegger and the *Daodejing*? It is the most frequently mentioned Asian text in his works and it is evoked through numerous indirect references. Previous chapters of this book elucidated how Heidegger extensively engaged with the *Daodejing* in the early 1940s, even attempting (as discussed above) a cotranslation of the text with the visiting Chinese scholar Paul Shih-yi Hsiao, who attended his lecture-courses. Heidegger initiates his reflections on the emptiness of the thing in relation to *Daodejing* 11 in the conclusion of the 1943 essay "The Uniqueness of the Poet" (GA 75: 43–4). There, emptiness is depicted as "in-between" (*Inzwischen*), which he elsewhere described as "the openness" (*die Offenheit*) of being and the spacing of "the between heaven and earth" (*das Zwischen von Himmel und Erde*).

In a series of reflections from the 1940s and 1950s, Heidegger engages the image of emptiness and the "empty vessel" (expressed in *Daodejing* 4 and 11, and pictured by Heidegger as an empty jug), more powerfully evoking the *Daodejing* than in his 1943 essay while no longer naming Laozi. In the first dialogue of the 1944/45 *Country Path Conversations* (GA 77), the first 1949 Bremen lecture (GA 79), and the 1950 essay "The Thing," emptiness proves to be the condition of gathering of the elemental and of materiality itself in the thing. As gathering: "The thing things world."[28] That is to say, as much as the artwork, the thing discloses and opens a world and there is no disclosure and openness without the thing.[29]

Heidegger described in "The Thing," considered earlier in Chapter 3, how when the jug or pitcher is filled, the liquid flows into and from its emptiness as it receives, retains, and gives. The jug is not the physical container. Emptiness is that which conditions and contains the materiality of the container. This emptiness, as a nothingness belonging to the pitcher and making it that which it is, is what the pitcher is as a containing container. This signifies that "[t]he vessel's thingness does not lie at all in the material of which it consists, but in the emptiness that holds" (GA 7: 171; Heidegger 1971: 167). This emptiness is its own emptiness or self-emptying, not the voidness of generalized physical space, which we must allow to be in its encounter and "let the jug's emptiness be its own emptiness" (GA 7: 173; Heidegger 1971: 168).

The emptiness, or "the void" as Albert Hofstadter translated *die Leere*, is what accomplishes the vessel's holding. The empty space, this nothingness of the jug, is what the jug is as the holding vessel. Yet as the holding is enacted by the jug's emptiness, the potter who shapes and forms the vessel on the potter's wheel does not create, make, or produce the vessel but shapes materiality in its emptiness. Things are shaped rather than fabricated by human practices and techniques. In not only shaping the material clay, but also its very emptiness, the potter participates in the forming and shaping of emptiness into a specific form. Emptiness acquires a determining and formative character in Heidegger's account, which is familiar from Daoist discourses while being either absent or precluded in Occidental philosophy, as is apparent in Hegel's thinking of "Oriental nothingness" as a primitive opposite overcome in Occidental becoming.

III. The Hermeneutics of Emptiness

6. Between Hegel's Being and Laozi's Nothingness

Heidegger's thinking of emptiness is formed through his earlier confrontations with Hegel's dialectical conception of emptiness, nothingness, and negativity. Hegel dismissed Oriental nothingness and emptiness as lacking substance, indeterminate and unproductive in that it does not lead to the positive (Hegel 1986b: 210–11; Hegel 1986c: 84). As Heidegger argues in his 1938–1939 drafts on Hegel's negativity, negativity in Hegel is relative, dependent on consciousness and operating as an intermediate means toward positivity; there is no genuine recognition of the abyssal and elemental nothingness of being nor of the source of the negativity that he dialectically deploys (GA 68: 3–57). Hegel's negativity is not genuinely negative as it is conceived through and must return to positivity and affirmation.[30]

According to Heidegger, nothingness needs to signify both a genuine nothingness and at the same time the nothing of being. Hegel posits emptiness as the indeterminate that must be overcome, while Heidegger perceives—in affinity with and perhaps due to his reading of the *Daodejing*—its generative and formative character. Perhaps recalling his early methodological ideas of hermeneutical anticipation and formal indication, which destructures and empties absorption in a particular concretion to open the possibilities of concreteness, Heidegger maintains that "emptiness is simply the origin of philosophy."[31] Hegel wishes to overcome this initial emptiness and indeterminacy in a determinate logical necessity that is constantly confronted with its own contingency and arbitrariness.

The beginning origin (*Anfang*) stays with what is unfolded, despite all negation and synthesis, whereas the beginning start (*Beginn*) is superseded (GA 68: 52). Hegel's beginning origin is being conceived through the Cartesian paradigm of consciousness and the affirmation of the primacy of being over nothingness as its secondary derivative negation. His system cannot escape this defining paradigm of idealism and logicism to encounter either thing or nothing as something exceeding reflection, and the representational object of being-as-entity. Heidegger traces how it is nothingness that is the genuine origin, albeit repressed and unthought, of Hegel's affirmative deployment of negativity. Hegel fails to master the radical nothingness and negativity that his dialectic postulates and utilizes without appropriately fathoming.

Heidegger's confrontation with Hegel's onto-theological thinking of negativity and nothingness does not mention Buddhist emptiness, Daoist nothingness, or their dismissal by Hegel. It does open the space for a dialogue that was impossible on Hegel's terms. Heidegger's subsequent account of formative emptiness in "The Thing," which draws on Laozi, indicates its determinateness to the extent that it is in the specificity of this nothingness and emptiness that the vessel's thingliness genuinely lies.

In addition to the Daoist background of Heidegger's interpretation of the thing's emptiness, it is also worth observing how the relation of emptiness and form (which evokes for East Asian readers the Buddhist interplay of emptiness and form or color) is co-constitutive of reality in perfection of wisdom (*prajñāpāramitā*) sūtra literature. As described previously, the *Heart Sūtra* asserts: "Form is emptiness; emptiness is form; form is not different than emptiness; emptiness is not different than form."[32] Form and emptiness are not static realities or qualities of things. These two expressions would be better translated as forming and emptying. This analysis is particularly salient if the emptying of Heidegger's "The Thing" (which addresses Laozi's empty thing) is joined with the emptying of his "From a Dialogue on Language" (which concerns Japanese Buddhist forms of emptiness). Earth, sky, thing, memory, and saying are sites of gathering and world-disclosure, through their emptiness in these East Asian informed and co-resonant texts.

7. Two Interpretations of Emptiness

As elucidated throughout Part Two of the present book, Heidegger should not be considered a thinker of emptiness as static spatial voidness but, instead, as a thinker of the illuminating clearing and emptying that clear, unfix, and free the way. Emptying is enacted in a comportment and praxis. Emptying plays a twofold role in his 1950s writings that call back to the methodological emptying of "formal indication" in the 1920s, destructuring reifying fixations and allowing things to be encountered in their myriad concrete ways of being.

In the conclusion to "The Thing," Heidegger reflects on both the emptying that constitutes the thing and the emptying comportment that allows the thing to address us as the thing that it is, in its own way of being in emptiness. There are accordingly two functions of emptiness in this context: (1) the emptying that is the gathering of the thing and (2) the emptying that allows the thing, as world-gathering and disclosing, to be experientially encountered and addressed in interpolation. Emptiness is a condition of world-disclosure and the formation of meaning in the communication between things.

The emptiness of being is correlated with practices of emptying as attunement and *ethos* in Heidegger. Emptying undoes by traversing perspectives and fixations. It is the preparation of a pathway. The clearing of the thing is its self-emptying. This requires a respectful and reverent (yet arguably inadequately responsive) distance and reserve that avoids absorption and consumption. Japanese aesthetics (as interpreted by Kuki) understands respectful reserve in the encounter as detachment (compare Nara 2004). In the step back (*der Schritt zurück*), in letting distance and the genuine between (*das Zwischen*, which the modern loss of distances and uniformity of space has disrupted) to reappear with the thing, one is called by the thing as thing, and then perhaps one can begin to hear toward it and respond more appropriately.

The distinctive yet overlapping and entangled notions of emptiness and nothingness operate in Heidegger as the highest expressions for being. These notions are interwoven with his understanding of Daoism and Zen Buddhism and with his philosophy's East Asian reception. Nothingness has an intimate relationship with the thing that cannot be objectified into an object and its qualities. In the self-emptiness of being, the thing and its sense are not annihilated, but rather it can be as the thing in the fullness of its own way of being. Heidegger once again appears to echo East Asian discourses, as in the sentence from the kōan attributed to Qingyuan Weixin mentioned by Nishida: "in the awakening of emptiness, mountains are directly mountains, and waters are directly waters" (Nishida 1943: 119). In the pluralistic relational logic of Huayan, this would be the return to the particular in its very particularity as mirroring and encompassing every other particular and the whole.

Kitayama's 1940 German translation and commentary on Dōgen's *Genjō Kōan* 現成公按 clarifies the movement from things to nothingness back to things, through the forgetting and falling away of the self and its constructs that separate it from things. This is the self-illumination of a holistic relational selflessness in which each thing is singularly itself just as the dewdrop can reflect the moon (Kitayama 1940: 4, 10-11). Still, this is neither a static abstract harmony nor a mere moment to be sublimated into a new harmonizing order. The logic of the kōan that confronts the fixated self and places it into question is antinomian, paradoxical, and without conceptual resolution. Kitayama describes how it leads the meditator into a "dead-end" (*Sackgasse*) without any recourse, which is fractured in a breakthrough in which the obstructing duality of being and knowing, object and subject, falls away (Kitayama 1940: 15). As Kitayama's earlier works show, Heidegger and Buddhist philosophy coincide in dismantling conceptual and experiential dualities.[33]

According to Kitayama's 1943 Nishida article, with its critique of Occidental spirit and its fixation on being, Heidegger's thinking of being continues to conceive nothingness in an Occidental fashion. This precludes the illumination of absolute nothingness that is unrestricted by (and otherwise than) being no matter how radically it might be thought (Kitayama 1943b: 268-9). This is not the decay of difference into an "empty unity of opposites unconcerned with one another," of which Heidegger warned in his analysis of the essential relational strife of earth and world (GA 5: 35; Heidegger 2002: 26). Rather, Kitayama elucidates Nishida's absolute nothingness as entailing an accord within complete contradiction—that is to say, a self-determination and self-identity encountered in the intensification of cacophony, contradictoriness, and multiplicity of singular phenomena—and reality itself. The danger here is that such a totalizing identity of contradictions (found in readings of Hegel, the Kyōto school, and dialetheism) does not take radical nonidentity, multiplicity, and singularity sufficiently seriously.

8. Transforming the Philosophy of Nothingness

The Japanese reception of Heidegger's hermeneutical strategy of approaching nothingness embraces one of its primary elements while diverging over a second key element. First, Heidegger's thinking is perceived as approaching "Oriental nothingness," far more than Hegel or Schopenhauer (despite moments of irreducible negativity and nothingness), insofar as nothingness needs to signify a genuine nonderivative non-negational nothingness in its own terms. Secondly, however, the Japanese reception is divided over the adequacy of the second facet of Heidegger's hermeneutical strategy. Heidegger repeatedly noted the first element of affinity in speaking of his Japanese reception. It is notable that he does not directly mention the second Nishida-inspired critique that was known in German language sources (Kitayama, Lüth, and Schinzinger). This situation might be glimpsed in Heidegger's judgment that Nishida reproduces Hegel's dialectic or in his hesitancy and reserve in interconnecting his own and "Eastern" encounters with emptiness and nothingness.[34]

At the same time, there are ways to reply to this criticism. As one encounters nothingness *qua* nothingness, Heidegger insists that it must be encountered as the nothingness *of* being. This step suggests a fall back into the logic of affirmation and being for Nishida's early German language interpreters. Schinzinger and Kitayama imagine a pure nothingness beyond all being. However, in Heidegger's defense, the nothingness *of* being cannot be reduced to either the positivity and presence of being or the absence and nihility of pure nothingness. It is not secondary or derivative. It has an elemental role as the nothingness, emptiness, and clearing that are deployed to characterize being *as* being.

Heidegger's limits teach as much as his insights. He suggestively yet inadequately anticipates a more groundbreaking thinking of nothingness, emptiness, and the clearing. He intimates further steps beyond the Occidental history of being, but he cannot twist free from it. He proposes an Occidental Greco-German conception of the history of philosophy without recognizing how this emphasis distorts its intercultural formation.

The preceding point is applicable to both Heidegger and Kitayama, who teach through their failures if one can draw the appropriate lesson. They are not proponents of multi- or interculturalism in any contemporary sense. Nor are they cultural purists in their interpretive practices, despite perhaps their own intentions given the virulent nationalism of the 1930s and 1940s, insofar as they offer highly mediated, interculturally, and intertextually entangled conceptions of nothingness, emptiness, and the thing. Engaging Kitayama's neglected philosophy of nothingness, which draws on Heidegger, Nishida, and classic East Asian sources, resituates the complex formation of increasingly intercultural and critical practices and discourses of emptiness and nothingness; these are practices and discourses that cannot be subsumed under and can potentially dismantle the reified collective subjects of nationalist discourses in National Socialist Germany, Imperial Japan, and contemporary authoritarian and totalitarian imaginaries.

Contrary to Kitayama, and movements such as Imperial Way Zen (*kōdō Zen* 皇道禅) (Victoria 2003; Ives 2009), emptiness does not stop at placing the ego or individual in question, subsuming it into a national identity or social totality. It more radically dismantles the very assertion and violence of identity itself. Such hegemony-seeking totalizing identities do not empty fixations and allow the gathering of thing, environment, and world. They require de-individuation through appeals to substantialized and mythicized collective subjects and their sacrificial logic that legitimates human and environmental devastation.

An alternative approach to emptying as a practice of freeing language and attunement has emerged in this work. Emptiness is correlated with practices of emptying. If emptiness undoes static identity by dismantling borders constructed between subject and world, what then might be said—as a formal indication and critical model—of emptiness, nothingness, and the clearing? Emptiness is the specific emptiness of something. Nothingness is the emptiness of being. It is the enfolding generative darkness and the clearing in which each thing can freely and easily enact its own shifting, transformational course.

9

Reimagining the Ethics and Politics of Emptiness

Emperor Wu of Liang asked Bodhidharma, "What is the first principle of sacred truth?" Bodhidharma replied, "Vast emptiness, not sacredness."

1. Introduction

Heidegger is principally a philosopher of formal indication, as an emptying that points toward existential concreteness and of thinking on the way and underway. It is this way that reveals the absence and presence (in their verbal senses), the emptiness and fullness, of being and beings, and of sense and meaning through nothingness and the ontological difference.[1] Heidegger's "way-ism" is historically and conceptually entangled with his interpretations of the "way-ism" of the *Daodejing* and the *Zhuangzi*, which indicate ways of freely-wandering-in-the-world. This work has offered a "ziranist" critique and reconstruction of Heidegger's thinking based on the Daoist and quasi-Daoist dimensions of Heidegger's own thought. The present philosophical reconstruction of *ziran* 自然 formally indicates nature as inevitably myriad (singular-plural) and transforming, demanding recognition in each moment. This sense of *ziran* draws on Daoist sources to contest naturalism as the reductive, anthropocentric projection of identity onto nature as a reified object.

The primary motivation for this book has been to outline Heidegger's interactions with East Asian philosophy in the context of questions of the thing and nothingness. A second undertaking has been to suggest its critical and emancipatory potential in leaping-ahead for the sake of things in the context of our current existential situation. Early Chinese experiences of self-so-ness, particularly the self-naturing of the thing (*wu* 物) and the nothing (*wu* 無), allows us to think both with and beyond Heidegger as shown throughout this work. This means to think against Heidegger's refusal of democratic self-interpretation and mutual interaction, and his other prejudices, and with his existential individualist, formally indicative, and ziranist moments in view of Daoist, Buddhist, and critical liberatory interpretive strategies.

As discussed in the previous chapter, there are questions concerning whether (1) the phenomenological and problematic political aspects of Heidegger or Japanese philosophers such as Kitayama can be disentangled, (2) radical nothingness necessarily entails or is a consequence of conservative and radical right-wing nationalist and racial politics, and (3) the philosophy of nothingness and emptiness can have a critical ecological (contesting the domination of nature) and emancipatory social-political (contesting the domination of persons) potential.

This interrogative hermeneutical tracing of barely visible and forgotten episodes and events in the intercultural history of the philosophy of nothingness leaves additional questions that need to be further addressed on other occasions. Such legitimate concerns encompass both (1) the reactive politics of nothingness in German and Japanese discourses and (2) the ethical and philosophical adequacy of a critical model and orienting *ethos* of nothingness.[2] In the cases of both Heidegger and Kitayama, one can repose Levinas's concerns about Heidegger formulated in the 1930s, and the interrogation of the politics of Buddhist nothingness in imperial Japan by Ichikawa Hakugen 市川白弦 (1902–1986) and recent critical Buddhism (*hihan bukkyō* 批判仏教).[3]

2. Alienation, Freedom, and Self-*Poiesis*

The complex philosophical and social-political contexts outlined in the closing chapters entail freely reimagining the philosophy of nothingness with and beyond its previous forms.[4] A few points can be addressed here, although it is a topic that calls for another work devoted to it. Deconstructing and emptying the individual self while fixating and glorifying a collective subject has catastrophic consequences, as Ichikawa and socially critical Buddhism have demonstrated.[5]

There are historical hints of different pathways. The early twentieth-century Korean thinker, reformer, poet, and Buddhist monk Han Yongun (Korean: 한용운; Chinese: 韓龍雲) (1879–1944), often called by his penname Manhae (만해; 萬海), suggested a different way of deploying Buddhist emptiness that led to a politics of egalitarian participation (Han 2008). According to Huayan Buddhism's pluralistic and interactive holism of mutually encompassing singular events, illustrated by thought-images of the infinite hall of mirrors, rafter-and-building, and the golden lion, the genuine whole that interpenetrates between each and all maintains the particular without reducing it to the fixation of a universal or a particular identity. The answer proposed in this work is to step back to retrieve the intercultural and critical elements of Heidegger's way and radicalize generative nothingness and opening emptiness. By doing so it is possible to release individuals as well as things and extend it to dismantle the reification of collective identities and authoritarian hierarchical social systems (to which Heidegger himself undeniably falls prey), systems that can be far more destructive than the fixations of individuals through which they operate and are reproduced.

The moment of nonidentity at work in distinctive ways in the discourses of Heidegger, early Daoist sources, and some varieties of Buddhist teachings indicates ways of resisting, undoing, and correcting for their own limits and fixations. Nāgārjuna stated that emptiness is itself empty and not to be taken as another substantive view (Siderits and Katsura 2013). Likewise, nonidentity needs to be thought as nonidentity against the persistent repetition of identity. Nonidentity, which is not Heidegger's expression but Adorno's, emerges in Heidegger's discussions of nothingness, difference, and event. Such ways of communicating are therapeutically justifiable, given the constant reassertion of reductive enframing identity in such conceptualizations, accompanied by reification and oblivion of the event of being in availability and usefulness. Heidegger's thinking here is an imperfect guide as it insightfully indicates basic problems while reproducing and inadequately breaking with them.

Rahel Jaeggi offers in recent works a helpful reconstruction of alienation and freedom for what her interpretation does and does not contain. She traced in her work on alienation how interpretations of freedom can restrict and open our consideration of practical possibilities. One sense of non-alienated freedom is no doubt the ability of the self to appropriate and individuate its material and social conditions with others (Jaeggi 2005). The freedom of non-alienation encompasses the co-appropriation of the realities of individual and social life; we might call this, with the early Heidegger, the self-world (*Selbst-Welt*) and with-world (*Mit-Welt*) (GA 16: 44). It would also need to encompass the third referentiality of the environing world (*Um-Welt*). This is predominantly pragmatic for Heidegger in the 1920s and subsequently extended (through twists and turns) to the priority of thing, place, and environmental life (by implication according to the present analysis).

Non-alienation is anticipated with reference to nature in the early Marx and in the early critical social theory of the Frankfurt school. Marx portrayed one of its most basic features as non-alienation from human and nonhuman nature in the *Economic-Philosophical Manuscripts* and *Theses on Feuerbach*. Alienation is systematically produced by a logic of use and uselessness operative between commodified humans and things. The production of useful and enchanted things correlates with the production of useless and disenchanted masses. Alienation is not only self-alienation but likewise alienation from things and the metabolic environment ("nature"). Some interpreters find a renewal of enchantment, mystification, and mythology in Heidegger, viewed as products of social reification and alienation. But, contrary to this misinterpretation, and, significantly for the focus of this work, Heidegger's most radical insights empty and encounter thing and world rather than mystify them and accordingly indicate exemplary models of other ways of comporting oneself and dwelling.

Adorno depicted in his aesthetic writings how the meaning of non-alienation also encompasses images of reconciliation with things and nature and the primacy of the object.[6] Another sense of freedom as non-alienation is (at least tacitly) operative in ziranist Daoist sources and Heidegger's later thinking. It calls for non-appropriation by the subject and the releasement of self, others, things, and world for them to thrive as themselves in their own event and ways of being. Mastery and domination are contested and transformed by means of indicative thought-images of nourishing life through co-appropriation, collaboration, and cooperation. If it is objected that the forms of releasement of *wuwei* and *Gelassenheit* are ultimately only anthropocentric perspectives, which human existence cannot avoid, the transperspectival priority of the thing and the fourfold world, the daily and seasonal alternations of earth and sky, and the usefulness of the useless, can all still be more salutary for human dwelling and flourishing in the thick of relational things and world. Such dwelling is not merely a purposive art or method of the self or the community: it is *poiesis* itself. According to Heidegger's late reflections, letting is fundamentally a letting go into being's *poiesis*

(GA 102: 182, 385). Poietic thinking is an element of the *poiesis* of being, to which it is respectfully attentive and attuned.

The preceding chapters cannot be described as interpreting or endorsing every statement made by Heidegger. It clarifies key elements of Heidegger's way in their intersections and entanglements with significant Daoist (in Part One) and Buddhist (in Part Two) themes: the way, the thing, and the nothing. These chapters offer an interpretation of the historical and philosophical contexts, claims, and implications of Heidegger's "Daoist" theses: those theses of the usefulness of the useless, the perfection of imperfection, the letting of thing and event in their own self-so character, and, further, how nothingness and emptiness, by undoing the borders and fixations of isolating identity, release and allow for more appropriate attunements and responsive encounters with things, places, and world.

3. The Anarchic Implications of Daoist Nothingness

Let us next consider how the *Daodejing* and *Zhuangzi* provoked anarchistic and libertarian interpretations in their European reception. Historically and conceptually speaking, Daoist generative nourishing nothingness and Buddhist self-emptiness have transformative ethical and social implications, particularly in their alignment with an *ethos* of maternal natality and nurturing care in life and acknowledgment of mortality and letting depart in death. Daoist or Lao-Zhuang nothingness is interlinked in the *Daodejing* with self-generativity and nurturing mother-like care (*ci* 慈) for the myriad things. Several passages in the *Zhuangzi*, the *Liezi*, and a polemical critique of an otherwise unknown figure, Bao Jingyan (who is alleged to advocate the abolition of ruler and ruled) by Ge Hong each indicate anarchistic and egalitarian self-ordering models of social life. This dimension of Daoism inspired a radical interpretation of Daoism in the early twentieth century. The brothers Heinrich Hart (1855–1906) and Julius Hart (1859–1930), best known as fin-de-siècle literary critics and advocates of aesthetic naturalism, promoted a Daoist inspired anarchistic socialism that influenced their friend Gustav Landauer, a socialist anarchist who perished in the suppression of the Munich Soviet Republic in 1919 and other intellectuals like the young Buber.

The younger Hart brother, the poet and literary theorist Julius Hart, claimed specifically to be a Daoist and unfolded a new intercultural poetics and anarchistic politics of Daoist nothingness. In the 1902 "Transformations" (*Verwandlungen*) and the 1905 "Tao," Hart adaptively interpreted the *Daodejing* as delivering a poetic, spiritual and anarchist emancipatory message. The Daoist poetic sensibility promised to revolutionize Occidental aesthetics and forms of life. Daoist nothingness was conceived here through the lenses of fin-de-siècle Orientalist enthusiasm and Jewish-Christian mysticism, with figures such as Meister Eckhart receiving a prominent role. Hart's revolutionary Daoist-informed mysticism would continue to resonate in the early writings of Landauer and Buber on mystical anarchism, and in Buber's 1910 edition of the *Zhuangzi* and his 1924 Ascona lectures on the political philosophy of the *Daodejing*.[7]

Sinologists have more systematically tracked the anarchistic aspects of early Daoist discourses. Angus Graham accentuated the agriculturalist strands expressed in the *Zhuangzi* and the *Liezi*. Each text contains radical political moments of dismantling the very distinction between ruler and ruled, identifying it with anarchism and utopianism. Appealing to the exemplary ancient agricultural sage-king Shennong 神農, this tendency stressed living in simple egalitarian agricultural communities without hierarchical leadership. Graham identified philosopher-farmers like Xu Xing 許行, whose conception of mutually shared simplicity and self-sufficiency was rejected for the sake of upholding hierarchical social distinction, in *Mencius* 3A4, with an agriculturalist "School of the Tillers" (*nongjia* 農家) located at the beginnings of the Chinese peasant utopian lineage that molded a history of peasant revolts (Graham 1989: 66–100).

Interpreted in view of its emancipatory social ecological potential, the much-criticized agrarianism and provincialism of Heidegger's thinking, accentuated by Adorno and Habermas among other critics, need not entail (as shown in this work) conservative or reactionary consequences.[8] At the least, the situation is more complex. First, historically speaking, agrarian utopian images have both reactionary and critical emancipatory uses as they can either refer to a closed localist identity, allergic to alterity or to a relatively equal and free self-ordering community that is open and receptive to the world. Heidegger's own ambiguities can lead to discarding the former elements in favor of the latter ones. Secondly, Heidegger's "provincial" agrarian conservativism led to his support for and his hesitancy toward National Socialism. His refusal to relocate to Berlin and aversion to the systematically racialized and totalitarian Nietzscheanism (as Heidegger considered it) of powerful National Socialist party ideologues, Alfred Rosenberg and Alfred Baeumler, indicate differences between, on one hand, his aesthetic and rural "fascist" inclinations of the 1930s and, on the other, the politically totalitarian and racialized fascism that remained irreconcilable with basic premises of his philosophy. These were initially articulated in *Being and Time* and then developed in the lecture-courses of the late 1930s and early 1940s that increasingly confronted the prevailing ideological appropriation of Nietzsche. To give a brief indication of this shift from the will to its critique: Heidegger could praise Baeumler in criticizing Klages's vitalistic biologistic and psychologistic reading of Nietzsche in the first Nietzsche lecture-course, but he contemptuously gestures at the "Berlin interpretation of Nietzsche" by 1941 (GA 49: 122). Such elements would allow his thinking to take a radically altered turn toward thing and world after 1943 that correlates and resonates with, even if not exclusively deriving from, his engagement with Daoist texts. These sources allow for an intercultural and anti-totalitarian analysis of core elements of Heidegger's thought.

As expressed throughout this work, four key threads in Heidegger's writings correlate with this European reception of Daoism (that centers around nothingness, the thing, and local agrarian forms of existence) and with a potentially emancipatory ethics and politics (or points toward critical models thereof): (1) the emptying enacted in formal indication contests sedimented concepts and values. In so doing, formal indication opens the concrete particularity of phenomena, and this methodology continues to resound in his subsequent language of opening the way[9]; (2) the leaping-ahead, making room for, and nurturing the individuation of others, which is constrained in *Being and Time* to other Dasein; (3) the Daoist-inflected articulation of releasement (*Gelassenheit*, as a freedom and letting uncompelled by use) in his mature thinking. This makes room for, opens the way of, and safeguards things in their own self-essencing or self-generative life; and (4) the safeguarding, preserving, and nurturing of interthingly places, environing regions, and—by implication—self-generative environments that constitute the conditions of human dwelling, building, and thinking.

These four threads intimate an adjusted attunement and comportment of responsive freedom with things, environing localities, and world that intimate a more appropriate environmental *ethos* and art of dwelling-in-the-world. *Ethos* here is understood as a responsively attuned comportment and mood that transperspectivally challenges and moves beyond the calculative anthropocentric subject toward the thing in the positionality of its own being and saying. Such an orienting and attuning *ethos* is one element of an appropriate answer to contemporary crisis-conditions if it is not taken as fatalistic resignation and aligned with a conception of political liberty as the formation and co-appropriation of material and social conditions in coordination with others.[10] Daoism can lead to fatalistic resignation, uncaring and unnurturing indifference, and merely reactive adaptation, as it does in some prominent interpretations, or to embracing a worldly relational freedom in which others and things have their own ways of becoming and are not assimilated to hidden powers and dogmatically postulated principles of "nature" or "spirit." The latter understanding of Daoist sources, and a Daoist reinterpretation of Heidegger's thinking, allows us to reorient the human-nature relationship. In addition to a conversion in human dwelling and *ethos*, for which ziranism offers critical transformative models, climate and ecological crisis-tendencies require scientific and technological inquiry and innovation as well as a participatory and pluralistic public sphere—as a formally indicative way taking individuals' communicative self-interpretation as its point of reference—capable of contesting and potentially reorienting the systemic power of the market and the state.[11]

4. The Consequences of Buddhist Emptiness: A Critical Huayan Interpretation

Secondly, based on the discussions of Part Two, what are the consequences of Buddhist emptiness for thing (as *shi* 事, the singular event, matter, or phenomena) and world? The primary purpose of Buddhist discourses and practices is not politics but the liberation of the self from its bondage. The basic meaning of Buddhist emptiness is the emptiness of form, nature, self-nature, and substance, rather than their generalized absence or negation. Emptiness is not an indeterminate nothingness but, conversely, a determinate "emptiness of" (self, form, nature, and so on) to be enacted through meditative and discursive practices.

Buddhist models of causal and karmic bondage, merit-making, meditative destructuring and freedom, and so on have a variety of ethical and social-political implications. Not all of these have been socially-politically emancipatory, as evident in the continuing entanglements of Buddhist teachings and institutions and ethnocentric nationalisms in modern South, Southeast and East Asia. Emptiness characteristically plays little role in these tendencies, with the notable exception of modern movements such as Imperial Way Zen and Japanese nationalist and Pan-Asianist thinkers such as Kitayama.[12] Structurally akin to how nothingness tends toward the idolatry of the presence and positivity of God in mystical and negative theologies, emptiness and nothingness circle around the reified images of the Emperor and the Japanese nation in these discourses.[13] This tendency is not limited to Kitayama writing in Germany. The wartime Nishitani and Tanabe also deployed absolute nothingness to dismantle the egotistical self and individual agency (which they could not differentiate) for the sake of collective Japanese existence and the totalizing Hegelian state (at least, as they interpreted it) embodied in the Emperor.[14] Nishitani accordingly declared that "the concentration of that total power is fundamentally impossible without a profound ethicality that would lead each and every Japanese to extinguish their private selves and be reduced, as a totality, to the nation-state."[15] Such fixating forms of nothingness and emptiness are ideologically imprisoning and can no longer destructure and release. They need to be themselves emptied, as illustrated by Mādhyamaka and Chan therapeutic strategies.

One can well question if the ostensive "reactionary" politics of nothingness and emptiness, insofar as such a political philosophy genuinely exists, attained an appropriate ethics and politics of the other and the "perfection of wisdom" in emptiness, given how śūnyatā is not only a tranquil attunement with and a letting releasement of things but is intrinsically intertwined with an ethics and responsive enactment of compassion (karuṇā), loving-kindness (maitrī), and generosity (dāna) toward the suffering world. This is evidenced in paradigmatic teachings of the dharma, such as Śāntideva's Bodhicaryāvatāra and that Schopenhauer recognized, based on a few imperfectly translated works, in his interpretation of Buddhism. This European transmission occurred in an ethical language of sympathy (Mitleid) and liberation from the will that, for Nietzsche, problematically linked Schopenhauer and the Buddha as nihilistic and, apparently, for the early Heidegger, conditioned and limited their understanding of it.[16] It is worth noting the background of such concerns: discourses of anti-pessimism and anti-nihilism were predominantly conservative forms of cultural critique, as the late nineteenth-century and early twentieth-century German social-political order (which includes Heidegger in part) perceived socialism/Marxism and pessimism/nihilism to be its utmost threats.

The interconnections between Buddhist emptiness and compassion and responsiveness, which are perfected in the figures of the Bodhisattvas and Buddhas who respond without conditions and limits, are crucial to its practice as an *ethos*. There have been regressive and also, one should recognize, progressive or emancipatory deployments of Buddhist emptiness in modern East Asia, that call for a more nuanced, complex, and critical engagement with it instead of uncritical acceptance or rejection.[17] For example, to briefly sketch a different encounter with Buddhist emptiness than its ideological deployments in Imperial Japan, Manhae Han Yongun is interesting due to his hermeneutical positionality, notwithstanding the controversies that surround him and his perceived compromises and failures in the complex situation of colonial Korea. He was a modernizing poet of the *eros* of the beloved (*nim* 님), a democratic socialist and anticolonial activist, and a Seon (선, the Korean form of Chan/Zen) monk and monastic reformer who perceived an emancipatory potential in emptiness.[18]

Given the complex varieties of Buddhist emptiness, we will consider only one of many germane Buddhist models at this juncture. Classical Tang era Huayan hermeneutical strategies and their Korean adaptation deeply informed subsequent East Asian Buddhist transmissions and played an exemplary role in Manhae's modern intercultural reconstruction of the Buddhist dharma. In Manhae's intriguing reimagining of the *Flower Garland Sūtra* (*Avataṃsaka Sūtra*; *Huayan Jing* 華嚴經), the principal sūtra of the Hwaeom 화엄 (*Huayan* 華嚴) Buddhist transmission that is named after it, the emptiness of self-nature of essence and substantiality (*svabhāva*; 自性) signifies non-obstruction. It allows the disclosure of the unobstructed mutual interpenetration and pervasion between particular phenomena and patterning principle (*lishi wuai* 理事無礙). Between each particular (*shishi wuai* 事事無礙) emptiness is elucidated as a meditative, poetic, and social-political practice, as mind is becoming embodied material form, and form is becoming mind in mutual aid and compassion.[19] In his political writings, emptiness consequently entailed and called for acting on equality as well as mutual interdependence. In his poetry, still widely read in Korea, he unfolded a poetics of emptiness in which emptiness operates as the space of erotic love, devotion to the occupied and oppressed Korean people, altruistic compassion for suffering beings, and receptivity to things that infinitely reflect the whole in their own concrete ways.

What then of Heidegger's postwar reflections on emptiness? In this reoriented and reimagined context informed by Huayan, his thinking of emptiness remains suggestive. Heidegger's most Buddhist informed writing, mediated through Japanese sources and interlocutors, is "From a Dialogue on Language." The emptiness of the thing in "What Is a Thing?" allowed the gathering of place. In the language dialogue, emptiness is a condition of opening for recipience, responding to, and saying toward the event. The emptiness of language allows the gathering and saying of words, following the Buddhist thought-image of the gathering and passing of clouds in the empty sky. Emptiness indicates paths of undoing the fixation of words, things, places, and world, thus making room for their other lives and possibilities and, accordingly, other ways of human dwelling with and amidst them.

Destructuring and emptying the individual self while reifying and exalting a collective subject (racial, national, or otherwise) that reduces individuals to expendable resources absorbed in a stratified totality have catastrophic social-political implications, as Ichikawa and other socially critical Buddhist scholars have extensively described. This destiny, however, is not the necessary outcome of Buddhist emptiness, much less Daoist nothingness. The latter is only drawn into modern nationalistic appropriations by Pan-Asianists concerned with constructing a mythical unitary "Oriental nothingness."

In the anti-reductive nonidentity logic (to deploy Adorno's expression again) exhibited in Fazang's prototypical Huayan discourse, to consider only one instructive model, a pluralistic interactive holism is introduced in which particular and whole interpenetrate and encompass one another without reduction. Huayan interactive and non-reductive mutual encompassing is not identical with Leibniz's preestablished harmony of isolated singular monads that mirror each other without contact. The infinite communicative relationality preserves the integrity of the six characteristics: wholeness and particularity, similarity and difference, and integration and dissemination. This comprehensive concomitance simultaneously preserves singularity. This non-reductive relationality is illustrated in Huayan thought-images of Indra's Net (*Indrajāla*), the hallway of mirrors in which the lamp is infinitely reflected, the rafter-building relation, and the golden lion. The genuine relational whole that interpenetrates between each and all events maintains the significance of each particular in their own way of being, while refusing to assimilate it to the identity of an essentialist biological organic or systematic totalitarian unity which would deny the elemental facticity of life and world: being myriad, interpenetrating, transpositional, and self-organizing.

5. Emptiness, Freedom, and the Political

This approach is inspired by hints in Manhae's articulation of a personal and social emancipatory Huayan model and the critique of identity conveyed in (if admittedly not all) moments of Heidegger's thinking. It indicates a different way of thinking of emptiness as world-disclosive in emancipatory strategies and practices of emptying. The answer then is radicalizing nothingness to release individuals as well as things in their particularity and to expand emptiness to confront and undo the reification and valorization of collective subjects and identities that are hierarchically centered on ethnicity, nationality, culture, or language.

A restricted deployment of emptiness might only take apart individuals and sacrificially negate them for the sake of the collective, as particularly evident in Japanese nationalist discourses from the 1920s through 1940s. Yet, analogous to the singularizing-equalizing of the *Zhuangzi* in which each thing is recognized as transforming of its own accord in its own self-naturing, the fullness of emptiness in Fazang's pluralistic Huayan sustains the singular event as well as the interdependent whole. This entails that fixating and totalizing collective identities should be undone for the sake of the other and the singular where freedom is genuinely enacted. This undoing of predetermined static identity is expressed in classical Huayan discourses of non-reductive yet holistic relationality and in Manhae's articulation of its radical social democratic potential. Adopting clues from Manhae's modern reinterpretation of Huayan, and resonating with Zhuangzi's equalizing and singularizing from nothingness, Huayan emptiness embraces anarchistic and egalitarian functions that disassemble and equalize constructed yet stratified sedimented inequalities, hierarchies, and distinctions.[20] Such insights indicate pathways, especially if loosened and unrestricted through formal indication as way, toward more democratic and environmental forms of life and a free and democratic (in an inclusive and participatory sense) ecological civilization.[21] Eco-fascism and other forms of eco-totalitarianism, by the very nature of identity and power that they presuppose, cannot genuinely resolve crisis-tendencies that want leaping-ahead releasement rather than leaping-in domination.

These brief closing considerations deserve further extensive analysis elsewhere. These reflections nonetheless reveal a distinctively critical and emancipatory politics of nothingness and emptiness. The enactment of emptying self and world contests the reification of the worldly material and intersubjective formation of the self (whether individualistic or collectivistic) and its underlying seeds and structures in ways that offer insights into contesting not only conceptual-linguistic but social-political reification and oppression. Buddhist self-emptiness need not and should not entail either nihilistic indifference or political conformity. Emptiness signifies the world's clarity and simplicity. It has been and can be extended in ways that contest and unfix structural inequalities and hierarchies that are not merely externally imposed upon selves but deployed to constitute existing forms of selves and societies.

This book has sketched paths through which we can interculturally think with and further than Heidegger on questions concerning the thing, nothingness, and emptiness. It is important in the current climate to be clear about the political implications of identity-thinking, given the contemporary global resurgence of authoritarian, hierarchically stratified, fundamentalist and nationalistic politics, in which the freedom of others requires (1) individual personal rights, (2) public participatory and political deliberative rights (as relational rather than requiring atomized possessive individuals or a collective general will), and (3) indigenous and intercultural rights and solidarities are restricted and endangered. New collaborations and conjunctures between decolonial and intercultural philosophy and critical social analysis could begin to address these complex issues and concerns.[22]

6. Hundun: In Praise of Self-Ordering Chaos

Substantive features of early Daoist and Sino-Japanese Zen Buddhist sources captivated Heidegger's attention throughout his life, to the degree that scholars have accused him of plagiarizing from their sources (Imamichi 2004). The *Daodejing* and the *Zhuangzi* are texts to which he recurrently returned in an environment of communication and exchange with East Asian students and intellectuals as well as their German interlocutors.

Heidegger returns throughout his philosophical journey to many Daoist-inflected thought-images such as letting things be themselves, preserving nourishing darkness, the silence where sincere listening and harkening occur, the emptying of the heart-mind in the encounter and the event, and the mystery of and beyond the mystery. Heidegger's Daoist entanglements permit this book's reimagining of his ziranist tendency (i.e., *ziran* as autopoietically self-naturing in its own way of being) that flourishes in his later philosophy of the releasement and the priority of thing, place, and world in their relational openness. This ziranist attunement does not preclude more attuned and humble forms of observation, inquiry, and involved action and participation; it would turn toward and encourage them.

Heidegger's direct and indirect allusions to the two Daoist masterpieces of the *Daodejing* and the *Zhuangzi*, which fascinated the younger and mature Heidegger, focus on a threefold configuration of questions that are operative in the center of his own thought and his broader engagement with interculturally mediated East Asian philosophies: nothingness/emptiness, thingliness, and indicative ways of dwelling and releasement. According to the reconstruction of Heidegger's pathway proposed in the present work, nothingness should not entail dismantling individuals for the sake of a monological collective identity or a monolithic cosmic reality that misses the ethically constitutive dynamics of the I-thou encounter and self-other relationship. Heidegger's key ziranist teaching, although inadequately unfolded from a Daoist perspective, can be seen in the call to unfix, jump ahead, and allow space for beings as a whole through releasement into nothingness and liberation from idols.[23] Altering the language of *Being and Time*, this *ethos* signifies to extend to things, to responsively leap-ahead through emptiness and step up for beings in their own ways of being, rather than leaping-in against them through the content and fixations of our own way of being. Emptying fixations and opening the space of the generative freedom of things and environments permit individuals to freely co-appropriate and individuate their own world in less compulsive, coercive, and violent ways.[24] This questioning of the sedimented structures and anthropocentric fixations of the domination of nature requires envisioning and nurturing different modes of attunement that nourish life. This entails co-appropriating and collaborating with human and animal others, with natural and artificial things, and enregioning places and environments.

Three flawed objections to early ziranist Daoism and this current in Heidegger's later philosophy need to be addressed. These are (1) that they assume that nature is kind, (2) they neglect humans in prioritizing nature or being, and (3) they negate action and intervention in the world. The ziranist *ethos* depicted here, as a way enacted in the world, need not presuppose that world and "nature" are intrinsically benevolent or compassionate: recall the statement in *Daodejing* chapter 5 that "heaven and earth are not humane." It thus signifies a sense that changing self-patterning natural systems need to be recognized and respected in their own ways of becoming, as humans adapt to them and act and intervene in them with unhurried reticence and humility. Humans and their motivations are not overlooked in indifferent nature or mere biocentrism, with its metaphysical presuppositions concerning *bios* and potential neglect of intrahuman inequities, but instead find their significance in being-with things, creatures, landscapes, and environments.

Action and intervention are not negated in mere inactive passivity; they are reconceived through their attunement and lack of attunement, their appropriateness and lack of appropriateness, with things, situations, and environments. One does not leap-in, attempt to help and improve by making identical and thereby kill Hundun (渾沌, a figure indicative of primal jumbled chaos in chapter seven of the *Zhuangzi*); one does nothing, mirroring the thing, responding without storing (Ziporyn 2020: 72). Insofar as this *Zhuangzi* chapter is describing mirroring responsive participation in the world, rather than passive apathy or resigned indifference, it entails what Heidegger analyzed as leaping-ahead for the other in their own individuation and way of being, allowing Hundun (self-ordering anarchic or dao-archic chaos) to adhere, as it were, to the course of its own self-generated transformations.

Zhuangzi is depicted in the "Perfect Enjoyment" chapter as crying with grief at the loss of his wife before letting go and singing and beating a drum when Huizi visits to console him (Ziporyn 2020: 145). This can be interpreted as another lesson in how to nourish life, as we need to nurture self-patterning chaos to flourish. What can no longer be nurtured due to its transformations is not rejected in indifference but generationally let go of in nourishing care. Hundun's fate does not entail excluding engagement and intervention for the sake of others, in neutral equanimity or indifference, nor leaping-in in coercive domination. Instead, it needs appropriate attunement to leap-ahead for the sake of nurturing environments and ecosystems that should be recognized as having their own ethical positionality. Forests, marshes, and oceans are self-patterning sympoietic systems that humans must care for and respect. This suggests, instead, according to the model of caring for and nurturing life that what is needed is intervention that attends to nourishing and restoring their own self-ordering or letting go as death and metamorphosis generate new autopoietic self-ordering relations. Heidegger's postwar discourse of healing and safeguarding things and places intersects with this Daoist sensibility. In its most radical moments, ziranist Daoism is an ethos and praxis of bio-spiritual and bio-political liberation of humans and things. Freedom signifies participation in the anarchic chaos and fullness of life, nurturing things and being nurtured by them in mutual interaction.

It is perhaps ironic that Heidegger can be more easily resituated in relation to pluralistic interculturality and anti-totalitarian freedom than many of his critics who remain ensnared in Eurocentric categories. Heidegger's encounters and entanglements with translated Daoist sources and Japanese thought can be said to be neither a fleeting and accidental curiosity (as claimed in Eurocentric readings of his writings), nor can they be appropriately understood as constituting a far-reaching "Daoist" or "East Asian" reorientation in his philosophical journey (as in overly optimistic comparative and transcultural interpretations). Heidegger's singular cross-cultural journey into things, nothingness, and language is one that can be reconstructed and reimagined for a formal indicative and therapeutic critical modeling of a sort that can orient and contest the present for the sake of nourishing living and nonliving things, interbodily and interthingly places and environments, and potentially self-aware mortals who dwell between the abyssal earth and the open sky with transitory gathering things that—in each case—have their own place and time.

Notes

Introduction

1. For an overview of Heidegger's journey, see Pöggeler 1990 and Sheehan 2014. *Sein* is translated as being and *Seiende* as a being or beings in this work.
2. On the centrality of formal indication in Heidegger's formation in the 1920s, see Kisiel 1993.
3. On issues of Eurocentrism and Orientalism in philosophy, see Davis 2016: 130–56; Heubel 2020; Heurtebise 2020; and Nelson 2017. The present work uses the terms "Orient" and "Occident" or "Eastern" and "Western" in scare quotes because of their essentialist and problematic genealogy. They are still mentioned because they are the discursive terms of the authors under consideration.
4. For instance, Heidegger criticizes *Being and Time*'s reliance on a framework of accessibility and understandability and identifies its transcendental elements with an inadequate appreciation of the radicality of Dasein and the truth of being in GA 82: 106, 382, 394. There is a large literature devoted to the status of transcendental philosophy (compare Crowell and Malpas 2007). I explain the approach deployed here (Heidegger relies on it and wishes to overcome it) in Nelson 2016: 159–79.
5. Such as the parable of killing Hundun 渾沌 (chaos) in chapter 7 or the appearance of *xingming* 涬溟 (primal darkness) in chapter 11. On Hundun, see Girardot 1983. Richard Wilhelm translated both *Zhuangzi* passages into the psychological language of the unconscious (Wilhelm 1912: 59–60, 80). Martin Buber's translation of chapter 7 does not state what Hundun is (Buber 2013: 74). His rendition of chapter 11, more pertinently, describes non-action as becoming empty, becoming like nothingness, giving things back into their primal condition (using *Urbeschaffenheit* to render *xingming*) in which each thing flowers from itself (Buber 2013: 78).
6. On the ethical-political problems involved in Japanese appropriations of Buddhism and Zen during this era, see Ives 2009. This book will only consider German-Japanese interactions that directly shaped Heidegger's milieu during this period and will not engage in an analysis of the Kyōto school that would need another volume.

Chapter 1

1. Interestingly, for the present interpretation, Buber relates Daoist self-generation and Judaic co-creation (*Mitschöpfung*), as both place creativity and generativity in the world and not only in a transcendent God.
2. On complexities of defining the thing, see Husserl 1973; Husserl 2003: 6, 114–15. Although *die Sache* and *das Ding* both refer to the thing in these statements, note the distinctive connotations of *die Sache* (thing, stuff, matter, case) and *das Ding* (thing, somethingness, object, entity) in German. Jacques Lacan distinguished in his

interpretation of Freud's psychoanalysis *die Sache* as the thing represented within the symbolic order from *das Ding* as the thing beyond signification and the symbolic order (Lacan 1992: 45, 62–3).

3   On the thing in Heidegger, Daoism, and Chinese philosophy, see Cabural 2020: 570–92; Chai 2014: 303–18; Kwok 2016: 294–310; Pang-White 2009: 61–78; Perkins 2015: 54–68. On Heidegger and early Daoism, see Burik 2010; Davis 2013: 459–71; Davis 2020: 161–96; Heubel 2020; Ma 2007; Michael 2020: 299–318; Nelson 2017: 109–57; Wang, Q. 2001: 55–71; Wang, Q. 2016: 159–74; Yu 2018. On issues of Eurocentrism, Orientalism, and Occidentalism in Heidegger's engagement with East Asian philosophies, see Davis 2016: 130–56; Heubel 2020; Heurtebise 2020; Nelson 2017. For contemporary interpretations of Heidegger and Daoism, see the essays published in Chai 2022. Note that expressions such as "Chinese" or "German" signify in the present work a contemporary cultural-linguistic configuration and "early" indicates preceding formations.

4   See Creel 1982 for a discussion of problems in defining "Daoism." I historically and conceptually differentiate different models in Nelson 2020: 4. As this book is about translation, Chinese and German expressions are used throughout it. Except when necessary to identify expressions and explain semantic shifts between different languages in the main text, longer Chinese and German expressions are often included in the endnotes.

5   Okakura 1919: 29; on the story of the gifted book and its possible influence on Heidegger, see Imamichi 2004: 123; Davis 2020: 161.

6   Buber 1910; critical edition in Buber 2013. Buber appears familiar with the language of Balfour, Giles, and Legge (Herman 1996: 4). On Buber's approach to the *Zhuangzi* in relation to Heidegger, see chapter 4 of Nelson 2017: 109–29. For an overview of Buber's translation and interpretation, see Herman 1996. On Buber's reception of Daoism, see Eber 1994: 445–64; Nelson 2020d: 105–20; Wirth 2020: 121–34.

7   Compare Pöggeler 1987: 52; Mendes-Flohr 2014: 5; Wolfson 2019: 14–15. Heidegger's familiarity with Buber's *Hassidic Tales* seems less attested. On Heidegger's relationship with Judaism, see Wolfson 2018 and Wolfson 2019.

8   "Verborgenheit ist die Geschichte von Lao-Tses Rede" (Buber 2013: 111). It is noteworthy that Buber stresses Laozi's abyss beyond conceptuality in a 1964 interview with Walter Kaufman, an abyss that is far more radical than Hume's skeptical questioning of conceptual claims (Buber 2017: 535).

9   Petzet 1993: 18. Heidegger revisited the joy of fish again in GA 12: 78. Heidegger was not the only philosopher interested in this dialogue of the joy of fish (translated in Buber 2013: 87 and Wilhelm 1912: 134) during the Weimar Republic. Otto Neurath, who had his own notable engagement with Chinese philosophy perhaps informed by Josef Popper-Lynkeus, cited it at the beginning of his 1921 critique of Oswald Spengler's irrationalism and pessimism (Neurath 1921: 4).

10 There is a rich literature on place in Heidegger that insufficiently explores its Daoist facets, such as the excellent analysis in Malpas 2008.

11 "In einer Umwelt lebend, bedeutet es mir überall und immer, es ist alles welthaft, 'es weltet'" (GA 56/57: 73).

12 One of the largest translation projects was from Sanskrit to Chinese. Early Chinese Buddhist *geyi* 格義 refers to the investigation and classification of meanings and not "matching concepts," as it is frequently misinterpreted. It refers to a problem rather than a method of translation in early Chinese Buddhism.

13 Compare Maly 2020: 15.
14 Compare Strauss 1870: 101, 134; Wilhelm 1912: 116; Buber 2013: 58.
15 See the August 1949 exchange between Jaspers and Heidegger in Biemel and Saner 1990: 177–82.
16 Eckhart identified *Gelassenheit* with Christian relinquishment (*relinquere*) of the world, detachment (*Abgeschiedenheit*), and the emptiness and freedom of self and things (Eckhart 1971: 528). The letting be or releasement of self and things signified an unchanging and unmoving constancy of the self (Eckhart 1971: 61). Things are in this context secondary to self and God in Eckhart. Heidegger's this-worldly thingly oriented releasement often functions more along the lines of responsive releasement (*wuwei*) to the self-so (*ziran*) event. On Eckhart, mysticism, and Heidegger, see Schürmann 1973: 95–119; Moore 2019. On the problems and prospects of employing the category of mysticism in early ziranist contexts, compare Nelson 2008: 5–19; Wenning 2017: 554–71. On *wuwei* as spontaneous responsiveness, which he identifies with syncretic Daoism, see Graham 1989: 186–93.
17 "Die Gelassenheit zu den Dingen und die Offenheit für das Geheimnis" (GA 16: 528).
18 GA 12: 187. "Essence" should be read as "essencing" in Heidegger. This and related texts will be elucidated in subsequent chapters.
19 "輔萬物之自然, 而不敢為" (Lou 1980: 166).
20 See Heidegger's August 1949 letter to Jaspers in which he denies Jaspers's assertion of Asian influence on his thought (Biemel and Saner 1990: 181). See Heidegger's letter to Hsiao dated 9 October 1947 (Hsiao 1987: 103) and Hsiao 1977: 119–27. Compare the same sentence in GA 13: 51 and GA 77: 118 and the similar discussion in GA 12: 187.
21 The problematic of natural and technologically framed things is found in the understanding of Daoism in Buber and Heidegger; see Nelson 2017: 109–29.
22 See Heubel 2020; Ma 2007; Nelson 2017: 109–57. This list does not include later editions mentioned in the last decades of Heidegger's life such as Jan Ulenbrook's 1962 translation.
23 On early Chinese and Daoist conceptions of the thing, see Chai 2014: 303–18; Kwok 2016: 294–310; Pang-White 2009: 61–78; Perkins 2015: 54–68. On the notion of "nature," see Chai 2016: 259–74; Nelson 2020; Perkins 2010: 118–36.
24 On sacrifice in early China, see Sterckx 2011.
25 For an overview of early uses of *wu*, see Pines 2002: 697–8.
26 See Perkins 2015: 57; Pines 2002: 697–8.
27 For English language translations and discussions of the *Fan Wu Liu Xing*, see Chan 2015: 285–99; Wang, Z. 2016: 49–81, 169–74.
28 In Chinese: "*baiwu busi* 百物不死" (Chan 2015: 289–90).
29 The Chinese text asks: "天何言哉? 四時行焉, 百物生焉, 天何言哉?"
30 On seasonality and temporality, compare GA 3: 259: "Time's power is expressed in the periods of the seasons and in the rhythms of the phases and ages of life."
31 Concerning the social-cultural importance of the *Yueji*, note Cook 1995: 1–96 and Steben 2012: 105–24.
32 The *Xiang'er Commentary* states, "精氣自然, 與天不親" (compare Bokenkamp 1997: 82). On *qi* and body in early Chinese thought, see Yang 1993.
33 On the ethical and environmental implications of these straw-dog passages in the *Daodejing* and the *Zhuangzi*, also note Nelson 2020: 58–9.
34 That is, self-so-ing (*wanwu zhi ziran* 萬物之自然 in Guodian A 6), self-transforming (*wanwu jiang zihua* 萬物將自化 in Guodian A 7), self-steadying (*wanwu jiang ziding* 萬物將自定 in Guodian A 7), and "self-guesting" (*wanwu jiang zibin* 萬物將自賓 in

Guodian A 10). Note that thing is *wu* 勿 in the Guodian excavated texts. For the Guodian *Laozi* texts and English translations, see Cook 2012: 244 and Henricks 2000: 44, 47, 54.

35 Erkes translates *wanwu zicheng* 萬物自成 as "All things are spontaneously perfected" (Erkes 1946: 170). "Self-" in these linguistic constructions signifies reflexive being itself rather than the human subject.

36 "Regarding the actions of the world: by neither avoiding nor partaking in them, they can happen of themselves" (舉天下之為也, 無舍也, 無與也, 而能自為也) (Brindley et al. 2013: 150).

37 In Chinese: "是故聖人能專萬物之自然, 而弗能為."

38 In Chinese: "復衆人之所過, 以輔萬物之自然, 而不敢為" (Lou 1980: 166).

39 Historically problematic categories such as Daoism, Huanglao, and legalism as they are introduced in the Han dynastic era or construed in modern Sinology are retrospective and frequently contentious terms that attempt to differentiate and unify a series of texts, ideas, and transmissions around the same or overlapping teaching.

40 On nourishing care (*ci* 慈), see Pang-White 2016: 275–94; on Daoist care and nourishing life, see Nelson 2020: 60–1. The maternal disposition of nurturing care, a model in which the sage is disposed toward affairs and things with motherly concern, is also interestingly discussed in the *Laozi* commentary in the *Jielao* 解老 chapter of the power-oriented "legalist" work *Hanfeizi* 韓非子.

41 Guodian *Laozi* A 16: "是以聖人之言曰: 我無事而民自富。我亡為而民自化。我好靜而民自正。我欲不欲而民自樸。" Note the slightly different rendition in DDJ 57 (Lou 1980: 150).

42 "聖人無常心, 以百姓心為心" (Lou 1980: 129).

43 See Okakura 1919: 29; Heidegger GA 2: 122.

44 Wang Qingjie takes the difference to be between "living longer" and "constant extension"; see Wang, Q. 2001: 55–71.

45 The received text reads: "若夫藏天下於天下, 而不得所遯, 是恆物之大情也。" Legge: "if you could hide the world in the world, so that there was nowhere to which it could be removed, this would be the grand reality of the ever-during Thing." Ziporyn 2020: 56 has "to hide the world in the world, so that there is nowhere for it to escape to, then it has the vast realness of a thing eternal." *Daqing* means the real natural affections of the people in the eclectic text *Yinwenzi* 尹文子 (*Yiwen* 佚文 3). The commentary ascribed to Guo Xiang 郭象 (Lynn 2022) supports taking the great affection as a disposition. As there is nothing that can be distinguished from things and their transformations, there is no difference between internal and external or life and death, and one remains harmonious with heaven and earth and undisturbed through the incessant transformation of things: "無所藏而都任之, 則與物無不冥, 與化無不一。故無外無內, 無死無生, 體天地而合變化, 索所遯而不得矣。此乃常存之大情, 非一曲之小意" (Guo 1961: 245).

46 See Brindley et al. 2013: 146. On the temporality of *heng*, see Wang, Q. 2001: 55–71.

47 Brindley et al. 2013: 147.

48 "侯王若能守之, 萬物將自賓" (Cook 2012: 253; Lou 1980: 81).

49 Compare Erkes 1945: 181.

50 Compare Lou 1980: 22–4, 81–2; Lynn 1999: 65–7, 108–9.

51 "我無事而民自富。我亡為而民自化。我好靜而民自正。我欲不欲而民自樸。" Compare Cook 2012: 273–5: "I serve no end and the people prosper on their own. I act to no purpose and the people transform of themselves. I am fond of tranquility and the people of themselves are rectified. I desire the lack of desire and the people of themselves become innocent."

52   Bao Jingyan is unknown outside of the "Interrogating Bao" (*Jiebao* 詰鮑) chapter of the *Baopuzi* 抱朴子 of Ge Hong 葛洪. One proposal is that Ge invented Bao for polemical or hidden political reasons. Given Ge's authoritarian Confucian-legalist political discourse, and his criticisms of the disorderly moral-political consequences of Lao-Zhuang, pure conversation (*qingtan* 清談), and mysterious learning (*xuanxue* 玄學) discourses, it appears unlikely that he was secretly advocating Bao's anti-authoritarian, egalitarian deconstruction of ruler and ruled. In addition to the question of Daoist "anarchism," varieties of biospiritual and biopolitical models are examined in Nelson 2020.

53   On the *Zhuangzi*'s background, structure, and content, see Kohn 2014. On the guiding role of generative nothingness in it, see Chai 2019. On reasons for a ziranist reading, as distinct from mystical, skeptical, and impersonal fatalistic interpretations, see Nelson 2008: 5–19.

54   Buber 2013: 56, 92. On Heidegger and the wooden bell stand (*Glockenspielstände*), see Petzet 1993: 59, 169. Heidegger's interest in this narrative is revisited later in the description of Heidegger's reading of the *Zhuangzi*.

55   Heidegger mentions the moods of "joy, contentment, bliss, sadness, melancholy, anger" in GA 29–30: 96.

56   Keyserling 1919, v. 1: 535. On *wuwei* and fatalism, also compare Kitayama 1942: 37–9.

57   The Yangist moments adopted from the philosophy of Yang Zhu 楊朱 were interpreted as a pessimistic deterministic egoism by Krause (Krause 1923: 88, 163). Wilhelm describes the fatalistic side of Daoism as a degradation of Laozi and links it with Yang Zhu (Wilhelm 1925: 104–5).

58   On Laozi and the White Rose, see Cantor 2023.

59   On reconstructing critical concepts such as alienation and ideology for the sake of a critique of contemporary society, compare Jaeggi 2005; Jaeggi 2014. Jaeggi's analysis shows how Heidegger's thinking can play a role in imagining new critical social models (Jaeggi 2005). While Jaeggi analyzes the appropriation and individuation of Dasein in *Being and Time* in her analysis of freedom as non-alienation, indicating its limits in the need to appropriate material and social relations, I hope to outline here the significance of Heidegger's later thinking of non-appropriation, releasement, and the freedom of things, spaces, environments, and regions.

60   "不自為也。天不產而萬物化,地不長而萬物育,帝王無為而天下功。" Ziporyn 2020: 111 translates this as follows: "They did not do anything themselves … Heaven does no producing of things, yet the ten thousand things transform. Earth does no growing of things, yet the ten thousand things are nourished. Emperors and kings do nothing, engage only in non-doing, yet the deeds of the world get accomplished."

61   Ziporyn 2003: 100. Guo Xiang reportedly borrowed from the now lost commentary of Xiang Xiu 向秀 (Liu 2002: 105–7).

62   Guo Xiang is frequently interpreted as a philosopher of freedom and individual authenticity (as in Ziporyn 2003). His own contemporaries, as the narratives of the fifth-century collection *A New Account of the Tales of the World* (*Shishuo Xinyu* 世說新語) make clear, were concerned not only with his individualism but with his determinism. On individuality and the culture of mysterious learning, note Balazs 1964: 226–54; Yü 1985: 121–55. The interaction between the relational whole of things (macrocosm) and the uniquely singular thing in its own moment (microcosm), the dewdrop that reflects the universe, remains a guiding question in the formation of early Chinese Buddhism.

63 This story is told by his friend the Bremen art critic Heinrich Wiegand Petzet (Petzet 1993: 18; Pöggeler 1987: 52–4). This topic is explored in greater detail below.
64 See Kroll 1996: 653–69.
65 The *Shishuo Xinyu* contains numerous anecdotes concerning Zhi Dun, including his new anti-deterministic interpretation of Zhuangzi's free and easy wandering (Liu 2002: 115–18). His lost *Xiaoyao lun* survives only in quotations and descriptions. It concerns wisdom (*prajñā*), equalizing things in emptiness (齊萬物於空同), and the emptiness of somethingness and nothingness that cannot be self-occurring. As it is empty of self-nature, the nothing does not self-nothing (無不能自無). Restating the mutual correlation between form (*rūpa*) and emptiness (*śūnyatā*) in the *Prajñāpāramitā* literature, nothingness is said to occur through material existence (form) just as material existence occurs through nothingness. See Zhi Dun's "Preface to a Synoptic Extract of the Larger and Smaller Versions [of the *Perfection of Wisdom*]" (*Daxiao pin duibi yaochao xu* 大小品對比要抄序) in Taishō vol. 55, no. 2145.
66 For instance, "integrate the myriad things and make them into one" (旁礴萬物以為一), "the myriad things are one" (萬物皆一), and so on. See the discussion of such expressions in Hsu 2019: 219. The fatalistic interpretation of Lao-Zhuang thought is expressed in Count Hermann von Keyserling's 1919 work *A Philosopher's Travel Diary*. He described *dao* as a preestablished concord that calls for resignation to the objective world order, in contrast to mystical unification with primordial spirit, in Keyserling 1919, v. 1: 535.
67 "變化齊一, 不主故常" in the "The Revolving of Heaven" (*Tianyun* 天運) chapter.

Chapter 2

1 Concerning Heidegger's discourse of the archaic Greek origins of philosophy, the first and other beginning, and the pluralistic alternative of Georg Misch (in Misch 1926), see Nelson 2017: 131–57. "Occident" translates Heidegger's "Evening Land" (*Abendland*) throughout this work.
2 GA 40: 17; also compare GA 35: 19.
3 See Plaenckner 1870: 32; Rotermund 1874: 6; Wilhelm 1911: 10; Misch 1950: 312. Rotermund notes both its natural and political functions in an interesting 1874 work on Daoist and Buddhist ethics.
4 On intercultural co-illumination, see Wirth 2019. On *Auseinanderzetzung* between distinctive philosophical and cultural forms of thinking, French and German in this case, see Heidegger's 1937, important yet relatively neglected piece, "Wege zur Aussprache" (GA 13: 12–21).
5 See Arendt 1976. This pivotal work can be read as an analysis of the collectivist nationalist and communist pathologies of modern republicanism in which the public is reduced to the state, individuals are absorbed in society, and "the people" is restrictively defined by race or class.
6 On the variety of Daoistic biopolitical models and their continuing relevance in a democratic context, see chapter five of Nelson 2020.
7 "Im anderen Anfang wird alles Seiende dem Seyn geopfert" (GA 65: 230). This sacrificial language from the mid-1930s has a more violent aura than the generosity and gifting that emerges a decade later, although Levinas and other critics identify a continuity between them.

8 The essay is reprinted in Bloch 1984: 365–84. Buber's politically oriented 1924 lectures on the *Daodejing* are published in Buber 2013: 227–68. On Buber's anarchistic reading of the *Daodejing*, see Nelson 2020d: 105–20. Buber's thinking of communal socialist self-organization is most developed in his writings on the kibbutz movement. On agrarian/agriculturalist propensities in early Daoist sources, see Graham 1989: 66–100. On Daoism and anarchism, compare Rapp 2012.

9 Derrida 2010: 319; Derrida 2017: 281. I now disagree with the claim in my first publication on Heidegger and Daoism in Nelson 2004: 69. Heidegger does not begin to substantively question the discourse of creative violence until his confrontation with these issues in his Nietzsche lectures of the late 1930s and the turn toward releasement and the thing in the 1940s.

10 See, for instance, GA 27: 220; GA 34: 42, 81. On Heidegger under National Socialism, see Bambach 2003; Nelson 2017b: 77–88. There is a notable linguistic and conceptual shift between the individual oriented liberation promised in caring-for in solicitude ("vorspringend-befreiende Fürsorge") in *Being and Time* and the collective violence ("befreiende Gewalt") of being and nature of the 1930s.

11 Arendt, Habermas, and Pöggeler interpret Heidegger's later notion of *Gelassenheit* as a response to the assertiveness of the will and collective life during the Nazi era while reaching different conclusions about its value. Arendt sees this shift as a needed correction and Habermas as an empty rhetoric (Arendt 2018b: 430; Habermas 1985: 168). Pöggeler notes the significant role of Daoism in this change (Pöggeler 1990: 248; Pöggeler 1987: 47–78). Concerning the will and its suspension in Heidegger, see Davis 2007. On the distinctiveness of Heidegger's later thought, see Pöggeler 1990.

12 GA 39: 144; compare GA 40: 66. On Heidegger, the Daoist thing, and the politics of the thing, note Cabural 2020: 570–92.

13 On "taking turns" and environmental generational justice, see Fritsch 2020. Also note the analysis of Heidegger and generational justice in Schalow 2021.

14 Note Adorno 1986, vol. 7: 152.

15 The expressions "heaven and earth" (*tiandi* 天地) and "humans and spirits" (*renshen* 人神) are used in parallel in post-Han-era sources, such as the *Records of the Three Kingdoms* (*sanguo zhi* 三國志), and in contemporary Chinese accounts of Heidegger's fourfold.

16 Wilhelm collaborated with Keyserling and Carl Jung in the 1920s. They shared an agenda of uncovering archetypes, the exemplary image (*Vorbild*) and prototypical primordial image (*Urbild*) in Asian philosophy and religion. Wilhelm preferred the language of exemplary models in his translations. The Sinologist Erwin Rousselle was Wilhelm's replacement as director of the Frankfurt China Institute and a frequent attendee of the early Ascona conferences organized around Jung and hosted by Olga Fröbe-Kapteyn. He discussed *dao* as *Vorbild* and *Urbild* in the 1935 Ascona conference, advocating the latter expression: "the *dao* of the universe is an exemplary model or, more correctly, a prototypical archetype for the unified human being" (Rousselle 1935: 197).

17 Pöggeler 1990: 248; Pöggeler 1987: 47–78.

18 Arguments for the roles of interculturally mediated Daoist sources in Heidegger's thinking are explored further in the following chapters.

19 Malpas 2008 offers an extended analysis of space and place in Heidegger's discourse.

20 Heidegger does not directly address political economy. On capitalism and the domination of nature, see the paradigmatic analysis in Adorno and Horkheimer 1979. On the need to confront capitalism for the sake of critically reimagining a more responsive and response-able environmental form of life, see the works of Donna

J. Haraway, such as Haraway 2013. On the necessity of critical social theory for a contemporary critical environmental philosophy, see Nelson 2020c. On Heidegger and ecology, compare Blok 2014: 307–32; Botha 2003: 157–71; Fritsch 2022; Schalow 2012; Schalow 2021.

21 "Critical models" can be employed to analyze the structural tensions and possibilities of a historical constellation. It is a strategy from Adorno that Heidegger explicitly rejected as ontologically nihilistic in a late note (GA 91: 664). I adopt it in modified form in relation to formal indication, which thereby takes on a critical function.

22 On the *Bremen Lectures*, in which themes of his later thinking are first presented in public, and the centrality of the fourfold in his later thinking, see Mitchell 2015.

23 GA 61: 33. On the centrality of formal indication in Heidegger's early development, see Kisiel 1993 and Nelson 2006: 31–48. Roughly put in a preliminary manner, and in need of further explication, Heidegger's "formal indication" empties a specific fixed content to open a way and Adorno's "critical model" immanently contests a structuring system from within, according to its own dissonances and contradictions that resist harmonizing identification. They each involve their own normativity, which does not entail positing a fixed set of normative principles and criteria. Habermas is correct that each discourse has its own normative presuppositions (Habermas 1985). However, contrary to Habermas's argument that every implicit normativity must be made explicit and determinate in a normative system, this normativity is anarchic to the extent that it cannot be fixed and limited to a specific ordering of normative criteria and prescriptive rules. As Daoist sources recognize, such ordering can in fact signify the loss of the ethical.

24 Rickett 1998, 2: 101. On water as thought-image and exemplary model, see Nelson 2020: 86. Thought-images are crucial in the history of philosophy as is particularly evident in those philosophers who privilege the concept over the image (Plato, Descartes, Hegel). As Walter Benjamin and Adorno have demonstrated, thought-images are dynamic configurations that can be misconstrued and fetishized as fixed pictures.

25 Heidegger argued that it is a later misconception to interpret the famous statement of Protagoras that "humans are the measure" in terms of mind and subject (compare GA 6.2: 114; GA 41: 35; GA 48: 161).

26 *Daodejing* 42: "萬物負陰而抱陽, 沖氣以為和" (Lou 1980: 117).

27 "Other-power" (*tali* 他力), a key concept of East Asian Pure Land Buddhism, was initially developed in South Asian accounts of the bodhisattva path in the *Saṃdhinirmocana Sūtra* (*Jieshenmi jing* 解深密經) and the *Laṅkāvatāra Sūtra* (*Ru lengjia jing* 入楞伽經) in which the Buddha enables the ultimate realization of bodhisattvas. In subsequent East Asian Buddhism, it is linked through universal buddha-nature not only with the saving power of bodhisattvas but at times with the other-power in natural phenomena.

28 Recall Chapter 1 note 42.

29 See the analysis of the thing in Kant and Freud in Lacan 1992: 55.

30 On the domination of nature, see Adorno and Horkheimer 1979. Despite their deep conflicting differences, Adorno's account of the domination of nature, the submersion of things in use and exchange, and the priority of the object in unencumbered mimetic and ecomimetic relations can be utilized to illuminate and reimagine Heidegger's later philosophy of the thing for a critical environmental philosophy. On Heidegger's ecological implications, see Blok 2014: 307–32; Botha 2003: 157–71; Fritsch 2022; Schalow 2012; Schalow 2021.

31 Note Heidegger, GA 4: 21; GA 7: 32; GA 11: 119.
32 Adorno underscored the "priority of the object" and criticized Heidegger in *The Jargon of Authenticity* and *Negative Dialectics* for an empty formalism that reduced things and beings, as entangled in capitalist material relations, to being. For more on Adorno's priority of the object and its implications, see part one of Nelson 2020c. On Adorno's critique of Heidegger in relation to Daoism, see Heubel 2020.
33 Rahel Jaeggi has analyzed how the phenomenology of the they-self and inauthenticity in Heidegger's *Being and Time*, read vis-à-vis Marx, can be interpreted as a critique of everyday alienation that can be adopted in contemporary critical social theory (Jaeggi 2005). Heidegger's later confrontations with reification and alienation of bureaucratic technological society are further sources for critical reflection on the present, as argued throughout the present work.
34 To flesh out Heidegger's claim that "Das Dichten is das Grundvermögen des menschlichen Wohnens" (GA 7: 197).
35 See Petzet 1993: 18; Pöggeler 1987: 52–4; Mendes-Flohr 2014: 5; Wolfson 2019: 14–15.
36 Buber 2017: 172. Buber's August 1924 Ascona lectures (published in Buber 2013: 227–68) emphasized an anarchistic, messianic interpretation of the kingdom in the *Daodejing*.

Chapter 3

1 Several Heidegger interpreters construe his thought as a choice between the centrality of being (Capobianco 2018) and meaning (Sheehan 2014). Both interpretive maneuvers are overly static. Heidegger himself accentuates the priority of way (*Weg*), path (*Pfad*), and movements of being on and underway. These would be glimpsed through indications, traces, and tracks in contrast to fixating interpretations of being or meaning.
2 Heidegger's ostensive "Daoist turn" is discussed in Heubel 2020; Nelson 2017: 109–57; Xia 2017. On Heidegger and Daoism, see also Burik 2010; Chai 2022; Froese 2006. On Occidentalism and Orientalism in Heidegger, see Heurtebise 2020. On the early Daoist thing, see also Chai 2014: 303–18; Kwok 2016: 294–310. I take it as an incomplete intercultural interaction with Daoist sources mediated by their German translations by Buber, Strauss, and Wilhelm and Heidegger's encounters and dialogues with East Asian scholars, beginning with Itō Kichinosuke, Kuki Shūzō, and Miki Kiyoshi in the early Weimar Republic. This third alternative differs from arguments that there was a radical "Daoist turn" (Xia 2017), or Heidegger in some sense plagiarized Daoist sources (Imamichi 2004), or Heidegger merely applied his own thought, with its "Occidental" presuppositions, without any genuine engagement or encounter.
3 On Brecht's interpretation and appropriation of Chinese motifs, see Detering 2008.
4 Buber 2013: 285–9; Keyserling 1919, v. 2: 812–13.
5 On Heidegger's thought during the 1930s and the question of failure, see respectively Polt 2019 and Trawny 2014. Otto Pöggeler interconnects Heidegger's reading of Laozi with releasement and his transformed thinking of the thing. Note how this point is formulated in Pöggeler 1987: 51.
6 Klages 1981: 1443. Klages could embrace Daoist emptiness in this work presumably because it expressed biocentric (*biozentrisch*) attitudes, in contrast with humanistic and logocentric (*logozentrisch*) ones (Klages 1981: 96, 130). Due to the Daoist

passages in his writing, Ernst Bloch criticized Klages for conflating the image for the thing and breaking Nietzsche's futurity by forcing the future to conform to the *dao* of the primordial past (Bloch 1959: 341).

7 The contextualizing-singularizing (historicizing) approach of interpreting in reference to a linguistic community and a form of ethical life is adopted from hermeneutics. Schleiermacher proposed linguistic interpretation as one side of hermeneutics, requiring the reconstruction of how words and sentences were deployed in a linguistic context. It need not imply that a given particular reader read a particular book, but the book reveals a linguistic and discursive configuration significant for interpreting the historical context of an author's works. On the hermeneutics of ethical life, compare George 2020. On hermeneutical issues in Chinese and intercultural philosophy, see Rošker 2021.

8 Fischer 1920: 165–6. Parts of this are cited and discussed in Klages 1981: 1443. Fischer's book is influenced by and dedicated to the life philosopher Klages. Fischer's works were familiar to Heidegger's friend the East Asian art historian and collection organizer Emil Pretorius.

9 Misch 1930: 52; Misch 1950: 311. On Dilthey's importance for Heidegger's development, see Bambach 1995; Kisiel 1993. The mediating role of Misch in Heidegger's interpretation of Dilthey has been underemphasized.

10 Compare Misch 1926; Misch 1930; Heidegger GA 8: 228; GA 70: 107. This issue is examined in chapters five and six of Nelson 2017. On the problematic of intercultural philosophy, see also Lau 2016.

11 "Das ursprüngliche Wort war eine Nennung, aber nicht eines bloßen Namens; vielmehr etwas, was in der Welt begegnet, wird angesprochen, wie es begegnet" (GA 17: 21).

12 Compare GA 11: 45; GA 79: 125.

13 GA 12: 187; Heidegger 1971: 92 (translation modified).

14 GA 12: 187; Heidegger 1971: 92.

15 Hsiao 1987: 103: "auf den Weg bringen (be-wegen)." Compare GA 16: 618; Petzet 1986: 58.

16 *Daodejing* 40: "反者道之動." Compare the different uses of *fan* (reversal, reversion, return, opposition) in *Daodejing* 15, 40, 65, 78. Wilhelm translates it in chapter forty as return: "Rückkehr ist die Bewegung des SINNS" (Wilhelm 1911: 44). He uses "return" throughout his translation and comments, speaking of the return to roots, determinacy, genuineness, simplicity, origin, and nature (Wilhelm 1911: 18, 21, 30, 57, 112). *Dao* is also described as self-reverting ("in sich zurückkehren") (Wilhelm 1911: 27).

17 *Liezi*: "無動不生無而生有" (Graham 1990: 22–3). *Fan* (反), *fu* (复), and *gui* (歸) are semantically related concepts in classical Chinese thought (Maier 1991: 29). For instance, they are interpretively linked in Wang Bi's commentaries on the *Daodejing* and the *Book of Changes*.

18 Inspired by *Daodejing* 1, "Twofold Mystery" was the name of a Tang-era Daoist movement that adopted elements from Madhyamaka Buddhism.

19 "In seiner Einheit heißt es das Geheimnis. Des Geheimnisses noch tieferes Geheimnis ist das Tor, durch das alle Wunder hervortreten" (Wilhelm 1911: 11). "同謂之玄。玄之又玄, 眾妙之門" (Lou 1980: 2). On the role of the gateway in Daoism, see Burik 2010b: 499–516.

20 "樸散則為器" (Lou 1980: 75).

21 Lou 1980: 75. Compare the different translation in Lynn 1999: 103.

22 On aesthetic senses of nature in early China, see Zhao 2006.
23 Compare Lou 1980: 77; Lynn 1999: 105.
24 Lou 1980: 113; Lynn 1999: 133.
25 Lou 1980: 170–1. This is interpreted differently here than in Lynn 1999: 174.
26 Compare Lou 1980: 89–90; Lynn 1999: 116.
27 Compare Lou 1980: 150; Lynn 1999: 159.
28 Compare Lou 1980: 190; Lynn 1999: 188–9.
29 See Lou 1980: 26–7, 93–4; Lynn 1999: 69, 119–21. This interpretation of Wang Bi and his philosophy of nothingness is developed in Nelson 2020b: 287–300.
30 "天地任自然, 無為無造, 萬物自相治理, 故不仁也" (Lou 1980: 13; compare Lynn 1999: 60). Revealingly, the *Heshanggong*'s one mention of self-governing (*zhili*) insists that the king achieves it in people (謂人君治理人民).
31 Translation modified from Lynn 1994: 53. On the significance of *yin-yang* in Chinese philosophy, see Wang R. 2012.
32 *Book of Changes*: "山上有澤。咸。君子以虛受人。"
33 Xu Gan: "人之為德, 其猶虛器歟。器虛則物注, 滿則止焉" (Makeham 2002: 51).
34 For Heidegger, see Hsiao 1987: 103; GA 16: 618; Petzet 1986: 58; compare Wilhelm 1911: 17. Heidegger's rendition of these two lines from chapter 15 has been widely discussed: "Wer kann still sein und aus der Stille durch sie auf den Weg bringen (bewegen) etwas so, das es zum Erscheinen kommt?" There has been little assessment of the interplay between Wilhelm and Heidegger. Heidegger's later references rely on Ulenbrook's 1962 edition.
35 The received text of chapter 11 states: "三十輻, 共一轂, 當其無, 有車之用。埏埴以為器, 當其無, 有器之用。鑿戶牖以為室, 當其無, 有室之用。故有之以為利, 無之以為用" (Lou 1980: 26–7).
36 Compare their three versions of this passage: (1) Strauss's translation: "Dreissig Speichen treffen auf eine Nabe: gemäss ihrem Nichtseyn ist des Wagens Gebrauch. Man erweicht Thon um ein Gefäss zu machen: gemäss seinem Nichtseyn ist des Gefässes Gebrauch. Man bricht Thür und Fenster, um ein Haus zu machen: gemäss ihrem Nichtseyn ist des Hauses Gebrauch. Drum: das Seyn bewirkt den Gewinn, das Nichtseyn bewirkt den Gebrauch" (Strauss 1870: 51); (2) Wilhelm's translation: "Dreißig Speichen treffen sich in einer Nabe: Auf dem Nichts daran (dem leeren Raum) beruht des Wagens Brauchbarkeit. Man bildet Ton und macht daraus Gefäße: Auf dem Nichts daran beruht des Gefäßes Brauchbarkeit. Man durchbricht die Wand mit Türen und Fenstern, damit ein Haus entstehe: Auf dem Nichts daran beruht des Hauses Brauchbarkeit. Darum: Das Sein gibt Besitz, das Nichtsein Brauchbarkeit"; (3) Heidegger's rendition: "Dreißig Speichen treffen die Nabe, Aber das Leere zwischen ihnen gewährt das Sein des Rades. Aus dem Ton entstehen die Gefäße, Aber das Leere in ihnen gewährt das Sein des Gefäßes. Mauern und Fenster und Türen stellen das Haus dar, Aber das Leere zwischen ihnen gewährt das Sein des Hauses. Das Seiende ergibt die Brauchbarkeit. Das Nicht-Seiende gewährt das Sein" (GA 75: 43).
37 For his Italian translation, see Hsiao 1941. Heidegger discusses Xiao in a letter to Jaspers in which he denies the impact of Chinese philosophy on his thinking (Biemel and Saner 1990: 181). Xiao also connected Daoism and the problem of modern technology in the context of his relations with Heidegger, in Hsiao 1956: 72–4; Hsiao 1977: 119–27. On Heidegger and technological modernity, see also Zimmerman 1990.
38 DDJ 11: "das Seyn bewirkt den Gewinn, das Nichtseyn bewirkt den Gebrauch" (Strauss 1870: 51). *Brauch* and *Gebrauch*, as thing and region appropriate or attuned practice and usage, are significant expressions in Heidegger's later works that appear

rooted in German translations of Daoist text; in particular, Strauss's translation of *yong* 用 as *Gebrauch* (Strauss 1870: 51).
39 As examined in Nelson 2017: 109–29.
40 Buber, Bloch, and Klages provide significant points of comparison, as they belong to Heidegger's context and directly discuss the Daoist thing in intersecting ways.
41 Heidegger's debts to Buber remain an underexplored topic. Heidegger was an avid reader of Buber's *Zhuangzi* and perhaps also his *Hassidic Tales* (Mendes-Flohr 2014: 5; Wolfson 2019: 14–15). Heidegger directly refers to Buber's *Zhuangzi* and indirectly refers to others, such as possibly *I and Thou* in GA 27, and mentions him in his correspondence. They met in person in Spring 1957 at Lake Constance (Mendes-Flohr 2014: 2–25; Pöggeler 1990: 340).
42 On *Geding*, see GA 73.2: 1121, 1205. Heidegger accentuates the archaic rather than subsequent meanings in German and Dutch that concern contractual associations and lawsuits.
43 See Wilhelm 1925: 50; Cysarz 1940: 73; Eckardt 1957: 161.
44 Schopenhauer has a few broad discussions of the *Daodejing* based on Stanislas Julien's 1842 French translation that also impacted its early German translations. Eduard von Hartmann published an 1870 review, entitled "A Chinese Classic," criticizing Reinhold von Plaenckner's 1870 German translation for distorting the text in an overly monotheistic manner, as words such as *heaven* and *father* have a distinctive meaning in the Chinese milieu (Hartmann 1876: 166–87).
45 Klages defends Daoist "not-willing" in contrast to "willing nothingness" in Klages 1981: 342, 496. Klages discusses the "empty jug" with reference to Otto Fischer's 1920 book (Klages 1981: 1443). Emptiness is for him the zero point of the unborn from which all arises and returns. He quotes Wilhelm's *Daodejing*, Buber's *Zhuangzi*, and Wilhelm's *Liezi* in this work. Heidegger briefly and dismissively lectured on Klages's book, and its contention that spirit is the adversary and sickening of life, as an example of vulgar *Lebensphilosophie* in GA 29/30: 105. Lukács links Klages and Heidegger throughout *The Destruction of Reason*, contending that Klages's objectivizing biological vitalism and Heidegger's subjectivizing existential decisionism are distinctive (Klages asserts the organic whole while Heidegger seeks it in fragmentation) yet complementary tendencies in Nazi Germany (Lukács 1955).
46 On non-willing in Heidegger and Schopenhauer, compare Davis 2007: 19–20. Nietzsche's initial formulations of the eternal return of the same appear to be composed in response to von Hartmann, the "worst of rogues," and his "apish" claim that death is to be accepted and that no one genuinely wants to live life again (compare Jensen 2006: 41–61).
47 Strauss 1870: 91, 120, 126, 226, 286.
48 Wilhelm 1911: 19, 25, 27, 34, 39, 56, 69.
49 Notably in Adorno's 1964 *Jargon of Authenticity* that ridicules Heidegger's agrarian imaginary. Adorno polemically criticizes Heidegger's categories as reactive, yet he also perceives how they contain a critical potential in relation to existing states of affairs. Adorno is correct to critique the residual idealism of Heidegger's rhetoric of anti-idealism until Heidegger's genuine turn to the thing's priority in the mid-1940s (compare Nelson 2016: 159–79). Adorno failed to adequately recognize this point in the *Jargon of Authenticity* and *Negative Dialectics*.
50 Strauss 1870: 349; Wilhelm 1911: 104; Eckardt 1957: 97.
51 Pfizmaier 1870: 285; Federmann 1920: 12, 57.

52 "Der seine Helle kennt, sich in sein Dunkel hüllt" (Strauss 1870: 140). It can also be translated as it was previously: "those who know lightness wrap themselves in darkness." On the question of darkness and light, also compare Burik 2019: 347–70.
53 Buber 213: 110. The hiddenness (*Verborgenheit*) and concealment (*Verbergung*) of *dao* appear in a variety of German translations (Buber 2013: 113; Federmann 1921: viii). Heidegger's remarks in 1930 indicate a familiarity with the use of these expressions in Buber's *Zhuangzi*. There are other sources. Wilhelm notes the self-concealment (*sich-verbergen*) of the sage in namelessness (Wilhelm 1911: iv). Plaenckner links *"verborgen"* (hidden) with *"geborgen"* (protected) that shares a common linguistic stem meaning safeguard and borrow (Plaenckner: 1870: 271). This might well be a source for Ernst Bloch's use of *"geborgen"* in speaking of Laozi as a sage "secured only in the ungraspable" ("nur im Unfaßbaren geborgen") and "always invisibly on the way of *dao*" ("ständig unsichtbar auf dem Weg des Tao") (Bloch 1959b, 2: 1444). Heidegger differentiates this language more extensively than Buber, Bloch, and others. He mobilizes a variety of expressions based on the stems of *borgen* and *bergen*. This includes the stem *bergen* (hold, hide, conceal), *entbergen* (unhold, unhide, unconceal), and *verbergen* (burry, disguise, obscure), a language that he deploys in his interpretation of early Daoism.
54 Heidegger, GA 16: 677, 712. These issues reappear in Heidegger's previously unpublished notes. For instance, intercultural East-West conversations require first understanding oneself in GA 91: 467–8 and Laozi is seen as a source of Chinese renewal and world-renewal in GA 91: 667. These two tendencies are not contradictory if the former, self-understanding, is the condition of the latter, encountering and learning from the other.

Chapter 4

1 Seekamp 1960: 71–2. This lecture was published in GA 80.2: 1041–63.
2 Seekamp names in one grouping: "Novalis, the two Schlegels, Schopenhauer, Paul Deussen, Karl Eugen Neumann, Martin Buber, Theodor Lessing, Carl Gustav Jung, and Karl Friedrich Duerckheim" (Seekamp 1960: 72).
3 Seekamp 1960: 72. Compare Ernst Bloch's claim that Laozi's *dao* appears to be simultaneously the easiest category to grasp and the most incomprehensible from the European perspective (Bloch 1959b, 2: 1445). Bloch also defines *dao* as a variety of life- and world-tact (Bloch 1959b, 2: 1438).
4 "知者不言言者不知" (Lou 1980: 147–8).
5 On *pólemos*, see Fried 2008. On Heidegger's 1933–1935 engagement on behalf of National Socialism, his subsequent disenchantment, and his unfolding conservative elitist critique of it, compare Bambach 2003; Habermas 1989: 431–56; Nelson 2017b: 77–88; Polt 2019.
6 Heidegger stated that it was "die größte Dummheit seines Lebens," according to Petzet 1993: 37.
7 On Nietzsche's roles in Heidegger, National Socialism, and the controversies of the 1930s, see Bernasconi 2013: 47–54.
8 To summarize, Heidegger was condemned as a "follower" (*Mitläufer*) by allied authorities, the fourth and lowest level of complicity and guilt between "lesser offender" (*Minderbelastete*) and "exonerated" (*Entlastete*). Heidegger maintained

after the war that he was unfairly identified with the movement given his marginality, the short duration of his active involvement, and the reintegration of more seriously engaged National Socialists into West German society and politics. Contemporary rightwing populists have appealed to Heidegger for intellectual legitimation. Yet Heidegger is an ambiguous source. He was an intellectual elitist critical of what he considered the vulgar elements of national socialism, preferring the poetic word to film, radio, and illustrated magazines (GA 40: 78; GA 47: 78). He rejected the category of race and advocated an anti-democratic and metaphysically transformed republican discourse of the collective self-determination and general will of the people that ultimately remained modernistic.

9   The aesthetic and charismatic dimensions of fascism were trenchantly diagnosed early by Benjamin, Helmut Plessner, and others. On the unrestricted public sphere and political participation as the basis of democracy, see Habermas 1990; Habermas 1994; Habermas 2022. Habermas is legitimately concerned with Heidegger's flawed politics while overextending this concern to his entire thought, thereby missing the significance of Heidegger's turn toward releasement and the thing (Habermas 1985; Habermas 1989).

10 On self-ordering agrarian tendencies in early Daoism, see Graham 1989: 66–100. An analysis of varieties of Daoist anti-politics and anarchistic politics is developed in chapters one and five of Nelson 2020. Sloterdijk emphasizes Daoist anti-politics in his 1989 portrayal of "Eurotaoism."

11 Compare GA 13: 27; GA 81: 23, 39, 57–8, 75, 215.

12 GA 74: 185. Also compare Petzet 1993: 169.

13 "大象無形" and "道隱無名" (Lou 1980: 113).

14 Heidegger states: "ein Gewebe eines Schleiers ist, der enthüllt, indem er verhüllt, nämlich das Bildlose des Wortlosen" (GA 74: 186).

15 "Solche Sammlung verlangt eine Bereitschaft für das Rätselvolle der Sachen und Sachverhalte, die uns im Gespräch an-gehen" (GA 74: 186).

16 See Nelson 2017: 120. Herman translates "wooden bell-stand" as "chime-post" (Herman 1996: 59). Compare Guo 1961: 658–9.

17 Compare the account of these two statements in Perkins 2015: 63, 67.

18 On the questions of freedom and determinism that this potentially raises, recall the previous discussion of determination and freedom in Guo Xiang and Zhi Dun.

19 For a detailed account of *Gelassenheit* in Eckhart and Heidegger, see Schürmann 1973: 95–119; Moore 2019.

20 "Dies Helfen [of the thinking of being] bewirkt keine Erfolge" (GA 9: 311; GA 13: 33).

21 On the development and significance of Heidegger's discourse of willing, not-willing, and *Gelassenheit*, see Davis 2007.

22 The "Letter on Humanism," examined further in the next chapter, provides a reflection on action and the problematic of activism that can be related to Daoist themes, as I initially explored in an inadequate way in Nelson 2004: 65–74. The letter questions the nature of the human in relation to nature and the inhuman that is also operative across the *Zhuangzi*. On humanism and anti-humanism in the *Zhuangzi*, see Perkins 2010: 118–36; Wenning 2014: 93–111.

23 GA 77: 206; Heidegger 2010: 133.

24 GA 77: 206; Heidegger 2010: 133.

25 GA 77: 207–8; Heidegger 2010: 134.

26 GA 77: 211; Heidegger 2010: 135.

27 GA 77: 212; Heidegger 2010: 136.

28 GA 77: 212; Heidegger 2010: 137.
29 GA 16: 563. On purposive and nonpurposive nourishing life (*yangsheng*), see Nelson 2020: 24–48.
30 On public and political participation, see Habermas 1990; Habermas 1994. For a more radical approach, compare Rosa Luxemburg's critique of Leninism and dictatorship for a proletariat public in Luxemburg 1922: 108–14. On the anarchistic and radical democratic implications of Lao-Zhuang ziranist Daoism, see Nelson 2020: 100–18 and Rapp 2012.
31 On these issues, compare Arendt 2006 and Arendt 2018b: 419–32.
32 On Heidegger's early enthusiasm for and increasingly ambivalent and critical response toward National Socialism, see Nelson 2017b: 77–88.
33 GA 77 227; Heidegger 2010: 140. On waiting without expectation and will, and the releasement of the worlding of world and pure arrival, see GA 97: 183. On Heidegger's conception of world and its development, see Trawny 1997.
34 GA 77 227; Heidegger 2010: 140.
35 The received text reads: "若一志無聽之以耳而聽之以心無聽之以心而聽之以氣。聽止於耳心止於符。氣也者虛而待物者也。唯道集虛。虛者心齋也" (Guo 1961: 186). Ziporyn's revised 2020 translation states that it is "a vacuity, a waiting for the presence of whatever thing may come. The Course alone is the gathering of this vacuity. This vacuity is the fasting of the mind" (Ziporyn 2020: 37).
36 GA 77: 220; Heidegger 2010: 143.
37 Wilhelm 1921, and Wilhelm 1948. Jung credited Wilhelm as a great inspiration in his life and thought, in "Richard Wilhelm: In Memoriam" in Jung 1966: 53–62.
38 Wilhelm 1912: 9; also note Nelson 2017: 67.
39 Wilhelm 1912: xiii, xxi, 8; ix, 116.
40 Buber 1962: 131. I show ways in which Buber's *I and Thou* is informed by his earlier interpretation of Zhuangzi in Nelson 2017: 109–29. On this Daoist dimension of Buber's classic work, see Wirth 2020: 121–34.
41 On Heidegger and Meister Eckhart's mysticism, see Schürmann 1973: 95–119; Moore 2019. The anarchy of Heidegger's releasement described by Schürmann is more likely due to Heidegger's ziranist debts than the mysticism that seeks to overcome things as well as the attachment to them.
42 Wilhelm describes how the *Zhuangzi* conveys the practical consequences of a "sovereign freedom" that is rooted beyond the entangling affairs of the world in the one. This leisurely unforced independence is free from every conditioning and limiting purpose, will, and striving (Wilhelm 1912: xiv).
43 Klages 1981: 342, 496. More recently, several works have emphasized the world-affirmative moment in Zhuangzi in relation to Nietzsche, such as Froese 2006 and Shang 2006.
44 See Guo 1961: 186; Wilhelm 1912: 36.
45 See Guo 1961: 936; Wilhelm 1912: 203–4.
46 GA 77: 239–40; Heidegger 2010: 156.
47 GA 77: 220; Heidegger 2010: 143.
48 GA 77: 227; Heidegger 2010: 147.
49 GA 77: 227; Heidegger 2010: 147.
50 GA 77: 229; Heidegger 2010: 149.
51 GA 77: 230; Heidegger 2010: 149.
52 See GA 96: 32, 91, 101, 162. In GA 97, this way of speaking is more closely interconnected with letting and concepts familiar from early Daoism.

53 Compare, for instance, Wohlfart 2003.
54 On the development and significance of *Gelassenheit* in Heidegger, see Davis 2007.
55 GA 77: 109: Heidegger 2010: 70.
56 On the significance of "nourishing life" in the *Zhuangzi* and nourishing co-creation in Buber, one of Heidegger's sources for understanding Zhuangzi, see chapter four of Nelson 2017.
57 GA 77: 237; Heidegger 2010: 155.
58 On Daoist self-ordering as an environmental, ethical, and political philosophy, see Nelson 2020. On the problems and prospects of Daoism for environmentalism, see D'Ambrosio 2013: 407–17. On Buber's anarchistic approach to Daoism, see Buber 2013: 227–68; Nelson 2020d: 105–20.
59 On how the forces of the state and capital systematically undermine and limit the public sphere, see Habermas 1990. On lifeworld and colonizing systems, see Habermas 1981, vol. 2. Arendt, Adorno, Habermas, and others have outlined the centrality of public and political participation since the 1940s. Heidegger rejected liberalism as overly narrow, dispersing and alienating the people from itself (GA 91: 176–7, 184–5). I argue in Nelson 2020c that liberal (in the sense of rights-oriented political liberalism as distinct from economic possessive individualist liberalism and neoliberalism) and social democratic political projects should be reoriented through alterity and nonidentity.
60 See Guo 1961: 39–40; Wilhelm 1912: 7; and Heidegger, GA 80.2: 1177–8. Compare Beaufret 1968: 15.
61 "[D]en Sinn wecken für das Nutzlose" (GA 80.2: 1176).
62 "Darum wirft die Besinnung, die ihm nachsinnt, zwar keinen praktischen Nutzen ab, gleich wohl ist der Sinn der Dinge das Nötigste. Denn ohne diesen Sinn bliebe auch das Nützliche sinnlos und daher nicht einmal nützlich" (GA 80.2: 1177).
63 "[D]as Sagen als das Zeigen und Erscheinenlassen des Anwesenden und Abwesenden, der Wirklichkeit im weitesten Sinne" (GA 80.2: 1193).
64 Heidegger's concerns here intersect with those of his critics such as Adorno and Horkheimer 1979. On Heidegger's appropriation of Daoism in the context of Adorno's critique, see Heubel 2020. On Adorno's philosophy and ethics of nature deployed at points in the present book, see Nelson 2020c.
65 "[D]ie Nähe des Ungesprochenen und des Unaussprechlichen bringt" (GA 80.2: 1195).
66 GA 12: 187; Heidegger 2009: 92.
67 For a stronger version of the argument for a Daoist turn in Heidegger, see Xia 2017.
68 Zhuangzi and Heidegger contest experiential reification and linguistic fixation through a variety of destructuring strategies: paradoxes, reversals of perspectives, and goblet words (*zhiyan* 卮言, expressions that spill over when full and refill when empty) in Zhuangzi (Wang Y. 2003), and paradoxical and poetic ways of speaking in Heidegger. On destructuring linguistic reification in Heidegger, see Rorty 1993: 337–57.
69 Hesse 1988: 158. On the German literary and intellectual fascination with Daoism during the troubled Weimar Republic, see Detering 2008: 31–2.
70 Jaspers 1966: 112. Concerning the *Zhuangzi*'s treatment of Confucius and critique of Confucianism, see Chong 2016. For an insightful interpretation of the *Zhuangzi*'s deconstructive and emancipatory uses of language, see Wang Y. 2003.
71 There are numerous discussions of Buber and Daoism, including Eber 1994: 445–64; Herman 1996; Nelson 2020d: 105–20; Wirth 2020: 121–34.
72 *Chinesische Geister- und Liebes-Geschichten* (Buber 2013: 131–226). Buber's Chinese translations based on English sources were widely read and discussed by the literary

modernists during the Weimar Republic. Heidegger's familiarity with the writings of these movements is unclear.
73 See Heidegger in GA: 8: 136; GA 11: 9; Husserl 1962: 331. Issues concerning the Eurocentric definition of philosophy are examined in Davis 2016: 130–56; Heurtebise 2020; Nelson 2017.
74 Compare Davis 2016: 130–56; Heurtebise 2020; Nelson 2017.
75 It is beyond this book's scope, yet the German philosophical reception of Daoism has continued unabated since Buber and Heidegger, in the utopian thinking of Bloch (Bloch 1959b, 2: 1032, 1438–50), Peter Sloterdijk's "Eurotaoism" (Sloterdijk 1989), and Ernst Tugendhat's reconceptualization of varieties of mysticism (Tugendhat 2003).
76 The administrative aspect of modernity, crucial to its analysis in Max Weber and the Frankfurt school, is frequently underemphasized in accounts of modernity in Heidegger. For a detailed portrait of Heidegger's therapeutic diagnosis of the pathologies of modernity, compare Zimmerman 1990.

Chapter 5

1 Heidegger and German translations of the *Daodejing* utilize two different expressions for mystery: *Geheimnis* means mystery as secret and *Rätsel* mystery as a puzzling riddle. Whereas much of twentieth-century Occidental philosophy is an attempt to reductively resolve the mystery, or dismiss it as nonsensical (the mystery does not exist), Heidegger is one of the few to emphasize preserving and nurturing the mystery for the sake of world, thing, and human dwelling.
2 For examples of self-criticism, see GA 82. Concerning Heidegger's notion of being-there and his critique of the subject, see Raffoul 1998. On Heidegger's difficult path to overcoming constitutive idealism, see Nelson 2016: 159–79. This book offers an alternative to Adorno's assessment that Heidegger failed to overcome constitutive idealism and identity-thinking.
3 On arguments for the priority of being or meaning, see Capobianco 2018 and Sheehan 2014. This debate appears misguided, given how Heidegger prioritizes a way in which these key concepts are rethought and is concerned with the sense *of* being rather than mere being, as if it were some sort of agent, or the transcendental (and hence ultimately anthropocentric) constitution of meaning. Heidegger himself ultimately rejected the logical, causal, transcendental, and semantic understanding of being's relationality as inadequate to its event character (GA 82: 552).
4 "Appropriating event" (*Ereignis*) does not refer to a conventionally understood ontic occurrence but should be interpreted in an ontological, singular, and verbal sense (*Ereignung, er-eignen*, GA 82: 552). Concerning the notion of the appropriating or enowning non-ontic event in Heidegger and its implications, compare Maly 2020; Nelson 2007: 97–115; and Raffoul 2020.
5 That is: "an-wesen-Weltisch-Weilen" (GA 98: 115). Its verbal character is noted on the following page.
6 See GA 6.2: 353; GA 67: 130. I interpret the "ownness" of *er-eignen* along ziranist lines as an autopoietic occurring "as" or "on its own." "Autopoiesis" is not an expression used by Heidegger and indeed he is a critic of "cybernetics," its closed systematic form. Still, it can be helpful in clarifying Daoist *ziran* and Heidegger's self-presencing if understood from their own contexts. I take autopoiesis to be plural and

interactive instead of as a closed totalizing system (as in Luhmann and his heirs). It signifies being sympoietically self-generative in relation to contexts and conditions in contrast to a determined collective or systemic self-reproduction (by "nature" or "society") that excludes singularity, normativity, alterity, and thus *ethos*.

7 "Auch der geringste Denkversuch muß wenigstens dieses Eine vermögen: immer auf dem selben Weg zu bleiben; und dies sagt: nie an der gleichen Stelle zu stehen" (GA 100: 9).

8 "Das vorläufige Denken ist noch kein Weg; es bleibt bei der Bewegung, beim Bauen eines Weges, im Bauen kommt der Weg am ehesten zum Vorschein" (GA 100: 185). On way-building, see GA 10: 77; GA 79: 133.

9 "An meinem Weg verkennt man bisher immer wieder—wissentlich oder unwissentlich—zwei wesentliche Be-stimmungen: 1. daß dieses Denken überall und stets sich als vor-läufiges versucht; 2. daß in dieser innegehaltenen Vorläufigkeit die ständig ursprüngliche Selbstkritik verankert ist" (GA 100: 55).

10 "Jede denkende Kritik des schon Gedachten ist Selbstkritik. nicht eine voraufgehende nur, sondern die wegbauende Besinnung unterwegs—der Versuch, dem Ungesagten der Fuge einzuwohnen" (GA 100: 174; compare GA 102: 22).

11 Chinese transmissions indicate how the freedom of *ziran* can be construed as a natural determination that calls for adaptive conformity. Spontaneous natural necessity and fatalism are issues in readings of the naturalization of *ziran*, in both the *Balanced Discourses* (*Lunheng* 論衡) of Wang Chong (王充) or in the previously discussed "sole determination" of Guo Xiang. Compare Ziporyn 2003: 56.

12 "Umwege, Seitenwege, Irrwege, Holzwege, Feldwege" (GA 100: 92).

13 GA 80.1: 397. On error, errancy, and freedom in failure in Heidegger, although without noting its Daoist elements, see Trawny 2014.

14 "Die Freiheit als das entbergende Seinlassen enthüllte sich als das Wesen der Wahrheit" (GA 80.1: 396).

15 Heidegger describes varieties of conditioning by the thing (*bedingen*) in, for instance, GA 101: 51. The later lines are from a thought-poem that in German reads: "dahin uns bedinge das wesende Ding? ruhig zu wandern im stetigen Andern … " (GA 97: 261).

16 *Daodejing* 25: "人法地, 地法天, 天法道, 道法自然" (Lou 1980: 65).

17 See Strauss 1870: 122, 176; Strauss 1879: 111.

18 Dilthey 2000: 4; Jaspers 1957: 299; Bloch 1959b, 2: 1438. *Daodejing* 67 refers to frugality (*jian* 儉), humility or nonassertion with respect to the world (不敢為天下先), and maternal-like nourishing care (*ci*) (Lou 1980: 170). Dilthey and other German authors call *ci* compassion. On the underappreciated roles of care in the *Daodejing*, which speak against interpretations positing a stance of neutral indifference, see Pang-White 2016: 275–94. On interpretations of ethics in the *Daodejing*, see D'Ambrosio 2022.

19 As in the lecture-courses published as GA 61; GA 62; GA 18.

20 GA 9: 183–7: GA 55: 214, 223. For an overview of ethics and its problems and prospects in and after Heidegger, see Raffoul 2010: 220–81.

21 "Das unter dem Anspruch der Anwesenheit Stehen ist der größte Anspruch des Menschen, ist 'die Ethik'" (GA 89: 273).

22 The recognition of the free (unclosed) self-generative autopoiesis of the myriad things is primarily a question of originary ethics and orienting *ethos* rather than self-reproducing totalities. This recognition need not require religious or mystical experiences or entail a theological position concerning gods, God, or the unity of

God and world. Heidegger himself never renounces his 1927 definition of philosophy as a-theological and his insistence on the abyss between a thinking of being/beings and a thinking of God/creatures (GA 80.1: 181–206).

23 "Wichtiger als alle Ethik ist das ethos. Wesentlicher als das ethos ist, sein Wesen als den sterblichen Aufenthalt im Ver-Hältnis des Ratsals zu bedenken" (GA 98: 345). On Heidegger's evolving conception of *ethos*, see also McNeill 2006.

24 GA 98: 345. See also the discussion of will and reserve in Davis 2004: 288.

25 A good example of Heidegger as a decisionist can be found in Habermas 1989: 431–56.

26 Habermas one-sidedly depicts Heidegger's sojourn as a development from heroic activist decisionism in *Being and Time* through his embrace of National Socialism; then, due to the conflicts and failures thereof, in Habermas's account, Heidegger subsequently switches toward the ostensibly passive fatalism and resignation of *Gelassenheit* (Habermas 1989: 431–56).

27 For a detailed account of the problematic of *pólemos* in Heidegger, compare Fried 2008. On Heidegger's thinking in the 1930s, see Polt 2019.

28 This is particularly the case in Lukács, who portrayed Heidegger and Klages as distinctive yet complementary expressions of the decay of bourgeois thought into fatalism and irrationalism (Lukács 1951; Lukács 1955).

29 Compare GA 43: 26–7; GA 49: 122; Bambach 2003: 275; Bernasconi 2013: 47–54.

30 For a nuanced account of holism, organicism, and vitalism during the National Socialist period, see Harrington 1996. A polemical critique is articulated in Lukács 1955.

31 See Heidegger's speeches and correspondence as rector, including the notorious rectorial address "The Self-Assertion of the German University," in GA 16: 81–274.

32 GA 6.2: 306; GA 50: 158; GA 67: 208–9. Deleuze's counter-argumentation that Nietzsche affirms a multiple pluralistic instead of unitary willing does not address Heidegger's underlying concerns that are directed at the priority of will and value as such (Deleuze 2006: 143, 191, 204). Heidegger's confrontation with Nietzsche is more radical than Deleuze's pluralistic reconstruction, insofar as will and value as such express truncated and problematic forms of being- and dwelling-in-the-world.

33 "Gelassenheit des Sein-lassens" (GA 75: 308). That is, letting-releasement correlates with the letting functioning of being that opens and allows the self-being of specific concrete beings. This strategy, intriguingly, and I have demonstrated non-accidentally, correlates with the *Daodejing*'s insight that the *dao* nourishes things and allows them to flourish as themselves. This exemplary *ziran-wuwei* model is enacted by sages through the practice of acting (in attunement with things) without acting (from the constructions and assertions of the self).

34 Three further points, which extend beyond this book's scope, should be mentioned. First, Heidegger and Adorno coincide in this analysis in ways that deserve a more detailed account than can be offered in this work focused on Heidegger and Daoism. Second, in addition to reimagining the classic Marxist concepts of alienation and ideology in social terms (Jaeggi 2005 and 2014), such concepts can be rethought in the anti-anthropocentric perspective of the domination of nature that was implicit in their formation in the early Marx and made explicit by Adorno and others. Third, shifting *ethos* and dwelling is one crucial aspect of questioning and imagining alternatives in our current environmental plight. Another necessary aspect, not articulated in Heidegger, concerns the political economic and material relationalities that need to be interrogated for an extended confrontation with current ecological crisis-tendencies. This entails that neither is sufficient by itself. Both *ethos* and

35 On Adorno's continuing significance for confronting the present crisis-tendencies concerning the environment and the natural world that encompasses and threatens humanity, see part one of Nelson 2020c.
36 GA 7: 149, 153; also compare GA 78: 149.
37 Zhuangzi: "夫復謵不餽而忘人, 忘人因以爲天人矣。"
38 Such as Cho 1993: 143–74. Heidegger's engagement with nature has been compared with, to give another example, the Japanese poet Matsuo Bashō 松尾芭蕉 whose "poetry is characterized by its closeness to nature and the simple life as well as to the thoughts of Laozi and Zen Buddhism" (Pieger 2000: 172).
39 Dehn 1948: 44–5, 53. Recall the previously quoted critique of Heidegger's Daoist-like nihilism by Klaus Mann (Mann 1949: 10). Another example of the early critical response to Heidegger's letter as a justification of atheistic mysticism against Sartre's atheistic humanism is found in Krüger 1950: 148–78. On the inhuman and human in ziranism, see Nelson 2014: 723–39.
40 Xunzi: "莊子蔽於天而不知人" (Li 1994: 478; also compare Nelson 2014: 723–39).
41 "Das Tun wendet sich so nicht in die Untatigkeit und das bloße Gleitenlassen; das Tun als Wesen der poiesis wendet sich in das weltische Freyen der Stille" (GA 98: 65).
42 Compare the 1935 accounts of violence in GA 40: 115–32; GA 65: 282.
43 GA 4: 42. Also compare GA 45: 3, 29. On the contexts, developments and shifts in Heidegger's reading of Hölderlin, see Bambach 2022.
44 On the early Chinese aesthetics of nature, see Zhao 2006. On the formation of aesthetics in mysterious learning discourses, with their new sense of affective subjectivity, and in the six kingdoms period, compare Cheng 1997.
45 On the sensibility of Wei-Jin mysterious learning literati, see Yü 1985: 121–55.
46 Heidegger and Adorno provide two different routes to contest the constitutive transcendental subject and conceive alternatives to it that can be interpreted as in part complementary. Adorno's critique is unfolded from *Against Epistemology* to *Negative Dialectics* through a critique of German Idealism and phenomenology. Adorno contends that Heidegger never adequately overcame this paradigm, while the current work shows how Heidegger's Daoist moments intimate alternatives.
47 As noted previously, a transformation of both the art of dwelling or being-in-the-world and the material-social conditions of human societies is necessary given the enormity of the environmental devastation that is currently occurring (this problem is considered in Nelson 2020c). The art of the self and the transformation of material-environmental reproduction are interconnected in specific configurations of the domination of nature and in dwelling as *poiesis*.
48 The distinction between purposive and nonpurposive forms of Daoism is made in Creel 1982: 1–24. The *Zhuangzi* and Wang Bi criticize purposive and instrumental techniques of nourishing life as contrary to its genuine nourishing (see Nelson 2020: 24–48).

Chapter 6

1 See Hegel 1986b: 210–11; Hegel 1986c: 84.
2 On water in early Chinese discourses, see Allen 1997; on images of primordial chaos at the origin of things, see Girardot 1983.

3   The present book extensively examined previously in Part One how Heidegger picked up on the *Daodejing*'s language of darkness and concealment. It is also interesting that the Chinese reception of *tathāgatagarbha* (*rulai zang* 如来藏) accentuated its concealed womblike nature as well as its storing character, in contrast to Tibetan interpretations that focused on the image of its being the embryo of Buddhahood. *Rulai* 如来 is a translation of "thus-come" (Sanskrit *tathāgata*) and the character *zang* 藏 signifies both to conceal and to store.
4   The most penetrating study of this topic remains Graham 1989.
5   On Wang Bi's life and thought, see Lynn 2015: 369–96. Some points in this section relate to previous research concerning Wang Bi's interpretive strategies and philosophy of nothingness in Nelson 2020b: 287–300.
6   Recall that a flexible pluralistic conception of Daoism resists more essentialist conceptions that would constrain it to one unitary philosophical or religious tendency that would exclude the others.
7   Religious varieties of Daoism are, according to my flexible pluralistic conception, also genuine forms of Daoism. They should not be dismissed in the name of a "classical" or "philosophical" Daoism, given the biospiritual elements in the latter, as well as how interconnected and complex their historical relations have been.
8   All these expressions occur in the *Zhuangzi* and subsequent Lao-Zhuang texts such as the *Liezi* 列子 and *Wenzi* 文子, texts that were heavily edited during the Han and post-Han eras. Not all these expressions appear in the *Daodejing*, suggesting an earlier textual formation. I take the *Daodejing* to be prior to the *Zhuangzi*, which presupposes and incorporates a more extensive variety of linguistic development, philosophical argumentation, and hermeneutical strategies.
9   On why this cannot mean the negation of nothingness in the *Zhuangzi*, which would undermine its significance, see Chai 2019: 4. On *wuwu* 無無 and *xuwu* 虛無 as the generative and destructuring functioning of nothingness in Zhuangzi and Wang Bi, see Nelson 2020: 87.
10 Lou 1980: 146; Lynn 1999: 156.
11 Lou 1980: 195, 2; Lynn 1999: 31, 52.
12 My translation of *Daodejing* 14 (Lou 1980: 31–2).
13 On generativity of nothingness, compare Chai 2019. On Daoist and deconstructive strategies, see Burik 2010.
14 On nothingness in mysterious learning discourses, see Chai 2010: 90–101.
15 Lou 1980: 93; Lynn 1999: 119.
16 Neo-Confucianism had an ambivalent and contested reception of *wuji* (the pole of emptiness) due to its perceived proximity to Daoism and Buddhism. Lu Xiangshan 陸象山 critically debated with Zhu Xi on the orthodoxy of *wuji*, which he considered an external non-Confucian teaching. Later heterodox "left-wing" neo-Confucians such as the Ming era philosophers Wang Ji (王幾, style name Wang Longxi 王龍溪) and Wang Gen 王艮 revealed the philosophical and social radicalness of negativity and nothingness. Huang Zongxi 黃宗羲 offered a paradigmatic critique of the popularity, heterodoxy, and dangerousness of the teachings of Wang Ji and Wang Gen in his *The Records of the Ming Scholars* (*Míngru Xuean* 明儒學案), accusing them of undermining Wang Yangming's teachings by conflating them with Chan Buddhism (Huang 1987: 165).
17 See Hegel 1986b: 210–11; Hegel 1986c: 84. Schopenhauer embraces negativity and nothingness in a more radical fashion than Hegel yet understands it as a relative expression (compare Schopenhauer 1977, vol. 2: 504–5 and Nelson 2022b: 83–96).

18 This negative language (*rittakaññeva, tucchakaññeva, asārakaññeva*) is used to describe form and perception as vacant, vain, and insubstantial, like foam and bubbles formed in water, in passages such as *Saṃyutta Nikāya* 22.95. The Buddha describes the emptiness of self and world in *Saṃyutta Nikāya* 35.85: "because it is empty of self and of what belongs to self that it is said, 'Empty is the world.'"

19 Recent critical Buddhist studies have critiqued "buddha-nature" and *tathāgatagarbha* as an East Asian substantialist aberration from "original" South Asian Buddhism. However, such expressions were already operative in proto-Mahāyāna South Asian Buddhist movements such as the Mahāsāṃghika *Tathāgatagarbha Sūtra*. Classic Tang dynasty–era forms of Chinese Buddhism, such as Huayan, with its non-reductive mirroring and mutual encompassing of particularities, did not understand buddha-nature as a fixed or static substance. Nor did they oppose buddha-nature to dependent origination and causal conditioning or principle to particularity. Dynamic mutually encompassing nature is disclosed through causality and emptiness. A clear example is Fazang's golden lion thought-image in which the gold (buddha-nature) operates in and through the causal conditions of the formed statue of the lion. On buddha-nature and Huayan, compare Hamar 2007.

20 MKK I.1. This text is cited as MKK plus chapter and verse numbers based on two different translations: Garfield 1995 and Siderits and Katsura 2013. For a more detailed account of the practical and determinate logic of emptiness, see Nelson 2023.

21 Sengzhao stated, "心彌虛行彌廣" (T1858: 160c23). On the practical orientation of emptiness in Nāgārjuna and Sengzhao, compare Nelson 2023.

22 See Heidegger, GA 11: 97, 129. Even within radical Hongzhou-style Chan, Mazu more frequently employs the language of buddha-nature, whereas Linji is depicted as disenchanting it and as expressing a performatively enacted emptying that undoes all distinctions, revealing the genuine person without rank who freely dwells with things and conditions through emptiness.

23 T45n1886; English translation and commentary in Gregory 1995.

24 On Zongmi's hermeneutical schematization of Chan Buddhist lineages, see Broughton 2009.

25 Haas 1909: 491–532 and Dumoulin 1938: 178–221.

26 The dynamic matrix of buddha-nature or the *tathāgatagarbha* (Gregory 1995: 134–40).

27 Gregory 1995: 163. Genuine nature is interpreted in Zongmi's revised Huayan model of the four dharma-realms and the difference/particularity maintaining mutuality and reciprocity between singular event and patterning principle. Genuine nature and buddha-nature in Huayan, as indicated by Fazang's analyses of the thought-images of the golden lion, the hall of mirrors, and rafter and building, are not statically existent; nor are these thought-images opposed to dependent origination and the causal matrix of reality, as critical Buddhist arguments against the East Asian buddha-nature paradigm maintain.

28 On Fazang's life, thought, and practice, see Chen 2007.

Chapter 7

1 GA 68: 47; also compare GA 66: 293.

2 Early Daoist autopoietics has been interpreted in the sense of functional-structural systems theories of maintaining equilibrium. This approach, stressing collective rather than interactive ordering, can be overly reductive, deterministic, and

inadequate for recognizing an *ethos* of interdependent freedom and nurturing care in responsive attunement (compare Nelson 2020).

3   On thinking "existentiality" in intercultural ways, see Kalmanson 2020.
4   The experiential and structural affinities and differences between the emptying of destructuring and formal indication in Heidegger, and negation and emptying in Chan Buddhist discursive and practical strategies, are examined in Nelson 2017: 225–52.
5   Concerning Meinong on nothingness, negative objects, and negation, see Jacquette 2015.
6   Windelband 1880: 355. On German pessimism, see Beiser 2016. On Buddhism, nothingness, and constitutive negativity in Schopenhauer, see Nelson 2022b: 83–96.
7   GA 29/30: 8. For a reconceptualization of freedom as world-appropriation, see Jaeggi 2005.
8   "色即是空, 空即是色。" See Taishō vol. 5, no. 220, 22a18 (*Mahāprajñāpāramitā Sūtra*; *Da bore boluomi duo jing* 大般若波羅蜜多經); Mattice 2021: 204. On the *Heart Sūtra*, its relation to perfection of wisdom discourses, and importance in East Asian Buddhism, see Mattice 2021.
9   Principle is at times directly identified with buddha-nature; more accurately, buddha-nature can only signify the complete interpenetration between principle and event without obstruction or duality. Emptiness is the entry into principle in Dushun 杜順 in his *Meditative Approaches to the Huayan Dharmadhātu* (*Huayan Fajie Guanmen* 華嚴法界觀門). I interpret buddha-nature as the entire dynamic of reality (the gold in the golden lion in Fazang's thought-image) that encompasses the mutual encompassing of emptiness and form, or principle and event. On Fazang and Huayan, compare Chen 2007. On buddha-nature in Huayan, see Hamar 2007.
10 On the originary not and not-ness (*Nichthafte*) of being, compare GA 9: 360; GA 65: 266–8, 481; GA 68: 102; GA 87: 64.
11 Schopenhauer has a deeper understanding of the "not" than Heidegger suggests here. For a detailed discussion of Schopenhauer and Nietzsche on Buddhism and nihilism, see Nelson 2022b: 83–96.
12 Buddhist "no-self" is misinterpreted in European discourses as advocating an absolute or generalized negation of the self in any sense giving rise to paradoxes in using and thinking the expression "I." This critique is exaggerated as no-self does not deny and seeks to free the conditional self by contesting fixations of the self as ego, essence, and substance. It thereby illuminates and transforms the ordinary conventional understandings of the self in the first- and second-person (I and thou) perspective instead of eliminating it. It shares some features with the critiques of the self in Hume, Nietzsche, and existentialism that contest constructed forms of the subject that are fixated as ultimately real. Buddhism typically does not solely deconstruct the self, as its negative mediative and linguistic strategies are correlated with discovering the relational interdependent self and freedom in compassion. The correlation of emptiness and compassion is evident in Madhyamaka (the emptiness school) as described in Śāntideva's description of the bodhisattva path in the *Bodhicaryāvatāra* (Śāntideva 1998: 105–32).
13 This connection was discussed in Leibniz's 1703 article on binary mathematics published by the Académie royale des sciences (Leibniz 1703) as well as in his correspondence and writings concerning Chinese philosophy that he interpreted through Jesuit sources (see Nelson 2011: 377–96).
14 Compare his remarks, from 1921/22 to 1951/52, in GA 61: 66; GA 55: 20, 151; GA 8: 42.
15 Significant alternatives were developed in rejoinder to Heidegger, such as Sartre's constitutive nihilation as formative of subjectivity rather than being (Sartre 1943).

16 For an overview, see Beiser 2016. He does not discuss the role of Buddhism in these controversies over pessimism.
17 Compare Habermas 1995: 128 and Nelson 2020c: 25–89. In the opening chapters of the latter book, I trace Adorno's analyses of nature as ideology and as critique.
18 Hans-Georg Gadamer credited Theodor Lessing's *Europa und Asien*, which he describes as dilettantish, with awakening his interest in Eastern thought during the Weimar era (Gadamer 1993: 480).
19 Compare Yusa 1998: 56; Petzet 1993: 153, 166–7; Heidegger, GA 16: 553–7, 712.
20 There is little discussion of how the cross-cultural question of nothingness intersects in their works. See Nelson 2011 on Leibniz, the *Book of Changes*, and the zero and Nelson 2022b on Schopenhauer, Buddhism, and nothingness.
21 For example, in GA 41: 94; GA 79: 158. The opposition between the history of Occidental philosophy as metaphysics and "non-Occidental" philosophical discourses—held in varying forms by Heidegger, Derrida, and Rorty—can no longer be maintained and requires a committed reimagining of the history of philosophy as an intercultural historical formation.
22 See GA 6.2: 357; GA 9: 382; GA 49: 199; GA 74: 23.
23 GA 81: 351, 356; also compare GA 65: 102.
24 On the subject in Heidegger, see Raffoul 1998. On expanding the initially much narrower formally indicative concepts of care and being-with, see Kanthack 1958 and Kanthack 1964.
25 See GA 67: 27; GA 69: 140; GA 74: 23.
26 Compare GA 5: 40; GA 9: 114; GA 68: 45–6; GA 74: 24, 28; GA 81: 351.
27 Such as Tsujimura Kōichi, Nishitani Keiji, Suzuki Daisetsu Teitarō, and Hisamatsu Shin'ichi. See GA 16: 553–7, 712; Petzet 1993: 153, 166–7.
28 On Buddhism and Heidegger in the Japanese context, see Umehara 1970: 271–81.
29 Tezuka's comments on their meeting and Heidegger's dialogue are translated in Buchner 1989: 173–80. Tezuka addresses the Buddhist character of nothingness/emptiness, as not negative, more clearly than Heidegger: *ku* 空 signifies emptiness, sky, and the open (Buchner 1989: 176).
30 See Taishō vol. 5, no. 220, 22a18, and Mattice 2021: 204.
31 In speaking of irreducible difference and nonidentity, Heidegger's discussion of the otherness of being (GA 65: 267) is being redescribed in part in the language of his critics (namely, Adorno and Levinas) in order to respond to the specific criticism of ontological totalization.
32 On the not-more and the not-yet, compare GA 7: 138; GA 8: 104. On remembering the flight of the gods of old and awaiting the arrival of the gods to come, see GA 39: 100.
33 Historicizing as singularization through contextualization is a strategy articulated by Dilthey (compare Nelson 2019: 10–36). On problems of contextualization regarding Heidegger, see Maly 2020: 15.
34 GA 16: 543; also compare GA 12: 246 on saying as showing, in which "address" expresses the said and "granting" expresses the unsaid.

Chapter 8

1 Carnap 1931: 241. Carnap's verdict on Heidegger's nothing (see Nelson 2013: 151–6) was shared by various positivists in the early 1930s: Oskar Krauss, David Hilbert,

Otto Neurath, and A. J. Ayer (Hilbert 1931: 485–94; Krauss 1931: 140–6; Neurath 1933: 8; Ayer 1934: 55–8).
2   For the former, see GA 12: 80–146; for the latter, see GA 77: 204, 218, 230.
3   On Heidegger and comparative and intercultural philosophy, see Buchner 1989; Davis 2013; Heubel 2020; Ma 2007; Nelson 2017; and Yu 2018.
4   Okakura 1919: 31; see also Imamichi 2004: 123; Davis 2013: 460–5.
5   "Juassa ... hat verstanden, was diese Vorlesung zeigen wollte" (GA 16: 712).
6   Heidegger remarked against those who identified his thought with Buddhism: "Kein Buddhismus! das Gegenteil" (GA 65: 171). Compare GA 7: 113; GA 43: 111.
7   "Für uns ist die Leere der höchste Name für das, was Sie mit dem Wort 'Sein' sagen möchten" (GA 12: 103).
8   This signifies that modernity and anti-modernity are interculturally mediated discursive and social-political configurations. This complex interpretive situation demands a critical intercultural hermeneutics that does not essentialize either one's own or the other's positionality, in contrast to both monoculturalism and multiculturalism (see Nelson 2017).
9   Nishida 1936: 126–7; also compare Nishida 1987. The present discussion of Nishida only focuses on the initial German translations and studies of his work between 1936 and 1944. For an insightful overview of nothingness in Heidegger and Nishida, see Krummel 2018: 239–68.
10 Pan-Asianism was, to be brief, typically "anti-colonial" in contesting Eurocentrism and Western colonialism, as well as nationalist in construing Japan as the inheritor, restorer, and culmination of "Oriental" culture and spirit that could defend Asia against Occidental encroachment. Kitayama and Kanokogi Kazunobu 鹿子木員信 were among the most active pan-Asianist intellectuals in Germany. Kanokogi wrote his dissertation with Rudolf Eucken in Jena in 1912 on "The Religious" and appears much more willing to directly advocate fascist ideology as director of the Japaninstitut in Berlin and subsequently in Japan (on Kanokogi, see Szpilman 2013: 233–80). Interestingly, Karl Löwith met Kanokogi during his time in Japan and thought poorly of him and other Japanese nationalist intellectuals for how they blended Confucius, Hegel, Hitler, and Shintō (Löwith 2016: 117–18). Löwith's experiences in Japan inform his skepticism concerning uncritical appropriations of Eastern thought.
11 Published in 1934 as Kitayama's *Metaphysik des Buddhismus; Versuch einer philosophischen Interpretation der Lehre Vasubandhus und seiner Schule*. Kitayama was among several rightwing Japanese intellectuals such as Kanokogi who studied in Germany and were active in German-Japanese relations during the National Socialist era. On Kitayama's links with German rightwing discourses and National Socialism, see Brightwell 2015: 431–53. On the intermixture of phenomenological and *völkisch* (racial and nationalist) geopolitical and georeligious predilections in Kitayama's philosophy of religion, see Kubota 2008: 613–33. Wolfgang Harich, an East German communist philosopher after the Second World War who helped Kitayama edit his German publications during the first half of the 1940s, describes Heidegger's influence on Kitayama and his activities in Germany, in Harich 2016.
12 See Nishida 1943: 140. On the early German language reception of Nishida's philosophy of nothingness: Kitayama 1943b: 274; Lüth 1944: 99–101; Schinzinger 1940: 38 and Schinzinger in Nishida 1943: 30–2.
13 In contrast to my therapeutic quasi-skeptical reading, which stresses freedom in non-assertion and non-affirmation rather than doubt, Graham Priest offers a (somewhat

reifying and identitarian) metaphysical account of Buddhist negation and emptiness in Priest 2018.
14 Schinzinger 1940: 31; Taketi 1940: 283–5; Imamichi 2004: 46.
15 A paradigmatic elucidation of "Oriental nothingness" is found in Hisamatsu 1960: 65–97 (also compare Hisamatsu 1994 and Hisamatsu 2002). On negation and nothingness in Continental and East Asian thought, see also Dastur 2018.
16 On Buddhism as world-affirmation, note Nishida 1939: 10–11 and Schinzinger's introduction to Nishida 1943: 51–2. *Tathātā* (thusness or suchness) designates in classical Buddhism either the negative breaking-off of discourse in emptiness (śūnyatā) or reality as such as disclosed through emptiness.
17 Barth concludes that Heidegger's nothingness is crypto-theological, whereas Sartre's is thoroughly atheistic (Barth 1950: 395).
18 Compare Buchner 1989: 169–72; Davis 2013: 460–5.
19 On Kuki and aesthetic theory, see Nara 2004.
20 Kitayama's *West-Östliche Begegnung: Japans Kultur und Tradition* was initially published in 1940 and revised and expanded in 1942.
21 Nishida 1939: 17. On how Nishida's circle of influence interpreted being and nothingness in early Chinese thought, compare Imamichi 1958: 54–64.
22 On the strategies of Wang Bi's philosophy of the nothing, see Nelson 2020b: 287–300.
23 The relationship between nationalist politics and the idea of nothingness in the Kyōto School is a highly contested one. On Kitayama's political context and motivations, see Brightwell 2015: 431–53; Kubota 2008: 613–33. On the social-political problems of modern Japanese discourses of "nothingness," compare Ives 2009 and Osaki 2019.
24 There is a profuse literature on the intersections during this era between German and Japanese thought, and between Japanese philosophy and politics, including Brightwell 2015; Kubota 2008; Ives 2009; and Osaki 2019.
25 The German text states: "das Nichts anfänglicher und wesender (ursprünglich das Seyn er-eignender) als das 'Etwas'? … Nichts hier besagt: überhaupt nicht ein Seiendes, sondern: Sein … Das Nichts entspringt nicht aus der Ab-sage an das Seiende, sondern ist anfängliches Sagen des Seyns, Sagen der Neinung in der Er-eignung" (GA 74: 24).
26 Note the assessment of Heidegger's nothingness as a radical yet insufficient step toward *śūnyatā* as absolute nothingness in Nishitani 1966, Nishitani 1983, and Nishitani 1989.
27 On the fourfold, see Mitchell 2015. On the East Asian contexts and resonances of the fourfold, see Part One.
28 "Das Ding dingt Welt" (GA 7: 182; Heidegger 1971: 178).
29 GA 5: 54. Much more could be said (than can be said in the confines of this chapter) about the complex interconnections between "work" and "thing" in the 1934/35 "The Origin of the Work of Art" and the 1950 "The Thing." Concerning the significance of the thing, see also Wang Q. 2016: 159–74.
30 "Hegels Negativität ist keine, weil sie mit dem Nicht und Nichten nie ernst macht, – das Nicht schon in das 'Ja' aufgehoben hat" (GA 68: 47). On Heidegger and Hegelian dialectic, note the helpful discussion in Kanthack 1968: 538–54.
31 "'Das Leere' ist also schlechthin der Anfang der Philosophie" (GA 68: 57).
32 "色不異空, 空不異色; 色即是空, 空即是色。" See Taishō vol. 5, no. 220, 22a18; compare Mattice 2021: 204.
33 Kitayama 1940 concerns Zen Buddhism. Non-duality is a significant facet of Buddhist argumentation, emphasized in Vasubandhu and Yogācāra (Kitayama 1934).

Heidegger's radical transformation of philosophy has been interpreted as contesting and overcoming the dualities (such as subject and object, ideality and reality) that structure previous Occidental philosophy (Kanthack 1964).
34 On nothingness in Nishida and Heidegger, see Krummel 2018: 239–68.

Chapter 9

1 Heidegger's thinking of being and beings, sense and meaning-formation, is structured through the emptiness and openness of nothingness and the ontological difference (compare GA 9: 134; GA 29/30: 521; GA 68: 20). Heidegger's way resists being reduced to the priority, presence, and positivity of either being or meaning. His later thinking contests being as presence, insofar as this prevailing paradigm forgets and suppresses indications of Daoist-like absence (as illustrated in Part One), concealment, darkness, mystery, and namelessness.
2 On the contemporary ethical and political implications of Daoist nothingness, see my account of the anarchistic and democratic potential of ziranist Daoist biopolitics in Nelson 2020: 110–18. I argue there for ziranist eco-democracy in opposition to eco-authoritarian tendencies. On Daoism and anarchism, also compare Rapp 2012.
3 Compare Levinas 1932; Levinas 1982. On Levinas and Heidegger on sociality and otherness, see Angelova 2010: 171–91. On critical Buddhism, see Ives 2009.
4 On the hermeneutics of reimagining, see the works of Donna J. Haraway.
5 Namely, the denial of individual and participatory rights, and militaristic nationalism and imperialism (Ives 2009; Osaki 2019).
6 See part one of Nelson 2020c for an analysis of the loss of nature, and critical models of alienation from and reification of nature, in the later Frankfurt school and the environmental implications of Adorno's dialectic of nature.
7 Writings collected in Buber 2013.
8 See Habermas 1985 and 1989. On Heidegger and Adorno in relation to National Socialism and Daoism, see Heubel 2020.
9 On the emptiness of formal indication in Heidegger and Chan Buddhism, see Nelson 2017: 225–52.
10 For a nuanced reconstruction of freedom as appropriation of and participation in material and social life, which intersects with aspects of Heidegger's more subjective and limited interpretation of individuation in *Being and Time*, see Jaeggi 2005. On early Daoist spontaneity, self-ordering, and participation as sources for democratic theory and practice, see Nelson 2020: 100–18.
11 The complex mediations between *ethos*, science, worldview, and politics indicate the need of developing a more adequate and comprehensive critical environmental and social theory and practice.
12 On the political entanglements of Japanese Buddhism and the Kyōto school, see Heisig and Maraldo 1995, Ives 2009, and Osaki 2019; on Kitayama, see Brightwell 2015: 431–53; Kubota 2008: 613–33.
13 Compare Victoria 2003: 120–4. The exponent of "soldier Zen," Gorō Sugimoto 杉本五郎 (1900–1937), stated in his popular, posthumously published work *Great Duty* (*Taigi* 大義): "The reason that Zen is necessary for soldiers is that all Japanese, especially soldiers, must live in the spirit of the unity of the sovereign and subjects, eliminating their ego and getting rid of their self. It is exactly the awakening to

the nothingness of Zen that is the fundamental spirit of the unity of sovereign and subjects. Through my practice of Zen, I am able to get rid of myself. In facilitating the accomplishment of this, Zen becomes, as it is, the true spirit of the imperial military" (Victoria 2003: 124).

14 Note Heisig and Maraldo 1995: 186, 194, 264, 273, 281, and 303. Löwith noted the fascination with Hegel while in Japan (Löwith 2016: 117–18).
15 Heisig and Maraldo 1995: 194.
16 On Nietzsche and Buddhism, see Wirth 2019. Despite Heidegger's expressions of interest in Zen Buddhism, he discussed and expressed Nietzschean suspicions concerning Buddhism on several occasions (GA 7: 113; GA 43: 111; GA 44: 68; GA 65: 171).
17 On the problematic of diagnosing progress and regression in a pluralistic context without a predetermined teleology of history, compare Jaeggi 2023. Pluralism is insufficient if it does not explicitly take an intercultural turn that contests the remnants of colonialism, and the Eurocentrism of theory and philosophy which predetermines and limits the multiplicity of available options and genuine possibilities.
18 For samples of Manhae's poetry and political thought, see Han 2005 and Han 2008.
19 Compare Han 2008: 154. Conflicting Tang dynasty era interpretations arose concerning which Huayan teaching is ultimate. The third Huayan patriarch Fazang prioritized, as the characterization of the primary reality-realm (*dharmadhātu, fajie* 法界), the mutual non-obstruction, interpenetration, and responsive interpolation between each phenomenal particular (*shishi wuai fajie* 事事無礙法界). These preserve both the uniqueness of the singular event and the interpenetrating character of the self-patterning whole; the fifth Huayan patriarch and Chan Buddhist Guifeng Zongmi 圭峰宗密 (780–841) prioritized, as the ultimate reality-realm (or characterization thereof), the non-obstruction and interpenetration between patterning principle and particular phenomena (*lishi wuai fajie* 理事無礙法界).
20 On Huayan and democratic socialist equality, see Han 2008; on Daoism and critical social theory, note Fritsch 2022, Nelson 2020c, and Wenning 2011: 50–71. It is also important to recognize countertendencies, such as the prominence of contemporary Chinese and Western Confucian discourses, in deploying an *arché* (such as hierarchical merit, relationality, rituality, and politeness) to critique liberty, equality, democracy, and human rights. More critical progressive conceptions of Confucianism, which do not reject democracy and rights in the name of authority and rites, were promoted by modernizing new Confucians such as Carson Chang (Zhang Junmai 張君勱) in the coauthored 1958 "New Confucian Manifesto" and in other works (Nelson 2017: 43–76). On the ethical and cross-cultural elements of Confucian relationality, compare Kalmanson 2020.
21 On "ecological civilization," see Schönfeld and Chen 2019.
22 Habermas and Jaeggi described the first two dimensions (individual-personal and public-deliberative) with respect to processes such as the colonization of the public sphere, reification, and alienation (Habermas 1990; Habermas 1994; Jaeggi 2005). Habermas 2022 and Jaeggi 2023 engage current dilemmas and pathologies. Still, less anthropocentric and Eurocentric perspectives are needed that offer more adequate accounts of the third intercultural dimension. This requires an approach that promotes both decolonial and intercultural conceptions and practices of the public, democratic will-formation and deliberation, as well as the protection of individual and political rights from state, market, and other oppressive forces.

Whereas indigenous subaltern voices and a critical intercultural discourse contest the oppression of individuals and groups, uncritical uses of multiculturalism can serve to legitimate essentialist identity, nationalist politics, and social-political oppression by placing existing cultural norms and practices outside of intercultural publicity, dialogue, and critique.
23 Heidegger: "das Raumgeben für das Seiende im Ganzen; sodann das Sichloslassen in das Nichts, d. h. das Freiwerden von den Götzen" (GA 9: 122).
24 A politics of material, environmental, and social liberty would require exemplars and models of the non-reification of creatures, things, and world, as well as the non-alienation of human selves (compare Jaeggi 2005). Although Heidegger cannot be described as a democratic thinker, his thought has noteworthy implications—as argued throughout this work—for our tenuous contemporary situation.

Bibliography

1. Complete Works of Heidegger

Heidegger, Martin. 1975–ongoing. *Gesamtausgabe*, 102 volumes. Frankfurt: Klostermann. [cited as GA plus volume number].

GA 1: *Frühe Schriften (1912-1916)*, ed. F.-W. von Herrmann, 1978.
GA 2: *Sein und Zeit*, ed. F.-W. von Herrmann, 1977.
GA 3: *Kant und das Problem der Metaphysik*, ed. F.-W. von Herrmann, 1991.
GA 4: *Erläuterungen zu Hölderlins Dichtung (1936-1968)*, ed. F. W. von Herrmann, 2nd edn. 1996.
GA 5: *Holzwege (1935-1946)*, ed. F.-W. von Herrmann, 2nd edn. 2003.
GA 6.1: *Nietzsche I (1936-1939)*, ed. B. Schillbach, 1996.
GA 6.2: *Nietzsche II (1939-1946)*, ed. B. Schillbach, 1997.
GA 7: *Vorträge und Aufsätze (1936-1953)*, ed. F.-W. von Herrmann, 2000.
GA 8: *Was heisst Denken? (1951-1952)*, ed. P.-L. Coriando, 2002.
GA 9: *Wegmarken (1919-1961)*, ed. F.-W. von Herrmann, 3rd edn. 2004.
GA 10: *Der Satz vom Grund (1955–1956)*, ed. P. Jaeger, 1997.
GA 11: *Identität und Differenz (1955-1957)*, ed. F.-W. von Herrmann, 2nd edn. 2006.
GA 12: *Unterwegs zur Sprache (1950-1959)*, ed. F.-W. von Herrmann, 1985.
GA 13: *Aus der Erfahrung des Denkens (1910-1976)*, ed. H. Heidegger, 2nd edn. 2002.
GA 14: *Zur Sache des Denkens (1962-1964)*, ed. F.-W. von Herrmann, 2007.
GA 15: *Seminare (1951-1973)*, ed. C. Ochwadt, 2nd edn. 2005.
GA 16: *Reden und andere Zeugnisse eines Lebensweges (1910-1976)*, ed. H. Heidegger, 2000.
GA 17: *Einführung in die phänomenologische Forschung (Wintersemester 1923/24)*, ed. F.-W. von Herrmann, 2nd edn. 2006.
GA 18: *Grundbegriffe der aristotelischen Philosophie*, ed. M. Michalski, 2002.
GA 23: *Geschichte der Philosophie von Thomas von Aquin bis Kant (Wintersemester 1926/27)*, ed. H. Vetter, 2006.
GA 25: *Phänomenologische Interpretation von Kants Kritik der reinen Vernunft (Wintersemester 1927/28)*, ed. I. Görland, 3rd edn. 1995.
GA 27: *Einleitung in die Philosophie (Wintersemester 1928/29)*, ed. O. Saame and I. Saame-Speidel, 2nd edn. 2001.
GA 29/30: *Die Grundbegriffe der Metaphysik: Welt – Endlichkeit – Einsamkeit (Wintersemester 1929/30)*, ed. F.-W. von Herrmann, 3rd edn. 2004.
GA 31: *Vom Wesen der menschlichen Freiheit: Einleitung in die Philosophie*, ed. H. Tietjen, 2nd edn. 1994.
GA 34: *Vom Wesen der Wahrheit: Zu Platons Höhlengleichnis und Theätet (Wintersemester 1931/32)*, ed. H. Mörchen, 2nd edn. 1997.
GA 35: *Der Anfang der abendländischen Philosophie (Anaximander und Parmenides) (Sommersemester 1932)*, ed. P. Trawny, 2012.
GA 39: *Hölderlins Hymnen "Germanien" und "Der Rhein" (Wintersemester 1934/35)*, ed. S. Ziegler, 3rd edn. 1999.

GA 40: *Einführung in die Metaphysik (Sommersemester 1935)*, ed. P. Jaeger, 1983.
GA 41: *Die Frage nach dem Ding: Zu Kants Lehre von den transzendentalen Grundsätzen (Wintersemester 1935/36)*, ed. P. Jaeger, 1984.
GA 42: *Schelling: Vom Wesen der menschlichen Freiheit (1809)*, ed. I. Schüssler, 1988.
GA 43: *Nietzsche: Der Wille zur Macht als Kunst*, ed. B. Heimbüchel, 1985.
GA 44: *Nietzsches metaphysische Grundstellung im abendländischen Denken: Die ewige Wiederkehr des Gleichen*, ed. M. Heinz, 1986.
GA 45: *Grundfragen der Philosophie. Ausgewählte "Probleme" der "Logik,"* ed. F.-W. von Herrmann, 2nd ed. 1984.
GA 46: *Zur Auslegung von Nietzsches II. Unzeitgemässer Betrachtung*, ed. H.-J. Friedrich, 2003.
GA 47: *Nietzsches Lehre vom Willen zur Macht als Erkenntnis*, ed. E. Hanser, 1989.
GA 48: *Nietzsche: Der europäische Nihilismus*, ed. P. Jaeger, 1986.
GA 49: *Die Metaphysik des deutschen Idealismus*, ed. G. Seubold, 2nd edn. 2006.
GA 50: *Nietzsches Metaphysik/Einleitung in die Philosophie – Denken und Dichten*, ed. P. Jaeger, 2nd edn., 2007.
GA 53: *Hölderlins Hymne "Der Ister,"* ed. W. Biemel, 2nd edn. 1993.
GA 55: *Heraklit*, ed. M. S. Frings, 3rd edn. 1994.
GA 56/57: *Zur Bestimmung der Philosophie*, ed. B. Heimbüchel, 2nd edn. 1999.
GA 58: *Grundprobleme der Phänomenologie (Wintersemester 1919/20)*, ed. H.-H. Gander, 1992.
GA 60: *Phänomenologie des religiösen Lebens*, ed. C. Strube, 1995.
GA 61: *Phänomenologische Interpretationen zu Aristoteles: Einführung in die phänomenologische Forschung*, ed. W. Bröcker and K. Bröcker-Oltmanns, 2nd edn. 1994.
GA 62: *Phänomenologische Interpretation ausgewählter Abhandlungen des Aristoteles zu Ontologie und Logik*, ed. G. Neumann, 2005.
GA 63: *Ontologie: Hermeneutik der Faktizität*, ed. K. Bröcker-Oltmanns, 2nd edn. 1995.
GA 64: *Der Begriff der Zeit (1924)*, ed. F.-W. von Herrmann, 2004.
GA 65: *Beiträge zur Philosophie (Vom Ereignis) (1936–1938)*, ed. F.-W. von Herrmann, 2nd edn. 1994.
GA 66: *Besinnung (1938/39)*, ed. F.-W. von Herrmann, 1997.
GA 67: *Metaphysik und Nihilismus*, ed. H.-J. Friedrich, 1999.
GA 68: *Hegel*, ed. I. Schüssler, 1993.
GA 69: *Die Geschichte des Seyns*, ed. P. Trawny, 1998.
GA 70: *Über den Anfang*, ed. P.-L. Coriando, 2005.
GA 73: *Zum Ereignis-Denken*, ed. P. Trawny, 2013.
GA 74: *Zum Wesen der Sprache und Zur Frage nach der Kunst*, ed. T. Regehly, 2010.
GA 75: *Zu Hölderlin/Griechenlandreisen*, ed. C. Ochwadt, 2000.
GA 76: *Leitgedanken zur Entstehung der Metaphysik, der neuzeitlichen Wissenschaft und der modernen Technik*, ed. C. Strube, 2009.
GA 77: *Feldweg-Gespräche (1944/45)*, ed. I. Schüssler, 2nd edn. 2007.
GA 78: *Der Spruch des Anaximander (1946)*, ed. I. Schüssler, 2010.
GA 79: *Bremer und Freiburger Vorträge*, ed. P. Jaeger, 2nd edn. 2005.
GA 80.1: *Vorträge, Teil 1: 1915 bis 1932*, ed. G. Neumann, 2016.
GA 80.2: *Vorträge. Teil 2: 1935 bis 1967*, ed. G. Neumann, 2020.
GA 81: *Gedachtes*, ed. P.-L. Coriando, 2007.
GA 82: *Zu eigenen Veröffentlichungen*, ed. F.-W. von Herrmann, 2018.
GA 87: *Nietzsche: Seminare 1937 und 1944*, ed. P. von Ruckteschell, 2004.

GA 89: *Zollikoner Seminare*, ed. P. Trawny, 2017.
GA 90: *Zu Ernst Jünger*, ed. P. Trawny, 2004.
GA 91: *Ergänzungen und Denksplitter*, ed. M. Michalski, 2022.
GA 96: *Überlegungen XII-XV: Schwarze Hefte 1939-1941*, ed. P. Trawny, 2014.
GA 97: *Anmerkungen I-V: Schwarze Hefte 1942-1948*, ed. P. Trawny, 2015.
GA 98: *Anmerkungen VI-IX: Schwarze Hefte 1948/49-1951*, ed. P. Trawny, 2018.
GA 99: *Vier Hefte I: Der Feldweg/Vier Hefte II: Durch Ereignis zu Ding und Welt (1947-1950)*, ed. P. Trawny, 2019.
GA 100: *Vigiliae I, II/Notturno: 1952/53 bis 1957*, ed. P. Trawny, 2020.
GA 101: *Winke I, II: Schwarze Hefte 1957-1959*, ed. P. Trawny, 2020.
GA 102: *Vorläufiges I-IV: Schwarze Hefte 1963-1970*, ed. P. Trawny, 2021.

2. Correspondence and Other Cited Works of Heidegger

Biemel, Walter, and Hans Saner, eds. 1990. *Martin Heidegger/Karl Jaspers: Briefwechsel 1920-1963*. Frankfurt: Klostermann and Munich: Piper.
Heidegger, Gertrud, ed. 2008. *Heidegger: Letters to His Wife, 1915-1970*. Cambridge: Polity.
Heidegger, Martin. 1971. *On the Way to Language*, tr. P. Hertz. New York: HarperCollins.
Heidegger, Martin. 1998. *Pathmarks*, tr. W. McNeil. Cambridge: Cambridge University Press.
Heidegger, Martin. 2002. *Off the Beaten Track*, tr. J. Young and K. Haynes. Cambridge: Cambridge University Press.
Heidegger, Martin. 2010. *Country Path Conversations*, tr. B. Davis. Bloomington: Indiana University Press.
Petzet, Heinrich Wiegand, ed. 1986. *Martin Heidegger-Erhart Kästner: Briefwechsel 1953-1974*. Frankfurt: Insel.
Pieger, Bruno, ed. 2000. *Martin Heidegger/Imma von Bodmershof, Briefwechsel 1959-1976*. Stuttgart: KlettCotta.
Quinn, Timothy S., ed. and tr. 2016. *Martin Heidegger and Ernst Jünger: Correspondence 1949-1975*. London: Rowman & Littlefield.

3. Other Cited Works

Adorno, Theodor W. 1986. *Gesammelte Schriften*, 20 volumes. Frankfurt: Suhrkamp.
Adorno, Theodor W. and Max Horkheimer. 1979. *Dialectic of Enlightenment*. London: Verso.
Allan, Sarah. 1997. *The Way of Water and Sprouts of Virtue*. Albany: State University of New York Press.
Anders, Günther. 2001. *Über Heidegger*. Munich: Beck.
Anesaki, Masaharu. 1915. *Buddhist Art in Its Relation to Buddhist Ideals*. New York: Houghton Mifflin Company.
Angelova, Emilia. 2010. "Utopia, Metontology, and the Sociality of the Other: Levinas, Heidegger, and Bloch." *Journal of Contemporary Thought* 31: 171-91.
Arendt, Hannah. 1976. *The Origins of Totalitarianism*. New York: Harcourt Brace.

Arendt, Hannah. 2006. *Eichmann in Jerusalem: A Report on the Banality of Evil*. London: Penguin.
Arendt, Hannah. 2018. *The Human Condition*, 2nd edition. Chicago: University of Chicago Press.
Arendt, Hannah. 2018b. *Thinking without a Banister: Essays in Understanding, 1953–1975*. New York: Schocken.
Ayer, A. J. 1934. "The Genesis of Metaphysics." *Analysis* 1.4: 55–8.
Balazs, Etienne. 1964. "Nihilistic Revolt or Mystical Escapism: Currents of Thought in China during the Third Century AD." in his *Chinese Civilization and Bureaucracy*, 226–54. New Haven: Yale University Press.
Bambach, Charles. 1995. *German Philosophy and the Crisis of Historicism*. Ithaca: Cornell University Press.
Bambach, Charles. 2003. *Heidegger's Roots: Nietzsche, National Socialism, and the Greeks*. Ithaca: Cornell University Press.
Bambach, Charles. 2022. *Of an Alien Homecoming: Reading Heidegger's "Hölderlin."* Albany: State University of New York Press.
Barth, Karl. 1950. *Die kirchliche Dogmatik: Die Lehre von der Schöpfung*. Zurich: Evangelischer Verlag A. G. Zollikon.
Beaufret, Jean. 1968. *La Naissance de la philosophie*. Guéret: Les Presses du Massif Central.
Beiser, Frederick C. 2016. *Weltschmerz: Pessimism in German Philosophy, 1860–1900*. Oxford: Oxford University Press.
Benn, Gottfried. 1951. *Probleme der Lyrik*. Wiesbaden: Limes Verlag.
Bernasconi, Robert. 2013. "Heidegger, Nietzsche, National Socialism: The Place of Metaphysics in the Political Debate of the 1930s." In François Raffoul, Eric S. Nelson (eds.), *The Bloomsbury Companion to Heidegger*, 47–54. London: Bloomsbury.
Bloch, Ernst. 1959. *Erbschaft dieser Zeit*. Frankfurt: Suhrkamp.
Bloch, Ernst. 1959b. *Das Prinzip Hoffnung*, 3 volumes. Frankfurt: Suhrkamp.
Bloch, Ernst. 1984. *Literarische Aufsätze*. Frankfurt: Suhrkamp.
Blok, Vincent. 2014. "Reconnecting with Nature in the Age of Technology: The Heidegger and Radical Environmentalism Debate Revisited." *Environmental Philosophy* 11.2: 307–32.
Böhme, Jakob. 1732. *Der Weg zu Christo*. Amsterdam: n. a.
Bokenkamp, Stephen R. 1997. *Early Daoist Scriptures*. Berkeley: University of California Press.
Botha, Catherine F. 2003. "Heidegger, Technology and Ecology." *South African Journal of Philosophy* 22.2: 157–71.
Brightwell, Erin L. 2015. "Refracted Axis: Kitayama Jun'yū and Writing a German Japan." *Japan Forum* 27.4: 431–53.
Brindley, Erica, Paul R. Goldin, and Esther S. Klein, tr. 2013. "A Philosophical Translation of the Heng Xian." *Dao: A Journal of Comparative Philosophy* 12.2: 145–51.
Broughton, Jeffrey, tr. 2009. *Zongmi on Chan*. New York: Columbia University Press.
Buber, Martin. 1910. *Reden und Gleichnisse des Tschuang-tse*. Leipzig: Inselverlag.
Buber, Martin. 1962. *Schriften zur Philosophie*. Munich: Verlag Lambert Schneider.
Buber, Martin. 1990. *Pointing the Way: Collected Essays*. Amherst: Prometheus Books.
Buber, Martin. 2013. *Schriften zur chinesischen Philosophie und Literatur*, ed. Paul Mendes-Flohr und Bernd Witte. Gütersloh: Gütersloher Verlagshaus.
Buber, Martin. 2017. *Schriften zu Philosophie und Religion*, ed. Ashraf Noor. Gütersloh: Gütersloher Verlagshaus.
Buchner, Hartmut, ed. 1989. *Japan und Heidegger*. Sigmaringen: Thorbecke.

Buddhaghosa. 2010. *The Path of Purification (Visuddhimagga)*, tr. Bhikkhu Ñáóamoli, 4th edition. Colombo: Buddhist Publication Society.
Burik, Steven. 2010. *The End of Comparative Philosophy and the Task of Comparative Thinking, Heidegger, Derrida, and Daoism*. Albany: State University of New York Press.
Burik, Steven. 2010b. "Thinking on the Edge: Heidegger, Derrida, and the Daoist Gateway (*Men* 門)." *Philosophy East and West* 60.4: 499–516.
Burik, Steven. 2019. "Darkness and Light: Absence and Presence in Heidegger, Derrida, and Daoism." *Dao* 18.3: 347–70.
Cabural, Mark Kevin S. 2020. "Daoism and the German Mission in Martin Heidegger's 'The Thing.'" *Frontiers of Philosophy in China* 14.4: 570–92.
Cantor, Lea. 2023. "Laozi through the Lens of the White Rose." *Oxford German Studies* 52. 1: 62–79.
Capobianco, Richard M. 2018. *Heidegger's Way of Being*. Toronto: University of Toronto Press.
Carnap, Rudolf. 1924/1925. "Dreidimensionalität des Raumes und Kausalität: Eine Untersuchung über den logischen Zusammenhang zweier Fiktionen." *Annalen der Philosophie und philosophischen Kritik* 4.3: 105–30.
Carnap, Rudolf. 1931. "Überwindung der Metaphysik durch logische Analyse der Sprache." *Erkenntnis* 2.1: 219–41.
Carus, Paul, tr. 1898. *Lao-Tze's Tao-teh-king*. Chicago: Open Court.
Cassirer, Ernst. 1955. *The Philosophy of Symbolic Forms*, vol. 2. New Haven: Yale University Press.
Chai, David. 2010. "Meontology in Early *Xuanxue* Thought." *Journal of Chinese Philosophy* 37.1: 90–101.
Chai, David. 2014. "Meontological Generativity: A Daoist Reading of the Thing." *Philosophy East and West* 64.2: 303–18.
Chai, David. 2016. "Rethinking the Daoist Concept of Nature." *Journal of Chinese Philosophy* 43.3–4: 259–74.
Chai, David. 2019. *Zhuangzi and the Becoming of Nothingness*. Albany: State University of New York Press.
Chai, David, ed. 2022. *Daoist Resonances in Heidegger*. London: Bloomsbury.
Chan, Shirley. 2015. "Oneness: Reading the 'All Things Are Flowing in Form' (*Fan Wu Liu Xing*) 凡物流形 (with a translation)." *International Communication of Chinese Culture* 2.3: 285–99.
Chen, Jinhua. 2007. *Philosopher, Practitioner, Politician: The Many Lives of Fazang (643–712)*. Leiden: Brill.
Chen, Shou 陳壽. 1975. *Sanguozhi* 三國志 [Chronicles of the Three Kingdoms]. Beijing: Zhonghua Shuju.
Cheng, Yu-yu 鄭毓瑜. 1997. *Liuchao qingjing meijue* 六朝情境美學 [The Aesthetic Realm in the Six Dynasties]. Taipei: Liren Shuju.
Chiang, Liang. 1938. *Die chinesische Wirtschafts- und Sozialverfassung zwischen Freiheit und Bindung ein Überblick bis zum Jahre 1937*. Würzburg-Aumühle: Triltsch.
Chiao, Kwan-Hua. 1937. *Darstellung der Philosophie des Dschuang Dsi*. Urach: Bühler.
Cho, Kah Kyung. 1993. "Der Abstieg über den Humanismus: West-Östliche Wege im Denken Heideggers." In H. H. Gander (ed.), *Europa und die Philosophie*, 143–74. Frankfurt: Klostermann.
Chong, Kim-chong. 2016. *Zhuangzi's Critique of the Confucians: Blinded by the Human*. Albany: State University of New York Press.

Cook, Scott. 1995. "Yue Ji 樂記: Record of Music: Introduction, Translation, Notes, and Commentary." *Asian Music* 26.2: 1–96.
Cook, Scott. 2012. *The Bamboo Texts of Guodian: A Study and Complete Translation*, vol. 1. Ithaca: Cornell University Press.
Creel, Herrlee G. 1982. *What Is Taoism? and Other Studies in Chinese Cultural History.* Chicago: University of Chicago Press.
Crowell, Steven Galt, and Jeff Malpas, eds. 2007. *Transcendental Heidegger*. Stanford: Stanford University Press.
Cysarz, Herbert. 1940. *Das Unsterbliche: Die Gesetzlichkeiten und das Gesetz der Geschichte*. Halle: Niemeyer.
D'Ambrosio, Paul J. 2013. "Rethinking Environmental Issues in a Daoist Context Why Daoism Is and Is Not Environmentalism." *Environmental Ethics* 35.4: 407–17.
D'Ambrosio, Paul J. 2022. "Approaches to Ethics in the Laozi (Lao-Tzu)." *Philosophy Compass* 17.2: e12810.
Dastur, Françoise. 2018. *Figures du néant et de la négation entre orient et occident*. Paris: Les Belles Lettres.
Davis, Bret W. 2007. *Heidegger and the Will: On the Way to Gelassenheit*. Evanston: Northwestern University Press.
Davis, Bret W. 2013. "Heidegger and Asian Philosophy." In François Raffoul, Eric S. Nelson (eds.), *The Bloomsbury Companion to Heidegger*, 459–71. London: Bloomsbury.
Davis, Bret W. 2016. "Heidegger on the Way from Onto-historical Ethnocentrism to East-West Dialogue." *Gatherings: The Heidegger Circle Annual* 6: 130–56.
Davis, Bret W. 2020. "Heidegger and Daoism: A Dialogue on the Useless Way of Unnecessary Being." In David Chai (ed.), *Daoist Encounters with Phenomenology*, 161–96. London: Bloomsbury.
Dehn, Fritz. 1948. *Vom Menschlichen im Menschen*. Berlin: Haus und Schule.
Deleuze, Gilles. 2006. *Nietzsche and Philosophy*. New York: Columbia University Press.
Derrida, Jacques. 1989. *Edmund Husserl's Origin of Geometry: An Introduction*. Lincoln: University of Nebraska Press.
Derrida, Jacques. 2010. *The Beast and the Sovereign*, vol. I. Chicago: University of Chicago Press.
Derrida, Jacques. 2017. *The Beast and the Sovereign*, vol. II. Chicago: University of Chicago Press.
Detering, Heinrich. 2008. *Bertolt Brecht und Laotse*. Göttingen: Wallstein Verlag.
Dilthey, Wilhelm. 2000. *Allgemeine Geschichte der Philosophie: Vorlesungen 1900–1905*. Göttingen: Vandenhoeck & Ruprecht.
Dilthey, Wilhelm. 2004. *Späte Vorlesungen, Entwürfe und Fragmente zur Strukturpsychologie, Logik und Wertlehre (ca. 1904-1911)*. Göttingen: Vandenhoeck & Ruprecht.
Döblin, Alfred. 1921. "Buddho und die Natur." *Die Neue Rundschau* 32.2: 1192–200.
Döblin, Alfred. 2013. *Die drei Sprünge des Wang-lun*. Frankfurt: Fischer.
Driesch, Hans. 1938. "Das 'Ding.'" *Synthese* 3.4: 136–42.
Dumoulin, Heinrich. 1938. "*Genninron*: Tsung-mi's Traktat vom Ursprung des Menschen." *Monumenta Nipponica* 1.1: 178–221.
Dvořák, Rudolf. 1895. *Chinas Religionen*. Münster: Aschendorff.
Eber, Irene. 1994. "Martin Buber and Taoism." *Monumenta Serica* 42: 445–64.
Eckardt, Andre. 1957. *Laotses Gedankenwelt nach dem Tao-te king*. Baden-Baden: Lutzeyer.
Eckhart, Meister. 1971. *Die Deutschen Werke*, vol. 2, ed. Josef Quint. Stuttgart: Kohlhammer.

Eichhorn, Werner. 1942. "Die dauistische Spekulation im zweiten Kapital des Dschuang Dsi." *Sinica* 17: 140–62.
Erkes, Eduard. 1945. "Ho-Shang-Kung's Commentary on Lao-Tse." *Artibus Asiae* 8.2/4: 119–96.
Erkes, Eduard. 1946. "Ho-Shang-Kung's Commentary on Lao-Tse II (Continued)." *Artibus Asiae* 9.1/3: 197–220.
Evers, Hans Gerhard. 1951. *Das Menschenbild in unserer Zeit*. Darmstadt: Neue Darmstädter Verlagsanstalt.
Faber, Ernst. 1877. *Der Naturalismus bei den alten Chinesen*. Elberfeld: R. L. Friderichs.
Federmann, Hertha, tr. 1920. *Tao teh King: Vom Geist und seiner Tugend*. Munich: C.H. Beck'sche Verlag.
Fischer, Otto. 1923. *Chinesische Landschaftsmalerei*. München: Wolff.
Fried, Gregory. 2008. *Heidegger's Polemos*. New Haven: Yale University Press.
Fritsch, Matthias. 2020. *Taking Turns with the Earth*. Stanford: Stanford University Press.
Fritsch, Matthias. 2022. "Heidegger's Dao and the Sources of Critique." In Hiroshi Abe, Matthias Fritsch, and Mario Wenning (eds.), *Environmental Philosophy and East Asia: Nature, Time, Responsibility*, 49–73. London: Routledge.
Froese, Katrin. 2006. *Nietzsche, Heidegger, and Daoist Thought: Crossing Paths In-Between*. Albany: State University of New York Press.
Gadamer, Hans-Georg. 1993. *Wahrheit und Methode: Ergänzungen*. Tübingen: Mohr (Paul Siebeck).
Garfield, Jay. 1995. *The Fundamental Wisdom of the Middle Way: Nāgārjuna's Mūlamadhyamakakārikā*. Oxford: Oxford University Press.
George, Theodore. 2020. *Responsibility to Understand: Hermeneutical Contours of Ethical Life*. Edinburgh: Edinburgh University Press.
Girardot, Norman J. 1983. *Myth and Meaning in Early Taoism: The Theme of Chaos (Hun-Tun)*. Berkeley: University of California Press.
Görres, Joseph von. 1810. *Mythengeschichte der asiatischen Welt*. Heidelberg: Mohr u. Zimmer.
Graham, A. C. 1989. *Disputers of the Tao: Philosophical Argument in Ancient China*. La Salle: Open Court.
Graham, A.C., tr. 1990. *The Book of Lieh-Tzu: A Classic of the Tao*. New York: Columbia University Press.
Graham, A. C., tr. 2001. *Chuang-Tzu: The Inner Chapters*. Indianapolis: Hackett.
Gregory, Peter, tr. 1995. *Inquiry into the Origin of Humanity: An Annotated Translation of Tsung-Mi's Yuan Jen Lun with a Modern Commentary*. Honolulu: University of Hawaii Press.
Guo Qingfan 郭慶藩. 1961. *Zhuangzi jishi* 莊子集釋 [Collected Annotations to Zhuangzi]. Beijing: Zhonghua shuju.
Gürster, Eugen. 1938. *Die Zukunft der Freiheit*. Zürich: Europa-Verlag.
Haas, Hans. 1909. "Tsungmi's *Yuen-zan-lun*: Eine Abhandlung über den Ursprung des Menschen." *Archiv für Religionswissenschaft* XII: 491–532.
Habermas, Jürgen. 1981. *Theorie des kommunikativen Handelns: vol. 1. Handlungsrationalität und gesellschaftliche Rationalisierung; vol. 2. Zur Kritik der funktionalistischen Vernunft*. Frankfurt: Suhrkamp.
Habermas, Jürgen. 1985. *Der Philosophische Diskurs der Moderne: Zwölf Vorlesungen*. Frankfurt: Suhrkamp.
Habermas, Jürgen. 1989. "Work and Weltanschauung: The Heidegger-Controversy from a German Perspective." *Critical Inquiry* 15: 431–56.

Habermas, Jürgen. 1990. *Strukturwandel der Öffentlichkeit: Untersuchungen zu einer Kategorie der bürgerlichen Gesellschaft*. Frankfurt: Suhrkamp.
Habermas, Jürgen. 1994. "Three Normative Models of Democracy." *Constellations* 1.1: 1–10.
Habermas, Jürgen. 1995. *Die Normalität einer Berliner Republik: Kleine politische Schriften VIII*. Frankfurt: Suhrkamp.
Habermas, Jürgen. 2022. *Ein neuer Strukturwandel der Öffentlichkeit und die deliberative Politik*. Frankfurt: Suhrkamp.
Hamar, Imre. 2007. "The Manifestation of the Absolute in the Phenomenal World: Nature Origination in Huayan Exegesis." *Bulletin de L'Ecole Francaise d'Extreme-Orient* 94: 229–50.
Han, Yongun. 2005. *Everything Yearned For: Manhae's Poems of Love and Longing*, tr. Francisca Cho. Somerville: Wisdom Publishing.
Han, Yongun. 2008. *Selected Writings of Han Yongun: From Social Darwinism to Socialism with a Buddhist Face*, tr. And ed. V. M. Tikhonov and Owen Miller. Folkestone, UK: Global Oriental.
Haraway, Donna J. 2013. *When Species Meet*. Minneapolis: University of Minnesota Press.
Harich, Wolfgang. 2016. *Frühe Schriften*, vol. 1: *Neuaufbau im zerstörten Berlin*. Marburg: Tectum Wissenschaftsverlag.
Harrington, Anne. 1996. *Reenchanted Science: Holism in German Culture from Wilhelm II to Hitler*. Princeton: Princeton University Press.
Hart, Julius. 1905. *Träume der Mittsommernacht*. Jena: Diederichs.
Hartmann, Eduard von. 1876. *Gesammelte Studien und Aufsätze gemeinverständlichen Inhalts*. Berlin: Carl Duncker's Verlag.
Hegel, G. W. F. 1986. *Phänomenologie des Geistes*. Frankfurt: Suhrkamp.
Hegel, G. W. F. 1986b. *Vorlesungen über die Philosophie der Geschichte*. Frankfurt: Suhrkamp.
Hegel, G. W. F. 1986c. *Wissenschaft der Logik*, vol. 1. Frankfurt: Suhrkamp.
Heiler, Friedrich. 1918. *Das Gebet: Eine religionsgeschichtliche und religionspsychologische Untersuchung*. Munich: Reinhardt.
Heisig, James W., and John C. Maraldo, eds. 1995. *Rude Awakenings: Zen, the Kyoto School, and the Question of Nationalism*. Honolulu: University of Hawaii Press.
Henricks, Robert G. 2000. *Lao Tzu's Tao Te Ching: A Translation of the Startling New Documents Found at Guodian*. New York: Columbia University Press.
Herman, Jonathan R. 1996. *I and Tao: Martin Buber's Encounter with Chuang Tzu*. Albany: State University of New York Press.
Herskowitz, Daniel M. 2020. *Heidegger and His Jewish Reception*. Cambridge: Cambridge University Press.
Hesse, Hermann. 1922. *Siddhartha: Eine Indische Dichtung*. Berlin: Fischer.
Hesse, Hermann. 1988. *Die Welt im Buch: Leseerfahrungen*, vol. 2. Frankfurt: Suhrkamp.
Heubel, Fabian. 2020. *Gewundene Wege nach China: Heidegger-Daoismus-Adorno*. Frankfurt: Klostermann.
Heurtebise, Jean-Yves. 2020. *Orientalisme, occidentalisme et universalisme: Histoire et méthode des représentations croisées entre mondes européens et chinois*. Paris: Eska.
Hilbert, David. 1931. "Die Grundlegung der elementaren Zahlenlehre." *Mathematische Annalen* 104.1: 485–94.
Hisamatsu, Shinichi. 1960. "The Characteristics of Oriental Nothingness." *Philosophical Studies of Japan* 2: 65–97.
Hisamatsu, Shinichi. 1994. *Die Fülle des Nichts: Vom Wesen des Zen*, tr. Takashi Hirata and Johanna Fischer. Stuttgart: Neske.

Hisamatsu, Shinichi. 2002. *Zen Talks on the Record of Linji*. Honolulu: University of Hawaii Press.
Hofmannsthal, Hugo von. 1979. *Gesammelte Werke in zehn Einzelbänden*, vol. 1. Frankfurt: Fischer Verlag.
Honneth, Axel. 2005. *Verdinglichung*. Frankfurt: Suhrkamp.
Hook, Sidney. 1959. "Pragmatism and Existentialism." *The Antioch Review* 19.2: 151–68.
Hsiao, Paul Shih-yi [Paolo Siao Sci-Yi], tr. 1941. *Il Tao-Te-King di Laotse: Prima Traduzione da un testo critico cinese*. Bari: Laterza & Figli.
Hsiao, Paul Shih-yi. 1956. "Laotse und die Technik." *Die Katholischen Missionen* 75: 72–4.
Hsiao, Paul Shih-yi. 1977. "Wir trafen uns am Holzmarktplatz." In G. Neske, *Erinnerung an Martin Heidegger*, 119–27. Pfullingen: Neske.
Hsiao, Paul Shih-yi. 1987. "Heidegger and Our Translation of the *Tao Te Ching*." In G. Parkes (ed.), *Heidegger and Asian Thought*, 93–103. Honolulu: University of Hawaii Press.
Hsu, Chiayu. 2019. "The Authenticity of Myriad Things in the *Zhuangzi*." *Religions* 10.3: 218–39.
Huang, Zongxi. 1987. *The Records of the Ming Scholars*, tr. Julia Ching. Honolulu: University of Hawaii Press.
Husserl, Edmund. 1962. *Die Krisis der europäischen Wissenschaften und die transzendentale Phänomenologie*. Den Haag: Martinus Nijhoff.
Husserl, Edmund. 1973. *Ding und Raum: Vorlesungen 1907*. Den Haag: Martinus Nijhoff.
Husserl, Edmund. 2013. *Transzendentaler Idealismus: Texte aus dem Nachlass (1908–1921)*. Dordrecht: Springer.
Imamichi, Tomonobu. 1958. "Das Seinsproblem in der Philosophie des Ostasiatischen Altertums." *Jahrbuch für Psychologie und Psychotherapie* 6: 54–64.
Imamichi, Tomonobu. 2004. *In Search of Wisdom: One Philosopher's Journey*. Tokyo: International House of Japan.
Ives, Christopher. 2009. *Imperial-Way Zen: Ichikawa Hakugen's Critique and Lingering Questions for Buddhist Ethics*. Honolulu: University of Hawaii Press.
Jacquette, Dale. 2015. *Alexius Meinong: The Shepherd of Non-Being*. Dordrecht: Springer.
Jaeggi, Rahel. 2005. *Entfremdung: Zur Aktualität eines sozialphilosophischen Problems*. Frankfurt: Campus.
Jaeggi, Rahel. 2014. *Kritik von Lebensformen*. Frankfurt: Suhrkamp.
Jaeggi, Rahel. 2023. *Fortschritt und Regression*. Frankfurt: Suhrkamp.
Jahr, Fritz. 1926. "Wissenschaft vom Leben und Sittenlehre." *Mittelschule* 40.45: 604–5.
Jahr, Fritz. 1927. "Bio-Ethik: Eine Umschau über die ethischen Beziehungen des Menschen zu Tier und Pflanze." *Kosmos: Handweiser für Naturfreunde* 24: 2–4.
Jahr, Fritz. 1930. "Gesinnungsdiktatur oder Gedankenfreiheit? Gedanken über eine liberale Gestaltung des Gesinnungunterrichts." *Die neue Erziehung* 12: 200–2.
Jahr, Fritz. 1933. "Gedanken über die liberale Gestaltung des Gesinnungsunterrichts." *Die neue Erziehung* 15: 200–2.
Jaspers, Karl. 1957. *Aus dem Ursprung denkende Metaphysiker: Anaximander, Heraklit, Parmenides, Plotin, Anselm, Spinoza, Laotse, Nagarjuna*. Munich: Piper.
Jaspers, Karl. 1966. *Anaximander, Heraclitus, Parmenides, Plotinus, Lao-Tzu, Nagarjuna*, tr. Ralph Manheim. New York: Harcourt Brace Jovanovich.
Jensen, Anthony K. 2006. "The Rogue of All Rogues: Nietzsche's Presentation of Eduard von Hartmann's Philosophie des Unbewussten and Hartmann's Response to Nietzsche." *Journal of Nietzsche Studies* 32: 41–61.

Jordan, Leo. 1932. *Schule der Abstraktion und der Dialektik: Neue Wege begrifflichen Denkens*. München: Reinhardt.
Jung, Carl G. 1966. *The Spirit in Man, Art, and Literature*. Princeton: Princeton University Press.
Kalmanson, Leah. 2020. *Cross-Cultural Existentialism: On the Meaning of Life in Asian and Western Thought*. London: Bloomsbury.
Kanthack, Katharina. 1948. *Max Scheler: Zur Krisis der Ehrfurcht*. Berlin: Minerva-Verlag.
Kanthack, Katharina. 1958. *Vom Sinn der Selbsterkenntnis*. Berlin: De Gruyter.
Kanthack, Katharina. 1964. *Das Denken Martin Heideggers: Die grosse Wende der Philosophie*, 2nd edition. Berlin: De Gruyter.
Kanthack, Katharina. 1968. "Das Wesen der Dialektik im Lichte Martin Heideggers." *Studium Generale* 21.6: 538–54.
Keyserling, Graf Hermann. 1919. *Das Reisetagebuch eines Philosophen*, 2 vols. Darmstadt: O. Reichl.
Kisiel, Theodore. 1993. *The Genesis of Heidegger's Being and Time*. Berkeley: University of California Press.
Kitayama, Junyū. 1934. *Metaphysik des Buddhismus: Versuch einer philosophischen Interpretation der Lehre Vasubandhus und seiner Schule*. Stuttgart: W. Kohlhammer.
Kitayama, Junyū. 1940. "Genjō Kōan: Aus dem Zen-Text Shōbō genzō von Patriarch Dōgen." *Quellenstudien zur Religionsgeschichte* 1: 1–15.
Kitayama, Junyū. 1942. *West-östliche Begegnung: Japans Kultur und Tradition*. Berlin: De Gruyter.
Kitayama, Junyū. 1943. *Heiligung des Staates und Verklärung des Menschen: Buddhismus und Japan*. Berlin: Limpert.
Kitayama, Junyū. 1943b. "Die moderne Philosophie Japans: Ein Beitrag zum Verständnis der 'Nishida-Philosophie.'" *Kant-Studien* 43.1/2: 263–74.
Kitayama, Junyū. 1944. *Heroisches Ethos: Das Heldische in Japan*. Berlin: De Gruyter.
Klages, Ludwig. 1944. *Rhythmem und Runen*. Leipzig: J.A. Barth.
Klages, Ludwig. 1981. *Der Geist als Widersacher der Seele*, 6th edition. Bonn: Bouvier Verlag.
Klein, Esther. 2010. "Were There 'Inner Chapters' in the Warring States? A New Examination of Evidence about the *Zhuangzi*." *T'oung Pao* 96.4: 299–369.
Kohn, Livia. 2014. *Zhuangzi: Text and Context*. St. Petersburg: Three Pines Press.
Krause, Friedrich. 1923. *Ju-Tao-Fo: Die Religiösen und Philosophischen Systeme Ostasiens*. München: Reinhardt.
Krauss, Oskar. 1931. "Über Alles und Nichts." *Philosophische Hefte* 2: 140–6.
Krieck, Ernst. 1934. *Wissenschaft, Weltanschauung, Hochschulreform*. Leipzig: Armanen-Verlag.
Krieck, Ernst. 1943. *Heil und Kraft: Ein Buch germanischer Weltweisheit*. Leipzig: Armanen-Verlag.
Kroll, Paul W. 1996. "On 'Far Roaming.'" *Journal of the American Oriental Society* 116.4: 653–69.
Krüger, Gerhard. 1950. "Martin Heidegger und der Humanismus." *Theologische Rundschau* 18.2: 148–78.
Krummel, John W. M. 2018. "On (the) Nothing: Heidegger and Nishida." *Continental Philosophy Review* 51.2: 239–68.
Kubota, Hiroshi. 2008. "Strategies in Representing 'Japanese Religion' during the National Socialist Period: The Cases of Kitayama Junyû and Wilhelm Gundert."

In Horst Junginger (ed.), *The Study of Religion under the Impact of Fascism*, 613–33. Leiden: Brill.
Kwee, Swan Liat. 1953. *Methods of Comparative Philosophy*. Leiden: Leiden University Dissertation.
Kwok, Sai Hang. 2016. "Zhuangzi's Philosophy of Thing." *Asian Philosophy* 26.4: 294–310.
Lacan, Jacques. 1992. *The Seminar of Jacques Lacan, Book VII: The Ethics of Psychoanalysis, 1959–1960*. London: W.W. Norton.
Lau, D. C. and Roger T. Ames, tr. 1998. *Yuan Dao: Tracing Dao to Its Source*. New York: Ballantine Books.
Lau, Kwok-Ying. 2016. *Phenomenology and Intercultural Understanding: Toward a New Cultural Flesh*. Cham: Springer.
[Leibniz, G. W. 1703] Leibnitz, Godefroy-Guillaume. 1703. "Explication de l'arithmétique binaire, qui se sert des seuls caractères O et I avec des remarques sur son utilité et sur ce qu'elle donne le sens des anciennes figures chinoises de Fohy." *Mémoires de mathématique et de physique de l'Académie royale des sciences* 3: 85–9. Paris: Académie royale des sciences.
Leibniz, G. W. 1842. *Œuvres de Leibniz*, vol. 2. Paris: Charpentier.
Levinas, Emmanuel. 1932. "Martin Heidegger et l'ontologie." *Revue Philosophique de la France et de l'Étranger* 113: 395–431.
Levinas, Emmanuel. 1969. *Totality and Infinity: An Essay on Exteriority*, tr. Alphonso Lingis. Pittsburgh: Duquesne University Press.
Levinas, Emmanuel. 1982. *De l'évasion*. Montpellier: Fata Morgana.
Levinas, Emmanuel. 1990. *Difficult Freedom: Essays on Judaism*. Baltimore: Johns Hopkins University Press.
Li, Chenyang. 1999. *The Tao Encounters the West: Explorations in Comparative Philosophy*. Albany: State University of New York Press.
Li, Disheng 李滌生. 1994. *Xunzi jishi* 荀子集釋 [Collected Explanations of Xunzi]. Taipei: Xuesheng shuju.
Liu, An, and John S. Major, tr. 2010. *The Huainanzi: A Guide to the Theory and Practice of Government in Early Han China*. New York: Columbia University Press.
Liu, Jung-Hsien 劉榮賢. 2004. *Zhuangzi waiza pian yanjiu* 莊子外雜篇研究 [A Study of the Outer and Miscellaneous Chapters of Zhuangzi]. Taipei: Lianjing chuban shiye gufen youxian gongsi.
Liu, Xiaogan. 1994. *Classifying the Zhuangzi Chapters*. Ann Arbor: Michigan.
Liu, Xiaogan. 2015. "Laozi's Philosophy: Textual and Conceptual Analyses." In Liu Xiaogan (ed.), *Dao Companion to Daoist Philosophy*, 71–100. Dordrecht: Springer.
Liu, Yiqing. 2002. *Shih-shuo Hsin-Yü: A New Account of Tales of the World*. Ann Arbor: Center for Chinese Studies, University of Michigan.
Lotze, Hermann. 1879. *Metaphysik*, vol. 1. Leipzig: Hirzel.
Lou, Yulie 樓宇烈. 1980. *Wang Bi ji jiao shi* 王弼集校釋 [Collection of Wang Bi's Works: Critical Edition with Annotations]. Beijing: Zhonghua Shuju.
Löwith, Karl. 1983. *Weltgeschichte und Heilsgeschehen: Zur Kritik der Geschichtsphilosophie*. Stuttgart: Metzler.
Löwith, Karl. 2016. *Mein Leben in Deutschland vor und nach 1933: Ein Bericht*. Stuttgart: Metzler.
Lukács, György. 1951. *Existentialismus oder Marxismus?* Berlin: Aufbau Verlag.
Lukács, György. 1955. *Die Zerstörung der Vernunft: Der Weg des Irrationalismus von Schelling zu Hitler*. Berlin: Aufbau Verlag.

Lüth, Paul. 1944. *Die japanische Philosophie: Versuch einer Gesamtdarstellung unter Berücksichtigung der Anfänge in Mythus und Religion.* Tübingen: J. C. B. Mohr.

Luxemburg, Rosa. 1922. *Die russische Revolution: Eine kritische Würdigung,* ed. Paul Levi. Berlin-Fichtenau: Gesellschaft und Erziehung.

Lynn, Richard J., tr. 1994. *The Classic of Changes: A New Translation of the I Ching as Interpreted by Wang Bi.* New York: Columbia University Press.

Lynn, Richard J., tr. 1999. *The Classic of the Dao and Virtue: A New Translation of the Tao-te Ching of Laozi as Interpreted by Wang Bi.* New York: Columbia University Press.

Lynn, Richard J. 2015. "Wang Bi and *Xuanxue.*" In Xiaogan Liu (ed.), *Dao Companion to Daoist Philosophy,* 369–96. Dordrecht: Springer.

Lynn, Richard J., tr. 2022. *Zhuangzi: A New Translation of the Sayings of Master Zhuang as Interpreted by Guo Xiang.* New York: Columbia University Press.

Lyotard, Jean-François. 1994. "Nietzsche and the Inhuman," interview with Richard Beardsworth. *Journal of Nietzsche Studies* 7: 67–130.

Ma, Lin. 2007. *Heidegger on East-West Dialogue: Anticipating the Event.* London: Routledge.

Mair, Victor H. 1991. "[The] File [on the Cosmic] Track [and Individual] Dough[tiness]: Introduction and Notes for a Translation of the Ma-wang-tui Manuscripts of the Lao Tzu [Old Master]." *Sino-Platonic Papers* 20: 1–68.

Makeham, John, tr. 2002. *Xu Gan: Balanced Discourses.* New Haven: Yale University Press.

Malpas, Jeff. 2008. *Heidegger's Topology: Being, Place, World.* Cambridge: MIT press.

Maly, Kenneth. 2020. *Five Ground-Breaking Moments in Heidegger's Thinking.* Toronto: University of Toronto Press.

Mandel, Hermann. 1912. *Die Erkenntnis des Übersinnlichen ein Grundriss der systematischen Theologie: System der Ethik als Grundlegung der Religion.* Leipzig: Deichert.

Mann, Klaus. 1949. "Europe's Search for a New Credo." *Tomorrow* 8.10: 3–11.

Mattice, Sarah A. 2021. *Exploring the Heart Sutra.* Lanham, MD: Lexington Books.

McNeill, William. 2006. *The Time of Life: Heidegger and Ēthos.* Albany: State University of New York Press.

Mendes-Flohr, Paul. 2014. "Martin Buber and Martin Heidegger in Dialogue." *The Journal of Religion* 94.1: 2–25.

Meyer, Hans. 1936. *Das Wesen der Philosophie und die Philosophischen Probleme: Zugleich Eine Einführung in die Philosophie des Gegenwart.* Bonn: P. Hanstein.

Michael, Thomas. 2020. "Heidegger's Legacy for Comparative Philosophy and the *Laozi.*" *International Journal of China Studies* 11.2: 299–318.

Misch, Georg. 1911. "Von den Gestaltungen der Persönlichkeit." In Wilhelm Dilthey and Max Frischeisen-Köhler (eds.), *Weltanschauung Philosophie und Religion in Darstellungen,* 81–126. Berlin: Reichl & Co.

Misch, Georg. 1926. *Der Weg in die Philosophie: Eine philosophische Fibel.* Leipzig: Teubner./1950. Revised and expanded edition. Bern: A. Francke.

Misch, Georg. 1930. *Lebensphilosophie und Phänomenologie: Eine Auseinandersetzung der Diltheyschen Richtung mit Heidegger und Husserl.* Bonn: Cohen.

Misch, Georg. 1950. *The Dawn of Philosophy: A Philosophical Primer.* London: Routledge and Kegan Paul.

Mitchell, Andrew J. 2015. *The Fourfold: Reading the Late Heidegger.* Evanston: Northwestern University Press.

Monk, Ray. 2014. *Robert Oppenheimer: A Life inside the Center.* New York: Anchor.

Moore, Ian Alexander. 2019. *Eckhart, Heidegger, and the Imperative of Releasement*. Albany: State University of New York Press.

Naber, A. 1947. "Von der Philosophie des "Nichts" zur Philosophie des "Seins selbst": Zurgrossen Wende im Philosophieren M. Heideggers." *En Gregorianum* 28: 357–78.

Nara, Hiroshi. 2004. *The Structure of Detachment: The Aesthetic Vision of Kuki Shūzō with a Translation of "Iki no kōzō."* Honolulu: University of Hawaii Press.

Nelson, Eric S. 2004. "Responding to Heaven and Earth: Daoism, Heidegger, and Ecology." *Environmental Philosophy* 1.2: 65–74.

Nelson, Eric S. 2006. "Die formale Anzeige der Faktizität als Frage der Logik." In Alfred Denker and Holger Zaborowski (eds.), *Heidegger und die Logik*, 31–48. Amsterdam: Rodopi.

Nelson, Eric S. 2007. "History as Decision and Event in Heidegger." *Arhe* 8: 97–115.

Nelson, Eric S. 2008. "Questioning Dao: Skepticism, Mysticism, and Ethics in the *Zhuangzi*." *International Journal of the Asian Philosophical Association* 1: 5–19.

Nelson, Eric S. 2009. "Responding with Dao: Early Daoist Ethics and the Environment." *Philosophy East and West* 59.3: 294–316.

Nelson, Eric S. 2011. "The *Yijing* and Philosophy: From Leibniz to Derrida." *Journal of Chinese Philosophy* 38.3: 377–96.

Nelson, Eric S. 2013. "Heidegger and Carnap: Disagreeing about Nothing?" In François Raffoul, Eric S. Nelson (eds.), *Bloomsbury Companion to Heidegger*, 151–6. London: Bloomsbury Press.

Nelson, Eric S. 2014. "The Human and the Inhuman: Ethics and Religion in the *Zhuangzi*." *Journal of Chinese Philosophy* 41.S1: 723–39.

Nelson, Eric S. 2016. "Heidegger's Failure to Overcome Transcendental Philosophy." In Halla Kim and Steven Hoeltzel (eds.), *Transcendental Inquiry: Its History, Methods and Critiques*, 159–79. London: Palgrave Macmillan.

Nelson, Eric S. 2017. *Chinese and Buddhist Philosophy in Early Twentieth-Century German Thought*. London: Bloomsbury.

Nelson, Eric S. 2017b. "Heidegger's Black Notebooks: National Socialism, Antisemitism, and the History of Being." *Heidegger-Jahrbuch* 11: 77–88.

Nelson, Eric S. 2019. "Introduction: Wilhelm Dilthey in Context." In Eric S. Nelson (ed.), *Interpreting Dilthey: Critical Essays*, 10–36. Cambridge: Cambridge University Press.

Nelson, Eric S. 2020. *Daoism and Environmental Philosophy: Nourishing Life*. London: Routledge.

Nelson, Eric S. 2020b. "Language and Nothingness in Wang Bi." In David Chai (ed.), *Dao Companion to Xuanxue 玄學 (Neo-Daoism)*, 287–300. Cham: Springer.

Nelson, Eric S. 2020c. *Levinas, Adorno, and the Ethics of the Material Other*. Albany: State University of New York Press.

Nelson, Eric S. 2020d. "Martin Buber's Phenomenological Interpretation of Laozi's *Daodejing*." In David Chai (ed.), *Daoist Encounters with Phenomenology*, 105–20. London: Bloomsbury.

Nelson, Eric S. 2022. "Heidegger and the German Reception of the *Zhuangzi*." In Kim-chong Chong (ed.), *Dao Companion to the Philosophy of the Zhuangzi*, 787–806. Cham: Springer.

Nelson, Eric S. 2022b. "Schopenhauer, Existential Negativity, and Buddhist Nothingness." *Journal of Chinese Philosophy* 49.1: 83–96.

Nelson, Eric S. 2022c. "Thing and World in Laozi and Heidegger." In David Chai (ed.), *Daoist Resonances in Heidegger: Exploring a Forgotten Debt*, 141–62. London: Bloomsbury.

Nelson, Eric S. 2023. "Emptiness, Negation, and Skepticism in Nāgārjuna and Sengzhao." *Asian Philosophy* 33.2: 125–44.
Nelson, Eric S. 2023b. "Martin Heidegger and Kitayama Junyū: Nothingness, Emptiness, and the Thing." *Asian Studies* 11.1: 27–50.
Neurath, Otto. 1921. *Anti-Spengler*. Munich: Callwey.
Neurath, Otto. 1933. *Einheitswissenschaft und Psychologie*. Vienna: Gerold & Co.
Nishida, Kitarō. 1936. "Brief an den Schriftleiter der Zeitschrift Risō." *Cultural Nippon* 4.2: 123–8.
Nishida, Kitarō. 1936b. "Logik und Leben." *Cultural Nippon* 4.4: 365–70.
Nishida, Kitarō. 1939. "Die morgenländischen und abendländischen Kulturformen in alter Zeit vom metaphysischen Standpunkte aus gesehen." *Abhandlungen der Preussischen Akademie der Wissenschaften*. Philosophisch-Historische Klasse 19. Berlin: De Gruyter.
Nishida, Kitarō. 1943. *Die intelligible Welt: Drei philosophische Abhandlungen*. Berlin: De Gruyter.
Nishida, Kitarō. 1987. *Last Writings: Nothingness and the Religious Worldview*. Honolulu: University of Hawaii Press.
Nishitani, Keiji. 1966. "Preliminary Remark" to Heidegger, "Two Addresses." *The Eastern Buddhist* 1.2: 48–59.
Nishitani, Keiji. 1983. *Religion and Nothingness*. Berkeley: University of California Press.
Nishitani, Keiji. 1989. *The Self-Overcoming of Nihilism*. Albany: State University of New York Press.
Okakura, Kakuzō. 1919. *Das Buch vom Tee*. Leipzig: Insel.
Osaki, Harumi. 2019. *Nothingness in the Heart of Empire: The Moral and Political Philosophy of the Kyoto School in Imperial Japan*. Albany: State University of New York Press.
Pang-White, Ann A. 2009. "Nature, Interthing Intersubjectivity, and the Environment: A Comparative Analysis of Kant and Daoism." *Dao: A Journal of Comparative Philosophy* 8.1: 61–78.
Pang-White, Ann A. 2016. "Daoist *Ci* 慈, Feminist Ethics of Care, and the Dilemma of Nature." *Journal of Chinese Philosophy* 43.3–4: 275–94.
Perkins, Franklin. 2010. "Of Fish and Men: Species Difference and the Strangeness of Being Human in the *Zhuangzi*." *The Harvard Review of Philosophy* 17.1: 118–36.
Perkins, Franklin. 2015. "What Is a Thing (*Wu* 物)? The Problem of Individuation in Early Chinese Metaphysics.". In Chenyang Li, Franklin Perkins (eds.), *Chinese Metaphysics and Its Problems*, 54–68. Cambridge: Cambridge University Press.
Petzet, Heinrich Wiegand. 1993. *Encounters and Dialogues with Martin Heidegger, 1929–1976*, tr. Parvis Emad and Kenneth Maly. Chicago: University of Chicago Press.
Pines, Yuri. 2002. "Lexical Changes in Zhanguo Texts." *Journal of the American Oriental Society* 122.4: 691–705.
Plaenckner, Reinhold von, tr. 1870. *Lao-Tse Tao-Te-King: Der Weg zur Tugend*. Leipzig: F. A. Brockhaus.
Pöggeler, Otto. 1987. "West-East Dialogue: Heidegger and Lao-Tzu." In G. Parkes (ed.), *Heidegger and Asian Thought*, 47–78. Honolulu: University of Hawaii Press.
Pöggeler, Otto. 1990. *Der Denkweg Martin Heideggers*, 3rd edition. Pfullingen: Neske.
Polt, Richard. 2019. *Time and Trauma: Thinking through Heidegger in the Thirties*. London: Rowman & Littlefield.
Priest, Graham. 2018. *The Fifth Corner of Four: An Essay on Buddhist Metaphysics and the Catuṣkoṭi*. Oxford: Oxford University Press.

Radhakrishnan, Sarvepalli. 1953. *History of Philosophy: Eastern and Western*. London: Allen & Unwin.
Raffoul, François. 1998. *Heidegger and the Subject*. Amherst: Humanity Books.
Raffoul, François. 2010. *The Origins of Responsibility*. Bloomington: Indiana University Press.
Raffoul, François. 2020. *Thinking the Event*. Bloomington: Indiana University Press.
Rapp, John A. 2012. *Daoism and Anarchism: Critiques of State Autonomy in Ancient and Modern China*. London: Bloomsbury.
Rehm, Walter. 1930. "Wirklichkeitsdemut und Dingmystik." *Logos* 19: 297–358.
Rickett, W. A., tr. 1998. *Guanzi: Political, Economic, and Philosophical Essays from Early China*, 2 volumes. Princeton: Princeton University Press.
Rorty, Richard. 1993. "Wittgenstein, Heidegger, and the Reification of Language." In Charles Guignon (ed.), *The Cambridge Companion to Heidegger*, 337–57. Cambridge: Cambridge University Press.
Rošker, Jana S. 2021. *Interpreting Chinese Philosophy: A New Methodology*. London: Bloomsbury Publishing.
Rotermund, Wilhelm. 1874. *Die Ethik Lao-tse's mit besonderer Bezugnahme auf die buddhistische Moral*. Gotha: Perthes.
Rousselle, Erwin. 1935. "Lau-Dsi's Gang durch die Seele, Geschichte und Welt: Versuch einer Deutung." *Eranos-Jahrbuch* III: 179–205.
Śāntideva. 1998. *The Bodhicaryāvatāra*, tr. K. Crosby, A. Skilton. Oxford: Oxford University Press.
Sartre, Jean-Paul. 1943. *L'Être et le néant*. Paris: Gallimard.
Schalow, Frank. 2012. *The Incarnality of Being: The Earth, Animals, and the Body in Heidegger's Thought*. Albany: State University of New York Press.
Schalow, Frank. 2021. *Heidegger's Ecological Turn: Community and Practice for Future Generations*. London: Routledge.
Schelling, Friedrich Wilhelm Joseph. 1857. *Sämmtliche Werke 2.2: Philosophie der Mythologie*. Stuttgart: Cotta.
Schinzinger, Robert. 1940. "Über Kitarô Nishidas Philosophie." *Monumenta Nipponica* 3.1: 28–39.
Schleiermacher, Friedrich. 2012. *Vorlesungen zur Hermeneutik und Kritik*. Berlin: De Gruyter.
Schönfeld, Martin, and Xia Chen. 2019. "Daoism and the Project of an Ecological Civilization or *Shengtai Wenming* 生态文明." *Religions* 10.11: 630–45.
Schopenhauer, Arthur. 1977. *Zürcher Ausgabe Werke in 10 Bänden*, 10 volumes, ed. Arthur Hübscher. Zürich: Diogenes.
Schürmann, Reiner. 1973. "Heidegger and Meister Eckhart on Releasement." *Research in Phenomenology* 3: 95–119.
Seekamp, Hans-Jürgen. 1960. "A Literary Bridge between Germany and Asia." *United Asia: International Journal of Asian Affairs* 12: 71–2.
Shang, Ge Ling. 2006. *Liberation as Affirmation: The Religiosity of Zhuangzi and Nietzsche*. Albany: State University of New York.
Sheehan, Thomas. 2014. *Making Sense of Heidegger: A Paradigm Shift*. London: Rowman & Littlefield.
Siderits, Mark and Shōryū Katsura. 2013. *Nāgārjuna's Middle Way: Mūlamadhyamakakārikā*. Boston: Wisdom Publications.
Sloterdijk, Peter. 1989. *Eurotaoismus: Zur Kritik der politischen Kinetik*. Frankfurt: Suhrkamp.

Spengler, Oswald. 1922. *Der Untergang des Abendlandes; Umrisse einer Morphologie der Weltgeschichte*, vol. 1. Munich: Beck.
Steben, Barry D. 2012. "The Culture of Music and Ritual in Pre-Han Confucian Thought: Exalting the Power of Music in Human Life." [Ajia Bunka Kenkyū] アジア文化研究 38: 105–24.
Sterckx, Roel. 2011. *Food, Sacrifice, and Sagehood in Early China*. Cambridge: Cambridge University Press.
Strauss, Victor von, tr. 1870. *Lao-Tse's Tao Te King*. Leipzig: Verlag von Friedrich Fleischer.
Strauss, Victor von. 1879. *Essays zur Allgemeinen Religionswissenschaft*. Heidelberg: Carl Winter's Universitätsbuchhandlung.
Szpilman, Christopher W. 2013. "Kanokogi Kazunobu: Pioneer of Platonic Fascism and Imperial Pan-Asianism." *Monumenta Nipponica* 68.2: 233–80.
Taketi T. 1940. "Japanische Philosophie der Gegenwart." *Blätter für Deutsche Philosophie* 14.3: 277–99.
Takeuchi, Yoshinori. 2004. "The Philosophy of Nishida." In Frederick Franck (ed.), *The Buddha Eye: An Anthology of the Kyoto School and Its Contemporaries*, 3rd edition. Bloomington: World Wisdom.
Trawny, Peter. 1997. *Heideggers Phänomenologie der Welt*. Freiburg: Alber.
Trawny, Peter. 2014. *Irrnisfuge*. Berlin: Matthes & Seitz.
Tugendhat, Ernst. 2003. *Egozentrizität und Mystik: Eine anthropologische Studie*. München: CH Beck.
Umehara, Takeshi. 1970. "Heidegger and Buddhism." *Philosophy East and West* 20.3: 271–81.
Ulenbrook, Jan, tr. 1962. *Lau Dse, Dau Dö Djing: Das Buch vom Rechten Wege und von der Rechten Gesinnung*. Bremen: Carl Schünemann Verlag.
Victoria, Brian. 2003. *Zen War Stories*. London: Routledge.
Wahl, Jean. 1957. *Traité de métaphysique*. Paris: Payot.
Wang, Youru. 2003. *Linguistic Strategies in Daoist Zhuangzi and Chan Buddhism: The Other Way of Speaking*. London: Routledge.
Wang, Qingjie James. 2001. "*Heng* and Temporality of Dao: Laozi and Heidegger." *Dao: A Journal of Comparative Philosophy* 1.1: 55–71.
Wang, Qingjie James. 2016. "Thing-ing and No-Thing in Heidegger, Kant, and Laozi." *Dao: A Journal of Comparative Philosophy* 15.2: 159–74.
Wang, Qingjie James. 2020. "On Chinese Receptions and Translations of Heidegger's *Dasein*." *Continental Philosophy Review* 53.4: 449–63.
Wang, Robin. 2012. *Yinyang: The Way of Heaven and Earth in Chinese Thought and Culture*. Cambridge: Cambridge University Press.
Wang, Zhongjiang. 2016. *Order in Early Chinese Excavated Texts: Natural, Supernatural, and Legal Approaches*. New York: Palgrave Macmillan.
Wenning, Mario. 2011. "Daoism as Critical Theory." *Comparative Philosophy* 2.2: 50–71.
Wenning, Mario. 2014. "Heidegger and Zhuangzi on the Nonhuman: Towards a Transcultural Critique of (Post) humanism." In Neil Dalal, Chloë Taylor (eds.), *Asian Perspectives on Animal Ethics: Rethinking the Nonhuman*, 93–111. London: Routledge.
Wenning, Mario. 2017. "Mysticism and Peace of Mind: Reflections on Tugendhat and Daoism." *Frontiers of Philosophy in China* 12.4: 554–71.
Wilhelm, Richard, tr. 1911. *Lao-tse: Tao te King: Das Buch des alten Meisters vom Sinn und Leben*. Jena: Eugen Diederichs.

Wilhelm, Richard, tr. 1912. *Dschuang Dsi: Das wahre Buch vom südlichen Blütenland. Nan Hua Dschen Ging. Aus dem Chinesischen verdeutscht und erläutert.* Jena: Eugen Diederichs.

Wilhelm, Richard, tr. 1921. *Liä Dsi: Das wahre Buch vom quellenden Urgrund.* Jena: Eugen Diederichs.

Wilhelm, Richard. 1925. *Lao-Tse und der Taoismus.* Stuttgart: Frommann.

Wilhelm, Richard. 1929. *Chinesische Philosophie.* Breslau: Hirt.

Wilhelm, Richard, tr. 1948. *Das Geheimnis der Goldenen Blüte: Mit Einem Europäischen Kommentar von Carl G. Jung.* Zürich: Rascher.

Windelband, Wilhelm. 1880. *Geschichte der Neueren Philosophie in ihrem Zusammenhange mit der allgemeinen Cultur und den besonderen Wissenschaften,* vol. 2: *Von Kant bis Hegel und Herbart.* Leipzig: Breitkopf und Haertel.

Wirth, Jason M. 2019. *Nietzsche and Other Buddhas: Philosophy after Comparative Philosophy.* Bloomington: Indiana University Press.

Wirth, Jason M. 2020. "Martin Buber's Dao." In David Chai (ed.), *Daoist Encounters with Phenomenology,* 121–34. London: Bloomsbury.

Wittgenstein, Ludwig. 1969. *On Certainty.* Oxford: Blackwell.

Wohlfart, Günter. 2003. "Heidegger and Laozi: *Wu* (Nothing): On Chapter 11 of the *Daodejing.*" *Journal of Chinese Philosophy* 30.1: 39–59.

Wolfson, Elliot R. 2018. *The Duplicity of Philosophy's Shadow: Heidegger, Nazism, and the Jewish Other.* New York: Columbia University Press.

Wolfson, Elliot R. 2019. *Heidegger and Kabbalah: Hidden Gnosis and the Path of Poiēsis.* Bloomington: Indiana University Press.

Wu, Shengqing. 2014. *Modern Archaics: Continuity and Innovation in the Chinese Lyric Tradition, 1900-1937.* Cambridge: Harvard University Asia Center.

Xia, Kejun 夏可君. 2017. *Yige dengdai yu wuyong de minzu: Zhuangzi yu Haidege'er de dierci zhuanxiang* 一個等待與無用的民族: 莊子與海德格爾的第二次轉向 [A Waiting and Useless People: Zhuangzi and Heidegger's Second Turn]. Beijing: Beijing daxue chubanshe.

Yang, Rur-Bin 楊儒賓, ed. 1993. *Zhongguo gudai sixiang de qilun yu shenti guan* 中國古代思想的氣論與身體觀 [The Concepts of *Qi* and Body in Chinese Ancient Thought]. Taipei: Juliu chubanshe.

Yates, Robin, tr. 1997. *Five Lost Classics: Dao, Huanglao, and Yinyang in Han China.* New York: Ballantine Books.

Yu, Jie. 2018. *The Taoist Pedagogy of Pathmarks: Critical Reflections upon Heidegger, Lao Tzu, and Dewey.* New York: Palgrave Macmillan.

Yü, Ying-shih. 1985. "Individualism and the Neo-Taoist Movement in Wei-Chin China." In Donald Munro (ed.), *Individualism and Holism: Studies in Confucian and Taoist Values,* 121–55. Ann Arbor: University of Michigan Press.

Yusa, Michiko. 1998. "Philosophy and Inflation: Miki Kiyoshi in Weimar Germany, 1922-1924." *Monumenta Nipponica* 53.1: 45–71.

Zhao, Jianjun 趙建軍. 2006. *Zuowei Zhongguo gudai shenmei fanchou de ziran* 作為中國古代審美範疇的自然 [Nature as an Aesthetic Category in Ancient China]. Beijing: Zhongguo shehui kexue chubanshe.

Zimmerman, Michael E. 1990. *Heidegger's Confrontation with Modernity: Technology, Politics, and Art.* Bloomington: Indiana University Press.

Ziporyn, Brook. 2003. *The Penumbra Unbound: The Neo-Taoist Philosophy of Guo Xiang.* Albany: State University of New York Press.

Ziporyn, Brook, tr. 2020. *Zhuangzi: The Complete Writings.* Indianapolis: Hackett Publishing.

Index

action/acting, way-making 125–9
Adorno, Theodor 49, 53, 74, 123, 130, 189, 205 n.20, 206 n.21, 206 n.23, 207 n.32, 210 n.49, 217 n.34, 218 n.35, 218 n.46
agency 124, 126, 127
alienation 188–90
All Things Flow in Form (*Fan Wu Liu Xing* 凡物流形) 23
Anesaki Masaharu 姉崎正治 177
annihilation, emptiness and 80–1, 94, 149, 150, 153
anti-humanism 120, 125
anxiety (*Angst*) 122, 150
aperture (*kong* 孔) 61, 137
appropriative/enowning event (*Ereignis*) 108, 215 n.4
Arendt, Hannah 86, 205 n.11
autopoiesis 7, 15, 42–3, 121, 163, 198, 215 n.6, 216 n.22, 220 n.2
  and sympoiesis 42

Baeumler, Alfred 121, 191
Balfour, Frederic Henry 16
bamboo manuscripts 5
Bao Jingyan 鮑敬言 190, 203 n.52
Barth, Karl 176, 224 n.17
Beaufret, Jean 101, 124, 125
Befindlichkeit (attunement, disposedness) 31
being-with/being and beings 9, 17, 22, 52, 59, 108, 187, 225 n.1
Benn, Gottfried 122
Bhikkhu Maha Mani 5, 171
biocentrism 120, 154, 197
bioethics 154
Bloch, Ernst 60, 116–17, 207 n.6, 211 n.53
Blochmann, Elisabeth 86
Bodmershof, Imma von 176
Böhme, Jakob 21, 99

Book of Changes (*Yijing* 易經) 24, 26, 28, 49, 94, 134, 136
The Book of Five Rings (*Gorin no Sho* 五輪書) (Miyamoto Musashi 宮本武蔵) 179
Book of Rites (*Liji* 禮記) 24, 135
The Book of Tea (Okakura Kakuzō 岡倉覚三) 15, 17, 154, 179
Book of Twists and Turns (*Buch der Wendungen*) (Brecht) 60
Brecht, Bertolt 60
Bṛhadāraṇyaka Upaniṣad 172
Buber, Martin 3, 16, 199 n.1, 211 n.53
  Daodejing 103
  on Daoism 57, 103
  on *Gelassenheit* word 96
  on hiddenness 16, 78
  "The Religious World-Conception" 57
  on things 72
  Zhuangzi 89, 103, 112
Buddhism 1–3, 5, 220 n.19
  Daoism and 8, 33–4
  European 154, 158–9, 168
  nihilistic morality of 140
  no-self 221 n.12
  nothingness and emptiness 134, 140–5, 152–5, 192–5
  perfection of wisdom 33
  and self-emptiness 140–2
  Zen Buddhism 160–1, 171, 173, 176, 184
  Zhuangzi and 33–5
Butcher Ding (Paoding 庖丁) 31

Cang Jie 倉頡 49
care (*ci* 慈) 9, 190, 202 n.40
Carnap, Rudolf 134, 153, 168
Carus, Paul 20
Chinese philosophy
  of *dao* in the *Daodejing* 60, 64
  images of gathering and emptiness 60–2

interpretations of empty vessel 67–8
landscape painting 62
negation and nothingness in 135–7, 139
Confucianism 23–6, 41, 116
   and Oriental nothingness 139–40
counterparting (*gegnen*) 76

Dao'an 道安 33
Daodejing 道德經 1, 3, 16, 196–7
   the *dao* in 60
   darkness 111–13
   emptiness in 61, 71
   event in 6
   Gelassenheit with 20–1
   guiding word *dao* 62
   mystery in 65
   not- expressions 137–40
   nothingness 136–7
   in *The Philosophy of Mythology* 65
   poetic thinking 127–8
   qi 器 in 65–6
   self-naturing in 28–9
   thing and world 1, 24, 59
   translation of 16, 20, 27, 64
   way of reversal in 110
   wuwei and *ziran* 72–4
   ziran 7, 72–4
Daoism 2, 3, 14, 74, 217 n.34
   anti-humanism with 125
   autopoiesis 42–3
   Bloch on 60, 116–17
   Chinese sources 5
   Daoistic Buddhism 33–4
   emptiness of 7–8, 15
   ethics and moral theory 117–18
   in European philosophy 3–5
   freedom 88
   German modernity 59–60
   image and word 89
   Lao-Zhuang 33, 51, 90, 177
   Laozi on 14
   nothingness of 7–8
   pluralistic conception 219 n.7–8
   purposive and nonpurposive forms 218 n.48
   religious 14, 136
   sense of life 5
   Ziranist 9, 10, 30, 130, 197
Daoistic Buddhism 33–4, 143–5

dao 道 2, 38, 96, 107–8
   as empty vessel 66, 68
   and *ethos* 9–10, 115–16
   freedom of 32
   gathering in emptiness 60–1
   as guiding-word 62–3
   images of 60
   objectives 4
darkness, sense of 15–16, 78–9, 111–13
Dasein-centric approach 6, 9, 37
decisionistic language 120
Dehn, Fritz 125
Derrida, Jacques, *The Beast and the Sovereign* 41
desertification 93
destruction of thing 23, 76, 80, 148
Dialectic of Enlightenment (Adorno and Horkheimer) 32, 56
Dialogue with Heidegger (Beaufret) 101
Die japanische Philosophie (Lüth) 177
Döblin, Alfred 59–60, 94, 154
Dōgen Zenji 道元禅師 173
Dvořák, Rudolf 60

earth and humanity 47, 80, 93
East Asian Philosophy 31, 51, 103, 105
   Daodejing (see *Daodejing* 道德經)
   Heidegger's entanglements with 170–1
   of nothingness 134, 135, 154, 168, 177, 187, 197
   Zhuangzi (see *Zhuangzi* 莊子)
Eckhart, Meister 20, 72–3
   Gelassenheit 20–1, 201 n.16
Eichhorn, Werner 32, 88
elemental nothingness 162–5
emptiness 2, 3, 15, 29, 50–3, 221 n.4. *See also* empty vessels
   of beings (*Seiende*) 180
   in Buddhist contexts 134, 192–5
   of Daoism 7–8, 15
   between Europe and Asia 171–6
   functions of 183–4
   gatherings in 60–2, 161–2
   Hegel's negativity 182–3
   in Heidegger context 148
   hermeneutics of 182–3
   holding (containing vessel) 78–9
   and humility 68
   implications of 70–1

Madhyamaka teaching on 142–3
openness of being 160–1
political implications 195–6
of self and world 220 n.18
and the singular 150–2
spacing of things 176–9
Theravāda and Mādhyamika teachings of 178
of words and things 179–84
empty vessels 65–7
availability and usefulness of the drink 74–6
Chinese interpretations of 67–8
in *Daodejing* 181
expansiveness 75–6
and nothingness 72
religious ritual and sacrifice 79
shaping of 80–1
the thing, and releasement 71–2
enregioning (*vergegnen*) 76
Ereignis (being's appropriating event) 63
errancy 111–13
essencing (*Wesen*) 108
ethos 9–10, 15, 217 n.34
action and 126, 128–30
conception of 116
dao and 115–16
ethics and moral theory 117–18
Laozian 30, 116
without mysticism 19–22
European Buddhism 154, 158–9, 168
"Europe's Search for a New Credo" (Mann) 168
Evers, Hans Gerhard 125
expansiveness 75–6

Faber, Ernst 60
fascism 124–5, 195, 212 n.9
Fazang 法藏 151, 194–5
Federmann, Hertha 21, 45, 75
Fischer, Otto, Daoism 62, 63
fourfold conception 45–6
freedom 15, 30–3
alienation and 189
essencing of truth 112
of stillness 109
stimulus-response model 31
with things 33–4, 98
of *ziran* 145, 216 n.11

Fundamental Verses of the Middle Way (*Mūlamadhyamakakārikā*) (Nāgārjuna) 141

gatherings in emptiness 60–2, 161–2
Gautama, Siddhārtha 140
George, Stefan 85
German contexts, Buddhism and nothingness in 152–5
Giles, Herbert A. 16
Gotthelf, Jeremias 41
Guo Xiang 郭象 5, 33, 34, 67, 95, 203 n.62

Habermas, Jürgen 100, 191, 205 n.11, 206 n.23, 212 n.9, 217 n.26, 226 n.22
Hakuin Ekaku 白隠慧鶴 176
Han Yongun. *See* Manhae
Hart, Julius 87, 190
healing 92–4, 99
Heart Sūtra (*Xinjing* 心經) 151, 162, 182, 221 n.8
heaven and earth 25, 32, 45, 49, 75, 76, 80, 95, 178, 203 n.60, 205 n.15
Hebel, Johann Peter 41, 165
Hegel, G. W. F. 133, 179
negativity in 147
Oriental nothingness 147, 172
Heidegger, Martin 209 n.36, 211 n.8, 211 n.54, 218 n.38–9, 218 n.46
"Art and Space" 52
Basic Problems of the Phenomenology 18
Basic Questions of Philosophy 54–5
Being and Time 6, 9, 17, 19, 28, 37, 71, 80, 113, 114, 119, 127, 150, 167, 168, 199 n.4
Black Notebooks 82, 93, 98, 100
in Bremen 85–6, 107
Bremen Lectures 76–7, 80
on Buddhism (*see* Buddhism)
"Building Dwelling Thinking" 124
communal identity 42
Contributions to Philosophy 40, 119, 164, 177
Country Path Conversation 61, 71–3, 92–4, 98
and *Daodejing* 15–17, 38, 51–2, 60, 64–5, 70, 215 n.1
on Daoism (*see* Daoism)

The Determination of Philosophy 17
empty vessel in 68–70
"The Essence of Truth" 78–9
"Evening Conversation" 96–7, 99–100
fourfold, conception of 45–6
"From a Dialogue on Language" 5, 39, 148, 161, 176, 180
"*Gelassenheit*" 50, 62, 76, 99
and German intellectuals 71
Hölderlin's Hymns 41
Holzwege 1
Husserl and 62, 63
Introduction to Metaphysics 37–8, 120
on joy of fish (*yule* 魚樂) 16, 200 n.9
"Letter on Humanism" 80, 92–3, 97, 102, 118, 123, 125, 126, 212 n.22
Nietzsche's philosophy 120–2
on nihilism 158–9
"On the Essence of Truth" 15, 112–13
"Origin of the Work of Art" 43–5
"The Origin of the Work of Art" 19
Petzet on 16, 17, 85
"Poetically Humans Dwell" 126
Pólemos and *Gelassenheit* 86–8
"The Principle of Identity" 63
"The Question Concerning Technology" 48
reliance on Wilhelm's *Zhuangzi* 96–7
on things 18–19 (*see also* thing(s))
as thinker of nothingness 167–70
"The Uniqueness of the Poet" 70, 86, 92, 181
On the Way to Language 63–4
"What is Metaphysics?" 46, 147, 155, 156, 161, 163, 167–72, 176, 180
words and images 89–92
writings 1, 3, 41
Wuwei 72–4
and *Zhuangzi* 17, 85, 90 (*see also Zhuangzi* 莊子)
Ziran 72–4, 90–1
Heiler, Friedrich 20
Heng Xian 恆先 27
hermeneutics (the art of interpretation) 2–3, 20
Heroic Ethos (*Heroisches Ethos*) 179
Heshanggong (河上公) 27, 67, 68, 136, 139
Hesse, Hermann 154

hiddenness (*Verborgenheit*) 3, 16, 38–9, 54, 78–9, 211 n.53
and darkness 78–9
Hisamatsu Shinichi 久松真一 174
Historical Records (*Shiji* 史記) (Sima Tan 司馬談) 14
History of the Myths of the Asiatic World (Görres) 60
Hofmannsthal, Hugo von 13
Hofstadter, Albert 181
holding vessel 78–9
Honneth, Axel 32
Hook, Sydney 175
Hsiao, Paul Shih-yi (Xiao Shiyi 蕭師毅) 21, 22, 69, 181
Huanglao 黃老, Daoism 27
Huayan Buddhism 8, 144, 162, 188, 192–5, 220 n.27, 221 n.29, 226 n.19–20
Hui Shi (惠施; Huizi 惠子) 136
Huizi 惠子 (Hui Shi 惠施), dogmatic skepticism 16, 17
humanism 80–1, 112, 124–5
Hundun 渾沌, (self-ordering anarchic/dao-archic chaos) 7, 33, 196–8, 199 n.5
Husserl, Edmund 14, 62, 63, 103–4
Ideas 14
Philosophy of Arithmetic 14

images
of *dao* 60
and word 89
Imperial Way Zen (*kōdō Zen* 皇道禅) 185
Itō Kichinosuke 伊藤吉之助 15, 146, 170

Jaeggi, Rahel 32, 189, 203 n.59, 226 n.22
Jahr, Fritz 154
Japanese philosophy, nothingness 170–1, 176–7, 184–5
Jaspers, Karl 21, 103, 142, 116
Jordan, Leo 168

Kanokogi Kazunobu 鹿子木員信 223 n.10
Kanthack, Katharina 9, 119, 156
Keyserling, Hermann von 31, 205 n.16
Kitayama Junyū 北山淳友 8, 172–5, 177, 185, 223 n.11
on *Genjō Kōan* 現成公按 184

philosophy of nothingness 178–9
  on things 180
  writings 178–9
Klages, Ludwig 60, 61, 103, 120, 210 n.45
  on nihilistic morality of Buddhism 140–1
  Spirit as Adversary of the Soul 122
koto 事 162
Krause, F. E. A. 31
Kreutzer, Conradin 50
Krieck, Ernst 121–2
Kuki Shūzō 九鬼周造 62, 162, 177
Kwee, Swan Liat 175

language 23, 102, 120, 162
Lao-Zhuang Daoism 33, 51, 90, 177
Laozi 老子 3, 6, 20, 173
  on Daoism 14, 16
  emptiness 67
  ethos 30, 116
  self and nurturing things 25
  in *On the Way to Language* 102
legalism (*fajia* 法家) 27, 45–6
Legge, James 16
Leibniz's question and nothingness 156–8
letting be learned (*lernenlassen*) 102
letting releasement of things 97–9, 123
Levinas, Emmanuel 19, 53, 56, 57
Liang Chiang (Liang Qiang 梁强) 87
Liezi 列子 29, 60, 64
Lotze, Hermann 13
Löwith, Karl 59, 223 n.10
Lukács, György 168
Lyotard, Jean-François 74, 86

Madhyamaka Buddhism 141
  emptiness 142–3
Mahāyāna Buddhism 141, 171, 172, 177
Mandel, Hermann 20
Manhae 188, 193–5
Marx, Karl 18, 189
"Martin Heidegger and Ontology" (Levinas) 168
Mazu Daoyi 馬祖道 144
Mencius (*Mengzi* 孟子) 135
Me Ti (Mo Di 墨翟) 60
Miki Kiyoshi 三木清 33
Misch, Georg 38, 61, 62–3, 104
  Occidental philosophy 104–5

modernity 82, 223 n.8
mortals 79–80, 123
moving-way (*be-wegen*) 109
myriad things 6, 24–6, 204 n.66
  self-ordering 29
mysterious learning (*xuanxue* 玄學) 64–5, 112

Nāgārjuna 142–3, 188
National Socialism 3, 86
  desertification of 93
  destructiveness of 100
  horrors of 121
nature/naturalism 7, 14, 37, 124–5
necessity of the unnecessary 98–100
negative philosophy 135–7, 139, 147–8
Neo-Confucianism 24, 25, 139, 219 n.16
Nietzsche, Friedrich 24, 72, 73, 96, 116, 120–2, 140, 150, 152–3, 158–9, 191
nihilism 7, 121–3, 133
  Buddhism and Daoism 159, 168
  Heidegger's references to 159
  Nietzsche's analysis of 158–9
  nothingness and emptiness 78, 180
"Nihilism and Existence" (Anders) 168
nirvāṇa 142, 149, 150, 153, 179
Nishida Kitarō 西田幾多郎 33, 171, 173–5, 177, 180, 184
non-alienation, freedom of 189
nothingness (*wu* 無) 2, 3, 7–8, 61
  anarchic implications of 190–2
  in *Being and Time* 167, 168
  in Buddhist contexts 134, 171–6
  in Chinese Philosophy 135–7
  of Daoism 7–8
  East Asian Philosophy of 177
  elemental 162–5
  emptiness and 72, 78
  between Europe and Asia 171–6
  in German thought 152–5
  in Heidegger context 147–8
  heroic *ethos* 179
  Huayan interpretation 194–5
  and individuation 150–2
  Japanese philosophy 170–1
  Kitayama's 8
  Leibniz's question and 156–8
  Nishida's notion of 171, 173–5
  nonidentity 188

Occidental and Oriental forms of 171–4
openness of being 151, 160–1
political implications of 224 n.23, 225 n.2
spatiality and temporality of things 29, 176–9
as temporalizing of factical life 148–50
transforming the philosophy of 184–6
Wang Bi on 67, 68

object 18. *Compare also* thing(s)
Occidental philosophy (*abendländische Philosophie*) 9, 14, 32, 53, 59, 81, 103–5
Occidental spirit 173, 179, 182, 184
Okakura Kakuzō 岡倉覚三 15, 22, 177
on Daoism 28
On Certainty (Wittgenstein) 16–17, 95
ontological revolution 86, 118–19
Oppenheimer, J. Robert 80
Oriental nothingness 7, 133–5, 172, 182, 184. *See also* nothingness (*wu* 無)
Confucianism into 139–40
nihilism of 174
Oriental spirit 173, 179, 184
originary ethics. *See* ethos
originary thinking 111
Origin of Humanity (*Yuanren lun* 原人論) (Zongmi) 144

The Path of Purification (*Visuddhimagga*) 142
"The Peasant and the Devil" 74
pessimism 121, 123, 149–51, 153, 158–9
Petzet, Heinrich Wiegand 15–17, 81–2
Encounters and Dialogues with Martin Heidegger, 1929-1976 85
Pfizmaier, August 75
The Tao-Teaching of Genuine Persons and Immortals 46
phenomenology 14, 54, 55, 177, 203 n.33
Phenomenology of Spirit (Hegel) 32, 56, 58, 72
The Philosophy of Symbolic Forms (Cassirer) 104
phúsis 38
ethos and 117
hermeneutics and politics of 39–43

self-emergence of things 39, 87
thing, work, and poetic 43–5, 69, 120
physiocracy 41
Plaenckner, Reinhold von 38, 210, 44, 211 n.53
poeticizing 127
Pöggeler, Otto 16, 90, 205 n.11
poiesis 113, 119, 126, 189–90
preparatory thinking 109
pre-Qin era 5, 26
presencing (*Anwesen*) 118–19, 153, 162
Pure Land Buddhism 161–2, 206 n.27
Pu Songling 蒲松齡 103

Qingyuan Weixin 青原惟信 175, 184
qi 氣 (material force) 23, 140
qi 器 (utensil, vessel) 65–6
Quesnay, François 41

Radhakrishnan, Sarvepalli 175
Record of Music (*Yueji* 樂記) 24
Rehm, Walther 20
relational freedom 2
releasement of things (*Gelassenheit der Dinge*) 3, 21–2, 50, 73, 97–9, 111, 123
religious Daoism (*daojiao* 道教) 14
reservedness 119, 133, 146
reversing movement 110. *See also* errancy
Rosenberg, Alfred 121

sacrificial ritual practice 23
Śāntideva, *Bodhicaryāvatāra* 193, 221 n.12
Sartre, Jean-Paul 120, 125, 168–9, 176
Schelling, Friedrich 65
Schleiermacher, Friedrich 20, 173, 208 n.7
Schopenhauer, Arthur 72, 149–51, 153, 210 n.44
Seekamp, Hans Jürgen 85, 86
Seghers, Anna 60
self-determination 32–4, 39–41, 166, 184
self-emptiness 140–2, 184, 190, 196
self-generating event of thing 113
self-naturing of thing 26–30, 114, 125
freedom and fate in 30–3
self-ordering anarchic/dao-archic chaos 196–8
self-presencing 118–19
self-relationality 35

selfsame (*selben*) way 109
self-so-ness 129–30, 187
Shang dynastic period 23
shepherding and safeguarding 124
Shishuo Xinyu 204 n.65
Sima Qian 司馬遷 14, 30, 136
Sima Tan 司馬談, *Historical Records* (*Shiji* 史記) 14
Sinitic language 23
Sojourning/lingering (*verweilen*) 75–6
Song-Ming Neo-Confucianism 24
Speeches and Parables of Zhuangzi (*Reden und Gleichnisse des Tschuang-tse*) 16
Spengler, Oswald, *dao* 63
stillness, things 50, 61, 65, 109–11, 123, 128–9, 140, 161–3
stimulus-response model 31
Strauss, Victor von 16, 20, 46, 51, 60, 61, 209 n.36
    empty vessel in 68–70
    light/darkness 78
    on sojourning (*verweilen*) 75
    on virtuosity 116
    ziran, translation of 73
suñña (empty, void, zero) 141

Takeuchi Yoshinori 武内義範 175
Tanabe Hajime 田辺元 161
Tang dynasty era 144, 220 n.19, 222 n.19
Tezuka Tomio 手塚富雄 161
thing(s) 5–6, 199 n.2
    animal and human life 113
    annihilation 81
    Buber and Heidegger on 57–8
    caring for 9
    carving and cutting 23
    in Chinese philosophy 24
    description 13, 72
    emptiness of 71–2, 179–84
    enframing and releasing 48–9
    ethos of 56–7
    explaining strategies of 113–14
    form and shape 23
    freedom with 33–4, 98
    gathering and emptiness 62
    measure of 49–50
    myriad 24
    mystical discourse 73
    nature and 56
    as object 14, 18–19, 25
    phenomenological strategies of 14
    place for 51–3, 77, 114
    poetic words and 13
    priority of 76–8
    questioning 55–6
    reification of 18
    releasement of 3, 21–2, 50, 72, 73, 98
    ritual and cosmic character of 24
    sacrificial entity 23
    self-acting of 32
    self-determination of 32
    self-generating event 113
    self-naturing of 26–30
    sense of things as 101
    straw-dogs 25–6
    thingliness of 43, 44, 48, 77
    thinking of 48, 73, 101, 114, 118, 130, 180
    uselessness of 89–90, 98–100
    in the work 44
    and world 1, 2, 5, 13–14, 17–19, 14, 107
    ziranist/generative 6
thing-mysticism 20
thinking (thought) 1, 3–4, 81–2, 110–11. *See also* preparatory thinking
The Three Leaps of Wang Lun (*Die drei Sprünge des Wang-lun*) (Döblin) 59–60
tianrendi 天人地 80
Tiantai 天台 Buddhism, emptiness 144
transmitted language 102
A Travel Diary of a Philosopher (Keyserling) 31
"Treatise on Emptiness as Nonsubstantiality" (*Bu Zhenkong Lun* 不真空論) (Sengzhao 僧肇) 143
truth, essencing of 112
Tsujimura Kōichi 辻村公一 82

unthought 1, 3
useful uselessness 67, 89–90, 100–2, 127, 128, 139

virtuosity (*de* 德) 116
von Hartmann, Eduard 72, 154, 210 n.44

waiting 73, 88, 93–4, 97–8
Wang Bi 王弼 5, 33, 65
  on the *Book of Changes* 139
  on *Daodejing* 30, 45, 139, 178
  light/darkness 78
  on nothingness 67, 68, 138
  nurturing life (*yangsheng*) 138
  world as spirit-vessel 66, 67
Wang Gen 王艮 219 n.16
Wang Ji 王幾 219 n.16
Wang Lun 王倫 60
Wang Wei 王維 178
wanwu (myriad things) 5, 6, 24
the way 1–2
  being-in-the-world 15, 59, 108–9, 123
  conceiving action 126
  event on 108
  mature thinking 111
  moving-way 109
  and mystery 63–5
  preparatory thinking 109
  releasement 111
  reversing movement 110
  selfsame 109
Wei-Jin era 5, 31, 33, 65, 67, 112, 128
Weiss, J. G. 31
West-Eastern Encounter: Japan's Culture and Tradition (*West-östliche Begegnung: Japans Kultur und Tradition*) (Kitayama Junyū 北山淳友) 173, 177
Wilhelm, Richard 5, 16, 38, 51, 60, 61, 205 n.16, 209 n.36, 211 n.53
  Daodejing 51, 65, 69
  empty vessel in 68–70, 79
  on *Gelassenheit* word 96
  Liezi 列子 95
  The Secret of the Golden Flower (*Taiyi Jinhua Zongzhi* 太乙金華宗旨) 95
  on sojourning (*verweilen*) 75–6
  for things 45
  "The Useless Tree" (*Der unnütze Baum*) 100–1
  Zhuangzi 91–2, 94–7, 103, 112, 213 n.42
  ziran 73, 89–91
will to power 119–24
Wittgenstein, Ludwig 16–17, 95
Wolin, Richard 121

words
  emptiness of 179–84
  and images 89–92
world
  Asia and Europe 81–2
  freedom and responsive participation in 30–3
  self and 2, 15
  as spirit-vessel 66
  thing and 1, 2, 5, 13, 46–7, 113–14, 123
  world-civilization 82
  worlding of the 17
wuwei 無為 21, 27, 32, 37, 49, 67, 72–4, 94
  acting out of nothing 139
wu 物 23

Xu Gan 徐幹, *Balanced Discourses* (*Zhong Lun* 中論) 68
Xunzi 荀子 24, 126

Yang Zhu 楊朱 32, 203 n.57
Yogācāra Buddhism 172, 178
Yuasa Seinosuke 湯浅誠之助 170

Zen Buddhism 160–1, 171, 173, 176, 184
zero (*śūnya*) 157
Zhanran 湛然 144
Zhi Dun 支遁 (Zhi Dao Lin 支道林) 33–4, 204 n.65
Zhuangzi (Zhuang Zhou 莊周) 10, 14, 16–17, 214 n.68
  and Buddhist reflections 33–5
  imperfectionism 67
  text teachings 103
  useful uselessness 67, 89–90, 98–100
Zhuangzi 莊子 3, 6, 28, 87, 196–7, 219 n.8
  action and inaction in 94
  dao in 2
  emptiness in 61
  equalization 35
  errancy 111–13
  freedom and fatedness in 30–3
  "Heaven's Way" (*Tiandao* 天道) 32, 50
  Heidegger's thinking in the texts 102
  "Horses Hooves" (*mati* 馬蹄) 65
  "Knowledge's Northern Rambling" 90
  Laozi and 30
  lone-transformation 33
  "Mountain Tree" (*shanmu* 山木) 90

nothingness 136-7, 219 n.9
nurturing life 93
objective idealism 95
poetic thinking 127-8
self-determination of the thing 32
stimulus-response model 31
usefulness and uselessness in 100-2
waiting in 94, 98
ziran in 30

Zhu Xi 朱熹 24
ziran 自然 7, 26-7, 32-4. *See also* self-naturing of thing
  Daoist texts 107
  and naturalism 14, 27, 30
  of the thing 29, 72-4, 77, 78
Ziranism 7, 14, 192
Zongmi Guifeng 圭峰宗密 34, 144-5, 165

www.ingramcontent.com/pod-product-compliance
Lightning Source LLC
Chambersburg PA
CBHW071822300426
44116CB00009B/1396